NORTH END SOULS 2

For my family.

Best wishes,

ISBN: 978-1-8380604-0-4

 Published by Fulwood End Media. Printed in Great Britain. www.northendsouls.com

FANTASY FOOTBALL

When I was young I used to play for North End. Up front, usually. At first I was Bobby Charlton, sweeping my schoolboy fringe into an unlikely comb over.

Then I was Alex Bruce. When everyone else was doing Marco Tardelli celebrations, I was always Brucie at Ewood.

I never even tried to be Mike Elwiss; like the time I attempted a Willie Naughton moustache, some things are just out of reach.

I wanted to be Peter Sayer, but I didn't have the curls. Same with John Thomas. I couldn't even pull off the perm like he did.

I was definitely Brian Mooney. Every Tuesday night after college I was King of the Plastic for an hour, playing on Deepdale and hearing imaginary chants from the back of the Kop as I missed another sitter: *'You're crap and you know you are!'*

I didn't want to be Vernon Allatt. But I was.

Even in my Summer League prime, I never made the first team - I just made the first team laugh. In the pub after the game, I was always John McGrath.

I was Tony Ellis for several years. And then I most definitely was not.

As I got older in the 1990s, I put my back out attempting an Andy Saville Scunthorpe Special. Who didn't?

When my pace (hah!) went and my backside grew, I dropped into midfield, clogging people and shouting classic Gregan orders: *'Two pints of lager and a packet of crisps please!'*

If I got injured, I was Ryan Kidd, battling through pain and giving everything for the cause. On the off-chance I banged one in, I was Jonny Macken.

A decent pass? Vintage Brian O'Neil.

Bit of both? Paul McKenna.

By the end, I was Hunts at the back, even though the only thing we had in common was the colour of our boots.

One day, the urge will pass. When that loose ball drops perfectly across my path in the park and I don't hear a little *'He's done superbly . . . he's done magnificently!'* in my head, I'll know it's time. Walking football beckons. I'll be Ian Ashbee.

Why am I telling you this? Because throughout my life, I've been obsessed with what it must be like to pull on a North End shirt and play for the club for real. I'm sure you've all done the same.

In the pages ahead, Gareth Ainsworth says it was his ambition just to play one game and he'd have been happy with that. Me too.

An old friend of mine did briefly make it into the first team. I still see him at games now and no matter what else happened in his future career as a roofer, I'm forever jealous.

He pulled on the shirt, he played in real North End games and no-one can ever take that away from him. He knows what it's like.

And that's what this book is all about; not the fantasy football of runaway imagination - but the reality of life as a professional for PNE over the past seven decades.

The changes have been incredible and it's been fascinating to hear how everything from training, tactics and team talks has transformed almost beyond recognition.

Seventy-odd years have passed since the oldest players on these pages began their journeys with the club.

From D-Day tanks parked at Deepdale to the birth of the Gentry, from Pontins to play-offs and all points in between, it's been a privilege to pull this second volume of North End Souls together.

Just like in the first book, every interview was an absolute pleasure and I can't thank the people involved enough.

More than once, voices cracked as the memories came flooding back; sometimes through emotion, often through laughter, never through anger.

Because the common theme was how much they'd enjoyed being part of North End. Players who had been elsewhere spoke of coming to Preston as a 'proper club, in a proper football town, with proper supporters'.

Several went away and couldn't wait to come back.

Others regret that they never got the chance.

One or two want to set the record straight.

Everyone wanted to tell their story, relive happy memories and get across how proud they were to have been at the club.

As one player quietly put it as I packed away the microphone: 'My time at Deepdale was the happiest of my life. I wanted it to last forever, but instead it was gone in a puff of smoke.'

That's the thing about Preston North End - it has a special effect on you.

Enjoy the book.

Keith Harrison, author

SIMON GRAYSON: STILL A WHITE

I'm told that when John McGrath arrived at Deepdale in 1986, he said he could tell it was a football town just by looking at the chimney pots.

Having met so many Preston fans over the years, I know what he meant; friendly, no nonsense, down-to-earth people, passionate about their team - and proper football supporters.

Like most northerners, they call a spade a spade and I'm a bit like that myself, so all in all . . . I think we were a good match for each other.

The fans just want to see their team reflect them in the way they want to be represented; hard work, give everything for the famous white shirt and do the basics right.

Not everyone is going to be the most talented player, but I know that if people are giving everything they've got, the North End fans will always be behind them.

And, for me, giving everything you've got is the minimum requirement.

I was lucky at Deepdale to have a group of players who would run through a brick wall for the club, the manager and the supporters.

Normally at this point I'd say 'not literally of course' . . . but with one or two of those lads, I'm not so sure!

Although the club wasn't in a great league position when I arrived, there was a good structure behind the scenes and, in Peter Ridsdale, a wise and experienced head overseeing affairs. I'd known Peter from my days as a young player at Leeds and kept in touch with him throughout my managerial career.

Everywhere I had been, I'd wanted to be part of long-term plans and when I looked at North End - the size of the club and where it could and should be - I was excited by the opportunity to turn it around and see where we could get to.

Peter and I shared the same vision and philosophy.

Our aim was to keep improving the playing squad in every transfer window - that was how we always looked at things.

And I think we were successful in achieving that, if you look at our progression from that first season, to the play-offs, then promotion and re-establishing ourselves in the top half of the Championship over a couple of years.

Yes, we had our ups and our downs at times, but I never felt pressure from above.

Without those key relationships behind the scenes and that clarity of everyone pulling in the same direction, it makes things a lot harder to be successful and I was always grateful for the support I had at Deepdale.

Moreover, I'll always be proud and humbled to have been asked to help carry Sir Tom Finney's coffin on that sad day back in 2014. It was such an honour, such a privilege, to be a part of paying tribute to the great man.

He wasn't just an iconic figure for Preston North End, or even the whole of England - he was an icon for the entire football world. You could see how much he meant to the people of Preston and it really meant a lot to me, too.

One of the first things I did when I joined the club was to go to see him at his home, because I didn't want to miss the opportunity to meet such a huge figure in the game.

Hopefully, we did him proud on the pitch and he would have been looking down on us at Wembley the following year when we were able to clinch promotion.

That final was a real test for the squad, because obviously we'd had the anguish of missing out on the last day of the season at Colchester.

It takes character to come back from a disappointment like that, but it speaks volumes for everyone involved - players and supporters - that everyone stuck together to seize a second chance.

And, of course, in the build-up to the final, people were going on and on about how North End had failed in nine previous play-off attempts.

'Oh really? No-one's ever mentioned it!'

I didn't want to dwell on anything that had gone on in the past - we couldn't affect that. Instead, we used previous failures as a motivational tool; we were going to be the ones to get that monkey off the club's back, once and for all.

I told the players that they can be the team that goes down in folklore at Preston North End - and thankfully that's what they did.

Rather than wallow after the game at Colchester, we kept emphasising the positive side of it; we'd been given a second opportunity, a chance to put things right.

We were glad the game at Chesterfield came round so quickly and we were able to get things out of our system with a solid performance there and then a convincing win in the second leg at Deepdale.

The scenes at the end of that game, with the fans on the pitch and the euphoria all around, I think gave everyone a psychological lift.

The supporters hadn't turned on us after the Colchester defeat, they were with us all the way and, again, that's a measure of the people of Preston.

After that, it was a case of doing all our preparations right; we changed the dimensions of the pitch at Deepdale to replicate Wembley exactly and made sure we knew how Swindon were going to play.

Credit to the players, because when the time came, they carried out every aspect of the gameplan to a tee; we let Swindon have possession and hit them on the counter-attack, we knew they were vulnerable at set pieces, we knew we had to turn them.

If we did all these things, we would get our opportunities - and that's exactly how it played out in a fantastic performance.

I've had some lows and some real highs in my career, including other promotions at various clubs. But to turn something around after such a huge disappointment is something that gives me an immense amount of pride and satisfaction.

It was a test of my man-management skills, of how to turn a negative into a positive, but when it came down to it, the players showed a lot of bottle, a lot of character and I'll always be proud of them.

I'd like to think I always had a good connection with the Preston fans and I think that day just cemented it a bit more - certainly one of the happiest days in my career.

I also look back at some of the players that we brought into the club over that period and am delighted to see how well they have developed and progressed in the game. When you bring people in that maybe the supporters haven't heard of, and you work with them every day to get the best out of them, it's massively rewarding.

The likes of Jordan Hugill, Callum Robinson, Alan Browne and Daniel Johnson have all been role models for any player who wants to fulfil their potential.

Their attitudes have been spot-on and they've taken their opportunities at every turn. It's incredibly satisfying to see lads who you brought in for small fees playing such a big role for the team years later - and being worth a lot more to the club than fifty grand.

It's down to the players themselves, Peter Ridsdale, the coaching staff - it's a real team effort and it goes back to what I was saying at the top; everyone pulling in the same direction. I knew when the time came to leave Deepdale that I was not only leaving some brilliant individuals, but collectively one of the best groups I'd ever worked with.

The culture, professionalism and standards set by the senior pros was absolutely spot-on; people like Tom Clarke, Paul Huntington, John Welsh and Paul Gallagher.

If you could bottle what those players bring, it would improve any dressing room in the land.

They are all natural leaders who would help the younger players out - on and off the pitch - and use their experience for the good of others around them.

The biggest thing that I felt I'd created at Preston was a unity, a team spirit, and a group of talented players that always came together collectively as a team.

So leaving was a real wrench and certainly not a decision I took lightly.

I'd had opportunities to leave in the past, but I was enjoying my time at the club so much and I'd built up such a relationship with the club, the supporters, the city - it's not an easy thing to walk away from.

But my ambition has always been to manage in the Premier League and I just felt I'd have a better opportunity at Sunderland than at Preston *(although obviously, in hindsight, it wasn't the best move I've ever made).*

I hope the North End fans understand the decision-making analysis though and recognise that it's no sleight on them or the club at all - my dream would have been to take that group of players into the Premier League. But, sadly, it wasn't to be.

Inevitably, whenever you leave in less-than-perfect circumstances, there's always a fear that it will taint all the work that you've done there over the years, so I was really touched to get such a warm reception when I came back as a visiting manager that season.

When Sunderland were 2-1 down, I didn't even mind the Mickey-taking from the Town End with the old 'sacked in the morning' chant.

Come to think of it, they were only a month or so out!

But it was a day I'll never forget, because it gave me a chance to acknowledge the Preston faithful for their brilliant support during my time at Deepdale and it was great to have such a warm reception in return.

You don't spend that long somewhere and not develop feelings for the place.

I've still got those feelings now.

I think it's a fantastically well-run football operation, a real family club and somewhere I have a lot of affection for.

They say you should never go back - and I've had some experience with that myself recently - but who knows what might happen in the future?

I think Alex Neil has done a great job in keeping things progressing and it would be absolutely brilliant to see North End get up into the Premier League - it's a club that deserves that type of success.

As for me, to get four-and-a-half years anywhere in football these days is quite rare and you get to know everyone there - not just the players, but the people in the offices, the ground staff, the tea lady, the stewards and even the the guy in the corner shop. They were exactly what I knew they would be - decent people who worked hard and wanted the best for their team. Proper football people at a proper football club.

No doubt in the chapters ahead, you will hear from players over many decades talk about the pride they had in pulling on the Preston shirt.

Whether they were Player of the Year or only turned out in a small number of games, that pride will last a lifetime and I hope you enjoy reading their stories here.

Maybe footballers get a bad press at times, but if you speak to them and work with them like I did, you know what it means to them to have been successful at Preston North End.

It certainly means a lot to me and I'll always be proud of what we achieved together.

Enjoy the book.

Simon Grayson

Chapter 1

GARETH AINSWORTH: WILD THING

You'd be amazed how many people think I'm actually from Preston. They know I started off there, they hear the Lancashire accent and they probably know how much I think about North End.

After all, I had four spells at Deepdale if you include a trial in my younger days.

So I hate to drop this on you, but I'm a Blackburn lad and grew up supporting Rovers with my dad from the age of about six.

For those of you who haven't turned the page (!), Howard Kendall was the manager around that time and Simon Garner was my hero - he still is, in fact.

They were great days and it was a proper working class upbringing; dad had two jobs, working as a clerk in a carpet factory and also as a driving instructor to make ends meet.

He was always grafting and I think that's where I got my own work ethic from. I always knew that no matter what you did, you had to work hard - that was instilled in me from a very young age and I carried it with me throughout my career.

The football on Saturday afternoon was always our release, walking down to Ewood Park, going with my mates on the bus - just a big adventure every week.

Everyone reading this will know that buzz you get from being part of something and supporting your local team. Whether it's Blackburn, Preston or Wycombe Wanderers, it's a special feeling that you just don't get from latching onto a 'big' club.

I wasn't really on anyone's books or anything from a young age - in fact, I didn't make the school team until I was about 13.

So we either had a really good side, or I was a bit of a late developer.

What I did know was that I was determined to make the most of every ounce of talent I had. I wanted to be a footballer and if it didn't happen, it wouldn't be through lack of trying. If there was any way I could make it, then I would, no matter what it took. I was quick, but there were probably faster lads than me, so I think it was my determination and attitude that caught the eye and when I was 16, I got taken on by Rovers on a two-year apprenticeship.

That was my absolute dream come true, but on my first day at Ewood, all I wanted to do was meet Simon Garner.

I was lurking around the changing rooms, just itching to say hello to him, but no sign. One of my jobs was to look after Frank Stapleton and Colin Hendry's boots, so I plucked up the courage to ask Colin where Simon was: 'Oh, he'll be out on the pitch son, go and say hello.'

I thought: 'Yes! That's what makes him the top man, the rest of the lads are still getting changed and he's already out on the pitch. What a star.'

So I headed up the tunnel at Ewood and looked out over the turf, but couldn't see him anywhere.

As I turned round to go back inside, I heard this little cough and were was Simon . . . sitting in the dug-out having a fag.

He poked his head out and - with that trademark grin - said: *'Alright son. Keep off these - they're bad for you!'*

So that's how I met my hero for the first time. What a player he was though, just a natural goalscorer (as I'm sure North End fans of a certain age will painfully remember).

In training, he could be the worst player out there, but when the games came around, well, he was different class, Garns.

After a couple of years there, doing all the rotten jobs that young lads had to do in those days, the crunch came on the day of my 18th birthday.

There were seven of us, including a young Peter Thorne, all waiting to hear if we were being kept on by Don Mackay, who had taken over as manager by then. I'd scored for the reserves in the week so I was feeling pretty chipper about things.

Instead, the news hit me like a hammer . . . the boss said I wasn't good enough and I was being let go. It wasn't quite that brutal, but it didn't half feel like it.

It was absolutely devastating. All I'd ever wanted to do was play professional football and now that dream was shattered. I held it together and fronted the lads up outside, as you do: 'Yeah, I'm alright, good luck boys, etc.'

But when I got outside round the corner in Nuttall Street, I just burst into tears. My world had fallen apart and, by the way . . . *Happy 18th birthday Gaz!*

Still, I was determined to make it and the thought of getting a 'real' job just never came into my head. My parents thought exactly the same; they were really supportive and straight away we set about getting back in the game.

I remember my dad in particular saying: 'Don't worry. You'll make it. I've seen enough of you to know you'll get there.'

There was no question of giving up and feeling sorry for yourself isn't going to get you anywhere. In those days, there was no email or anything - you had to write letters to clubs, so I put pen to paper and sent off to every club in Lancashire asking for a trial. First up, Blackpool said 'no thanks', but then North End gave me a call.

Walter Joyce was in charge of the youth team with Roy Tunks at the time and asked me in for a trial. My emotions at the time? Buzzing, relieved, excited - and bricking it.

That two-week trial turned out to be about three months long and in the end I was training with the first team squad. There was no sign of a contract, but as long as I was going in every day, I thought I was getting somewhere. The lads all welcomed me in, even though I wasn't signed on or anything and I wasn't getting paid.

David Flitcroft, Lee Cartwright and Lee Ashcroft were all around my age and they'd already made the first team, so I could see there was a chance for me, if I could just get a foot in the door.

Whether it was down to finances at the time or not, North End were giving young lads a go. What I probably didn't realise was that it had nothing to do with age - they were getting in because they were absolutely brilliant.

Ashy was so talented and fiery, while Carts was just unbelievable and ended up playing nearly 500 times for Preston.

For me, all I ever wanted to do was play ONE first team game in front of a crowd. At that point, that would have done for me, and I thought it was tantalisingly close with those lads breaking through.

I was busting a gut in training but unfortunately, in that first little spell . . . I got the dreaded *'can I have a word?'* knock.

Walter pulled me in one day and said: 'Look son. You've been here two or three months and I really appreciate it. But Sammy McIlroy at Northwich Victoria has inquired about a right winger and I've given him your name. It's Conference level and you're due down there on Tuesday night for training.'

Walter had been great with me, he wished me all the best and basically, that was that. I played a trial game for Northwich and scored two, so afterwards they were very keen to sign me on a contract.

Now, I never had an agent throughout my career, mainly because my dad always gave me the best advice going. Dad was absolutely brilliant and said that, yes, I'd love to play for Northwich, but no, I wouldn't sign a contract just yet.

So I wasn't getting paid any money, it was expenses only. But I didn't care.

Dad was convinced I'd catch the eye and get back in with a league club, which is probably why, as the weeks went on and I was doing well, Sammy was desperate for me to sign up.

The great Norman Whiteside was physio there at the time too and if anyone can get you to do something it's normally Big Norm (!) but I managed to hold off.

To be honest, I loved playing for Northwich and if that had been my career, at that point, that would have been good enough for me. I was playing in front of fans at a well-known club, getting used to the game a bit more and learning every week. There were proper derby games against Witton Albion and they'd kick you all over the park.

Well, you know me, I'd be kicking the hell out of them back and fronting up against real grown men. You had to show you weren't taking it, because if those lads sniffed weakness, well, it was going to be a long hard game.

My shins might not agree, but it was probably what I needed at that point and stood me in good stead for what was coming next.

One night, I was sat at the family home in Blackburn and the phone rang; there was only one phone in the house and luckily enough I got up to answer it in the hallway.

It was Ted Davies, a scout at North End, and he said: 'Hello, is that Gareth? We need a right winger to play for us against Shrewsbury on Saturday. Do you want to come down and play?'

It was either the wind-up of all wind-ups, or he was being serious.

Thankfully, it was the latter. Talk about being gobsmacked.

Think about it; this was Thursday night and Preston North End were ringing ME up to see if I wanted to play for them in a league match on the Saturday - less than 48 hours later. I'm not sure it would happen like that these days!

Obviously, I said 'yes!' straight away, but I was thinking: 'Why have they not taken someone from the youth team?'

Not that I was going to question it, mind you - I was bouncing off the walls!

My parents were like: 'Who was on the phone?'

Me: 'Well, you're not going to believe this . . .'

Then I suddenly realised: 'Oh crap, I'm going to have to call Sammy and tell him I can't play for Northwich at the weekend.'

When I rang him up, I just remember this long pause before he said in his lovely Irish drawl: *'. . . ohhhhh bloody heeeellllll.'*

He knew there was no contract in place and North End were nicking me for free.

I thanked Sammy for all his help and went to training in Preston the next morning. This was January 1992 and there wasn't a huge crowd down in Shrewsbury - 3,154 to be exact. But it made no difference to me.

That day, the old Gay Meadow on the banks of the River Severn was my San Siro, Wembley and Maracana all rolled into one.

I was lining up on the right wing with Ashy pushed over to the left. We had club legend John Thomas up top with Graham Shaw. There was Simon Farnworth in goals, Gary Swann was in midfield with Jeff Wrightson and Mike Flynn at the back. Big Steve Senior was behind me at right-back and Carts was in midfield, so there was at least someone I knew quite well.

Luckily, I sort of knew the lads from my extended trial a few months earlier, so it wasn't a case or learning everyone's names, but I didn't really know how they played.

It was the days of only one sub, so I played the full game and despite our decent line-up, we ended up getting beat 2-0.

Apart from the result, if it had all have ended for me there . . . I'd still have been happy.

I'd played a game of professional football, in front of a crowd, in the Football League. That was it; I'd lived the dream, even if it was for just one game.

My mum and dad came to watch the match and back home, they'd actually recorded the Radio Lancashire commentary on cassette.

When we got back, all they kept doing was playing back the bits where I'd done something or the commentators had said I'd had a decent game. I'm sure they've still got it somewhere.

I'll always remember on the Monday, the Lancashire Evening Post had the headline *'Gissa Job - Gareth'* and that summed things up perfectly!

By the following day, I'd signed a deal to the end of the season and that was my first professional contract. It wasn't a fortune by any standards, but it was absolutely priceless to me. I think I played about five more games that season and, in my mind, I held my own. I scored my first goal in an Associate Members Cup game against Hull. It was a classic of its kind - I kicked the ball out of the keeper's hands and put it in on the old plastic pitch, while all hell kicked off around me.

But I didn't care - that was a HUGE North End moment for me, even though it was in a cup competition, it was my first professional goal, a massive thing.

I thought I was doing OK; all I used to do was tackle back, get the ball, belt forward, get to the by-line and cross it. I remember both JT and Graham Shaw saying to me: 'Just keep putting those crosses in son - you're doing great.'

So I really thought I had a chance of extending the contract beyond that season. I'd got my hopes up - only to be smacked back down like an all-in wrestler once again.

It was all a bit of a blur, but almost 12 months to the day since I'd been rejected by Rovers, Les Chapman gave me the bad news again: 'Thanks for helping us out, but sorry son, we're not going to offer you anything.'

To be fair, I don't think there was a lot of money around the club at that time, so maybe that was part of it. (That's what I tell myself anyway!)

I remember we used to train on Moor Park quite a bit and there was a pitch behind the Town End that was horrendous - I'd played on better in Sunday leagues.

Sometimes, it felt like we were driving round the town, looking to see where we could get on to train.

We used to get changed at the ground, pile into cars then say: 'Right, where are we training today?'

I had my mum's Ford Orion, but Carts had this battered Triumph that he'd bought and us young lads used to jump into that. Then there'd be this little convoy driving round, looking for that day's pitch. In reality, the way training was back then, there wasn't a need for a super gym or perfect surface. It was still football as we loved it - in the raw; a bunch of fit lads who all got on together, good footballers, get out and play. I know it's easy to get nostalgic, but looking back, they were great times.

So despite being let go (again!), Preston will always be massive in my heart for giving me that first chance. Everything stemmed from there.

I don't know how he found out I'd been released, but the very next night, a scout called Glen Bonnell rang up.

I didn't know him at all, but there I was, on my parents' home phone in the hallway again, and he was very straight to the point: 'Seen you play. Think you're good enough. John Beck will turn you into a player. Get your ass to Cambridge.'

I was thinking: *'OK, who the hell is this guy? A talking Telegram?'*

He said he'd been down to watch someone else, but had seen me and thought: 'That kid's got something. He'll run through a brick wall. Becky will love that.'

So I was off to Cambridge for a week, with another North End youngster, Matt 'Lamby' Lambert, for them to have a look at us.

The funny thing is, at that point they were at Championship level with people like Dion Dublin and Steve Claridge, pushing for this brand new thing called the Premier League. So it was a higher league than North End were in.

I couldn't take my mum's Orion for the week - she'd have killed me - so we ended up going in Lamby's old banger, which really shouldn't have been on the road at all.

We used to call it The Speedboat, not because it went quick - it just handled like one. About half way down we had a flat tyre and were stuck there for ages at the side of the road sorting it out. By that point, I wasn't surprised there was a problem and I remember thinking: 'There's just something against me getting into football.'

To be honest, I was a lot more surprised that Lamby had a spare tyre in that car (!) but we just about made it down there in the end.

We had a trial game lined up and just before kick-off, one of the Cambridge people said to me: 'If you smash the left-back, John Beck will love you - he'll take you on for sure.' OK chief, message received.

Well, I was fired up anyway, but as the match went on, even I was feeling sorry for this poor full-back. I absolutely battered him at every opportunity; every tackle - *bang.* Every header - *bang.* Even if the ball was just in the vicinity - it's near enough . . . *bang.*

Obviously, I got up and down, did all the right stuff and got my crosses in too.

But looking at the battered, bruised and bitter left-back as we came off, I knew I'd shown what I was all about, attitude-wise. *(Sorry mate, but it had to be done!)* One of the coaching staff came over, shook my hand and said: 'Well done son, that'll do for Becky.'

True enough, a week later, John said: 'I want you to sign. You'll be brilliant down the wing for me.' Cambridge had reached the play-offs and were up against Leicester, who had a young Simon Grayson in their ranks, in the semi-finals.

They drew the first leg 1-1 at home, but went down 5-0 at Filbert Street in the return, with future North Enders John Vaughan in goals and Micky Norbury going on as a substitute. I was watching the game as a 19-year-old from the stands and had no real understanding that if John's team had got through, we'd have been playing in the Premier League.

Looking back, I think it would have been incredible for Cambridge United to have been in that first Premier League season - and, even more incredibly, I'd have been playing for them. But at the time, you don't take these things in. I was just excited, relieved and happy to have another chance at professional football.

As it was, we were still at Championship level and I finally got my chance in October. John had changed me into a midfield player by then and I scored the winner against Bristol City on my league debut (Andy Cole scored for them) and I thought everything was going great.

At last, I was in the team, I had a contract and a manager who believed in me.

What could possibly go wrong? Errr, well . . . you do know the story of my career so far, don't you?

Out of nowhere, there was a rumour going round that John had been talking to Preston, who had just sacked Les Chapman. I don't know if it was true, but the people in charge at Cambridge weren't impressed - they questioned John's loyalty and sacked him. I couldn't believe it.

I'd made my debut, scored the winner and thought finally - *finally!* - everything was going smoothly, when, just like that, the manager who signed me had gone.

Gary Johnson took over and the next game . . . he dropped me (!).

I was thinking: 'What the hell do I have to do here?' I was probably seen as 'one of John's signings' so I was out in the cold a bit and wondering what was going to happen. For a while, I was back to Square One, but North End were about to play another big role in my career.

Whether he'd been talking to them or not, John did get the Preston job and just before Christmas he came back in for me and Micky Norbury.

He bought me out of the contract at Cambridge and that's when I first thought: 'Wow, someone's actually gone out of their way to sign me.' Up to that point, it had been me saying *'gissa job'* - now someone actually WANTED me. There was no transfer fee, maybe a bit of compensation for the contract, but I felt 10-feet tall.

I raced back up north, moved back in with my mum and dad . . . and arrived at North End for the third time in just over 12 months! It was like fate was always pulling me back to Deepdale and I thought: 'Surely, this time it will go smooth.'

Straight away, John put me in as a central midfielder, sometimes alongside Flynny, where it's safe to say the pair of us quite liked a tackle.

It was on the plastic pitch, so we were in these leggings every week, while the opposition would turn out in just shorts.

We'd be able to go in for sliding tackles, whereas they would do it once, look down at the bleeding mass of flesh, sand and astroturf and think twice about it next time.

I also played right-back, out wide too; in fact I think I've played in nearly every position on the pitch for Preston - I was even centre half a couple of times.

The fans had welcomed me back again and I was loving it, just being out there on the pitch in any position; getting up and down, giving my all for the team. That was always my style and I think the fans saw that and appreciated it.

If I had to put my head in where it hurts then I'd always do it. It wasn't a macho thing, I was just trying to help the team. At times, it seemed that my shirt was covered in blood every week but I promise you I never set out to get it like that - it just happened!

Becky had got rid of quite a few people and brought a few in, like he does, so there was a bit of turmoil, as there always is when someone wants to make big changes in a short space of time. He wanted to shake the place up and there's no denying that he achieved that in many ways. There were things that he did that really brought the club and the town back together.

Me? I absolutely loved playing in front of the Town End.

If we were winning and it was bouncing, you'd hear the PNE chants and catch yourself thinking: 'I bet it's flipping great in there today!' I really felt I was maturing as a professional footballer; I was starting every game, learning all the time and getting valuable experience - sometimes in ways I never expected.

One time towards the end of that season, we were away at Port Vale on a Tuesday night when Simon Farnworth got a smack on the head after bravely diving at Alex Mathie's feet. His nose was all over the place and he was basically out cold - he couldn't carry on. In those days there was only one sub, so there was no keeper on the bench, either. We were winning 2-1 at the time and there were about 15 minutes left in a game where we really needed the points.

Becky looked around and said: 'Right, who wants to go in goals?'

No-one put their hand up, so I said: 'Well, I'll do it then.'

I wasn't the biggest lad on the team, but I was the only one up for it, so in I went.

I honestly didn't have a clue what I was doing - other than trying to do all those things keepers do; waving my arms about, shouting a lot, bouncing the ball, trying to look confident: 'Yeah, I do this all the time.' I vaguely remember punching a corner away and I thought I was doing OK: 'I might pull this off here!'

Within five minutes . . they'd equalised.

To be fair, it was a great goal from outside the area and I didn't really have a chance with it. Now they were really piling the pressure on, looking for the win, but the lads were brilliant in front of me and we held out for a valuable point.

Farny would have been proud, if he'd been awake to see it. When I came in for training on the Thursday, I thought I'd be getting a pat on the back from the boss.

Instead, the first thing he said to me was . . . 'Shoulda saved it.'

To this day, I don't know if he was being serious!

So we had our moments as a team but, on the other hand, there's no getting away from this . . . it was a terrible feeling to be getting dragged towards relegation as the weeks went by.

We lost four games on the trot right at the end and it all came down to the last game, away at Bolton, who were pushing for promotion.

The funny thing was, in the build-up to the game, there was no negativity; there was something about us and I really thought we were going to do it. In my mind, I kept picturing scoring the winner and celebrating with the fans at the end. Then we'd have a real go at the league the next season. Of course, it didn't work out like that.

We got beat, we got relegated - and it hit me like a train.

Preston had given me my chance and I felt I'd let them down. The club meant so much to me and I know how much it would have hurt the fans to go down.

The Bolton crowd piled on at the end but I remember going over to thank the Preston fans for their support, because there were thousands there that day; a sea of North End shirts, some lads with flat caps and funny hats on, banners, scarves - they'd been unbelievable for a team at the bottom of the league. I could see in their faces how heartbroken they were, but they were still applauding us off.

It was just incredible and I'll never forget that. In the end, the emotion just got too much for me and I broke down in tears as we left the pitch. I couldn't help it, it just hit me so hard. I didn't know it at the time, but the Evening Post photographer captured the moment and again I was on the back page on the Monday night.

But this time it was in much sadder circumstances. Gissa tissue.

The only thing we could take from a terrible day was tha . . . no, sod it, there was nothing we could take from that day.

Let's move on.

As we faced up to life in the bottom division, John brought in a raft of new players who epitomised his outlook in many ways; people who could play football, but you knew their attitude was always going to be spot on.

The experienced Paul Raynor and Mike Conroy came in, while David Moyes and Ian Bryson arrived as the season got going. For a younger player learning the game like me, these were fantastic signings - just to see how the likes of David and Brys conducted themselves and approached things was an education in itself.

For John, I think they were his own signings - putting his stamp on the team.

As a coach, he would find what you were good at, work on it and make it better.

He was an amazing motivator and, you may have heard this before, he was tough - by God, he was *tough*. But I always knew I was the fittest I'd ever been under him, because training was hard; it was disciplined and regimented and strict.

Yet, believe me, some managers still use what he pioneered even today, even if John doesn't get any credit for it.

You look at the ice buckets and things, but they weren't that far off from some modern techniques around now, with people having cold showers before games. Getting players together to eat after training, making sure they got the right food, this is all common practice now - but it wasn't back then. He was one of the first to do it.

And he also went out of the way for his players, even little things like making sure the bus got us home as soon as possible after long journeys, he would always do everything he could to put the players first.

He would go in to fight for the players, whether it was something inside the club, the FA, referees, whatever, he would lead from the front. Admittedly, he could rub people up the wrong way and he was a one-off character, but I don't have a bad word to say about him. OK, some of his rollockings took on legendary status and I was never on the end of one, so I can't speak for those that were.

And there's absolutely no doubt you had to be mentally tough to deal with him at times. But if he saw you weren't that robust, he wouldn't destroy you - he would build you up to make you tougher. It wasn't in his interest to grind people into the floor - why would it be? The bottom line was, if you gave everything you had, he was fine.

You weren't necessarily doing it for him, you were doing it for the supporters, who would give anything to be out there in your shoes.

That's what I always thought. I looked back on me as a kid on the terraces at Blackburn thinking: 'If ever I got out there, I'd do everything for that shirt.'

So when I got to play for Preston, I knew I wasn't just living out my dream - I was living out the dream of everyone coming to watch. And to earn that, to carry that responsibility, you can't give anything less than 100 per cent.

That's the way I always looked at it and I think John appreciated that.

At times, I think his playing style became an easy get-out for people to hide behind a bit: *'We'd have won if we didn't have to play these stupid tactics.'* There's an argument that maybe he was so focused with getting the ball 'in behind' that it stopped us playing much football at times, but that was his philosophy and it wasn't pie-in-the-sky - there was science behind it and it had worked for him at Cambridge.

He was very keen on putting pressure on the opposition right from the kick-off; Ryan Kidd would knock the ball high and long towards the left-back, hanging it up to give me time to get there. I would just be pelting down the line to get a challenge in and it was often just a case of throwing my body at this poor soul, who was about to get smashed in the first 10 seconds.

I knew what was coming, John did, Kiddo did - *even the North End crowd did* - but if the opposition hadn't done their homework, it was a hell of an introduction to the game! In all seriousness, there was a lot of method in what he was doing tactically; getting teams turned, wearing them down, turning them again and again and again.

We'd do it more than anyone else, but even people who criticised it could see that it worked in that first season after we went down. We ended up second top scorers in the league, with Tony Ellis - not a typical John Beck player - getting 26 goals, so it wasn't as one-dimensional as people might think.

For me as a young lad, I never questioned it. He turned me back into a right winger and we went on a great run, winning five games on the trot and beating Shrewsbury 6-1 at Deepdale, where I got two and Mike Conroy got a hat-trick.

That was the start of me really enjoying my football and, while I never rested on my laurels, I started to relax a bit more in my surroundings. I didn't have the 'Wild Thing' tag at that point, but I was known as a little bit crazy and if there was any messing about going on, I'd probably be at the centre of it. I'm an extrovert so I'd always be entertaining the lads and taking on daft challenges.

If Moyesie says I could head a pool ball across the room, then maybe - maybe - I did. I've no recollection of it, but I do have plenty of lumps on my forehead, so possibly that explains it!

On the pitch, John was building a really strong, fast team around his front men and the crowds were up, even though we'd been relegated. It was something different, but it was exciting and I think he brought the place back to life.

I think it was John who started looking at Springfields as a training ground and getting better infrastructure behind the scenes. There were little things like getting the cheerleaders on the pitch when the team came out.

Again, teams do it everywhere now, but 30 years ago it was new and it was all for us; just a little mental motivator as you go out: 'You're the team, you're important, don't let these people down.' He raised our profiles in the town, improved communication with the fans, made us more accessible. There was so much more to it than just what people saw on the pitch.

And really, we had an amazing season that year, finishing fifth and going through that epic play-off against Torquay; talk about atmosphere, passion and drama - that night had the lot. The celebrations at the final whistle were just unreal and again, something you dream about being part of as a footballer.

I think everyone who was there took something special from that night - including big strips of the plastic pitch, which the fans were ripping up around us at the end.

For me to get to Wembley as a 21-year-old was just a dream come true.We were properly together as a team; there was this real bond between us. Another way John was clever was that he didn't mind if some of the lads didn't like him, as long as they liked each other. Sometimes he'd manufacture situations that you look back on and you can see what he was doing; it was purely designed to bring the team closer together. Maybe someone would mess up in training and he'd make you feel guilty by punishing everyone for the mistake.

But the whole thing was to improve us and make us a really solid outfit.

Come the final at Wembley, it was just unbelievable to step out in that stadium, onto that pitch. You're trying to focus on the game but it's impossible not to try and take everything in. I don't have many superstitions, but I always liked to go out third in the line and these days, the pictures from that day are up at Adams Park so I see them all the time. There's Martin O'Neill leading Wycombe out, John leading us, there's Moyesie and just behind, there's me; this pale, skinny lad with an army-style haircut.

So I'm constantly reminded of that game down here, but the good news is - I look so young, no-one can believe it's me! *Where's the long hair, for a start? And the wrinkles?*

Obviously, it was a great day for Wycombe, but with all Preston's history, it's not one that will feature highly in Lancashire. They beat us fair and square though and, of course, my hero Simon Garner scored. You'd have thought those cigarettes would have caught up with him by then, but sadly not. I was gutted at the end, but he came up, gave me a hug, told me to keep going and was great with me. He's a proper person, Garns, one of those that even opposition fans liked, because he was such a character.

You couldn't help loving him, even though he'd just broken our hearts.

I've always loved to sing - I think I get it from my mum, who was a professional in the 1960s and had a beautiful voice. I think she'd have preferred me to be a singer than a footballer, to be honest.

At the end of the day, neither are exactly bad career options (!), so to be able to combine the two is a dream for me, even if we're not exactly headlining Glastonbury.

I've played in various bands down the years and these days front The Cold Blooded Hearts. (What do you mean, you've never heard of us?) When I was at North End, I'd always get up on the karaoke and we had some memorable nights out, trying to match the 'singing' to the song. I'm not saying I'm Bono or anything, but some of the lads should been nowhere near the mic.

Me? I'm a big Jim Morrison fan, so anything by The Doors is fine by me. Light My Fire is probably my 'go-to' tune, but I'll give anything a go.

We released a cover version of The Wanderer (of course) last year and I've also been in a few other bands down the years: APA, Road to Eden and Dog Chewed The Handle.

I've also fronted an INXS tribute band as Michael Hutchence - albeit with a bit of a Lancashire accent instead of an Aussie one. Hey, you can't ignore your roots can you?

As for us, it was a case of dusting ourselves down and going one better the following year. We would be aiming for automatic promotion, but be better prepared if it came to the play-offs.

I began to feel like I belonged as a professional a lot more and I was in the team again the next season, starting every game.

One thing that stands out for me is after we beat Gillingham away in September 1994, where big Mark Sale got two and the prolific Terry Fleming grabbed the other. I hadn't scored but I'd had a good game and maybe got an assist or two.

Moyesie asked to have a word with me after the game and took me to a quiet corner. He was the captain and I was thinking: *'Oh crap, what have I done wrong?'*

But he looked me in the eye and said: 'Gareth, you keep playing like that and people will start taking notice. I'm telling you now, you're going to play in the Premier League.' He was deadly serious and it had a big impact on me. I thought: *'Wow. Moyesie thinks I can achieve that.'* We all had so much respect for him as a player, as a man, as a leader. It was a massive thing for me to hear that from him.

Maybe it was one of the first signs of how good he was going to be as a coach and manager, because he has this presence, this intensity and authenticity about him that makes him such a great motivator. He was still one of the lads and he wasn't always serious, but when he was . . . you listened. I always took on board what he said and I remembered his words all the way through my career.

We'd lost Tony Ellis by then *(I can't remember where he went)* and for whatever reason we suddenly dropped into a terrible run - losing seven on the trot in the league.

To shake things up a bit, John put me up front with Micky Conroy for the FA Cup game against Blackpool when we won 1-0 in front of the TV cameras.

That was a great night and I can imagine people watching it at home, listening to the atmosphere and thinking: 'Blimey!' The win wasn't enough though and not long after that, Becky was sacked.

I'll be honest, I was gutted when he went.

When you're only 21 though, you don't see the politics and the stuff that goes on, I was just disappointed that it had come to that.

Gary Peters stepped up and he liked me, but not as much as Becky did. I picked up a knee injury in the reserves and then I was in and out of the team even when I was fit. Understandably, Gary wanted to do things his way and maybe one or two of us John Beck-type players weren't at the centre of his thinking.

We had a couple of bust-ups, because players get like that when they're not being picked. But I've nothing against Gary, he's a good guy and he was successful with North End, so he was getting it right, no matter what I thought at the time.

I'd just got back in the team when one Friday afternoon, he called me in and told me he was signing this 17-year-old from Man United on loan. He said: 'You've got to kick on Gareth. I'm bringing this kid in from United and he's going to be starting ahead of you. He's taking your place and it shouldn't be like that.'

I was thinking: 'Damn right, it shouldn't be like that! I haven't been that bad, and he's getting some snotty teenager in ahead of me!'

Of course, the 'kid' was David Beckham and the rest is history.

As soon as he started training with us, I was like: 'Ohhh, hang on . . .'

Becks was just incredible even at that early age and I look back and think how lucky I was to have been with him when he was just starting out. Years later, when I played for Wimbledon against United in the Premier League, he came up to speak to me and said: 'Hello Gareth, remember when we were at Preston?' It was a nice touch from a class act, but I know he always speaks fondly of his time with us at Deepdale.

Even when he returned to United, however, I still didn't get a run in the team as we made it into the play-offs and ended up losing to Bury that year - more play-off heartbreak.

Andy Saville and Steve Wilkinson arrived that summer and, in all honesty, I was all set to fight for my place and show that I could do a good job putting in the crosses for them.

But just a couple of weeks into the season, it was all change - I was on my way out to a new club. To be fair to Gary, with everything that had gone on with Becky, he had to change the style to a degree and there's no doubt he wanted us to get it down and play more football.

I think it probably came down to a choice between me and Lee Cartwright in his team and Carts was definitely more of a player than I was; we both had good engines, but he had the vision and could always pick a pass. I was more about getting past people and whipping balls in. I'm under no illusions about my strengths, I was quick, fit, physical, up-and-at-'em, never-say-die, all that type of stuff.

But Lee had all that and passing ability too, so the way Gary wanted to play, I'd probably agree with him that Carts was the better man for it. Plus, he went on to be a legend who played hundreds and hundreds of games for North End, so I've got to respect the decision all day long.

Having said that, I still reckon Lee was better in central midfield - but that's probably only because he kept me out of the team on the right!

Silky Paul Raynor could play there, too, so I was a bit down the pecking order when I got another one of those abrupt phone calls at home from Glen Bonnell.

'Becky wants you. Get your ass to Lincoln.'

'Yes Glen. Will do.'

The club had accepted an offer and John was reuniting quite a few of the Preston lads there; Terry Fleming, Stevie Holmes, Barry Richardson and his ponytail. So there were plenty of familiar faces and it was a real catalyst for me in many ways.

I moved out of my mum and dad's and had to stand on my own two feet. Also, someone had paid money for me, an actual transfer fee of £25,000, which was an amazing feeling, but also a bit surreal.

Lincoln finished in the bottom half that year as North End won the league, but I was absolutely chuffed for everyone back at Deepdale - no bad feelings whatsoever. I was delighted, but I would have loved to have been a part of it. To think about the Town End at the end of the season when the lads were getting the trophy . . . wow. It must have been amazing, the type of scenes that fans and players never forget.

Obviously, things went well for me at Lincoln and then a big move to Port Vale, who were in the Championship, before a £2 million transfer to Wimbledon, where I fell in with the Crazy Gang. It was Kenny Cunningham who first nicknamed me 'Wild Thing' there after seeing my attempts at a golf swing.

That's the official story, although there may have been other reasons too!

It's funny but apart from playing football, I'd never really been to London before, so I was this classic Northern lad in the capital; bright lights, big city - it was an unbelievable experience. I was really proud to play in the Premier League and had some great times up there, scoring a couple of goals at Newcastle - including a last-minute equaliser - was an unforgettable feeling.

The sad thing was though that I wasn't able to fulfil my potential in the top flight.

I'd hardly missed any games in my career up to that point, but I suffered a pelvic injury that took me more than a year to recover from and by then we'd been relegated to the Championship. It really knocked me sideways and took me a long time to get over.

The only positive was that when I was coming back from the injury, it allowed North End to come in for me on loan in 2002.

Kelham O'Hanlon had just taken over from Moyesie and the team was pushing for the play-offs at the top of the Championship. He rang me up and it was almost full circle from 10 years earlier: 'We need a right winger, can you play?'

A chance to go back to Deepdale? I was setting off before he put the phone down.

The first game back I came on as a sub against Portsmouth - ironically replacing Carts - and I was taken aback by the welcome from the crowd. It was just an amazing reception and I was determined to repay the supporters. A couple of games later, I made my first start against Coventry on a glorious sunny afternoon at Deepdale.

Sadly Kiddo had just retired, but obviously Carts was still playing and Paul McKenna, who'd been on the books when I was first there, too. Mick Rathbone was physio and what a legend he is too, by the way.

But there was a new generation of North Enders: Sean Gregan, Graham Alexander, Richard Cresswell - really good players and top professionals.

Deepdale itself though was virtually unrecognisable. Only the old Pavilion was still in place, the rest had been developed with three beautiful stands - they'd done a really good job of it, keeping that feel of being a 'proper' football ground. The floodlights themselves are a thing of beauty and you could see how far the club had come over the past decade.

The funny thing is, although it's a brilliant stadium now . . . part of me still misses the old ground. It was a real honour to play in front of the old Town End, I feel privileged to have experienced it, I really do.

It was where thousands of people crammed together as one entity; noisy as hell, scary at times and always on your side. It was so, so good to play in front of.

The Preston fans were always a good crowd and that hadn't changed on that afternoon against Coventry. I was so, so happy to be back, lining up at Deepdale, big crowd, sunny day - I couldn't wait to get going.

We won 4-0 and not only did I get Man of the Match, I managed to score a late goal at the Fulwood End. Talk about a dream come true. One of the lads got clattered putting the cross in, but I got in at the back post and caught it on the half volley.

I had my head bandaged up, shirt untucked, blood all over it - it was just like the good old days and I remember kissing the badge in celebration. I know that can be a bit of a 'football crime' to some fans *(sorry!)* and it's not something I usually did, but I was just so pleased to be back and the club meant so much to me.

Without Preston North End, I wouldn't have gone on to have the career I had, it's as simple as that and I will always, always, always be grateful.

We just missed out on the play-offs that season, but I could see the club was in a really good place with a great set of lads and I was desperate to return.

I was back home in Lancashire, with a club that I loved and a good chance of success the following season. I had an agreement with Kelham and Derek Shaw to sign permanently that summer and I went away happy as anything, thinking it was all sorted. When I came back from holiday though, it wasn't down to Kel any more.

Craig Brown had taken over and well, in a nutshell, he didn't want me. I don't think he'd ever seen me play, but he wanted to bring his own people in and you've got to respect that. I get it and I've no axe to grind with Craig at all, managers have to make these decisions, as I know only too well.

It was a real blow though, because I would have loved to have been a part of things at Deepdale again and maybe see my career out there.

That loan spell just re-emphasised to me what a special club it was. I was always pleased to be wanted anywhere, but to have Preston come calling for me had been the dream move.

When it fell through, it was a really worrying time because the ITV Digital deal had just gone belly up and money was really tight in the game.

Luckily, I signed for another year at Wimbledon then after that had long spells at QPR and Wycombe, first as a player and now for the past eight years as manager.

I've been back to Deepdale as a player and come up against North End in the FA Cup with Wycombe. I'm always taken aback by the reception I get from the supporters - especially as the people who first saw me nearly 30 years ago will be probably be getting on a bit now *(aren't we all?)*.

There's still that connection there though and there always will be for me - the North End result is always one of the first I check when the scores come in.

It was great to chat to some PNE fans over the phone during the Coronavirus crisis recently and relive some great memories.

It's the same whenever I'm up there and people spot me around town; once they've taken the Mickey out of my hair, we always get talking about this game, that goal, this incident - I absolutely love it.

I'm just so proud to have played for the club, to have forged such good friendships and to have those supporters still think highly of me.

If I ever get round to writing the story of my life, Preston North End will be a long, happy chapter.

Chapter 2

JON MACKEN: WHAT'S THE STORY?

It's funny how little moments can have such a big effect on your life, without you even realising it. When I was about nine years old, I was playing for my junior team and we were getting beat 2-1 at half-time.

I hadn't been playing fantastic or anything, but as we came off at the interval, I was saying: *'Come on boys, we can get back into it! We can win this!'*

I just wanted us to keep going and going. I didn't realise it at the time, but there was a scout there that day and he overheard me geeing the lads up.

To this day, I think that's what swung it for me to get a trial at Manchester United.

I was a late addition to the long list of young lads they were looking at and I don't even think it was down to ability - it was the attitude I'd shown that day.

On the day of the trial, I was sent home from school because I wasn't very well. Sheer nerves and I probably lost a few pounds in weight that morning, I can tell you!

Even when I got there I thought I was going to be overlooked. The trial was split into three 20-minute games. The first one; I wasn't involved. The second one; not involved again. I was bobbing around the coach, trying to get noticed (as you do), but when they read out the teams for the last game . . . I wasn't on the list again.

I was gutted, thinking I wasn't going to get a chance.

So I did the biggest warm-up you've ever seen right next to the coach and - *finally* - I got on for the last 10-15 minutes. *Right, let's go.*

Thankfully, I did really well - scoring two and setting one up. After that, they said they wanted to sign me and, well, that's how the story starts.

Brian Kidd was at the School of Excellence at the time and he was great with me; he took an interest in my education, made sure I got to training and he was a top class coach. One time he said he wanted me to meet someone at Old Trafford and as we went along this corridor, I kept thinking: 'What's that funny smell?'

He knocked on a door and as we went in there was this haze of pipe smoke almost filling the room - it was like an indoor fog. I could see this figure sitting at a desk and as the haze cleared I saw the unmistakeable figure of Sir Matt Busby.

Brian said something like: 'This is Jonathan Macken, Sir Matt, he's going to be a very good player in the future.'

Of course, at the time, I was just a kid and the enormity of meeting such a legend of the game only really sinks in years later. I wish I could remember exactly what he said, but it was along the lines of: 'Hello son, I've heard good things about you, keep working hard, etc . . .'

But just to have met him and had a brief chat is almost surreal, looking back on it. Brian moved up the ranks at United, but the other coaches there were top class too;

ex-PNE manager Nobby Stiles was great and people have probably heard of Eric Harrison, who brought through the Class of '92.

However, Jim Ryan was absolutely fantastic for me personally. He pushed me on and really furthered my career at that young age more than anyone. I think he saw something in me and believed in me and I'll always be grateful to him.

As things developed, I worked my way through the levels at United and broke into the reserves, when out of the blue I got a call-up to the England Under-20 team.

Ted Powell was the manager at the time and I made it into the squad for the World Youth Championship in Malaysia in 1997 where there were some unbelievable players; Thierry Henry and David Trezeguet of France, Juan Riquelme of Argentina - while we had Liverpool's Michael Owen and some kid called David Lucas of Preston North End.

We got knocked out by Argentina in the last 16, but it was an amazing experience and something that again helped me develop as a player.

Before setting off for the tournament, I'd been offered a new contract by United and my intention was to sign it.

But when I got back, there were a few teams interested in signing me - Bradford and Wrexham were interested and I was a bit like *'mmmm'*. But then Gary Peters came on from Preston.

I could have stayed at United, but I had got to a point where I wanted to play first team games and if I could do that in the right environment at the right club, then I thought that would be a good move for my career.

So I took the plunge to sign for Preston - and never regretted it for a single minute.

It was the classic case of taking a step back to move forward in the long term and that's exactly how it turned out. Not only that, but there seemed to be a real United connection to Preston down the years.

Obviously, Sir Bobby Charlton and Nobby had managed the club and Brian had been there too. Another of the young United lads, big Colin Murdock, had just signed at Deepdale and he'd let me know that they were interested in me, so when Gary gave me the call I couldn't wait to get up there.

I drove up to see Gary and remember looking round the stadium thinking: 'Wow - this is fantastic.' I was trying to keep a lid on it, but inside I was like: 'Where do I sign?'

The Sir Tom Finney Stand was in place and there were plans for the rest of the ground too; the crowds were really good for the level they were at and I just got the feeling it was a club 'on the up'.

I'd never even been to Deepdale before, although I knew Becks had been there on loan a few years earlier and loved it. I didn't get chance to ask him about it though because it was all done in a day. It was a case of going up to Preston, looking around, agreeing a contract, doing some photographs and then heading back to The Cliff to pick up my stuff. So it was a hectic old day and - *just to top things off* - we broke down on the M61 on the way home!

At the time, I was only a young lad of 19, so the enormity of it all, having someone pay a transfer fee for me before I'd even played a first team game, didn't really sink in. Yes, there was a bit of pressure, but I don't remember thinking about it too much - I just remember being excited and couldn't wait to get out there.

I wanted to be part of something special; to play in a winning team, score goals and create great memories for the supporters who came to watch. I just got the feeling that Preston was about to really take off again.

Gary sold me his vision for the club very quickly and it was just really exciting to be part of. He gave you the belief that you could go out and achieve things - he'd always give you that extra push and get you to *dream big, aim high*.

The dressing room culture reflected that outlook, too - everyone was really hungry for success no matter what stage their careers were at. Me, Colin and Michael Appleton were just starting out, but there were people like Gary Parkinson, David Reeves, Sean Gregan - all massive characters who had been around the block.

It was obvious to everyone that the club had recruited players with the right sort of personalities; all good lads who could have a laugh and a joke, but deadly serious about winning games. Lots of Northerners with proper 'no messing' attitudes; battlers like Ryan Kidd, Michael Jackson and Simon Davey, along with the flair of people like Kurt Nogan and David Eyres.

(I'm hoping that when you read this, you're smiling as much as I am when I think about those lads!)

It was a bit of an eye-opener at first, because obviously I'd come from youth football where it's not as physical and nowhere near as vocal. If that scout thought I'd geed the lads up in that junior game, he should have heard Moyesie at the back!

Suddenly, I stepped into playing with men who'd been around football for many years and were battle-hardened in every way.

There was no pussy-footing about. It was a real toughening-up process; in training, in the dressing room and, most of all, in matches.

Greegs was probably the biggest personality and he let us know what was required: the team had to win, no matter what. No excuses. Just win.

The unwritten rule was that it's not about individuals, it's about playing your part for the team - and winning. That was the culture in a nutshell.

Of course, I was only 19 and when you're that age, even though you're really a young lad, you think you're a man. You think going into a man's game will be a doddle. *Yeah, right.*

It was such a big jump for me. I hadn't been out on loan before or anything, so it was simply a case of: 'Here you go - deal with it.' It all took a lot of adjusting to; the intensity, the pressure to win.

No-one was getting paid huge amounts of money at the time and win bonuses played a big part in your income. People were fighting for their livelihoods, for their careers, to pay the bills. As a young kid, that's where the pressure came from. I was thinking: 'I've got to really perform here, I don't want to let anyone down.'

Luckily, I hit the ground running by getting off the mark in my second match at Rotherham and then scoring on my home debut against Millwall. Lee Ashcroft put the ball over for me, it took a bit of a bounce and I nodded it in at the Kop end.

It was just a fantastic feeling to hear that roar from the Preston fans when it went in. I remember running over to the Sir Tom Finney Stand and just seeing everyone going crazy - it's almost indescribable really.

Coming from United, I thought I was a fiery character at times - but that was before I met Ashy. New levels, that lad. I remember as we walked off at half-time he was going mental at me for not passing him the ball when he thought I should have done.

I was thinking: 'Wow! What's going on here? I've just scored and this guy's giving me a rollocking.' That was Lee though; great player, a brilliant lad and Preston through and through.

Sadly, my good start didn't last and I was in and out of the team a bit as I got to grips with the step up to playing at League 1 level. Realistically, I probably wasn't physically ready and probably not as mentally tough as I needed to be when we hit bumps in the road. When you're older and you've played a bit more, you know you're going to come through things - the tide is going to turn at some point. But when you're young, it all weighs really heavily on your shoulders and affects you.

I suppose I was shielded a bit because I was in that 'young prospect' comfort zone, seen as someone with potential. But, young lad or not, the brutal truth in that first season was that I wasn't doing what I'd been brought in to do - score goals.

When it's like that, what I probably needed was an 'arm around the shoulder' approach, but when results aren't going for the team and there's a lot going on, it's hard for the manager to do that, especially if he's fighting for his job.

We were getting some good results, but not with any consistency and by January we were hovering just below mid-table. Gary was changing the team quite a bit and for me personally, without three or four games on the bounce, I couldn't get any momentum going. I understand it, because he was looking for a winning formula and sometimes if a young lad's not doing it, it's a natural instinct to turn to more experienced players, so I was sub quite a bit.

Nowadays, I say to young players who are on the bench: 'Look on it as a chance to learn.' Listen to the manager and the coaches, understand what's happening and you'll have more chance of affecting things when you come on.

Of course, back then, I used to get so frustrated at not starting that I'd be on the bench getting angry and not realising what I could learn. Because when you're 19, you know it all, don't you?

Eventually, the penny dropped and I realised that by paying attention, it gave me a much better understanding of what was required when I came on. It was probably the first time that I'd not been playing matches regularly. So, again, that brings a new challenge about staying sharp, how to be match ready, how to handle things mentally.

Another thing was, I wasn't used to losing. At United, we tended to win most games and now I was in a dressing room where we were losing a few. And this was league football. It mattered. Not just to the players, the manager and the staff, but also to the 10,000 people who were paying to watch us.

You soon understand the responsibility of representing those people and knowing what it means to them. They're a really good crowd at Preston, but like all football fans, if you're losing, they'll let you know what they think. It was a whole new world for me, but you just had to handle it and I grew up so much over that period.

If we got beat, there were arguments, people pointing fingers, big inquests on what had gone wrong - because the culture of the North End dressing room was the right one; there was no acceptance of defeat. Fans going mad at us as we left the pitch should know that we didn't get in and just shrug it off; we were just as naffed off as they were.

It may have been painful at times, but the experience was invaluable in the years ahead. It wasn't the glamour of being on Man United's books, it was something much more useful.

It was proper football; the nitty-gritty reality and if you want to be a professional footballer, you need to see things as they really are - the good and the bad.

Obviously, I was really sad when Gary eventually stepped aside, because he'd been great with me - he brought me in and I knew he rated me. Everyone liked him and could see how hard he worked and how much he cared for the club.

Thankfully, the board had faith in Moyesie and, as everyone now knows, that was a masterstroke. Straight away he told us what he expected, what the standards were and how hard we were going to work. No problem.

He'd already been doing some coaching, so it was a smooth transition. He pulled me to one side early on and said that he'd been to watch me with Gary before I joined and it was the pair of them had pushed for the club to sign me. That was a big thing for me and meant a lot, that he had the same belief in me as Gary had.

It didn't happen straight away, but results-wise things picked up as that season went on and David's training and approach started to pay dividends.

Once things started to pick up, we got some momentum and you could feel us moving in the right direction towards the end of that first term.

I remember we played Blackpool in April and it was the first time I'd been involved in that derby game. Blimey - talk about intense. The atmosphere was just cranked up like I'd never seen before at that point.

We were drawing 2-2 when the keeper parried a shot and I managed to slot it in right in front of the old Town End to put us 3-2 up. Scoring against Blackpool at Deepdale? New to it or not, I knew what that meant. *Get in!*

In those days, there were a lot more standing areas and I could just see people jumping around going absolutely crazy everywhere I looked. I was like: *'Blimey - look at that!'*

Punching the air in celebration, here comes the noise, the mayhem, the lads . . . what a feeling.

We all loved games like those, and it gave us a real taste for getting more success. We knew that if we could light the blue and white touch paper, the club would really take off.

Over the summer, Moyesie's pre-season training was just fantastic and you could feel that the group had really started to look a lot stronger. The sessions were hard as hell and people were pushing each other, spurring each other on - no-one was allowed to slip from the standards expected.

As that new season went on, I was starting nearly every game and again that was a great boost for me because I got sharper, more used to playing in that environment - and the more you do something, the easier it gets. I wasn't actually scoring loads of goals, but I was holding the ball up well, bringing others into play and contributing a lot of assists. All that builds confidence and I think laid the groundwork for me being able to score more in the seasons ahead. I'd shown that I could do it at that level and having that confidence is a massive thing.

The buzz of starting week-in, week-out becomes infectious and I couldn't wait for the games to come around.

Moyesie drilled into us such a strict positional sense, we always knew where we should be on the pitch, no matter what the situation.

I felt that even when I went home at night, I'd know where Kurt Nogan would be.

(Well, with Kurt, maybe not . . . but you get the picture!)

It was a thing of beauty to play in when it got like that; the rhythm of our play, like a machine with all these parts, ticking over, then - *bang!* - suddenly going through the gears.

One of the games everyone remembers from that season was when we beat Man City at Maine Road. I don't know what it was but we all just fancied ourselves in the build-up.

We played really well on the night and when we got the penalty, with about 20 minutes to go, there was never any doubt Gary Parkinson was going to score.

Some of the free-kicks he scored were the best I've ever seen and his shots from outside the box were just unstoppable at times - a hell of a player. I got brought down for the penalty and before I'd even hit the deck, I think Parky was setting off to take the pen. I just knew he was going to score - I don't think I ever saw him miss one.

But that night - *wow* - he nearly took the back of the net off. I think Nicky Weaver dived out of the way to avoid it! An absolute rocket in a pressure situation - Parky had nerves of steel, that lad.

I think it was Kurt *(who else?)* who'd said in the run-up to the game that if we scored we should do a daft celebration. So when it went in, we ended up doing a rowing boat celebration back to the halfway line. Don't ask me why! I look back on it now and think: *'What the hell??'*

But at the time, that was the spirit that we had. City at Maine Road? Yeah, OK, let's enjoy this if we win. And we did.

The other one people remember was the Arsenal FA Cup game. Again, it was a case of us puffing our chests out and saying: 'Right, let's have it!' We wanted to show them what Preston North End was all about - and thankfully we weren't alone.

There must have been more than 20,000 packed into Deepdale that night and the atmosphere was just incredible. Watch the highlights now and you can hear the crowd backing every challenge, every tackle, screaming for free-kicks - I don't think we heard the Arsenal fans unless they scored.

One of the funny things about it is that everyone thinks I helped set up the first goal for Noges - but, sorry, it wasn't me. The commentator on TV says something like 'Macken keeps the ball in . . .' but it was actually Eyresy - I was out wide in the build-up.

We had similar haircuts at the time and I think in the excitement, even North End fans got mixed up. But, hey, it was a goal so no-one cares *(well, apart from Eyresy, who never lets me forget it!).*

It was a great night for the club and we were all pleased to have stood up well against a world-class side. But again, we weren't slapping each other on the back afterwards. We'd lost, so y'know . . .

It did help spur us on in the league again though and we built up some real momentum. Steve Basham came in on loan and was a great addition, although he's behind one of my most controversial goals.

And when I say 'behind', I mean about the length of a stud. We were 2-0 up at home to Northampton and Bash had got both on a glorious day at Deepdale.

With about 20 minutes to go, the ball came in just on the edge of the area and it was almost perfectly dropping between us.

Steve went for it. I went for it. And - *bang!* - we caught it virtually together as the ball flew in the back of the net; 3-0. Job done.

Of course, Bash was on a hat-trick though and to this day, people say to me that it was his goal. But I know I got there first - because I felt Steve whack the bottom of my foot as I hit it! After the game he had this big cut where he'd caught my studs, so there was physical proof, too.

Look, I'm a striker; I claim goals - especially when I've scored them!

We didn't have the best run towards the end of the season, but we finished fifth and came up against Tony Pulis' Gillingham side in the play-offs. They were all big, big lads and it was always going to be a tough game against them; they always seemed to have something over us when we played them around that time - a real bogey club.

It wasn't just that though, they were a good side with a lot of lads who went on to have really good careers. Bash was doing really well, so in all honesty, I didn't think I'd be starting. But then he turned his ankle in training and I was in the team.

We weren't disgraced and on paper it was tight as we lost 2-1 on aggregate. In reality they were horrible games, but as ever, we took something from them in terms of where we needed to be the following season.

There was no resting on laurels and saying we'd done well to get in the play-offs - it was a case of seeing where we needed to improve.

David was so focused on improving us that the pre-season that year was ***the*** hardest I've ever done. I'm wincing just to think of it now, but there were no complaints, no grumbling.

I don't quite know how to describe this, but when we got together for the first day back in training that summer, you could really feel something special about us as a group. It wasn't just one or two of the lads were absolutely 'on it' - it was the entire squad. We'd been together for two or three years by then and the determination about us was tangible.

David was bringing good quality signings in and he installed in us a real belief that we could go on and achieve something special. Our aim was automatic promotion - simple as that. I know people will say that at clubs every year, but for us, it was non-negotiable. Honestly, the mindset of that squad was unbelievable.

And so were our haircuts.

Me and Eyresy were rooming together pre-season and we heard that Tepi Moilanen had cut someone's hair really short. I'm not sure if Tep was a qualified barber (nothing would surprise me!) but Dave and I said: 'Come on, let's have it done.'

You look back and think . . . oh my God, as if we let Tepi loose on us with clippers!

Why, why, why??!

We looked like skin-headed army recruits, but the next thing, the lads were all lining up to have the same trim. Jacko, Kiddo - those lads looked scary enough without the crew cuts, but now . . ! It was a sign of the team spirit we had. One for all and all for one - that was our mentality.

As for Tepi, the only thing I can say on the record is that he was so loopy, he made Dave Lucas look sensible. Goalkeepers - say no more.

Our first game of the new season was away at Oldham. A hot sunny day everywhere else, but - as always - about minus six over there! I got the winner and I just remember the away end there being absolutely packed with North End fans, maybe three or four thousand of them - noisy as hell, brilliant support. When the goal went in, well, the entire end just went up. It was almost a surreal moment, it makes the hairs on the back of my neck stand up just thinking about it.

You could see the belief was in the supporters too - I think they knew we were on the verge of doing something great. The fans were feeding off the team and vice versa. Again, mentally, that gives you a real lift and the games can't come around fast enough.

What can you say about that season?

We had the ability, we were driven, we were organised - and we were relentless. For me, I was coming into my peak and scored 25 goals that year, probably because it was such a good team to play in. The defence was rock solid, Greegs and Ranks were dominating midfield every week and Eyresy was still doing his magic on the wing, even though he was about 50 by that point!

The element that brought it all together though was Moyesie. He was absolutely brilliant with me, because I knew he cared about me. He was always offering me advice about things, believing in me, looking after me, taking an interest. Sometimes, it wasn't even football stuff - just how to live your life properly, advice on outside stuff. You could tell he cared, because he was a proper genuine person.

It made a big impact on me. Not just in my career, but in my life too.

When you've got someone like that, it just makes you even more determined to do everything you possibly can to be successful. You couldn't wait to get in every day, because it was like being part of a family.

And if you bumped into any North End fans out and about, everyone was smiling, happy, urging you on, part of it too. It was just a brilliant time.

We felt like we could take anyone on, so when we were drawn away at Arsenal in the League Cup, we were well up for it. Parky was injured at the time but was doing the radio commentary and I'll always remember him saying to me before the game: 'You're going to score tonight Jon - when you do, don't forget to give us a wave.'

Kanu put them 1-0 up, but a few minutes later the ball looped in to the edge of the box and I managed to catch it first time. It dropped over David Seaman at the famous Clock End and we were level - I couldn't wait to get over and give Parky a shout!

They just about saw us off 2-1 in the end, but again we'd stood up against some world-class players and not been intimidated. We'd actually gone into it thinking we were going to win - that was the way we looked at every game, no matter who we were playing.

Moyesie had said not to swap shirts but I'd come off in the second half and managed to get Ray Parlour's. It wasn't a swap though, boss - he just gave me it. For some reason he wasn't interested in having mine in return.

Back in the league, we were just flying; if we got our stride, we were playing great football. If a team wanted to battle with us, we'd battle and grind it out.

Either way, we were getting results.

I got a bit of a knock at Scunthorpe towards the end of the season, but was back on the bench for the home game at Millwall at Deepdale where we were able to celebrate winning the league.

You look back on moments in your life and just think: 'Wow, how lucky was I?'

It's hard to imagine a more perfect scene . . . a glorious sunny day and Sir Tom Finney leading us out at a packed Deepdale when we'd just won the league.

What a moment, what a memory, what a thing to experience as a footballer.

Again, I relive it in my mind and it gets the hairs standing up even now. How can it not? That's what football is all about, that's what you come into the game for.

It's not money or flash cars or any material stuff. It's memories like that - things no-one can ever take away from you.

People talk about players earning this and that, but I don't care if they're the richest people in the world; if they've not had that feeling, they're missing out.

Same with the open-top bus parade through the town. I wish I could just go back and experience it over and over again, because at the time, you don't really take it all in. You're caught up in the moment and you can't believe your eyes at how many people have turned out.

The celebrations, the singing, the banners, BAXI shirts everywhere, everyone in the club colours - just seeing what it meant to the town and the fans.

You think you know when you're at the games, but then you see something like that, all of Preston turning out, and you realise just how much it really means.

If you could bottle the energy and emotion from that day, you could power the National Grid for years. It was unbelievable and I just wish I could go back and thank everyone personally.

It was typical of Moyesie and the club that they kept faith with us as a group that summer. There was no great spending spree, we were given the chance to show we could do it at a higher level and it was an opportunity we seized on.

Players were still coming through the ranks and Paul McKenna was establishing himself in midfield as an unbelievable talent. In training, if he was on your team, you'd always win the five-a-sides. You couldn't get the ball off him and he had so much energy; buzzing around, putting a foot in, scoring goals - he had the lot.

On top of all that, he had a fantastic attitude - always giving everything he had. He's hilarious Kenna, too - sharp as a tack and really funny. He remembers everything; you think you might have got away with something from months ago, but he'd bring it back up and slaughter you for it. A great lad, who fitted right in with the team and it was no surprise to see him as captain for many years later on.

Out on the pitch, I didn't find the higher league as big a step up as I'd thought it was going to be - and I think the lads were all the same.

We'd been playing Championship standard football in the league below, so when the time came, the difference wasn't that big. It might sound a bit arrogant, but we'd always been geared up to that higher level.

People were calling us a surprise package when we started doing well, but it wasn't a surprise to us - we knew what we had in the group. Yes, we were up against bigger clubs now, but they still only put 11 lads out against us, so bring 'em on.

And anyway, who's to say we weren't becoming a bigger club ourselves? Crowds were up again, the stadium was really taking shape and, don't forget, we were Preston North End. It's not exactly a little-known team, is it?

Clubs with far fewer fans *(no names mentioned)* have made it to the Premier League, so why not us? There's no doubt in my mind that North End would be a credible team in the top division if and when they get there. We certainly thought it at the time and I still think so now. Moyesie thought it too and gave us that belief every day along the lines of: 'We've come a long way, but there's another step to go yet.'

And don't forget, David was still developing us with his coaching.

Don't get me wrong, there's no doubt it was tougher in the Championship, the general standard of players was better and you didn't get as much time on the ball, but we adapted right from the start.

We put down a marker on the first day at Grimsby and again it was great to score in the very first game. You always want to get a goal so you're up and running. If it doesn't happen for a few, it starts to prey on your mind.

So it was great to announce ourselves on that first day. I remember the ball going through and I was tussling with the defender a fair way out from goal. I managed to get away from him, take the ball forward at full sprint, round the keeper and slam it into the empty net where the North End fans were to make it 2-0.

Hey, we're here, y'know? OK. Bring it on.

We carried on like that all season really; bigger teams, big crowds, but we played with no fear. If anything, it was like being let off the leash on a Saturday afternoon and we couldn't wait to get at people.

Fulham were on an absolute charge all season and had Louis Saha up front, with Jean Tigana in charge. They'd been unbeaten for ages at Craven Cottage, but we went down there, paid no attention to reputations or anything, worked hard and beat them.

We felt we were on a journey to the Premier League, simple as that.

I remember Blackburn were pushing for promotion just above us and they clinched it in a night match at Deepdale that they needed to win. Matt Jansen scored their goal and just afterwards I hit the post. Henning Berg came running up to me saying: 'What are you doing? You don't want to get us in the play-offs!' I was like: 'Do one, mate. If you think we're lying down, you've got the wrong team!'

Fair play, they deserved to go up that year, but trust me, to have a local rival celebrating promotion on your pitch is something that, *errr,* jarred with us. If anything, it made us even more determined in those last few games.

As for those games against Birmingham, well, what can anyone say?

That second leg at Deepdale . . . wow. Just an incredible, incredible piece of sporting theatre. If you put that night in against any sporting spectacle, it would stand up. The drama, the emotion, the excitement, it just had everything.

In the build-up we used the Gillingham experience to give us extra fire in our bellies; we knew how much that had hurt and didn't want to feel like that ever again.

As for the match itself, well . . . who doesn't know the story?

I remember feeling really tired in that last minute - we'd given everything and we knew time was almost up, so it was a case of one last effort, go right to the very end.

It was back to being that junior kid the scout saw years earlier: 'Never give up.'

And when Stan Lazaridis went through and missed, it gave us one last bolt of energy.

The lads worked it forward and I managed to get it on the edge of the box, feed Dave Healy, he took a shot and . . . I just saw the net almost burst and the roof come off in the same split second.

Everyone was chasing around and piling on in celebration and I was like: '*Who scored? Who scored? Ranks! No way! What the hell was he doing up there?!'*

The fact that Ranks had been that far forward to get that goal just gave us even more belief that this was our night, our year.

Think about it, Mark Rankine had just scored - it MUST be written in the stars.

I came off in extra time and it was understandable really; I'd never really taken penalties, Richard Cresswell always brought new energy to the team and, most of all, I was absolutely knackered.

It's funny, because although I was dog-tired, the adrenaline and the enormity of the game keeps you going while you're out there. But as soon as I came off, it hit me and I was absolutely shattered.

After that, I think the Trevor Francis rigmarole probably affected the Birmingham players. How could it not? You might be annoyed about taking penalties at the home end, but your main focus has to be making sure your team is ready. Keep calm.

We just took it in our stride really. Moyesie had us all so well prepared and Dave Lucas was brilliant in goal, a real character, a great keeper - and a proper Preston lad. For another local boy like Kenna to step up and hit the winner was just perfect really and after that, well, it was all a bit of a blur.

The noise, the fans on the pitch, coming back out with the flags and Champagne and stuff - again, just an incredible celebration. We ended up going out round the town afterwards and everywhere we went people were out singing North End songs.

It was just a brilliant, unforgettable night. I think as a group we were very down to earth and we had a real bond with the fans. There were top lads there like Kiddo and Lee Cartwright and if we went up, they'd have played in all four divisions for the club. What a story that would be . . . if we could just beat Bolton.

One more game and we've cracked it.

Come the final, we prepared really well, there was no question about confidence or belief . . . but the bottom line is, it was a game of football - and we lost.

Obviously, there's more to it than that - and anyone who's ever watched it will agree it wasn't a 3-0 game. It was 1-0 right up to the very end, when I think we'd even chucked Colin Murdock forward to try and get something right at the death.

I had a chance early on when Gudni Bergsson missed a cross right in front of me and I got a header in that I *'should probably have done better with'* as the pundits say.

At the time, it all happens in a split second between the defender missing the ball and me getting my head on it. I've looked at the replay and people say it's actually not an easy chance. They're probably right, it's not a sitter by any means, but I know it's scorable and, in any game, those fine margins count.

I think if we'd have gone 1-0 up, we'd have won and I don't think we were out of it at any point until the very last minute. Dave Healy forced a good save from the keeper in the second half and we had them under real pressure at times.

But the key difference was they were just very 'matter of fact' about the whole thing. They were down to business from the minute they came out, very focused. They had people like Colin Hendry who'd captained Scotland at the World Cup against Brazil. Whereas for us, I hate to say it, but maybe the occasion got to us a little bit, even if only subconsciously. We weren't inexperienced, but a game of that magnitude was still a big thing for us.

If we'd have been able to stay together and get in the play-offs again the following year, I'm convinced we would have won them because we'd have had that extra know-how up our sleeves. We were the type of team who learned from setbacks and defeats. We asked questions of ourselves and tried to find the answers next time out.

And I'm convinced that if we had have gone up, we'd have gone on to have as successful a period as Bolton in the Premier League.

On the day, it was just painful. We'd given our all, but we hadn't really shown what we were about. We'd had brilliant support, but fallen at the final hurdle. I think the thing that kept us going was knowing that we had it in us to come back and do better the following season. And I genuinely think we were capable of doing that.

Chris Lucketti joined at the start of the season and after a bit of a play-off hangover, we were into our stride by the time we played Man City at Deepdale in October.

City had people like Stuart Pearce and Darren Huckerby playing, as well as Eyal Berkovic, who was probably the best player I ever played with in my career.

We were 1-0 down at half-time before Dave Healy got us level, but all the way through I'd been noticing Nicky Weaver coming out off his line. I kept thinking: 'If I get the chance from a long way out here, I'm having a go.'

And I did. I remember when the ball dropped that I was ready for what I was going to do. I knew where he was, I knew where the goal was and, as soon as I hit it, I thought: *'Ohh . . . winner!'*

It was just one of those perfect moments; it was a great goal, it was on TV, the ground was packed, I had loads of family and friends there - and it was City, a massive game. Looking back, it all seems a bit surreal. Again, the atmosphere from both sets of fans was off the scale and to get the victory against a team that was flying high under Kevin Keegan was just another marker to everyone around us.

We weren't one-season wonders. We were a good side, we wouldn't back down and we were going for it again that year. We don't care who you are, try and stop us.

People were sitting up and taking notice of us - but that soon became a double-edged sword in many ways. We weren't a 'surprise package' any more, people knew how good we were. And other clubs started showing an interest in taking some of us elsewhere - including me.

When you get stuff like that, you attempt to shut it out, but no matter how hard you try, it's a distraction. Wolves came in for me with a couple of big bids, Blackburn were sniffing around and I found myself talking with David about things that had never arisen before.

I wasn't getting the greatest advice at the time and in the end, with everything swirling around, I put in a transfer request. It was a mistake and, with hindsight, something I bitterly regret.

But I made that decision and I've got to take responsibility for it. Deep down, I didn't want to do it and it's not something I'm proud of. It could and should have been avoided, but there was a lot going on with the club and, unfortunately, it happened. Even at the time, I never felt comfortable about it. I'd never really wanted to leave and I was so pleased when things got resolved, I came off the list and signed a new contract with North End. For me, that was it, done and dusted.

I was really happy and just looking forward to pushing on for promotion again. Moyesie had stuck by me throughout and there was never any issue between us. Don't get me wrong, he wasn't thrilled and he told me in no uncertain terms what he thought of it. If he thought I wasn't pulling my weight I'd be out on my ear, but that had never been in doubt, so once it was all sorted it was a case of 'head down, crack on'.

I thought that would be the end of it but then, a couple of weeks later, we were in training and Moyesie pulled me to one side and said: 'Listen Jon, the club's accepted a bid. It's a big one and it's Man City. I think you should go.'

Genuinely, at that point, in my head I thought I was going to be a Preston player for the foreseeable future, so there was a big part of me that didn't want to go. I knew I would massively miss David, the lads and a place where I'd been so happy.

However, knowing the club had accepted a record £5 million bid, I realised that the die was cast - I had to leave. I hugged Moyesie, thanked him for everything and went to City where everything was done within a day really.

In hindsight, you look back and think: 'Was it the right time to move?' I honestly don't know. But I do know these opportunities don't come around very often, for players or the club. The fee had reached the level where North End wanted the money, City wanted me and that was that.

It happens in football all the time, but players aren't robots and I had massive feelings for Preston, so it was a sad day in many ways. It was the end of a brilliant chapter in my life and a step into the unknown.

If I'd stayed, could we have gone one better than the year before? Possibly, it certainly wasn't beyond the group, but we'll never know.

Not long after I left, David went to Everton and that was a far bigger thing than me leaving. He was at the heart of everything we did and the driving force in the club.

I know Greegs left at the end of that season too and it was the start of a new era, with Craig Brown and then Billy Davies leading the club back to the play-off final.

Graham Alexander says he was always telling Billy he should try to bring me back, but sadly nothing ever came of it. If it had, trust me, I'd have been there like a shot!

(Ironically, Billy signed me when he was at Derby and I think he's a fantastic manager and a top coach. Very intense, very focused, very good.)

As for me, I started well at City and we went up into the Premier League. But a nasty knee injury meant I didn't play as many games as I would have liked, even though I had some personal highlights and scored against United in the first derby match at the Etihad.

That, for me, is what it's all about - creating memories. The amount of players who have been in and around the game but not really achieved anything in terms of winning cups and titles is huge when you think about it.

It doesn't happen very often, so you've got to create your own moments, your own reasons for people to remember you and, while I may not have played 200 games or whatever, I made more than 50 City appearances and had those special moments that I will always remember.

Kevin Keegan was always great with me and I moved on in my career through Crystal Palace, Ipswich and Derby before joining Simon Davey, Kelham O'Hanlon and Ryan Kidd at Barnsley. I loved it there. The training, the way they were, they were just spot on. They all still had those values and the camaraderie that we'd shared at Preston.

But, without question, I was always happiest at North End.

That's where I found out what it meant to be a professional footballer, what kind of player I was and what kind of person I was.

It's a club that will always mean so, so much to me.

I'm focusing on coaching and managing now and, having had a taste of success at Radcliffe FC, my top ambition is to help North End in some way, to repay them for everything they have given me.

I try to use everything I've learned throughout my career to bring out the best in people and help them fulfil their potential.

The ultimate goal would be to manage North End and, although that might seem a long way off, that's the target to go for. Like Gary Peters used to tell us: *'Aim high.'*

That's not me saying I want Alex Neil's job right now or anything, it's just to emphasise how much Preston means to me and if I ever get the opportunity to help bring further success to the club in the future, that would be my dream.

It was great to be asked to chat to some North End fans over the phone during the Coronavirus lockdown recently and relive some happy days.

Similarly, I hope getting these words down in writing brings back as many great memories for you as it does for me.

What I wouldn't give to turn back the clock, pull on the old BAXI shirt and score one more goal at the Town End - even if the ground's all locked up and there's no-one there.

Someone fetch a ladder and I'll grab my boots.

Chapter 3

ALEX BRUCE: BLESSED

From the very first minute I kicked a football, all I ever wanted to do was score goals. That thrill of putting the ball in the back of the net was what I played for. I never thought I was very good as a player - there were plenty out there better than me.

But I had a knack of scoring; I wouldn't give things up in the penalty box, I'd always try to find space and, like all strikers - I was a bit greedy at times.

Well, OK, I was a lot greedy!

But when your role in the team is to score goals, that's what you do.

I probably - *no, definitely* - drove some of my managers spare down the years by not concentrating on other parts of my game, tracking back and the like. However, if I had my time again, I'd do it exactly the same; to me, I was a striker, a centre forward - and I was there to score goals.

I grew up in Dundee and you couldn't keep us kids off a football; in the park, a patch of grass or just in the street. I had a great family upbringing and we lived in a place called Douglas, which was quite a tough council estate.

Round our way, there was no leisure centre or artificial pitch or anything so we'd play whenever, wherever. There wasn't as much traffic about in those days and it was proper 'jumpers for goalposts' stuff. *(Jeez, how old do I sound here?)*

They were the kind of matches that people reading this will remember well; about 20-a-side, no referee and no time limit either - we used to play for hours, no bother, until it got dark or you were called in for your tea.

One of my earliest football memories was going to watch Dundee United where we had a centre forward called Fin Dossing, a big Danish lad who was a brilliant player and a hero of mine growing up.

Scottish football was in somewhat better health in those days and I remember watching Dundee United in the Fairs Cities' Cup in 1967/68 when we beat Barcelona - *yes, Barca* - at Tannadice 2-0.

In the next round, we beat Juventus at home - Fin Dossing scored - but lost 3-0 in Italy and went out. They were great games though and I absolutely loved those days, watching my home town team beat Barcelona and Juventus. Unforgettable times.

My dad was a plasterers' labourer and we didn't have much money. He was a proud, tough Scot, honest as the day is long and we lived in a tenement block when I was younger.

I had a milk round, so had to get up at about 4.30am then off to school where I progressed from primary school football, to the secondary school team and ended up as captain of Dundee Schoolboys.

I also played for a local amateur team, so by the time I was 15, I was playing three matches on weekends and ended up getting scouted for North End by Jimmy Scott, who was based in Dundee and had previously brought the likes of Archie Gemmill down to Deepdale.

I could have signed for Dundee United and I also had talks with Rangers, who wanted to sign me over in Glasgow. I have a brother called Eddie who is seven years older than me and was an excellent footballer. He signed for Chelsea as a schoolboy, leaving Dundee for London.

Eddie spent a few years at Chelsea then had a spell at St Johnstone before playing junior football in Dundee. I used to watch him play and really admired his skills on the park and often thought he just didn't get that break that we all need, because he was such a fabulous footballer. Believe it or not, I went down to Manchester United for a trial then turned down trials at Chelsea and Aston Villa. My Dad and I discussed things and agreed PNE had a great reputation in signing Scottish players and I might have more of an opportunity joining a club of their stature in football.

I was still only 15 when I signed as an apprentice for North End in April 1968 and coming away from Dundee was quite hard for me as a young lad. I got picked up at the station and took me to my digs in Farringdon Park and that was it - you were just left to it. Luckily, there was another Scottish lad there - Andy O'Halloran - so I wasn't totally on my own.

After a while, the club opened a youth hostel near Moor Park and that was better, because there were more of you in together after training.

The wages were £10 a week, but there was a bit of tax on it and the club charged you £5 a week for the digs - so I had about £2 a week left over and that was it.

Don't spend it all at once, y'know?

That baptism into football life was quite a shock really; you think *'wow, I've signed for a professional football club'*, but the reality was a bit less glamorous than I'd maybe imagined.

You go in and you end up doing a lot of general tasks; you're responsible for keeping the players' boots all cleaned and if there was a game on the Saturday, you'd spend Monday sweeping out the old West Stand, top to bottom.

North End had some great players around at that time, but don't ask me whose boots I cleaned - I did them as little as possible!

The set-up was that there was the first team squad, the reserves and then the A team. It was a strict hierarchy so even to go into that first team dressing room was a big thing. If you went in there in the afternoon to give the players their boots, you'd get all the stick under the sun. And if you were a 15-year-old Jock, with long ginger hair and freckles . . . you can imagine the grief I used to get. They were great lads really - but there was no mercy, I can tell you!

On the plus side, we were in full-time training which was great, even if it was quite hard to get used to. We'd train on one pitch up on Willow Farm and the first team would be away on another and you never got near them until you worked your way up. That was your goal and it gave you a real hunger.

The manual work, the training, the division between the players and the apprentices; these days, I think it's all very different. Young lads are pampered a bit and I'm not sure it's a good thing.

If I came down at 15 and someone was laying my kit out for me and I had a dietician preparing my meals, I don't think it would have been as good an apprenticeship. You need to come in and graft and start right at the bottom with the goal of getting into that first team squad.

Occasionally, we'd play practice matches against the first team and it was people like George Ross, Graham Hawkins, Ken Knighton and John Ritchie.

I remember looking at them and thinking 'my God, not only are these men hard - they *look* hard', too. All 1970s sideburns, long hair, moustaches - they weren't male models those boys; proper men - absolutely terrifying for a young lad like me.

Even when you got in the first team squad, actually, some things weren't exactly glamorous. I'm not saying this is right, but the kit man used to just come in with a big bag and empty it onto the dressing room floor and you grabbed what you could. It was all washed, but if you came in late you were in the raggy stuff and that was that.

The players I played with though, when we look back on it, none of us would swap it for nowadays.

Media training? It would drive us mad - just give us a ball.

Bobby Seith was the manager who signed me, but I rarely saw him as he was always with the first team, which was fair enough.

By the time I made my debut in May 1972, Alan Ball Senior was manager and was giving a few of us our first run-outs in the last game of the season against Swindon at Deepdale; me, Gary Williams and David Hughes.

I just remember being really excited and when you look at the list of names that day there were some great players; George Ross, John Bird, Ricky Heppolette. Alan Spavin wasn't in the team that day, but I loved playing with him the following season. He was brilliant at getting the ball into your feet and was always good for advice about movement, where to look for the ball and things - a fantastic professional.

We used to go away before away games and pre-match you'd get offered soup, toast - or steak. Well, coming from Dundee where we didn't have much money, I'd never had steak before so I was piling into it, as you can imagine. But I was sat with Spav one day and he said: 'Don't be eating that before a game. You need to go on the pitch hungry.' I was gutted - I was loving my first taste of proper steak, y'know?

But Spav said: 'Go in hungry and you'll be hungry for the ball. Look for it and, trust me, I'll get it to your feet.' And he did. He wasn't looking for 'glory' balls, he was just probing all the time, trying to find you in space - as a striker, that was the best food and drink you could get.

Mind you, I did miss those steaks.

The 1972/73 season was the first season I played regularly in the first team. I made 35 appearances in the league and got 13 goals to finish top scorer.

It wasn't a vintage season for the club and by the last game, we needed a point at home against Burnley to stay up - while they needed a point to go up into what is now the Premier League. Alan Ball pulled every trick in the book before the game; they had two good wingers - Steve Kindon and Dave Thomas - so he narrowed the pitch to give them no space. He also got the fire brigade from Fulwood in to flood the pitch so it was really boggy on the day, all sorts of little things. Classic Bally.

There were more than 21,000 at Deepdale and Alan Lamb piled down what was left of the wing - he probably could have shot, but he squared it to me and I managed to put us in front.

They equalised in the second half, and I think both teams were happy with that - that score suited everyone. They were up, we weren't down.

But nobody had said anything to me about easing off or anything, so I was still charging about, going for a winner.

I remember with about 15 minutes to go, I got through and fired a shot just wide and their centre half said to me: 'Brucie, do that again and I'll break you legs.'

I just laughed, but then his partner at the back joined in: 'We mean it, you have another shot and we'll do you, son.'

I was like: *'Blimey, these guys are serious.'*

And just like our defenders, they were hard, hard men.

The last 10 minutes were played out almost entirely in the middle of the park with neither side doing any attacking at all. A 1-1 draw, everyone was happy.

Years later, I was talking to Paul Fletcher, the Burnley centre forward that day and he said: 'What about that game at Deepdale, Brucie? I was only 20 and you won't believe what your centre halves were saying to me - they were going to break my legs and all sorts if I had a shot.'

It turned out that our defenders - Graham Hawkins and John Bird - had been saying exactly the same to Paul as the Burnley lads were saying to me. No wonder it ended as a draw . . .

The following season, we were a bit in and out again at the start, but I was getting games and scored a few goals. Even though we weren't doing great, I was confident we would stay in the division and there were no thoughts in my mind about leaving.

Anyway, one day in January, I picked Jim McNab up from Penwortham to go to training and as soon as he got in the car he said: *'I see you're getting sold today Brucie! Newcastle United - it's in the morning paper.'*

That's the way it was in those days, no internet, so the newspapers really were first with the news. I couldn't believe it - I'd never heard anything about any move so I didn't know what to do. It was totally out of the blue.

When I got to Deepdale, Bobby Charlton called me into the office and just said: 'Sorry son, we're selling you'.

There were no agents or anything, you were expected to do as you were told. I puffed my cheeks out a bit and said: 'But I'm really happy here - I don't want to go. I've only had one season in the first team. I've just moved house six weeks ago and I've got a 20-month-old son.'

Deep down, one of the big things was that I wanted to be a one-club man at Preston like Tom Finney - that was my dream. But Bobby just said: 'No, you need to go. I cannot guarantee you a place in my team here.'

It was a real bolt from the blue, especially as I'd been top scorer the season before and Bobby had said that he wouldn't sell me at any price. There we were a few months later and it was made clear to me that I had to go.

Joe Harvey, the Newcastle manager came down and by lunchtime that was that - they'd sold me for £120,000 - more than a million in today's climate.

No-one said anything but I think North End probably needed the money at the time and I've no axe to grind with Bobby. He was a nice man, but nice men don't always make good managers. He was always very pleasant with me, but when he left Deepdale, I wasn't surprised that he called time on his management career - I think he could see he wasn't really cut out for it.

I was 21 when I signed for Newcastle. It was a bigger club and better money, but I was hardly rolling in it. First off, I had to get a better car to get up there - so I splashed out on a Datsun Cherry (!). I had a black and white telly, so we upgraded to colour, and by the time I'd moved into a new semi-detached house, I was back skint. No better off than I had been at Preston!

There was a lot of messing about when I first went up there, too. At first they promised me a club house and what not, but that never materialised. I ended up back at the ground with my wife, only to discover the team were away in Buxton preparing for a big FA Cup game. This Geordie chap came up and asked: 'Oh, are you Brucie?'

I said yes and he kindly showed us around some housing schemes in the area in his car, really proud of the area. It was only later that I realised the old chap was the legendary Jackie Milburn, who did a bit of work for the local press, a lovely guy.

But mainly, it was all a bit chaotic - an awful time. After a few weeks, Joe Harvey had me in, apologised and said they would fix me up with a hotel. I thought that it would be somewhere nice and near the stadium so I said: 'Oh right, which hotel?'

'Lovely place,' he said, 'It's called The Airport Hotel.'

And true enough, there it was by the side of the runway, miles from St James' Park and not exactly great for a good night's sleep.

I didn't even know why they'd signed me; I was up against Malcolm McDonald - probably the best striker I ever played with and there was no way I was going to get him out of that side. It was a disaster, really.

The previous year at Preston, Bobby Charlton had had the brainwave of mixing up our shirt numbers to confuse the opposition in a game at Millwall. I don't know what it did to the opposition, but it bamboozled us and we got beat 4-1. I'd worn the number 3 shirt, but I played up front. Joe Harvey called me in one day and said: 'I remember seeing you away at Millwall last year . . .'

I thought: 'Oh God, I know what's coming here!'

He said: 'You were in midfield that day.'

I said: 'No boss, I was up front.'

'Yeah, but you had the number 3 on.'

I said: 'Honestly, I was up front.'

As the conversation went on, I started to think: 'Jeez, this guy's not even seen me play!'

Looking back, I'm convinced of it. Especially as a month or so later, I bumped into his assistant Len Richley in the gents. He was a nice guy, but I said: 'In all honesty Len, I don't know why you've signed me.'

He said: 'Ah well Brucie, it was coming up to the end of the tax year and we had to either spend some money or hand it to the government.'

So that was a great confidence booster, too!

The following year, Gordon Lee had taken over as manager up there and actually gave me a run in the team - in midfield. That was a nightmare for me, but that was the best run in the team I had. Even though I was playing in front of 30,000-40,000, it was hard work for 18 months. But when the chance came to come back to Deepdale in the summer of 1975, things weren't exactly smooth either.

Again, you used to find things out from the newspapers in those days and one morning I read that Newcastle were after John Bird from North End and were willing to offer me in part exchange.

A deal was set up and we met in a hotel on Garstang Road; me, Bob Bolton, Alan Jones and Tom Gore. Trevor Hemmings was involved in the club by then but he was down south with Pontins, so he was on the other end of the phone.

The only issue was, things were all flaring up about Bobby Charlton resigning if the deal went through. He didn't want to lose John Bird and he'd come out saying I wasn't good enough for his team and whatnot.

It was all a bit messy and I didn't want to return amid any controversy so I said: 'Look, I'm not going to come back if Bobby's going to resign.'

Alan Jones then said: 'Even if you don't sign . . . he'll still be leaving the club.'

He said the board would love to have me back, Harry Catterick was going to be the new manager and he had no problem with the deal - the wheels were already in motion. He said: 'Whether you come back or not, Bobby Charlton will no longer be at the club.'

So I thought: 'Well if that's the case, I'll sign.'

Nothing against Bobby, I just couldn't wait to get back to North End and pick up where I left off. Harry Catterick came in and was OK, but he wasn't a tracksuit manager at all - Nobby Stiles used to do a lot of the training and he was great.

While I was away, the club had signed Mike Elwiss and Nobby used to just say to us: 'Go out and play. Do whatever it takes to hurt the opposition.'

That was it. There was no great tactical structure or rules we had to stick to. It was 'get out and play, score goals, win games'. It sounds simple, but it worked.

I was really lucky at North End to have had great people like Hughie McIlmoyle and John Smith up top with me, helping me out and making me look good.

Mike was the best of the bunch - such a brilliant player and we clicked right from the start. I'd be in the middle watching him do his stuff and I'd just be thinking: 'I've got to get on the end of this when it comes in.'

It was instinctive - I found space and Mike found me. We never really practised our partnership like they would nowadays; one comes short, one goes long, and all that. We just seemed to have that understanding from the outset.

And in all the games we played, I never saw his head drop once. He'd get kicked all over the place, but he was brave as a lion and just kept coming.

Me and Mike had great years together where everything went well for us, we played off the cuff and were really successful - it was the peak of my career playing alongside him, but in all honesty, I think he would have made anyone look good!

Training was never really tactical, it was just knowing that if someone had the ball, you made a run or you supported them. I don't think that was unusual for the times, you put out 11 good players and whoever played best on the day won.

I think you can complicate it for players at times and you see that a lot in the modern game. Some players won't run from one 'zone' to another because they've been told not to. I know everything has moved on, but losing that instinctive bit of play is a crying shame I think.

For me, I never lost that thing from being a schoolkid; I just wanted to score goals. I wasn't interested in defending and I suffered a bit for it - although probably not as much as the managers who tried to get me to track back.

Mark Lawrenson was just breaking into the team when I got back and he was brilliant - a great player, even though he was playing up front at first!

I've got huge admiration for Mark, not just for what he achieved in his career, but also what he's gone on to do since and, as anyone will tell you, he's still the same down-to-earth lad that he ever was.

In my first year back 1975/76 we did OK and finished eighth in Division 3, which is now League 1 level. The following year, I played all 46 league games and scored 24 goals as we finished sixth in the league.

I thought Harry Catterick was doing alright, we'd had two decent seasons under him - so it was a bit of a surprise when he was fired at the end of that season.

You didn't see much of him during the week, but he'd been Everton manager and he'd done OK so it wasn't a decision that you expected. You're always worried when a manager who likes you gets fired, but luckily Nobby took over and things went up a gear straight away.

I thought he was a really good manager and a great coach and with Alan Kelly there as well, it was a really strong backroom team. Nobby was really down to earth, but he instilled a confidence in you that made you feel ten feet tall. He was similar to Alan Ball in that he would just encourage me and Mick to go and play where we wanted.

Well, I knew where Mick was going to be and he knew I'd always be in the penalty box so it worked brilliantly - we scored more than 100 goals between us in three seasons. It was a period where you just felt everything was going right for us both and he was the best strike partner I ever had without a doubt - an absolute dream to play with.

But it wasn't just us; we had a really good side that year, Roy Tunks in goal, Mick Baxter, Sean Haslegrave, Gordon Coleman, Ricky Thomson - all great players.

What's funny about that season is that we really only used 16 players. Steve Uzelac and Spav made a couple of appearances each, but mainly it was the same tight group of lads all the way through. Don't forget, in those days you only had one substitute, which probably made a big difference.

As a player, you were gutted if you got subbed.

I always think that if I was playing now, with three subs who almost always come on, I probably wouldn't have finished a lot of games. When you're a poacher, you're not always in the game a lot and people might look at me and say: 'He's not had a touch, get him off.'

But when you're that type of player, you're looking at the whole 90 minutes; you might have to wait until the 89th minute for that half a chance and get it in.

Sometimes now, I think they'd probably have me off for not working hard enough, not being involved or whatever. But it's a different mindset when all you want to do is score goals - you know you might have to be patient.

We played a lot of games, but I never felt tired and never wanted to be 'rested' or anything. If I'd been 'rotated', I'd have wondered if I'd done something wrong and breaks like that can affect your rhythm. *No thanks, keep me in.*

The midfield players probably had to work harder back then because they were always being told to make these long runs to get in the box, then get back to help out the defence. These days, it seems a lot more rigid in where players are supposed to be.

Don't get me wrong, I get it - it's a different era and a different style of football. But it's frustrating sometimes when you watch good players and you're thinking: 'Why doesn't he just go for it and get in the box?'

It's all so tactical and I think sometimes people overthink things.

I have sympathy for modern strikers too; with the best will in the world, you're not going to score every chance that comes your way, so you might need two or three before you put one in. Some games I watch now, the ball isn't flying into the box like it used to do, where you might pick up a ricochet and get a half-chance.

It's worked backwards and sideways then maybe backwards to start again while the striker has to reset his position and hope it comes in next time.

So every time he gets a chance, you're hoping he's going to get it in because they're not coming round as often as they used to. He might get two or three chances in a game where we would get six or seven half chances maybe.

The other big difference is the pitches. You look at Deepdale now and it's perfect all year round. There have been massive improvements in the way they are maintained and when you look back on some of the old TV clips, you can see the state of the surfaces back then.

Our home pitch was never one of the worst, but we'd go away sometimes and it would be like a quagmire; thick mud, bare patches, no true run of the ball. We've all had passes that bobble away from you, but it cracks me up sometimes when you see players in the Premier League make a mess of a shot and look to blame the surface.

I just think: 'Aye, look at it - it's like a bowling green, what more do you want?'

All this is just different times, though. Like I said, I understand it - the game's moved on. I'm not even sure the kids use jumpers for goalposts any more!

Anyway, back in 1978, we were moving on too.

But it was a close-run thing, I can tell you. Peterborough were breathing down our necks and we had to play Shrewsbury at home in the last game of the season aiming t nail down third place and promotion - no play-offs in those days, we'd be straight up.

Mike scored, but they were on top and 2-1 up before I managed to get an equaliser with nine minutes to go - my 30th goal of the season.

It was tense stuff as the game ended 2-2. The fans piled on the pitch but we couldn't celebrate promotion as Posh had a game in hand, so it was a really strange situation.

Back then, it wasn't all orchestrated for TV and they had to play on the Easter Monday at Wrexham who had already been crowned champions.

Plenty of North End fans went over to watch them only manage a 0-0 draw, which meant we were up . . . on goal difference. *Phew!*

Like I say, it was a close thing but I think we deserved to go up. It was a great feeling - and a great relief, I can tell you.

To top things off, I'd scored 27 of our 67 goals in the league that season and won the adidas Golden Boot award as top scorer.

I haven't got it on display at home or anything - it's up in the loft somewhere. But I remember my wife bubble-wrapped it, so it should still be in good condition!

When I went to collect the award, it was a glittering do in London, but it took me right back to a family caravan holiday in Anstruther, Fife, in the summer of 1966. There, I watched the World Cup Final and I can recall it being strangely quiet during the game - as the Scots didn't want either England or West Germany to win!

But me? Well, I was in awe watching the great Geoff Hurst scoring a hat-trick.

When I was fortunate enough to win the Golden Boot, Nobby said we would be sitting with one of his mates during the presentation in London. He never said his mate would be Geoff Hurst. I felt deeply honoured and amazed to be in such fine company and only managed to say hello and goodbye! It was a great highlight of my career, especially winning it as a PNE player.

We were back in Division Two - the Championship now - and couldn't wait to get started. But that summer, Crystal Palace, who were in the same league as us and managed by a young Terry Venables, came in and bought Mike Elwiss for £200,000.

It was big money - a club record at the time - but I was devastated. I think we both thought we'd have many more seasons together at Deepdale so it was a massive blow.

Obviously, when you're a player, how the club is run is nothing to do with you.

But the problem with North End going back many, many years is not just that they've sold players - every club has to do that apart from the really big boys - it's that they've sold to teams who were in the same league as them.

When I went to Newcastle, at least they were in the top division, but Palace were in the second tier with us when we sold Mike. We sold Lawro and Gary Williams to Brighton, who were in the same division. I remember playing against Mark and wishing he was still on our side. But, at the time, you've just got to get on with it.

We did really well in that first season up; I got another 21 goals and we finished seventh in the league, with players like Eric Potts shining for us.

One goal that everyone remembers is a volley I got against Blackburn at Ewood in March that year - probably because it was on TV, which was a real rarity for us in those days. It was Graham Bell's debut and he swung this long cross in that I just managed to catch right. It could have gone anywhere I suppose, but it went right in the bottom corner to give us a 1-0 win.

I was pleased with the goal - *as you can see on the replays!* - but people don't believe me when I say I got as much pleasure from the six-yard box goals. I always used to think, if I get in there and score on from there, I'm doing my job right.

That season, I was going for the Golden Boot again and my big rival was Pop Robson at West Ham. We both got 26 goals; I got 21 in the league and five in the cups and he got 26 in the league so he won the trophy.

I'd played every game that season right up until April. But I'll always remember, just three games or so after that Blackburn game, Nobby called me in on a Monday afternoon and told me I was dropped for the following game against Newcastle.

He said I wasn't working hard enough to keep the full-backs in - I was absolutely gutted. I'll never forget it. I was top scorer in what is now the Championship and it was a big game against my ex-club, who I'd scored against at their place a few weeks earlier. And I was dropped for not closing down full-backs - *I wasn't even sub!*

Anyway, I came out of the meeting and was moping round the Deepdale pitch on my own when I bumped into Sir Tom Finney. He asked what the problem was and I told him what Nobby has said.

He was very nice about it and he thought it was a nonsense. He said: 'That's not your job - you just keep doing what you're doing.'

To hear that from someone like Sir Tom lifted my spirits - clearly I wasn't the only one who thought the priority was scoring goals.

The Newcastle game was on Easter Monday and finished in a 0-0 draw. The following night - *yes, two home games in two days* - we played Leicester and I was back in and scored two as we won 4-0.

I don't think it was a motivational thing or anything from Nobby because, to be honest, sometimes I was my own worst enemy.

My mind was so focused on getting that ball in the back of the net and sometimes I thought: 'I'm not going back to defend - that's someone else's job.'

I don't think I ever even heard the phrase 'tracking back' when I played. And if I had, I would probably have pretended I hadn't!

Mick Robinson was also bursting onto the scene that season and scoring lots of goals, so the club was keen to tie me and him down to long-term contracts.

In those days, if you got a two-year contract, you thought: *'Wow - great stuff!'*

A three-year deal was almost unheard of - you had to be really tearing up trees to get one of those.

So it was fantastic when North End offered me and Micky three-year contracts.

We were both over the moon and there was a signing ceremony upstairs in the old boardroom in the Pavilion stand. I thought it was brilliant they were tying Mick down to a long-term contract - it was a real marker for the club's ambitions.

And within about four weeks . . . he'd gone.

We heard that Malcolm Allison's Manchester City came in with a lower bid and the board said no, but they kept going up and up until it was an offer they couldn't refuse.

Fair enough, it was around £750,000 which was big, big money at the time - another club record fee - but another massive loss on the playing side.

It was so, so sad to hear of Mick's death recently; he was a real football man, a brilliant player and a great guy.

He had a fantastic career and will be really sadly missed by everyone.

A couple of people have asked whether there was any chance of a call-up from Scotland around 1978/79, but I never got the call and it's not something that ever bothered me.

It was an era when Scotland had a lot of far better players than me, with the likes of Kenny Dalglish and Joe Jordan up front - *not bad, those two!*

I got an Under-23 cap a few years earlier and the attitude towards players who were down in England was a bit frosty, to be honest.

There was this view of: *'Well, you've left to go and play in England. Scotland not good enough for you is it?'*

I was a bit taken aback by it to be honest, but it was a real thing at that time.

I remember not long after that call-up, Jimmy Scott phoned me up and said: 'One of your Dundee United heroes Dennis Gillespie is having a testimonial, do you want to come up and play in it?' I said yes straight away and couldn't wait to get up there when the time came. It's a long drive so I fixed up with the club to have a few stretches on the pitch when I arrived, before anyone else got there.

Anyhow, I was spotted by Jim McLean, the legendary Dundee United manager, who was well known to have, *errr,* a bit of a fiery nature.

He came over and after a few pleasantries, he gave me an almighty rollocking: 'You left Scotland, you could have stayed here in Dundee, you could have signed for Rangers, but you went to Preston instead and that's the problem with you young players . . .'

I thought: 'Blimey, I've driven 250 miles to play in a testimonial and here I am getting a telling off from Jim McLean. Welcome home!'

I had a knee operation at the end of that 1978/79 season which disrupted me going into the following campaign, too.

By then Steve Elliott was establishing himself and he was a lovely player who could do everything; pass, shoot, score with his head, great touch, good pace, the lot. He's probably the most stylish teammate I ever had at Deepdale, his all-round game was outstanding and he was a really classy player.

I had a bit of an in-and-out season through injury mainly and managed only 24 starts in the league, scoring 10 goals. We weren't in any relegation trouble though and ended up finishing 10th.

Mick Elwiss came back on loan from Palace towards the end of the season, but sadly had to retire through injury that summer, which was a really terrible blow, as he was only 27 and it was terrible to see his career cut short.

Maybe it would have been a different story these days, because - without being unkind to anyone - there wasn't a great deal of knowledge around at that time about injuries.

It was the same at other clubs too. Some of the treatment you had wasn't the best. I remember one time I got caught a deep cut on my shin away at Orient; really bad, you could see the bone through it.

After the game, I was sat in their treatment room waiting for stitches when one of their guys came in and said: 'The doctor's had too much to drink - you'll have to get it done at hospital.' But the North End fella said: *'We can't take him to hospital - we're on the seven o'clock train out of Euston!'*

So that was that - no stitches for me and instead of being out a week, I was out for a fortnight.

Prior to that, Alan Lamb broke his leg away at Southend . . . and they brought him back on the coach without getting it fixed. *From Southend!*

Every bump on the road, he was in absolute agony.

Another time, Mel Holden got a whack on the shin in the Deepdale gym and you could tell it was a bad one. When we got him to the treatment room, they just said: *'Oh, just go back to the hostel and rest it son.'*

About six of us were virtually carrying him back over Moor Park - he was sweating buckets, his leg was swelling like you've never seen and he was really in pain. He couldn't get to sleep at night so in the morning the landlady sent him to the hospital.

Diagnosis - broken leg.

And these are just a few examples.

But it wasn't just the home players. People reading this might remember Kenny Burns, a proper Glaswegian centre half from the 1970s. *Hard? Blimey - like granite.*

One time, he split his head open at Deepdale and after the game we could hear him screaming blue murder in the room next door. Harry Hubbick was the physio at the time; a lovely man but really, he wasn't the best physiotherapist.

The doctor was nowhere to be seen and instead Harry was pulling these stitches through Kenny Burns' head in a way you might mend an old jumper or something.

You can imagine the language he was coming out with: *'Where's the effing doctor? He's supposed to do this!'*

But Harry was just 'Ah, now come on - hold still son!'

Knit one, purl one.

We were cracking up, but deep down, we were just grateful it wasn't happening to us. All joking aside, the treatment was awful really at that time and I think a lot of our generation are paying the price now. I've got two serious knee operations coming up and I know a few other ex-players from back then who are in the same boat.

It could have been worse though - I really wouldn't have fancied playing on the artificial surface a few years later, so we had a lucky escape there, from rug burns if nothing else!

As we headed into the 1980s, something really strange happened, not just at Preston, but for the game in general.

Our opening game against Bristol City attracted just 6,058 fans and a few weeks later that was down to 5,500 against Cambridge. In October, we played Newcastle in front of just 5,300 - these days they'd bring more than that in away support.

I don't know if it was hooliganism, poor facilities or whatever, but crowds dropped away dramatically. It was a tough season and everyone remembers the Swansea game at the end when they were going up and we were heading in the opposite direction.

We didn't actually go down that day though - we went to Derby for the last game of the season and beat them 2-1 to give us a chance of staying up against all the odds.

We went from the high of an 88th minute winner to getting back to the dressing room and finding out . . . we'd been relegated in the same way we came up - on goal difference.

Cardiff had got a draw against champions West Ham and we were down.

It was a terrible feeling, as you can imagine. Just silence. Everyone just on the floor - one measly point, y'know? It was so disappointing.

You look back at things over the season, but there's nothing you can do. It's done and you just feel empty inside, sick to the stomach. The funny thing is, we were playing well when we went down - we lost only one of our last six matches.

One more point and the course of the next few years could well have been a lot better for North End.

Instead, to make a bad situation a lot worse, the club sacked Nobby, which I still genuinely think was a terrible decision.

He was a World Cup winner, he'd got us promoted, done OK in the previous seasons up there and he was learning all the time. OK, there were mistakes along the way, but given time I think he would have got us back up.

I think that decision to sack him set the club back many years.

His replacement was Tommy Docherty and, well, what can you say about The Doc? He wasn't exactly shy about letting you know his opinions was he? I was one of the fortunate ones because he picked me and kept me in the team, but others weren't so lucky. He put quite a few of the first team lads in the away dressing room and basically told them they weren't wanted, they weren't part of it. He made his mind up about people very quickly and split the squad up accordingly. To me, that was wrong.

We're talking about good professionals and they shouldn't have been treated like that. We didn't start well at all and won only one of our first 12 games that year.

But still it was a shock one morning in December when Tunksy rang me up and said: *'Brucie, you'll never believe it - they've just sacked Tommy Doc!'*

Roy had been at Rotherham when they'd had him in charge there and he'd cleared out loads of players. Maybe that's what North End were thinking too: get the Doc in, clear out a load of players and rebuild.

But the results just weren't there and really, I'm not sure they were going to come. There was too much turmoil behind the scenes in a short a space of time. It was all just too much and something had to give.

The next guy through the door was another big name, but - *agh!* - my heart sank.

Gordon Lee had managed Everton and been my boss at Newcastle - but it was a nightmare for me when he arrived. He wasn't really my type of manager at all and right away I thought the writing was on the wall.

Newcastle may not have been perfect under Joe Harvey, but the one thing they did do was entertain. When Gordon took over, he put a stop to all that.

He sold Malcolm McDonald to Arsenal, got rid of Terry Hibbitt and Terry McDermott and set about building a team that was a lot more workmanlike. He was always alright with me, but he was just so negative as a manager - it wasn't exactly fun to play for him.

We'd be there before a game and he'd say things like a 0-0 draw at Deepdale would be a good result. We'd be looking at each other going: *'Is this for real? A draw at home would be a disaster.'*

We finished mid-table in his first season and I played every game, scoring 18 goals. I knew it wouldn't last and by the second year, I was in and out of the team.

In November, he called me into the office and asked me: 'What do you think your role is in the team?'

I said: *'To score goals.'*

He looked at me and said: 'OK, tell me what your first four priorities are.'

'Well, I'm a penalty box player, that's what I've always been and my role is to score goals.'

He said: 'No, it's not.'

'It is.'

He said: 'I'll tell you what your role is - you keep the full-backs in, get back for corners, back for free-kicks, make the fifth man in midfield . . . and THEN you look to score goals.'

I said: *'No. I look to score goals FIRST and anything else is a bonus.'*

So we went on like this for a while and ended up having a bit of a fall-out.

In the end he said: 'I'm not going to play you for eight weeks.'

I just said: *'OK, don't play me for eight weeks then.'*

This didn't go down well either and he had another go at me, saying I should be doing whatever it takes to get back in.

I said: *'If you mean coming back in, defending all the time and scoring goals as my FIFTH priority then . . . no. My job is to score goals.'*

I stuck to my guns and, to be fair, so did he.

It wasn't quite eight weeks, but I didn't play again until New Year's Day. We played Wigan at Deepdale, I was back in the team, scored two and we won 4-1. I stayed in for a while after that, but I knew he didn't really want to play me.

He brought me back in for a game away at Millwall, but played me up front on my own. Away at The Den, in January. I got lots of kicks, but not of the ball. And, yes, we got beat.

As for the players coming in, Willie Naughton was around by then and he was a great dribbler of the ball, while lads like John Kelly were also coming through.

In the end though, Gordon just killed it for me and quite a few players.

He was just negative, negative, negative all the time - not the inspirational figure you want from a football manager. I was 30, I'd had a knee operation and with him wanting me to be a defender, I just thought . . . *I cannae play for this bloke.*

I wasn't enjoying it and I don't think many others were. We had a few more run-ins and my last start was against Cardiff at home in March. I scored in a 2-1 win, so at least that was a nice way to sign off.

But it was no surprise when I came in one day towards the end of the season and he called me in and said North End weren't retaining me. It was a sad day, but it wasn't unexpected by then so I'd had time to get my head round it.

In those days there was no great send-off or anything; when the time came, I went in, got my boots and went home. There was the annual presentation night and Keith Leeming came over and thanked me for my service to the club. That was nice of him and he was one of the few to make the effort.

Also, Trevor Hemmings was always very good to me and it was through the board, not the manager, that I had my testimonial match at the end of that season. It wasn't something I was pushing for and we just played against a team of ex-North Enders. Bobby Charlton came along, Tony Morley, Lawro and Archie Gemmill, so it was a nice night and I was grateful to everyone and to the fans who came for their support.

The things is, I'd been in football a long time by then so I'd got used to the business. I knew it was the sort of profession where sentiment didn't really count for anything and when your time was up, well, that was that. I had no agent or anything so I went home and wondered what I was going to do next.

A few weeks later, I was at a dinner and I was sat next to Gordon Lee of all people *(I'd like to thank the organisers for that)*. Anyway, while we were there, someone came over and said: 'Hey Brucie, Hull City want to speak to you . . .'

Gordon raised his eyebrows a bit, but inside I was thinking: *'Hey, you see that? Someone DOES want me to play for them!'*

So Hull were interested and wanted me to keep fit over here while something was sorted out. Tunksy was at Wigan and invited me there for pre-season and I enjoyed it so much I ended up signing there for Harry McNally.

For anyone who remembers Harry . . . yes, you can say he was mad *(!)*, but he was a really funny guy - great with me - and I had two happy seasons at Springfield Park.

Following on from two years under Gordon Lee, it was chalk and cheese and just nice to go back into training again with a smile on your face. After a couple of years there, I was reserve team coach and youth team coach, which I loved, but my knees were playing up. The doctor said I needed maybe two cartilage operations to get another year or two out of me as a player. But Harry had been sacked and I'd decided I just didn't want to stay in football at that point.

I'd done my bit and had some great times, so I called it a day.

Like everyone else at that time, I hadn't made a fortune from the game or anything. You didn't play for money and there was very little gap between what the players were earning and what the fans were probably taking home.

OK, it wasn't entirely for the love of the game, you still had to put a roof over your family's head, but money really wasn't the driving force.

I'd had a good career, bought a house and I really appreciated every minute of it. I started off in a tenement, then a council semi and then when I came down here I eventually got my own house.

By the time I finished my footy career I thought: 'How lucky am I? I'm blessed - I've had a great life.'

I was always just really grateful for having the chance to make a career playing football. The money wasn't important - not that it was there in the game anyway.

And to be honest, what would I do now if I had a million quid?

I wouldn't know what to do with it.

To me, money is neither here nor there, the memories I've got are priceless - that's something of real value.

When I finished playing, I was like a lot of pros . . . wondering what I could do next. If you're a footballer, that's all you ever focus on from a very young age and I could kick myself now that I didn't stick at my education a bit more.

In the end, me and my wife sat down to see what I could make a living out of now that I'd finished playing. We got a piece of paper out and said we'd jot down everything I was good at.

And at the end of the night the only thing we'd got written down was . . . *snooker!*

We'd spend hours playing in the old supporters' club after training, so I was pretty good - but nowhere near professional level. So it was back to the drawing board and, like most players, it was pretty traumatic when my career was over.

I was fortunate that a great PNE supporter Colin Monk greatly assisted me in having a career in the Leisure Industry at South Ribble Borough Council. I also had a short spell at Ribble Valley Borough Council, where Nigel South also assisted me and I'm greatly in their debt. My new career progressed and I ended up as contract manager for South Ribble Council before taking early retirement a few years ago. I've never regretted it and if you keep busy, there's always plenty to keep you occupied.

I still come back to watch North End and it was a huge honour a few years back when the fans voted me a Legend of the Town End.

Even when I was injured or out of form, the fans were always great with me and I'll never forget that. I really appreciated the bond I had with them.

Since stopping as a player, I've been a fan myself through thick and thin and I know we had a really hard time in the mid-1980s for a while.

I'm just glad the club got through that period and has become the modern organisation we see today; the stadium, the pitch, facilities at Deepdale, community work, professionalism - it's all absolutely top drawer.

Nowadays, I still love coming to watch games with my grandchildren, Angus, Tilly, William and Toby. People are always really nice and it's just humbling to be remembered in all honesty.

I'm really proud of what me and my teammates achieved; I played with some great players, had some fantastic experiences and always, always, always tried my best.

Quite simply, they were the best days of my life and I wouldn't have missed them for the world.

So it goes without saying that I always wore that famous white shirt with pride.

It's Preston North End - who wouldn't?

Chapter 4

PAUL McKENNA: RIGHT PLACE, RIGHT TIME

Is it that time already? Memoirs in a North End book? It doesn't seem like two minutes since I started out, let alone finished playing. Might make me feel old, this.

Hell of a journey though; from the plastic pitch and the club not having two pennies to rub together, to knocking on the door of the richest league in the world three times.

From struggling for kit and wide open terraces, to a stadium fit for the Premier League. When you step back, the progress was incredible.

People talk about being in the right place at the right time and I suppose a bit of that applies to me and North End.

I'd been on the books of Manchester City as a young lad - my dad was a scout there in the old days under Tony Book. I wasn't exactly a City fan, but we used to get tickets to Maine Road every now and then so I'd go to watch with him occasionally.

But when I got to 14, they didn't offer me any terms as they mainly took on lads who were going to their School of Excellence every week, whereas I just used to go down in the school holidays for three or four days at a time.

I'm from Eccleston and was always playing football with the year above my age group with my mates back then. The team I was in packed up though when they got to Under-15s, so I dropped back into my own age group in the Chorley league and, having had the experience with the older lads, I found the standard quite easy if I'm honest.

I don't want to sound big-headed *(I'm really not!)* but I knew I was a good player and found that the game came easy to me. When teachers would ask what I wanted to be when I grew up, I always said 'footballer'.

I had a natural understanding of the game and I think the only thing that held me back at that age was that I was quite small.

I say *'at that age'* - I never developed into a six-footer or anything, but I filled out as I got older and never felt I lacked physical presence on the pitch.

So, anyway, I stood out a bit as a young lad and was called into the league team, then became captain soon afterwards. It was around then that I started coming on the radar a little bit and a few clubs started getting in touch.

One of my mates was at North End and used to train on the astroturf. One day I went down with his mum and dad just to watch him from the sidelines at Deepdale.

By that time, I'd been playing against a few of the lads that were there and they pointed me out to the coach in charge. Next thing, he came over and asked if I wanted to join in the session. Luckily, I was wearing a tracksuit and had my trainers on, so I got involved and that was that really . . . for about the next 15 years!

They asked me to come back the following week and I signed schoolboy forms a couple of months later. It was Sam Allardyce who signed me up and he was there for the first six or seven months before going off to take the Blackpool job in the summer of 1994.

At the time, money was tight at the club and it was often 'first in, best dressed' with our kit as young lads; you grabbed what you could - *quick*.

I was lucky because my mum and dad were always involved in everything I did and were a great support for me throughout my career.

Where we played, we had a little kitchen, so my mum suggested starting to make cups of tea and selling them to parents and supporters to help raise some funds for the team. It soon progressed from cups or tea to bacon butties and raised a tidy sum for our kit and whatnot. Later on, the lady who did the catering at the club packed in and my mum and dad took over making lunches and stuff for the first team after training.

They were always very supportive for me - the kind of people who, if they were doing something, threw themselves into it 100 per cent. I like to think some of that rubbed off on me too.

Anyway, I played a couple of years at Under-15 and Under-16 before North End offered me a Government-funded Youth Training Scheme deal. So that was it - I left school at 16 and started full-time the following week.

The first year, I didn't really pull up any trees but in the second year, I started to get a chance in the reserves and thrived in among better players at that level. I just seemed to carry on progressing, while some of the lads stopped at a certain level.

I think that's where I started to kick on, my game improved and I never looked back. Not everything was right at the club though; there were times when I thought it was a bit of a shambles. There were players coming in from all over the place on trial and sometimes it looked like people could just turn up with their boots and join in. It didn't really have the standard of professionalism you might expect nowadays, but looking back, it was the 1990s; different times and miles away from the way things are done in the modern era.

I was 19 when I made my debut against Wycombe in February 1997 and Gary Peters was the manager.

When you look back at that team, you can see it was packed with experience: Kelham O'Hanlon in goal, Greegs and Mark Rankine in the middle, Moyesie at the back, Ian Bryson and David Reeves - loads of good, experienced pros.

And then there was me and Kev Kilbane to balance things out - and bring the average age down by about ten years!

I remember being nervous, just wanting to do well, and luckily I had a dream start, scoring after 15 minutes.

I had a shot from about 25 yards out that went in, so that settled my nerves and it's a memory I'll always cherish. OK, it got a deflection, but I'll take it, thanks very much.

They equalised, but Simon Davey got a winner in the second half so it was a winning start and I got a decent reception from the Deepdale crowd when I was replaced by Dean Barrick in the last minute.

I think I took it in my stride; don't get me wrong, I was really chuffed - especially as we'd won - but I was pretty level-headed about it. I always had belief in myself and was pleased I'd not looked out of place. I was also happy that I'd repaid the manager for having faith in me and I've got a lot to thank Gary Peters for.

On the other hand, I think he could have given me more opportunities sooner. I'd been in the reserves for about six months and was doing really well every week and getting a lot of good reviews from people, so I was champing at the bit.

Gary signed me as a pro, but to be honest, the deal I signed was probably worse than my YTS contract. It wasn't about the money, but on a YTS you got an allowance for your bus fare - so my dad had to go down and ask Gary if I could have a bit more, just so I'd be on the same as the YTS.

That should give you an idea about how lucrative it was!

I played quite a few games that season, including a TV match at Crewe and felt like I was progressing and breaking through a bit.

But in my second season, I got less of a look-in. I travelled everywhere with the first team, but wasn't even making the bench. I felt I was being dragged up and down the country, but wasn't involved in the matches at all so it all got a bit frustrating. I was still playing in the reserves every week and doing really well, while the first team were struggling in the league at that point. I felt I should have been getting a chance as I knew I could do a job, but he never played me.

Fortunately, I'd been around David Moyes for a couple of years and I knew he rated me. So when he stepped up to take over from Gary, he pulled me to one side and said: 'Listen, we're in a bit of a dogfight at the bottom at the moment - but as soon as I know we're safe I'll get you in.'

Thankfully, results picked up and four games before the end of the season, Moyesie was true to his word.

I played away at Northampton, then stayed in the side for a 3-3 draw at home to Blackpool, before a draw against Wrexham and a last day win over Bristol City.

That was that, really. I established myself from there and the following season, I played about 40-odd games under David, at a time when we had a really good team developing.

Graham Alexander signed and we had the three Manchester United lads in - Jon Macken, Michael Appleton and Colin Murdock, as well as people like Michael Jackson, Ryan Kidd, Tepi Moilanen and Dave Lucas.

Alongside Greegs and Ranks, the nucleus of our team for the next few years was in place. No offence to Gary, but as soon as Moyesie took the reins, things went up a level in terms of professionalism and approach. He wasn't just putting sessions on and hoping we'd be better than the next opponents. He really worked on the team and we were all incredibly well drilled about what we needed to do.

We had freedom going forward, which was great for me, but we had an unbelievable defensive structure within the team. As soon as we lost the ball, everyone knew exactly where they needed to be, depending what the situation was.

I always say it was like rehearsing a script. If you learned it and did it well, then you knew you would play. If you weren't prepared to do the work, then you wouldn't. You had to do the defensive side of things and understand your responsibility to the team. If you weren't doing that, then Moyesie would get someone who would.

It was as simple as that.

There are things that people take for granted in training manuals these days, but we were doing them back then under David and it was unusual at that time. The shape drills that players have come to expect were all new things back then and David's methods were at the forefront of those changes. Years later, when he'd gone to

Everton, I used to watch some of their games and see that organisation still in place. I felt I could slot into that team and know what I was supposed to be doing, based on our training all those years before.

One of the games we played in his first full season was against Arsenal in the FA Cup, live on Sky with the ground absolutely packed to the rafters.

Shy, quiet Kurt Nogan put us two goals up before they turned the screw a little bit, David Eyres got sent off and we ended up losing 4-2.

I came on as a sub and, although we were under the cosh, it was great to be involved. I think, as a team, we put down a marker that night for what was to come.

It just goes to show that you can take things from defeats and use them positively, which is what we did for the rest of that season.

In the end, we came up against Gillingham in the play-offs and they were a bit of a bogey side for us around that time. They were a classic Tony Pulis team; all big lads and, while I think we were a better footballing side, they just had too much for us over two pretty horrible games.

Looking at it positively though, our progress was impressive. We'd been in a relegation scrap at times the year before, then rallied under Moyesie and now we were knocking on the door in the play-offs.

We went into the next season full of belief, especially as David had brought in more players who were better with the ball. He inherited some good players, but he recruited some great players too, with Steve Basham and Rob Edwards coming in.

You're always watching new arrivals in their first few sessions to see what they're like and a good test was always on a Friday morning in training. We'd set up six versus two in a ten-foot-by-ten-foot box, with the lads in the middle trying to get the ball. It was a test of how clever you were as footballers; thinking quick and getting out of tight situations. That was a good gauge of someone's ability and the standards were always very high.

The rest of us would be looking at each other with a little nod and know we'd got a good lad on board - or maybe an eye-roll at times too.

Overall, David's methods were paying off and we were having one of those seasons that take on a momentum of their own.

We were pushing at the top of the league most of the season and gave another good account of ourselves in the FA Cup at Everton, even though we lost 2-0 late on.

We were like a machine at times in the league and I'll always remember the game away at Wigan where our fans took over an entire side of their ground. Incredible.

You looked at that level of support and knew the supporters believed as much as we did that we were on the verge of something special. They were up around us at that time and were a good side, with two Manchester United lads - Michael Clegg and Terry Cooke - on loan for them in midfield. I'd played against them since my youth days, so it was great to get one over on them in a senior game when Michael Jackson scored and we won 1-0.

(I say 'great', but that's underplaying it really - that night was flaming brilliant.)

It put the seal on things for us really and we went up as deserved champions with some amazing scenes of celebration in the town - I'd never seen anything like it.

The presentations on the pitch, Sir Tom leading us out, the open topped bus parade - just amazing. It's hard to describe how good that feeling is; being with your mates, looking out and seeing thousands of people cheering you through the streets.

Honestly, it doesn't seem real at the time - it's like something from a film. The buzz about the place was incredible and us players fed off that a bit when we went up.

Having tasted that success, we were desperate for more.

Apart from David Healy coming in, the club didn't throw money at big new signings, so the same nucleus of lads stayed together in the Championship.

There was a big step up in standard; you could tell there was a massive difference in the players you were up against.

Luckily, through a combination of ability, attitude, the right environment and a great manager, we had a team that was able to make that transition to a higher level.

It made you a better player, just by being there. After having a season in the Championship, I was a far better player than the one that ended the title-winning season in League 1.

You had to be fitter, think faster, be sharper on the ball - the better players used the higher standard to improve themselves and that was the vast majority of the squad. We all progressed together and that bonded us even more tightly as a group and a unit.

And don't forget, we're talking about players who hadn't really been at that level before; Greegs, Grezza, Rob Edwards, Jacko, Kiddo, Lee Cartwright, Dave Lucas - some people who had come through the leagues with the club and were now performing just outside the very top division. There were people who went on to have really good careers, both at Deepdale and beyond.

That sort of recruitment doesn't happen by accident and credit must go to David - and Gary Peters before him - for not only bringing in talented players, but also the right sort of characters, too. I know there was a lot of work done behind the scenes to find out about players before they arrived, so that no-one coming in would rock the boat or upset the team spirit.

Undoubtedly, David created the right environment discipline-wise on the pitch and everyone knew the boundaries off it, too. That's not to say there weren't one or two scrapes at times.

There's quite a well-known story about Moyesie and Tepi having a bit of 'handbags' on a night out in Germany. Dave had playfully jabbed me in the ribs and when Tep heard about it he got the wrong idea.

I think he thought he was riding to my rescue, but he really didn't need to - Dave was just messing about, I thought nothing of it and went off to the loo.

I came out to find the lads all going crazy about how the two of them had had some sort of scuffle because Tep thought Moyesie had genuinely punched me.

We can laugh about it now and I just remember getting back to the hotel reception later on to find Moyesie a bit dishevelled, in full Glaswegian mode, giving it: *'I don't care hoo big he is . . !'*

There was no long term damage between them though. Tepi was a great keeper and a lovely guy - but probably the oddest bloke I've ever met in football.

When he first arrived, he used to turn up for training on an old shopper pushbike - the type with the big basket on the front. He was about six foot six inches tall and would come riding in with his training gear piled into in the basket.

New lads would ask: 'Who the hell's that?'

And we'd be like: *'Yep . . . that's our goalkeeper.'*

Then there was the time we were on the back of the bus one day and we kept hearing these strange noises from down at the front; *parp, squeak, parp, squeak.*

After a while I went down to investigate and found Tepi buried in a musical instruction manual . . . with a harmonica between his lips, making a right racket.

'Oooo, hi Kenna,' he said (in his thick Finnish accent), 'I've always wanted to learn how to play one of these. What do you think?'

A flipping harmonica? You can imagine what I thought.

It was between Tepi and Dave Lucas that season as they were two top keepers, but Lukes was in goal for our final run-in and the games against Birmingham in the play-offs.

To be honest, they were an established club at that level and could attract much higher-profile players than us. I remember the first leg down at St Andrews was a really tough game and we got away with a 1-0 defeat really. It was backs-to-the-wall stuff at times, but when we looked at the result, it gave us hope that we could turn it around at Deepdale. Obviously, Dave Healy put us one up with a great goal early on, but Geoff Horsfield equalised for them.

Everyone reading this probably knows two real shocks that came next: Graham Alexander missed a penalty and Mark Rankine scored a goal.

I don't know which was the bigger surprise to be honest!

Seriously though, I think Ranks' goal was just reward for the way we'd kept going and refused to accept defeat that night. Obviously, once that went in, I think we had the upper hand mentally, so I was hoping we'd score in extra time to avoid penalties.

But . . . no such luck.

When the final whistle went, I thought: *'Blimey, here we go now.'*

I wasn't a great penalty-taker, but my dad had been talking to me around that time about having more confidence in myself. Michael Owen had been coming through at Liverpool and dad was saying to me: 'Look at him, he's a young lad like you and he's doing everything . . .'

So really, it was those conversations that pushed me into saying I'd take a penalty that night. If it wasn't for that, I would have quite easily sat on the fence and let someone else step up.

What had happened though was that we'd been practising spot-kicks regularly in training. Moyesie had said to us: 'Make a decision and practice the kick you're going to take on the night, so that there's no changing your mind at the last minute. Know exactly where you're going to put the ball.'

He took any indecision out of it. We knew - and he knew - where we were putting our kicks. I think that was a great way of approaching it. We knew Greegs was going to smash it *(there's a surprise, eh?!)*, Grezza was going high left, I was going low to the left - we'd all spend timegetting these kicks just right, over and over again.

We knew who was taking the kicks, but we hadn't set the order. So when we got together at end of the game, I was hoping to be first or second - get it over with.

But Moyesie just said: *'Kenna - five.'* I tried to look calm, but deep down I was thinking: 'I'm right at the business end there!'

The good thing was though that Moyesie's preparations had taken a lot of doubt out of it. You put it where you'd planned and if it got saved, well, it was out of your hands. I think if anyone had gone differently to what they'd practised, Moyesie would have had something to say about it, let's put it that way.

Obviously the penalties went well for us and Rob Edwards stepped up to win it - I was praying for him to score . . . well, you know the rest. Then I was waiting for their guy to take his kick, praying he would miss, but knowing full well that he'd score.

So that was it - time for me to step into the pressure cooker.

The commentator on TV described it as 'the most important kick of a Preston football for half a century'. Thank God I couldn't hear him at the time!

People ask what was going through my mind, but what is there to say? I'm not going to pretend I wasn't nervous, but I also knew I had to stay calm, stick to what I'd practised and get the job done. Keep it on the floor, hit it hard - you can't start thinking about anything beyond that and anyway, you don't have time to.

They say it's a long walk from the halfway line, but really it's a few seconds, which is probably a very good thing.

I got a good connection, the keeper went the right way, but he couldn't get to it and then . . . just **RELIEF**.

There was no joy initially, just pure, absolute relief: 'THANK GOD FOR THAT!'

After that I didn't have time to think about anything really, because it seemed like the entire population of Preston was on the pitch with me.

I just dived into the arms of these lads who piled on and couldn't get anywhere near the rest of the players for ages, there were so many fans everywhere. Just amazing.

We went out afterwards and the town was absolutely buzzing. We were like rock stars for the night - except we were only in Squires!

Anyway, it was a fantastic night, and we believed we could go one further - the club was flying, the players were flying and it was a case of 'bring on Bolton'.

Looking back, to beat Birmingham was almost like winning a final itself that night and I can understand when people say maybe the drama and the emotion took something out of us. You wouldn't be human if it didn't.

But we had 10 days to get ourselves right and I think we went into the final very well prepared. The bigger issue was probably that Bolton were a quality outfit that season. They'd finished well ahead of us in the league and, yes, they had lots of 'big game' players. They had four or five internationals and the nucleus of their squad kept them up for the next 10 years.

So, yes, we didn't play as well as we could, but maybe they were just better than us on the day. Probably not three goals better and the two they got very late on puts a spin on the result.

We gave them a game and you could see their relief when they got the second towards the end, because we were still in it at that point.

It was a tight game and I don't think we were out of it until those last couple of minutes. We never felt outplayed, but 3-0 in the end puts a different look on things, doesn't it?

As a player, obviously, it was a huge disappointment. But it was a great experience and showed how far the club had come in such a short space of time. Maybe we'd gone too far, too fast, because the following season we became victims of our own success.

Our best players had become well known in the Championship and now there were different eyes looking at them. Obviously, the manager's success was being noticed and other clubs started to show an interest.

If we'd have beaten Bolton and gone up, there's no doubt we could have kept David, Jon Macken, Greegs and one or two others.

But because we stayed down, it was only a matter of time before offers started to come in for them and within 12 months we'd lost Moyesie to Everton, Jon to Man City and Greegs to West Brom, who had already taken Micky Appleton from us.

The frustrating thing is that we gave it a real good go that following season and only just missed out on the play-offs again, finishing seventh despite Moyesie leaving. Kelham took over from David and tried to keep things going along the same lines, but it's never the same when your spearhead leaves.

You could just sense that things were stuttering a bit, which was inevitable, and we lost a couple of games we really shouldn't have done.

I still say that if the club had held its nerve with a couple of things and waited to the end of that season, we'd probably have made the play-offs again and then who knows?

The following summer Craig Brown arrived as new manager and obviously, he was very well known in football for what he'd achieved with Scotland. He was a fantastic bloke and I've got a lot of time for him, but if I'm being honest, he was probably the most frustrating manager I played under.

In many ways, he was the opposite of Moyesie.

Things were quite disorganised at times and occasionally he seemed more bothered with what we looked like than how we played. He wanted us to go to the games in suits and we turned up looking like young executives - Mortgage Advisors FC.

I understand that you're representing the club, the city and everything - but I'd rather turn up in a sack of spuds and win than be all smart suits and lose.

Sometimes, team talks veered off into making sure we all had our socks rolled up. (Come on . . . what's that got to do with anything?) I think Craig was maybe happier to play well and get beat than to win ugly. It's admirable in some ways, but on the other hand, as a group, we were all about winning matches by hook or by crook.

In a nice way, it was a bit like having a kindly old relative in charge at times and his knowledge of the game was encyclopaedic, no question about that. His scouting system and contacts were just amazing - I'd never heard of Ricardo Fuller when he signed for us.

I think the first time I saw him he must have only been about 21, but he looked so old in his movement; all knock-kneed and jerky. There were a few raised eyebrows among the lads at first and a bit of: 'Who's this lad?'

But then, of course, we trained with him . . . and it was just jaw-dropping.

We were like: *'What the hell is this??'*

I'd never seen anything like it - he could run rings round the entire team. I know that phrase is overused, but he genuinely could. He was so quick, so strong, so skilful and he could stop on a sixpence, it was just incredible.

People ask who was the best player I ever played with and, for me, before he did his knee, it was Ricardo for sure. At that time, I would have backed him one-on-one against any defender in the world. I'm not exaggerating either. You just couldn't stop him - he was phenomenal.

And he wasn't the only great signing around under Craig, Youl Mawene came in and he was another top, top, player and a great addition to the dressing room. Claude Davis and Callum Davidson also arrived and the recruitment was absolutely spot on.

When you look at the players Craig had available to him, the lads he inherited and the ones that he signed, we should have absolutely walked the Championship.

But he just couldn't gel them together and I think we were always 'less than the sum of our parts'. There wasn't enough emphasis on tactics and he couldn't mould all the talent in the squad into what it should have been.

Moyesie had arguably got good players to overachieve, but with Craig, it was the other way round sadly. I remember we were 2-0 up at Wimbledon one day and one of the centre halves got injured.

Instead of just swapping like-for-like, he changed the entire formation, we went five at the back and I ended up left wing-back. I'd never played there before in my life, so that lasted about 20 minutes. Then he put Dickson Etuhu, not the greatest defender you've ever seen, there. Then he switched it again and put me back there. It was just bizarre and the lads were pulling their hair out over it.

We ended up drawing 3-3 and I remember that during the game, even one of their players said to me: 'What *is* your gaffer doing?'

I feel a bit bad saying anything negative about Craig though, because he was great with me on a personal level and he genuinely is a really nice bloke. I've got a lot of time and respect for him. But if I had to sum up his time at North End, for me, it was frustrating. We could and should have achieved so much more.

What's surprising is that Billy Davies was the assistant and he was all about tactics, preparation and intensity, so working under Craig must have been frustrating for him too. When he stepped up to take over it was like polar opposites. Craig had been so laid-back but Billy was probably too intense for his own good at times.

They say opposites attract and it looked that way with those two.

As soon as he took over, things switched dramatically overnight and I was left thinking: 'If this is the way he wants to run his ship, how has he worked under Craig for all this time?'

He must have been tearing his hair out, but for us, him stepping up was like a breath of fresh air. Training became shorter, but way more intense. There was a clear plan, a pressing game, an emphasis on tactics, organisation and preparation and a high-energy, incredibly hungry manager. I don't think Billy cared if your socks were down or not - just win the flipping game.

It was a bit like being back under Moyesie again and I loved it.

Billy took the same players Craig had had and transformed us in a very short period into the top Championship outfit we should have been.

In all honesty, I think that year when we reached the play-off final against West Ham was our best chance of reaching the Premier League in my time at Deepdale.

The Bolton game maybe came a bit too soon, but the squad that we had at Cardiff in 2005 was more experienced by that point. We maybe had a bit more quality and, of course, we'd beaten West Ham home and away in the regular season.

Yes, they had a lot of big names in their team, but quite a few of our lads went on to play in the Premier League too and it was a high standard all over the pitch in that play-off final.

I don't know if it was nerves, but I remember after only about 10 minutes being so fatigued and tired, whereas normally I felt like I could run all game. We were really confident going into it but it was a poor game overall, both teams just seemed to nullify each other.

I don't think they were any better than us and it could have gone either way. All it took was one slip and a bit of luck for them to nick it on the day. After they scored, we were chasing the game and that's really hard. They're running down the clock, breaking up play, lads are snatching at things and you know time is running out.

We kept going, but it wasn't to be and I remember being really deflated afterwards - as low as it got in my career, I think. I remember sitting in the changing room afterwards and saying to Julian Darby: *'That's my last chance gone.'*

He pulled me up a bit, because I was only 27 at the time, and said it would come again.

But I just felt like North End never had the money behind us that other clubs did. They weren't going to throw the kitchen sink at it and we'd missed out on a real chance that day. We were on this crest of a wave that year where everything had gone right for us, without spending a fortune.

We'd got lads like Dave Nugent in for a pittance really, signed some great players on free transfers like Brian O'Neill and Youl Mawene, and yet there we were - toe-to-toe with West Ham United, packed with players they'd signed for millions, earning a fortune every week.

Could you really bank on that happening again anytime soon? In a league as tough as the Championship?

You knew that bigger clubs would spend big the following year and that we wouldn't. You feared that players would start to be picked off by bigger clubs or at least have their heads turned. Our hope was just trying to keep the squad together and obviously, I'd seen what had happened after we lost in 2001. So that worried me.

Maybe we were punching above our weight a bit in the first final against Bolton, but we went into the West Ham one thinking we could really do it.

And obviously, if we'd managed it, it would have been life-changing for the players and the club. The revenue coming in would have changed Preston North End for the next 10 years, probably more.

I didn't care about the money - I just wanted to play in the Premier League, up against the best at the best stadiums, week in, week out. That was my goal - it wasn't about earning millions of pounds. It was a sporting thing, a football thing.

Instead, it was back to the Championship to see if we could repeat the feat next time out and go one further.

We went away to regroup and that summer Stoke City came in for me with an offer of about £750,000. North End refused it and that was that really. I wasn't angling for a move or anything and I was really enjoying being at a club close to my heart.

Despite losing in Cardiff, Billy was sticking around and I thought we'd have another good crack at the league the following season. Having said that, if Preston had accepted the offer, I'd probably have gone. It would have been a sign, not just about me personally, but about the direction of the club.

I won Championship Player of the Year for 2004/05 and it was nice to get noticed, so the interest was flattering really. I was coming on the radar and there were a few clubs interested in me round that time.

We played Malaga in a pre-season friendly that summer and they were doing quite well in La Liga at that time. Apparently, they showed an interest in me after the game too and Billy asked if I was interested in going there. I turned that one down flat though - there was no way I was going abroad, I just never fancied it.

North End gave me a new contract but looking back, to achieve my dream of playing in the Premier League, maybe I should have kicked up more of a fuss and worked my way into a move. Some lads do, but it's just not in my nature.

My biggest regret in my career is that I never got the chance to play at that top level, which is what I really wanted to do.

That's nothing against Preston and it was nothing to do with money - just from a personal footballing ambition, I look back and think maybe I could have done things differently and had more of a chance elsewhere. But it's all ifs and buts and maybes.

I can't complain with the career I had and I'm not bitter about things at all; I loved playing for North End and it is what it is.

We had another chance to go up the following season, finishing fourth and facing Leeds in the play-offs. Nuge put us one up and I think we did a good job on them after that, right up until Eddie Lewis equalised with a last-minute free-kick.

That changed the complexion of the tie and was the moment we were undone, really. Billy came out with his 'job done' statement to the press and that definitely riled them up a bit.

In the second leg, we went with a strange line-up that no-one had been expecting and it was one of those nights when everything seemed to go against us.

We seemed to be playing about five centre forwards, with Marcus Stewart, who'd barely played for us, starting at Deepdale. He was a good player, but he had a hamstring strain, wasn't even fit, and had to come off at half-time.

Brett Ormerod had broke his leg after about 10 minutes, so by the start of the second half, we'd used two of our subs and were still playing this strange formation we weren't used to. I don't know if Billy panicked with his team selection, but it certainly wasn't the tried-and-tested line-up we'd been using all season.

The strange thing is, he didn't need to do anything radical.

At home, against Leeds, we would probably have had enough to see them off. No-one liked coming to Deepdale - especially for a night game - so you'd fancy us, without having to change the team around so much. I think a few of the lads were a little miffed by that team selection and obviously, that's never good either.

So that was another year, another missed opportunity and, I'll be honest, by this point I was starting to wonder whether I was ever going to get to the Premier League with North End.

Maybe Billy thought the same because he left for Derby that summer and Paul Simpson came in as his replacement.

To be fair, he brought some decent players in - the likes of Neil Mellor, Liam Chilvers and Sean St Ledger - and for a while we were doing really well.

But it's a bit like when Roberto Martinez took over from Moyesie at Everton. At first, the Goodison team was still tight at the back and he added an attacking flair, so everything was looking good. The players at the back were well-drilled and well-organised from their time under the previous manager.

But if you don't do those drills every day in training, things start to erode pretty quickly and the same thing happened at Preston as happened at Everton. At first Billy's influence was still there, but after a few months, things started to fall away.

Paul Simpson inherited a squad that had been in the play-offs two years running and had some fantastic players at his disposal. It was such a good opportunity for a manager - normally, they come in when someone's been sacked.

But he was handed a successful team right from the start. All he had to do was continue doing what we were doing - but that wasn't his way.

He had this paranoia that the older pros were running the dressing room and so he had to break it all up. *Why? I'll never know.*

Of course, the senior pros had an influence on the dressing room - but it was a positive thing; they set the standards.

He shoved Graham Alexander out of the door - our captain, who'd been there for 10 years, a club legend farmed out to our local rivals. It was just a crazy move.

There had been no mention of it and I remember getting a call from Grezza early one morning when I was still in bed. He said: 'Guess where I am? I'm on the M65 going for talks with Burnley. North End have accepted an offer on me.'

I thought it was a wind-up - I genuinely couldn't believe it, but next thing you know, Graham had left Preston, a club he absolutely loves.

Similarly, Brian O'Neil is my best friend in football and I still speak to him every week. As well as being a great footballer, you can't meet a better pro and a better bloke to be around. Simpson treated him like dirt in my opinion, until in the end, Brian just had enough and retired early.

We also lost Danny Dichio around that time too and these were all good professionals and top lads who had been a major part of our success.

And the thing is, the spirit in the dressing room had really been the key to that success. There were no Big Time Charlies, everyone knew the standards, the work ethic - it was part of the culture, the way we'd done things for years.

But that was all taken apart pretty quickly and inevitably, results suffered. He just broke up this fantastic dressing room that we had. I know he was a young manager and maybe felt a bit threatened by senior pros, but there was no need to break things up the way he did.

And to make matters worse, he was bringing in people who were not only not good enough as players, some of them weren't good lads either.

I was vice captain when Grezza left and not long afterwards I was upstairs with the physio having some treatment on an injury. While I was up there, the manager called a meeting downstairs. He got all the squad together and announced that the new captain was going to be Kevin Nicholls, his new signing from Leeds.

I was vice captain, with hundreds of appearances for the club, been there all my career and he didn't even have me in the meeting - that was the level of respect he showed me. It was a very poor way of dealing with things and of all the managers I had, I've got the least respect for Paul Simpson.

There's a certain way of doing things and that's just not it.

Nicholls had come in from Leeds on big money, but was injured at the time and couldn't even play. To be blunt, the lads weren't having him.

They used to call him 'Captain Catchphrase' because he was always shouting out slogans like *'There's no 'i' in team!'* - cringey stuff like that.

It was embarrassing and all a bit of a smokescreen - anything to cover the fact that he couldn't really get about the pitch. Results weren't going well and I remember we were playing away at Hull City. I'd been back in the team after injury for about three or four weeks and we all knew Simpson's job was on the line.

He'd finally dropped Kevin Nicholls - I think even he realised he couldn't stand by him anymore, he was that bad.

So he pulled me to one side before the game and said: 'I want you to be my captain today.'

Everything in me wanted to say: *'Shove it up your backside.'*

But I knew he'd love that. He would have run to the press, making out I didn't want to be captain and calling me a disgrace for sure.

I knew it was a last-ditch attempt for him to save his job but I bit my tongue and said: 'Yep, fine.'

Captain or not, we got beat 3-0 that day because, well, the club was in a mess at that point. We were 2-0 down at half-time and he took off Andy Carroll and Chris Sedgwick. It wasn't good.

We had a line-up that had Andy Lonergan in goal, Youl and Sean St Ledger at the back with Callum Davidson and Matt Hill - all proven to be very good players, but we were never in it. We were just so disorganised.

After the game, he ripped into us, saying stuff like: *'I've had a good career, so it doesn't matter to me if you lot want to toss yours off. I couldn't care less - you're a disgrace, blah, blah, blah.'*

I think he realised the end was nigh and, true enough, he was sacked on the Monday morning. To be honest, when that happened, I really wished I had told him to stick it up his backside. But either way, I was glad to see the back of him.

As a footnote, we played Hull in the return fixture at Deepdale a few weeks later with virtually the same team . . . and won 3-0.

By that time of course, Alan Irvine was in charge and the difference was just like chalk and cheese. He was probably my favourite manager in my entire career.

Just a proper, stand-up guy, straight down the line, man of his word, always time to talk to you - a great bloke. I loved playing under him, but it nearly never happened.

After that Hull game, the club had another offer from me; Crystal Palace came in with a £750,000 bid. I spoke to their manager Neil Warnock and, while I didn't really want to go to London, they were offering to double my money and I thought: 'I can't turn this down.'

By that time, I'd been in so many play-offs and pushes with North End, I was pretty resigned to that fact that it wasn't going to happen for me at Preston.

Brian O'Neil was my agent by then and the deal was fairly done and dusted. I'd never met Alan before, but on his first day, Brian and I arranged to see him in his office.

He was very complimentary and said he felt like he knew me already because he'd seen me play so many times and heard so much about me from Moyesie at Everton.

He'd heard about the Palace deal already so I just said: 'I want to go. I've done everything I can for the club over many years and I think the time is right.' I'd never said that to any other North End manager and it was a big thing for me, a real wrench.

Alan was very calm and just said: 'The thing is, you're the club captain, we're in a relegation battle and this is my first day in the job . . . if I sell you, I'll get lynched.'

I was a bit taken aback, but he said: 'I understand where you're coming from and all I can promise you is this; if we can work together and get the club out of this mess, then the next opportunity that comes along, I'll do everything I can to help that move happen. But not this one - I need you.'

I could have been a bit of a dick about it, but I respected the way he was totally honest with me, so I agreed to stay. No problem, head down, crack on, let's go.

Almost straight away, we improved dramatically. I think from the date Alan arrived to the end of the season, we got more points than anyone in the league - that's how much he transformed us.

He was like Moyesie in many ways; quite intense, made sure you were all fit, very disciplined, but fair as well. We went back to being well-organised, confident, motivated - as a player, the coaching sessions were brilliant.

We were well clear of relegation by the end and who knows what we could have achieved that season if he'd been in from the start.

He also had an eye for a good player and not long into the next season he made a big signing in every sense when Jon Parkin arrived.

He'd been around for a few years but hadn't had much experience in the Championship at that point; he'd been a bit-part player at Stoke, but never really nailed a regular place down.

Now, I like players who work hard, train hard and look after themselves properly. That's what our success had been built on.

I'm not sure Parky fitted that model in the traditional sense!

But obviously Alan Irvine had seen something in Jon that we could make work and that's exactly what happened.

My wife wasn't a big football fan, I think she watched me about 10 times in 15 years, but when we were on Sky she'd always have it on for the kids. So we played a televised game at West Brom and the camera zoomed in on Jon, waiting to come on as a substitute, with his belly bulging out of his shirt - the classic Parky look.

When I got home she said to me: *'Who's that fat lad they were bringing on?? He looked like he'd just come out of the pub!'*

I said: 'Yeah, I know . . . that's our new centre forward.'

But, of course, he was a good player and scored some great goals for North End, as well as being a big influence in the dressing room.

They broke the mould when the made Jon - and I'm not sure we'll see his like again in the modern game. They probably couldn't find a mould big enough!

Neil Mellor was back firing under Alan and Chris Brown was still around, so we had good options up front and with Alan at the helm, we were pushing up around the play-offs in 2008/09.

I think the game that everyone remembers is the 6-0 win over Cardiff at Deepdale; Parky was almost unplayable that day and everything just went right. That wiped out their goal difference over us and gave us belief going into an away game live on Sky at Birmingham. They just needed a win to go up into the Premier League and the build-up was all about them sealing promotion. They maybe forgot we were a decent side ourselves, especially after they went 1-0 up.

Lee Bowyer and Lee Williamson then got sent off for a bit of handbags before I scored one of my favourite goals to level things up - a curling shot into the top corner from about 30 yards out. Then in the last minute, Ross Wallace pinged an absolute screamer in from a free-kick and we had well and truly ruined Birmingham's day.

They'd been asking the fans to 'keep off the pitch' in the celebrations at the end, but instead got booed off.

It set things up for us to beat QPR at home on the last day. Parky and Ledge scored on a beautiful sunny afternoon at Deepdale and we sneaked into the play-offs courtesy of goal difference after a 2-1 win. *Tense?* Just a bit, like. But the table doesn't lie.

We had some good players, a really good manager and we'd been on an unbelievable run, so we'd deserved our place in the top six. It's not like Cardiff could complain - we did put six past them.

But going into those play-offs, hand on heart, I didn't think we were good enough to win them.

On paper, they were two close games against Sheffield United and they only beat us by one goal in the end. However, when you're playing in games you get a sense of whether you're on the ropes, or gaining the upper hand.

Over those two games, I felt they were better than us.

We went 1-0 up at Deepdale through Ledge again, but I never felt we were fully in control and it ended 1-1. The equaliser just after half-time killed us and I knew we were up against it at their place.

Alan switched our formation around for the second leg and made a couple of changes, which maybe affected our rhythm, but there were probably other things too. Bramall Lane is a tough place to go and going there with a 1-0 lead would have given us something to roll our sleeves up and defend.

Going there and needing to win was always going to be a tough ask.

Being brutal, it wasn't like 2005 where I thought we had the better team - Sheffield were better than us that year. I think we had lots of good players with the ball, but we didn't have too much when we lost it. I felt I needed more help around me in midfield to do some of the ugly work.

Ross Wallace was a great player on the ball going forward, but he gave you nothing on the defensive side of things. I knew we needed to match them physically if we were going to get anything from the two legs, but I just didn't feel we had that in the squad. We needed a bit more bite, a bit more desire in those games - people like Brian O'Neil and Callum Davidson maybe, who could put a foot in, break things up.

So even though it was only 1-0 and we pushed right to the end, I think they won quite comfortably.

Losing in the play-offs again was a massive blow for everyone at the club; fans, staff and players. At Wembley, I was really pleased to see Grezza finally make it to the Premier League when Burnley beat Sheffield. I don't think anyone could have deserved it more than Graham.

But it also brought home to me that nagging feeling that if I wanted to get there too, it would probably have to be away from North End. We'd had too many chances and not taken them for one reason or another. You can only talk about luck for so long.

Again, I knew the club was not going to throw loads of money at things, so I didn't have that feeling that we were going to take that next step.

We had a good squad at Deepdale, but it wasn't the strongest I'd been involved in over the years and I didn't think we were going to win the Championship the next year. I was also 31 by this time and I felt that the clock was ticking for me a bit.

I knew Nottingham Forest had been monitoring me that season, as Billy Davies was there, but they were struggling at the wrong end of the table.

Billy had said that as long as they stayed up, he would come in for me that summer. They'd spoken to Brian and the outline of the contract and things was in place even before the end of the season.

So that was in the back of my mind at the end of the play-off second leg at Bramall Lane . . . this could well be my last appearance for North End.

That was a big thing for me when we lost and saying goodbye to the North End fans in the away end that night was emotional.

True enough, Forest came in with a bid that summer and Alan Irvine was true to his word in helping the deal go through.

Obviously, he was gutted that I was leaving - I was his captain and we had a great relationship. But he kept his promise to make sure things went smoothly when the offer was accepted. The previous summer, the club had stopped him going to West Brom so I think he understood my situation.

I loved North End, but I wanted to give myself the best chance of reaching the Premier League. Yes, the money was better at Forest, but that was never my motivation - if it had been I could have forced things a lot more over the years.

It was a footballing decision, pure and simple.

Alan gave me a glowing write-up in the Evening Post and I don't think there was any great animosity over me leaving Deepdale from the fans or anyone really.

Everyone who had seen me play knew I'd given my all for the club over many years and I think they understood my reasons for going in the end. I just knew if I was ever going to get a chance to play in the Premier League, I had to go.

Billy had been given an open cheque book at Forest because they really wanted promotion and, while I knew it was a big club, I didn't realise quite how big until I got there.

Ideally, I wanted to get in the Premier League with Preston - but now I felt I was somewhere where the money they had might make all the difference. The day I arrived, Billy made me captain and there were loads of talented players there.

But it was like babysitting them at times; they were all quite young and didn't know how to play without the ball. I used to finish every game hoarse from shouting to get them where they should be on the pitch.

Just before Christmas, I got my first goal for Forest, a half-volley from the edge of the box against . . . who else? It had to be North End.

Lonners got a punch out from a corner and it just sat up nicely for me and flew into the far corner. I had too much respect for the Preston fans and the club to celebrate and if you watch it, there's just a little shake of my head.

Of all the teams to score against . . . unbelievable.

Mainly though ,I felt vindicated; that game and Forest's good season showed that I was right to go there. That win put us second in the league and I was really hopeful of finally going up. Things were going really well, but in March I did my medial ligament and missed the entire run-in for that season. I made it back for the play-offs, but I wasn't fully fit when we lost to Blackpool *(I know)* so that was a double sickener, especially as I felt we were a better team than them.

The following year we lost out in the play-off semi finals again to Swansea, who went up in the final thanks to a Scott Sinclair hat-trick. We hadn't gone up, but we'd had two good goes at it, so it was a bit of a shock that summer when the club sacked Billy and not long after that, they said I could leave on a free transfer.

I think they saw me as one of Billy's players and they wanted a clean sweep.

Possibly, they expected me to go back to North End, who had been relegated by then, but I didn't have any contact with them around that time.

I did go back to Deepdale for a game during the Graham Westley era and it was sad to see how things had gone downhill behind the scenes.

The atmosphere was totally different to how I'd remembered it just a few years earlier. It was like the heart had been ripped out of the club. When I left it, everything was well-run and the club was pushing at the top of the Championship.

Within a couple of years, it was worlds apart; everything was doom and gloom, the staff were all down in the dumps, there was about 7,500 on for the game and I just thought: *'What the hell has gone on here? What's happened to the club?'* It was shocking.

The chance of going back never came up though, because I thought I still had something to offer in the Championship and within days of Forest saying I could go, I joined Hull City for a couple of seasons. I think I did OK there before reuniting with Graham Alexander at Fleetwood for a last hurrah.

These days I have a property company where I buy, sell - and sometimes build - houses. I also do some of the co-commentaries for North End games on the club website and that's something I really enjoy doing. The fans are always great and I'll never forget more than 9,000 turning out for my testimonial game against Moyesie's Everton side in 2006 - that really meant a lot to me.

It's great to see that over the last four or five years, we've got back in the Championship and re-established ourselves at that level as a really decent team and a proper club once more.

It's well-run again, but some of the issues that were around in my time haven't gone away. We're not the biggest team in the league, so Preston is always going to be a selling club. We tend to have teams of players who haven't cost a fortune, are well organised, will work hard and are always tough to play against. It's a blueprint the club has had for many years and it has been largely successful.

While that will get you so far, when you come up against the bigger teams, they have that extra bit of quality that puts them out of reach over the course of a season.

Together, North End are a formidable unit and in a one-off game, they can match anyone on their day. But when push comes to shove, unless they can properly invest in more creativity and quality, I fear they are always going to be behind the top two or three in a Championship campaign.

The risk then is that the best players get picked off and the process starts all over again. We've seen that happen before and I just hope that the club can find that one season when everything comes together to get us over the line.

For me, I had great times at Deepdale and look back with pride on what we achieved there - I'm not sure there's ever been a period of progress like it in the club's history.

Players, managers, directors, staff and supporters all came together to make it happen.

To have been a part of that is very special.

Chapter 5

PAUL HUNTINGTON: MAGIC

I see you're back from the dead again then.' That was the text message I got from Joe Garner after coming into the North End team after ten long months of being left out.

It was typically deadpan of Garns and I couldn't help but smile. After all, there's many a true word spoken in jest. Because that's what it felt like to me deep down; some people may have written me off, but now I was part of it again.

I'd had a good game against a decent West Brom side in December 2019, so I could barely have been happier - apart from the result.

That had been a travesty after a very dodgy penalty where their lad had clearly dived, so obviously that tainted events quite a bit, because it's all about winning games, isn't it?

The positive thing was that I'd pulled on the white shirt again, but I was much happier a few days later when we beat Fulham and got the three points.

That night, I got the Sky Sports Man of the Match and loved walking off, clutching the award with the cheers of the Town End ringing in my ears.

When I got back to the dressing room the lads gave me a round of applause as I walked in and I couldn't stop smiling.

I'd taken my chance and shown what I could still do. I was back and I was absolutely chuffed.

It's been a bit like that a couple of times for me at Deepdale, people thinking my time was up, but I've always come back fighting and nailed down a place in the team.

You could say it's the story of my career; from making my debut as a teenager in the Premier League and playing in the UEFA Cup to a decent transfer to another big club and then before I knew it - being out of contract and wondering what to do next.

All by the time I was 22.

I'd packed a lot in before I came to Deepdale, but once I arrived I don't think I've ever felt more at home.

You may know I'm from just up the road in Cumbria (!) and by the age of 10, I was signed up by Newcastle, so two or three nights a week I was going over there; Monday, Wednesday, Friday with games at the weekend as well.

I was actually a ball boy from the age of about 10 to 14 at St James' Park and would go over there with my dad after playing for the youth teams on a Saturday morning.

All that travelling was a big commitment for my dad really - over an hour each way on the A69. I'd get in from school, do a quick change and we were off. A sandwich in the car for tea and go training.

That was the routine for years and I'll always be grateful for his help and support.

My dad still comes to my home games now and some of the northern away games, too. Same with my wife, I remember her coming to Sunderland a couple of years ago and it was about -5 degrees - but she loved it because we won 2-0. Having that family support always means a lot to me.

On top of that, I carried on playing locally, too for a while. I don't know if you're meant to, but they were my mates, y'know?

There was a time around about 14 or 15 when I wasn't enjoying the coaching at Newcastle and I thought about moving clubs, but I stuck it out and things got better from there. When I was 16, I left school and straight away signed as an apprentice there and it was a really big step for me; moving away from home and into digs, with a house parent and things like that.

I missed home like mad that first couple of years; it was really difficult - all your mates back home were going out on the drink, going off to uni and whatnot and I was a bit homesick. But playing football full time really helped me and I soon came to enjoy it. After all, here I was - playing football for a job.

OK, I was very much learning my craft, but what a job to have.

I played up above my age group quite a bit and got into the reserves, so I was heading in the right direction. I signed professional terms and ended up playing something like 60-odd games for the reserves. Getting the experience at that age was great, playing with established professionals like Scott Parker, Shola Ameobi, Lee Clark and James Milner, who I still speak to now.

Alan Shearer was there and he was great with me. When you played against him in training, he would take you to one side afterwards and give you pointers: *'You're not doing this, it's better if you do that.'*

He was always interested in you and how you were getting on. It was a bit mad really, Alan Shearer talking to you, but he was fantastic with us young lads. He'd retired from England by then, so when it was international breaks, there'd only be him and a few of the first team with us youngsters. He'd just sit and talk to us for ages; he'd want to know about you, rather than the other way round.

Graeme Souness was the manager and I started being involved a bit more with the first team; travelling with the squad a few times, warming up with the team, etc.

We do it with some of the young lads at Deepdale now and it's a great way of getting them a bit more prepared for when their time comes.

Glenn Roeder had come in as Academy Director and I really liked him. When Souness left, he became manager and obviously knew a bit about me.

With a few injuries and suspensions I made it onto the bench for quite a few games without getting on, until we played Blackburn at Ewood Park in December 2006. It was a Premiership game and they had the likes of Tugay and Robbie Savage, while we had Shay Given in goal, Nicky Butt in midfield and Obafemi Martins up front.

I came on at right-back after 86 minutes when we were winning 2-1 and they were throwing everything at us.

I remember Brad Friedel came up for a corner and I cleared a good chance off the line, heading it away from under the bar. With the keeper out of position, we broke away and Martins scored a third to make it safe.

So that was a fantastic start and, as luck would have it, Alan Shearer was a pundit on that night's Match of the Day.

He did a little section on me, which was unbelievable, saying how he was delighted for me with how hard I'd worked, how I'd made this important header and helped set up the third goal. I was only 19 and it was my first game so I was absolutely made up, as you can imagine.

That was on the Saturday and I started the following Wednesday, away at Chelsea who were flying under Jose Mourinho with Frank Lampard, John Terry, Ashley Cole, Michael Ballack, the whole crew.

That was my full debut; playing right-back against Arjen Robben under the lights at Stamford Bridge. *So, yeah, a bit of a test!*

We did quite well and only lost 1-0 late on to a Didier Drogba goal.

I hadn't really come through as a full-back, but it was case of 'needs must' and I was lucky that whenever I played there, James Milner - the fittest guy ever - would always be working back right there with me, helping out. He wasn't an older player himself, but he looked after me and we had a great relationship.

I played quite a bit that season, up against the likes of Rooney and Ronaldo at Man United and scoring against Spurs at White Hart Lane. In those days, I had a boot deal and got a bonus payment for scoring so I was doubly delighted!

We lost 2-0 in the last-16 of the UEFA Cup at Louis Van Gaal's AZ Alkmaar and went out on away goals, but it was good to get a taste of European competition and everything was going in the right direction.

But even though I was in and around the first team, I knew I had loads to learn and would have to work hard.

Around that time, I stopped drinking and I don't drink alcohol to this day. It wasn't a problem for me or anything, I just wanted to give myself the best chance to succeed in my career.

When we were younger, we'd be out over the weekend, then play a youth or reserve game early the next week and I could still feel the effects at times. If I wanted to be at my best, I knew I'd have to lay off the beer, so I just stopped almost before I'd started.

I still go on nights out with the lads and all the rest and I don't think it makes me boring or anything - you'd have to ask them.

On second thoughts, *don't!*

After that first season, Glenn Roeder was sacked and Sam Allardyce came in. We all had to have meetings with him at his penthouse in a top hotel. He was very laid back and met me at the door wearing a robe, saying: *'Alright son, come on in . . .'*

He's just like he comes across when you see him on TV and I got on OK with him. But he signed four or five defenders straight away for good money back in the day - six, seven, eight million - and I was pushed down the pecking order.

He wasn't particularly keen on the younger players who were around with me at the time, lads like Andy Carroll and Tim Krul, who I lived with in digs. They only really came through when he'd left. In hindsight, I should have stuck it out as Big Sam didn't last very long and if I had my time again, I'd have stayed.

But at the time, I was young and naive, so when a number of clubs came in for me on transfer deadline day 2007, I was interested. By then, I was back in the reserves, but I'd had a taste of the first team and I wanted to play. Tony Pulis wanted me at Stoke, Brian Laws at Sheffield Wednesday and Phil Brown was keen at Hull.

In the end, it was a whirlwind day; I turned up for training as normal on a Friday and by that evening, I'd signed for Leeds under Dennis Wise and Gus Poyet.

It had all happened so fast and was a big change for me, as I'd been at Newcastle from the age of 10.

Leeds started my first season on minus 15 points for going into administration, but still finished fourth, losing 1-0 in the play-off final to Doncaster at Wembley with me, Jermaine Beckford and Neil Kilkenny in the side and former PNE keeper Dave Lucas on the bench. Obviously, we felt hard done by at the time, as without the points deduction, we'd have gone straight up.

Dennis and Gus left and Gary McAllister came in and he was great, but the expectation there is huge. I had a few injuries, we had a sticky spell, Gary was sacked and Simon Grayson came in. The timing wasn't great. I was having all sorts of issues; groin injuries, hernia issues - I just couldn't get fit.

Mentally it was hard; you get to thinking: 'Will I ever be right again?'

Again, Simon had brought in a lot of established players and I don't think he liked throwing the younger lads in.

I went out on loan to Stockport, which, with hindsight wasn't the best move. I'm not saying I was better than the players that were there, but you go from being with lads at a certain level to players who weren't as good. The team was struggling and I found it really hard mentally to adjust.

I was in the last year of my deal, things came to a head and I ended up getting my contract paid up at Leeds. I could see I wasn't going to play, so we had a clean break.

I didn't have any big falling out with Simon, it was just one of those things.

Now I was out of contract again, my career seemed to be going backwards and I remember being affected by it all. We went away that summer and my wife said I was just like a different person, really down about things and wondering where I was going to go next. In the end, I had to give myself a wake-up call.

Yes, I'd had a setback. But now it was a case of knuckling down, getting back out there, getting my career back on track, finding a place where I could start to move my career forward again.

So I went to Yeovil, which was a lovely League 1 club and at that time it was a bit of a place where people went to rebuild or restart their careers.

There were lots of good players there who have gone on to have good careers; Alex McCarthy, Byron Webster, Luke Ayling, Luke Freeman, Kieran Agard, Ed Upson, people like that. You could just go there and concentrate on your football.

I could have stayed up north, but I knew I had to find somewhere where I could start enjoying playing again.

I'd played against the manager Terry Skiverton and he's a really good guy, while Nathan Jones, who recently managed Luton and Stoke, was player coach and was one of the best coaches that I've ever had - I still keep in touch with him now.

I was captain for a lot of the time I was there and I was playing 40-odd games per season - just what I needed.

When I've been fit, I've always been a big part of things and that's why any time out of the line-up at Deepdale has always been so hard to take.

I've got nothing but fond memories of my time at Yeovil; it's a lovely part of the world and I'd stay there during the week and just go home at the weekends.

However, it's a long trek to Carlisle on a Saturday night and there were times when I'd catch a glimpse of Deepdale from where the motorway and I used to think to myself: 'Wouldn't it be amazing to be able to play there.'

Not just because it was nearer to home, but because of the whole nature of the place; it has this feeling about it.

It just looks like a proper football ground, proper floodlights, surrounded by rooftops and sticking out like a prized jewel on the skyline.

I'm sure people reading this will know the view I'm on about and have thought the same thing. I know it's based on the Sampdoria stadium in Genoa and I just love it, I absolutely love turning up and playing at home.

I'd played there before for Yeovil and was always impressed; good pitch, good atmosphere, just a proper football club. After two years, my contract was up at Yeovil. Gary Johnson had taken over and offered me a deal, but I knew I should really move on. I'd played a lot of games, established myself again and done what I set out to do - I was back on an upward curve.

I'd been Player of the Year in my first year and fans' Player of the Year the following season, so there were a couple of teams interested in me; decent, top six League 1 sides. But I'd made up my mind that if there was any chance to go to Preston, I'd be there in a flash. Thankfully, I got the call.

Of course, it was Graham Westley managing North End at the time and the signing process was a bit like going for a job interview.

Well, not just one interview - several, in fact.

I met him down at the offices at the ground, then I spoke to him on the phone, then he was texting, then he wanted to meet again - it was all quite intense.

He'd obviously done his background work on me and got references from people about my attitude, etc. We talked for hours and he was telling me in detail what the daily routine was going to be like and what his philosophy was, etc.

I just thought: 'Well, if it works out great and if not, there will be another manager coming in and it'll be a clean slate.'

There was a huge turnaround in players around that time; something like 20-odd lads coming and going.

And, to be fair, we weren't disastrous at the start of my first season. We were up and about the top six until around Christmas when we had a few injuries, results started to suffer and it was then that issues with the training and the texting and the methods started to take their toll on the squad and it all got a bit much.

It was so intense, it just consumed you and probably distracted you from the games, rather than focusing your mind on them. I genuinely didn't mind his training methods and the hours and whatnot; it was different, yes, but we gave it a go.

It's sad because there genuinely was method in the madness at times.

And I'll always be very grateful to him for bringing me to the club, along with players like Garns, John Welsh and others who served North End well. So I can't be too harsh on him and also I don't think it was an easy job.

He'd obviously been told to sort out the budgets and he was trying to change the culture of the place and bring in his style that had been successful elsewhere.

I think his heart was always in the right place and I remember when we went up at Wembley he was there, a few rows back when we went to collect the trophy, cheering us on and loving it.

He sent a few of the lads he'd brought in a text saying: *'I knew you were a winner when I signed you, etc'*, so he was obviously pleased the club had been successful, even after he left.

But when Simon Grayson came in, it was like someone had flicked a switch.

We went from being dull, down and disappointed to being upbeat and enjoying coming in every day. Probably the first thing that Simon did was put smiles back on faces again. We knew we had a half decent squad and we'd been under-achieving.

He made a few changes, things got a bit more tactical and results really picked up. It was a bit of a strange situation for me though.

Obviously, I'd worked with Simon before and the lads were asking me what he was like. I just said: *'Don't ask me, he bombed me out at Leeds!'*

Looking back, I understood it; I was just a young defender and he preferred to bring in more experienced players. Leeds got promoted, so it worked for him and you can't argue with that. When he was coming in at Deepdale, I was probably 100 games down the line, mid-20s and I think I fitted the mould he was looking for a lot better.

We didn't really talk about what had happened at Leeds and I'd never burned my bridges with him. In fact, the summer I signed for North End, I bumped into him on holiday - in Barbados, bizarrely. I was walking out of a restaurant there and I didn't see him, but I heard this shout and there he was with his family.

I stopped and we had a quick chat; he said he'd seen how well I'd done at Yeovil and was pleased it was all going well for me. So there was no ill-feeling or anything between us from what happened at Leeds; I was a young player with quite a bit to learn and he was looking for something else at the time.

He picked me for North End right from the start and I think we had a really good end to that season, finishing comfortably mid table - OK, not where we wanted to be, but there was a belief that we'd turned a corner.

Obviously, Simon had got quite a few teams promoted from that league - including Leeds - and he just had the air of a bloke who knew what he was doing. We brought in Kevin Davies and although he wasn't playing so much, I learned quite a lot off him and so did quite a few of the lads.

The thing with Kev is that he looks a bit like a choirboy but he's an absolute beast, who's been there and done it at the top level.

He's a great guy, who I still keep in touch with, and brought a different perspective to things in training, even though he might not have been playing every game.

The season started well and we had some great results - beating Blackpool at home, what a night that was.

The atmosphere, the fans, the passion, the result - everything you come into the game for and a fantastic way for Tom Clarke to introduce himself to the fans.

It helped set us up and I played nearly every game until around March when Simon changed the team - just like that - and that was it for me that season.

It was really strange, because we hadn't hit a run of bad results or anything, in fact the last three games I played we won three and drew one. But suddenly I was out.

Simon was going with Bailey Wright and Clarkey, sometimes Jack King, sometimes someone else - and I didn't get a look-in. I was in the squad and made the bench a couple of times - and I came on for the last few minutes when we were 6-1 up against Carlisle. However, I had gone from playing virtually every game to basically not getting a kick. There'd been no bust-up or anything and nothing was really said.

I was just really disappointed and inevitably you start to feel like you're not part of things. You've just got to keep your head up, work harder than ever and make sure you're ready if and when you're needed.

You can't sit around sulking, you've just got to suck it up. The only thing I can say, is that the team was doing well without me and made it to the play-offs.

However, for the games against Rotherham, I was travelling with the team, but not even in the squad so I was gutted not to be involved at all.

You just try and be there for the lads, wish them all the best and whatnot, but it's hard to go from playing nearly every game to not even being close to the team. You've got to be smiley at times when it's really hard to take.

People sometimes get the wrong idea about footballers, thinking they don't care, they get paid anyway, etc.

Trust me, they do and they all want to play.

I won't deny there are some lads who see others in their position and think *'I hope he has a stinker'* but they've been few and far between at North End down the years. And they haven't lasted long.

One thing I always do is look after my own boots and bring them to games myself.

It's not a sleight on the kit people or anything, it's just that I always want to know they're there and they're right.

Same with my shin pads and flip flops. I've seen enough players lose them down the years, so it's just one less thing to worry about.

I haven't got a boot deal with a supplier and I clean them myself too, like most of the lads. We don't have boot boys anymore, that's gone from the game a bit now.

And, yes, the boots are always, always black.

I don't know where it comes from, probably from just when I was starting out really - football boots were black and that was that.

I've just always liked black.

I once had to borrow a pair of Clarkey's blue ones for a session at UCLan and it was weird.

Every time I looked down I felt as though I was putting my foot too close to the ball, or moving it too far away.

Some of the new lads turn up in orange boots and we let them know that's not going to go down well with the fans, for obvious reasons.

Clarkey's been a bit close to the line a few times, but he's like: 'No, no - they're peach, honest!'

I'm in Nike at the minute, but I've changed down the years; Under Armour, adidas.

These days I have them specially adjusted by a guy who goes under the name Toots Boots - Darnell Fisher and Billy Bodin use him too.

He's the brother of Matt Tootle (who played for Crewe for many years and does a lot of work for MIND, the mental health charity that I want to give a shout-out to).

He does 'black-out' services, sole conversions and all sorts of things and it doesn't cost a fortune, probably around £40, depending what you want doing.

He's a really clever bloke who not only sorts out the trims and things, but also customises your studs, so you can have a mix of moulded and screw-ins, a specific number, etc.

For defenders it's normally studs, not blades or anything - I've tried them and I was like Bambi on ice. No thanks. No messing. Back to black.

At that time, I had a year left on my contract and it was pretty clear that if the club got promoted, they'd be looking to bring in new defenders and I realised that would probably have been the end of it for me, really.

If I wasn't getting in the team in League 1, I wasn't going to get picked in the Championship. But you put all that to one side and you still want to go up, obviously. Personal situations don't come into it, not for me anyway. If the team's winning, I'm happy. I wanted us to go up and then I could look back with pride on the games I did play earlier in the season. So I was gutted when we lost at Rotherham and ended up staying down for another year.

I remember I went away determined to come back flying and force my way back into the team the following season.

Unfortunately, that didn't look like happening.

One day that summer, I was playing golf with a mate back home in Carlisle when I got a call from Glynn Snodin, Simon's assistant.

He was basically saying: 'Well Hunts, you've got a year left on your contract, but we won't stand in your way if you get fixed up elsewhere. What are you thinking?'

I'll be honest, it really hurt me at the time.

I was thinking: *'I've just played about 30 games, I love being at the club, I'm going to keep working hard and I want to get back in the team at Preston - nowhere else.'*

It was really hard, because if felt like Snods was ringing me every couple of days, asking if I wanted to go here or there. There were teams in Scotland in for me, decent teams in League 1 - some good clubs.

Every time I said 'no' straight away, but it started to get me down a bit. It felt like they wanted me to accept that my time at North End was up, but I wouldn't.

I spoke to my wife and she said: 'Just keep working, keep doing your best and prove them wrong.'

After a while, I said to Snods: 'Look, you can keep asking, but I don't want to go anywhere else. I want to stay here and fight for my place and that's what I'm going to do.' I hadn't sulked, I'd kept my attitude right and I wanted to be a big part of things.

I tried to use it as a motivational thing, sort of like 'you think I'm done here, do you? OK, I'll show you'.

I went on holiday to Ibiza - not a lads' trip, just a quiet one - and I really blasted the running up and down the seafront, listening to 'My Love' by Route 94 *(give it a listen if you get the chance, it's a great tune)*. I was absolutely determined to force my way back in, it was like an obsession almost.

In pre-season training, I'd normally be somewhere in the middle of the pack. But that year I came back flying, out at the front, really putting it in. It got to the point where Simon was joking about it, saying: 'Who's this guy? Is it Hunts' twin brother?'

At first, it didn't do me much good. Simon was sticking with Clarkey and Bailey Wright and I wasn't even making the bench in the League Cup.

I played a couple of Johnstone Paint Trophy games - we won both, but I was back out for the next league game. Again, it was hard because I felt I was training better than certain people, but they would still be in the squad.

You've just got to suck it up, keep going and make sure you give a good account of yourself when you do play. I'm not the type to go knocking on the manager's door; I just keep working hard and hopefully get a chance to get back in.

But then early in October we were away at Gillingham. I think Bailey was ill, Tom was injured, so there was only me and Jack King fit to play at the back.

Kingy was a good lad who loved a tackle, but I don't think he really liked heading the ball at the back too much - he was more of a holding midfield player.

We flew down and, while no-one said anything to me, I thought: 'Well, he's got to play me now.'

True enough, it was me and Jack at the back; there was no great fuss when the team was read out. I played right side, did well on a horrible windy night and scored the only goal in a 1-0 win. Get in.

On the journey back, I was just so pleased to have put in a good performance in a good away win and I thought: *'Surely, he can't drop me again now . . .'*

Thankfully, he didn't and I was in for the next home game - against Fleetwood at Deepdale. Of course, fifteen minutes in and we were 2-0 down in a local derby.

I was thinking: *'Well, that's out of the team for another six months!'*

Thankfully, we got ourselves together at half-time and Garns scored a hat-trick in the second half to turn it around for us. Cheers Joe!

On the Tuesday, we went down to Orient and me and Callum Robinson scored in a 2-0 win and things just went from there really.

I played nearly every game for the rest of the season and every game I knew I'd have to be absolutely spot on. Whether it was deliberately motivational by the manager, I don't know, but I knew that I almost had to prove myself to him in every game. So that's what I did.

It's partly why playing for Preston means so much to me; because there have been challenges put in front of me and questions asked of me at the club and I feel I've answered them.

I feel like I fought so hard to prove people wrong and when you've fought for something, you're invested, you never want to give it up.

Don't get me wrong, I know I haven't got a divine right to be in the side - then or now - but all I've ever wanted was a fair crack of the whip, the same as everyone else.

After that, it's stand or fall on how I perform and I can live with that. I was back in the team when we played Man United in the FA Cup and I think we gave a good account of ourselves that night.

Scotty Laird scored a wonder goal *(he'll tell you alllllll about it if you ever meet him)* and we thought: 'Come on! We can beat these!'

Normally, me and Clarkey, being the old heads sometimes don't go sprinting in for the goal celebrations if they're at the far end, we sort of wait until the lads are coming back to our half.

That night, we both legged it to join in the pile-on near the tunnel!

The noise was incredible and I really thought we had a chance. Sadly, they got back into it and ended the night with a dodgy penalty. Wayne Rooney and me had been talking throughout about how poor the ref was that night - really arrogant (the ref, not Rooney). Next thing he gives them that penalty and two minutes later Rooney's still saying 'oh, he's still rubbish'.

I just said: 'Tell me about it!'

The ref was all first name terms with the United players - *Wazza and things like that* - when he was talking to them. With us, he looked at us as if to say: 'Who are you then?' So it's not great when they get like that.

The best ref I ever had was Howard Webb, always very clear and fair with you, and Michael Oliver, who's fantastic in games.

I remember absolutely nailing El Hadj Diouf in a game for Newcastle (I wasn't the first) and all the Bolton players piled in, players squaring up all over the place, but Howard Webb just stepped in and within seconds it was all calm again. He had that authority that players accepted.

There are one or two who are still reffing now so I have to be careful, but hopefully, I've developed a way of talking to them that gets through. What I do know is that shouting in their faces doesn't work at all. You've got to try and reason with them at times to get your point across.

Most times, you'll just want them to be consistent; you'll see one of our lads wiped out and get nothing, whereas if Pearo goes in for a tackle, they can't get the cards out fast enough at times.

It's a reputation thing and that shouldn't come into it. It should be on the incident itself, but we don't always get the rub of the green at times.

We didn't that night against United either, losing 3-1 in the end, but the game set us up for a long unbeaten run. For a long while, it looked like we were going to claim automatic promotion but we ended up drawing too many games in the run-in.

We drew away at Port Vale, when they got a dodgy penalty, and all the time . . . the MK Dons were staying with us, point-for-point in the race to get in the top two behind Bristol City.

Callum Robinson knew Dele Alli, who was at Milton Keynes, from the England set-up, and he was getting texts from him after every game saying: 'We're coming for you boys.'

We beat Swindon in our last home game, which really helped us, even though they put out a reserve side as they were already in the play-offs.

And then it was down to Colchester - win that and we were up. Simple, on paper. OK, they were fighting for their lives and needed a win to stay up, but we just didn't turn up in the first half.

I've no idea why. It wasn't an attitude thing, we just couldn't get going. A few of the lads were having a pop at each other at half-time and we improved a bit second half, but you could feel time slipping away and things started getting a bit more pressurised all over the pitch.

They then missed a penalty and you start to think: *'Right, come on, that's our let-off, let's put this to bed'.*

I remember Jermaine and Callum going for a header and getting in each other's way - it was starting to look like one of those days.

Then they scored. Obviously, it was a big goal for them and the crowd were right up for it. After that, the rest of the game flew past in a blur, if I'm honest.

They were going down, slowing things down a lot and before we knew it . . . we'd got beat, MK Dons had won and we were down in the play-off places.

Maybe we'd got a bit ahead of ourselves in the build-up, because there was a party organised for everyone after the game to celebrate promotion.

But that was all off now, obviously.

We got back on the coach on the way to the airport and no-one said a word. I was just staring out of the window and filling up a bit in all honesty, because it meant that much to me.

After a while, Simon stopped the bus and gave us a speech saying we still had 'a chance to put this right' and the main thing now was that we took it.

He could see everyone was shell-shocked, but we weren't out of it and we couldn't feel sorry for ourselves - it was down to character now.

That's one of the things I'd say about Simon, he wasn't as tactical as Alex Neil, who is probably the most switched-on tactical manager I've played under.

But Simon was great at getting a team full of strong characters, proper good lads and I think we were a band of brothers that season in particular.

We still are now.

Preston aren't a team that goes out splashing out big money on flash signings, so there's no 'big star egos' or anything to deal with.

You do get that at other clubs, normally there's one or two bad eggs that you hear about, but since I've been at Deepdale the groups have all been sound lads. Clarkey, Gally, Ben Davies, just the best type of lads you could wish for on and off the pitch.

It's interesting that we tend to just sign British or Irish lads mainly, people who understand the league and North End's position in it.

We've had one or two Scandinavians and obviously we've got Patrick Bauer now, but largely it's a home-grown dressing room. (Pat, by the way, is a great lad, who has really fitted in with everyone from Day One.)

Also, we quite often sign people who have a point to prove, either coming from other clubs' reserves or from lower leagues and everyone knows it's up to them to make the most of the opportunity.

It was like that when I joined and it's still like that to this day.

Anyway, after the Colchester defeat, we had a day off, moping around, then got straight back into it. Against Chesterfield away, it was a classic workman-like performance where Becks nicked us a goal and then we defended for our lives.

They might have thought we'd be on a downer, but if anything the mood was just the opposite. We were absolutely determined.

At home, Sam Johnstone made a great save from Sam Clucas and then we battered them with Becks and Joe getting the goals to send us to the final.

We had a night out in Manchester to celebrate and then had a few days off, which you don't normally get at that stage of the season.

There's a bit of a gap to the final and it was a bit like being in pre-season again as we didn't have the game for such a long time. I remember we had a few sessions on Deepdale and ended up with an 11 v 11 game, where the reserves absolutely battered us. I was thinking: 'Oh my God, we're all over the place here.'

So we had to pull our socks up and get our heads back to where they'd been against Chesterfield pretty sharp. It was probably a good wake-up call.

For the final itself, there was no big celebration or anything organised for afterwards at all.

There'd been talk of a trip to Vegas before the Colchester game. Now it was all about winning the final and forget what might come afterwards.

We trained at Brentford, did all our sightseeing at Wembley the day before and Simon made sure there was nothing put out on social media.

We had to make sure we weren't overawed and that was all part of it; forget the occasion, we're here to win a game of football.

On the day, well . . . Becks was unplayable.

But Swindon played right into our hands; they were using a high back line and trying to be tippy-tappy.

We were just getting the ball off them in midfield and going straight in behind.

It was like - *bam!* - we've got the ball and we're in. Time and again.

I'd got a few goals that season and it's one of those where I always think if I get one, I'll get a few over the next few games. It just gives you confidence and you back yourself a bit more.

I think I ended up with nine goals that season and the deliveries in from Gally were just a dream, every game. When he's on the pitch, you always feel you've got chance of getting on the end of things.

Ironically, that day he hit the first man from a corner, but Welshy won a great tackle on the edge of the box and I stayed up as Swindon quickly tried to get back in position.

This time Gally hit a perfect cross in and I could see that it had plenty of pace on it.

I also knew their keeper was a strange one; he always seemed to go for things with his feet. He didn't like diving around so much.

So in that split-second I just thought, I'll just try to guide it in, get it on target and wrong-foot the keeper, rather than leather it at him.

When it went in I didn't know what to do for a second so I just kept running; ran past Gally - *high-fived him* - ran to the bench on the way back, pointing to my family in the stand and then, errr, just kept going!

It's funny now when I watch it back - I'm just running and running and trying to look cool. But for the next five minutes I was just a mixture of buzzing - and blowing out of my backside after all the celebrations.

Obviously, Becks got a brilliant third before half-time and that killed the game, really. I remember sitting there at half-time, 3-0 up and we couldn't believe it.

Simon was saying 'it's not over' but straight away in the second half, Becks got through again. Swindon hadn't learned from their mistakes and, with being 3-0 down, they were having to go for it, leaving even more room in behind.

Becks just missed that one but a few minutes later, I think Joe played him through on the keeper again and that was that - 4-0. Happy days!

Again I piled in on the celebrations and being right next to a TV camera, I let the watching audience know that it was 'a flipping beauty'. Or words to that effect!

Strangely, they never bleep it out, so you can still hear exactly what I thought whenever it's re-shown on Sky.

To be honest, I was glad it was a 4-0 game because the size of the pitch was massive and it was a really humid day.

I remember at the start thinking 'I hope this doesn't go to extra time' because it's going to be hard work out here.

At 75 minutes, I was really feeling it in my calves and cramping a little bit but I was just determined to be on the pitch when we clinched promotion.

The other thing - *and I hesitate to mention it* - was that we were all so delighted to be putting that flipping hoodoo to death. It's all the press guys ever asked about: 'Are you aware that Preston have never won the play-offs, etc?'

Yes mate, of course we know about it!

But that wasn't us and now we're going to put an end to it.

The past is the past. This was a new group of players and we didn't want to be weighed down by things from years earlier. It's daft to start putting that in people's heads, so we were chuffed to finally put an end to it.

I remember keeping one of the Champagne bottles in my bag and it was just a fantastic day. I've got the programme, my medal and my shirt all framed up at home and as Alex Neil always says: 'You want to be remembered for doing something.'

It's great to be remembered as a good player, but really, you want to be remembered as part of a promotion-winning team.

After that, you want to be in the first team to lift this club into the Premier League. And that's been our target ever since that game against Swindon.

To round off that season, I was named Player of the Year and presented with the Sir Tom Finney trophy, which was just an unbelievable honour. It meant - and still means - so much to me, especially as I wasn't in the team at the start of the season.

So to get in the starting line-up, nail down a place and be a part of a successful season was everything I could have wished for.

The following season in the Championship, Simon kept faith with a lot of the lads who had won promotion and we did better than the teams that had come up with us.

Some of his signings were inspired; Greg Cunningham and Jordan Pickford came in and Adam Reach was another great loan signing out wide.

I loved playing alongside Greg at the back. He was such a calming influence, fantastic in every aspect of his game really and brilliant to play alongside.

I think Simon wanted to keep things tighter in the higher league and, although it might not have been as pretty to watch at times, I think we did really well.

We didn't create loads and we played 4-3-3 quite a lot, which didn't suit Joe's style up front, leaving him a bit isolated at times. But it was pragmatic; keep a solid defence, stay in games and see if we can nick it 1-0.

I think with Alex now, we would try and score again but you can't knock it under Simon in that first season back up, because we finished eleventh - so it worked.

The only times I think we were really found out were against Huddersfield and Brentford, who were playing a type of 'total football' that we just had no answer to at times. But in the main, we adjusted well and built a platform to go from again.

I enjoyed that season, but we started the following one badly, losing 1-0 away at Reading and then I was out of the team for a while.

It was disappointing, but I thought I would get another chance. It wasn't a case of *'here we go again'*, as Simon was quite honest and open about things. It was Tom and Bailey for a while and by that time we'd also got Tommy Spurr and Alex Baptiste in so there was quite a lot of competition.

Clarkey is one of the most solid players and blokes you could ever wish for; he gives everything for the cause and - *you probably already know this* - is just a warrior on the pitch.

Like I say, when you're in the Championship, you're bound to strengthen and that's a good thing - you want the squad to be as strong as possible, and you've just got to step up accordingly. Unfortunately, one of the games I did play, was when Simon recalled me for the League Cup tie away at Newcastle in October.

My father-in-law had died the day before and, to be honest, my head was all over the place. We played a reserve side, Alan Browne got sent off early on and we ended up losing 6-0.

I remember still being so upset after the game that I couldn't do any media interviews or anything, I just wanted to get home and be with my wife. It was a really difficult time. I shouldn't have played, but I did because I thought it would make my father-in-law proud and he would have wanted me out there. Of course, come the game itself, emotions take their toll and mentally I wasn't in the right place.

I also felt bad for the fans, as we'd taken a good following over there in midweek and got thrashed, never in it really. I always feel for them when they've spent their hard-earned money to follow us and it's not gone well.

The cost of going to some games these days is getting ridiculous.

I know Leeds charge crazy prices and I'm not surprised that some fans choose to boycott them - I think I'd do that myself. But I always want to thank the fans for their support at the end of the game. Genuinely, without them, we'd be nothing.

It's a great feeling when we've won and you go off to applause and the 'Cumbrian Cannavaro' etc.

So it's just as important - *sometimes more so* - to acknowledge the supporters when you've got beat. You might be thinking: 'Uh-oh, we're going to get slaughtered as we walk off here.'

But you've still got to do it. These people have paid to come and see you, they've maybe travelled hundreds of miles, maybe given up their entire day, finished work early; they're passionate about Preston North End and I'm passionate about the club too. I always feel proud when I see someone with a 'Huntington' shirt on and I'm really grateful for the support I've always had.

We might not have as many in the stands as some clubs, but you know their feeling for North End is 100 per cent.

I went down to watch Arsenal versus Southampton one time and was amazed that people were on their phones, chatting, whatever, rather than watching the game they'd paid to see - at London prices, too!

I don't think our fans are like that; you see the huge turnouts in the local derbies at Ewood and places and you know it means something to these people. They're proper supporters.

So it's part of your responsibility to thank them for turning up. After all, what's a club without its supporters?

And when you're a player; you know you're one of the lucky ones. You're getting paid to be at a great football club, to pull on the shirt like those fans would love to do just once.

Anyone who doesn't appreciate that shouldn't be in the game, let alone the club.

I remember Forest away when Louis Moult scored and we won 1-0. I was walking over at the end of the game and the hairs on the back of my neck were just standing up with the reaction from the fans that day.

No-one had given us a chance there and we'd taken three points at a big away ground. It was just electric at the end and there's that bond between the fans and the players that you don't get at every club.

Some places you go, it's well-known that if you can keep them out for the first 20 minutes or so, their crowd will turn on them and that makes it easier. It's not like that at Deepdale, they stick with you.

Yes, they let us know if they're unhappy at half-time sometimes, but we always come out to a big roar for the second half. And if we are still rubbish - well, sometimes you just have to take it at the end of the game.

Like I say, the fans are passionate and if you don't want to be booed off . . . do better next time out.

Sometimes though, you get results you don't deserve - good and bad. I remember we went down to Brighton a couple of years ago. We got pumped for almost the entire game, we were just scrambling through it, making blocks everywhere, hanging on.

They were absolutely all over us but we were still only 2-1 down in the last minute.

Out of nowhere, big Simon Makienok grabbed a last minute equaliser and we were all just like: *'Oh my God! How have we done that?!'*

It was hilarious. I know Glenn Murray, who's from Cumbria too, and he just couldn't believe it. We got back on the bus and were all just cracking up; me, Pearo, Davo laughing our heads off on our table on the bus as we pulled away from the AMEX. Absolute daylight robbery. So it's good when it goes for you. Obviously, not so much when you're on the other end of it.

I got back into the side that year just before Christmas, a couple of weeks before Bailey left for Bristol City and thankfully I stayed in for almost every game after that.

Jordan Hugill had really developed up front and become our main goalscorer as the season went on. He's a great lad who works hard for everything he gets and another one who'd taken his chance at North End.

Aiden McGeady was our player of the season and had the quickest feet I've ever seen - he's up there with Gally as the best player I've been alongside at Deepdale. DJ is another top quality player, trying to get the ball off him in training is impossible and he just always seems to have time.

We finished that season 11th again in what was a tough league but the following one, 2017/18 started with a shock.

We arrived at Springfields for pre-season training to be called in for a meeting with Peter Ridsdale in the video room. He announced that Simon was in talks with Sunderland and the likelihood was that he wouldn't be coming back.

We were all a bit surprised; we'd heard a few rumours, but personally, I didn't think he'd go there.

Not long after that, Alex Neil arrived and it was a great appointment by the club.

He's incredibly knowledgeable about the game and tactically spot-on.

We always know what the gameplan is and how we're going to go about things. You can talk to him about anything and have a laugh with him, but when it comes to training, it's intense and you know the standards he drives and expects.

Everyone is aware that you can't slip back from that and from the start, the intensity in training went through the roof.

I started the first game of the season partnering Tommy Spurr at the back. Some people had said we wouldn't be quick enough together and this and that, but we both know the game and know how to deal with things.

For example, if you're up against someone really quick, just give yourself an extra yard. Get in a good position to give yourself the advantage. Read the game; lock the channels, edge strikers into areas you know they don't really want to be.

Be available for Pearo, or whoever the holding midfielder is.

Towards the end of the game, know how to play 'keep ball' - frustrate the opposition, turn them, do all the things to them that you don't like being done to you.

Whatever you do, don't make it like a basketball game with quick turnovers and keep giving the ball away. I think a lot of that comes with experience, which is why most players get better with age.

You look at Gally and his mind is so sharp at those crucial stages of games; he knows exactly how to manage things if we're getting a result and where to put it if we're chasing a game a bit. He's got that through playing hundreds of games.

Same with Tommy Spurr, who sadly got injured quite early on in that season. Then Ben Davies came in and has just been magnificent ever since really.

I was at the club when he made his debut under Graham Westley and it's been fantastic to see him come through the ranks and flourish into the player he is today.

He's my room-mate on trips and we get on great, with a good understanding on the pitch, having been around for so long together. The lads say that if I'm the Cumbrian Cannavaro, he's the Barrow Baresi - just fantastic to play alongside and a great bloke, too.

Back on the pitch that season, things were going OK and it was turning out to be great for me on a personal level.

Not only did I chalk up 45 appearances in the league, but I also managed to score one of my best goals - a low shot into the bottom corner - from outside the box.

Obviously, I'm used to scoring headers in the six-yard area so to get that one from that far out, with my left foot too was a rarity for me.

I didn't quite know what to do with the celebration - so I ended up doing a bit of a Klinsmann dive, probably the one and only time I've ever attempted it!

Overall, the team stepped up again as the season progressed and we were unlucky to finish seventh. We lost at home to Derby and drew to Norwich in games that could have just pushed us over the line, so that was disappointing, but we'd established ourselves as a very good side and I don't think anyone fancied playing us.

Ever since I've been at Preston, we're known as a side that will always work hard and give you a tough game.

Personally, I feel like that was my best season, playing week in, week out and having a good partnership with Ben, who just reads the game so well.

That summer, I signed a new three-year contract with the club and I was just so happy to be able to stay.

There was interest elsewhere, but I didn't want to leave; I was really happy at North End, playing regularly, great relationship with my teammates, the fans, and enjoying my football. The contract would take me up to being 33, but hopefully that wouldn't be the end of things for me at Deepdale.

The following season, I started off on the bench as Alex Neil went with Clarkey and Ben. But after beating QPR on the opening day, we made a bad start and didn't win again in the league until October when we beat Wigan 4-0 at home.

There was a fair number of changes as the season went on as injuries really hit the squad, and I was in and out of the side, playing most games overall until January.

We had a bad run and I came off at half-time against Swansea with a groin injury.

After that, we went with Ben and Jordan Storey, who had come in and was doing well as we went on a run of winning five away games on the spin.

It's been a bit like that with us; our results come in little bursts - we'll go on a great run, followed by a poor run.

I can't put my finger on why it comes like that, I suppose a lot of it comes down to momentum when you're flying and lack of confidence when you're not. But for whatever reason, after coming off injured at Swansea I was out of the team again.

At first, I was making the bench and then suddenly . . . I wasn't.

It was a similar situation to the one I'd had under Simon Grayson; playing lots of games and then just seemingly out of the picture.

To be fair, the team was flying again, on a good run of ten or eleven games unbeaten, so I thought: 'No problem, you can't complain at that.'

I didn't realise that I wouldn't start another league game until December - ten months away and into a new season. I went from being a big part of things to maybe making the bench.

In fact, the only action I saw for the rest of the season was as a late substitute against Sheffield Wednesday in a 3-3 draw after they brought that giant Nuhiu lad on.

Again, it's a hard situation to take. You try to keep sharp, keep fit, I do extra running on my days off - a 10k, just like I do in a game normally.

For whatever reason, the season just petered out after the last international break. We only won one of the last eight games, against a poor Ipswich team and our play-off hopes fell away.

At the end of the season, we had our chats with the manager and he told me I'd not been at my best over the season. I accepted that, but said I needed more games, a decent run to get properly match sharp.

However, I'm honest enough to know that I can do a lot better and at times I hadn't been good enough. Having said that, there were times when I thought I could have been brought back into the team to help out and add experience, but I wasn't called upon. He told me to go away for the summer, work hard and come back as good as ever next time out. No problem, that was exactly what I was planning anyway.

At the start of the 2019/20 season, with Patrick's arrival, it looked like I was fourth choice at the back and some people were asking what my plans were.

A couple of teams were asking about me, but I wasn't going to go.

For me, it was simple and it still is; I want to stay at Preston as long as possible.

My contract runs to 2021 and I've no plans to go anywhere else. But at the start of the season, I wasn't even travelling with the team for the opening game away at Millwall.

I was back home running and trying to keep fit while the lads were down in London for the game. That's mentally hard to get your head round, when you've been a big part of things over many years and I suppose the easy thing would have been to think that my time was up and look at offers elsewhere.

But I didn't want to do that. I wanted to fight for my place and get back in the team.

So that's what I did.

Again, it's not been easy and there have been plenty of times I've had the dreaded call into the office to tell me I'm not travelling with the team. That hurts, but you've just got to keep your head up. As Alex Neil says, you're a lot less likely to get back in the team if your attitude is wrong, so you've got to keep going and keep setting the standard as a senior professional.

So that was that, really. Black boots at the ready, I kept working behind the scenes, kept myself properly prepared if called upon and waited for my chance to come again.

I played and scored in the League Cup against Hull but had to wait until injuries to Ben and Pat saw me back in the side for that visit of West Brom alongside Jordan.

We did well to keep them out until the last couple of minutes when . . . *well, everyone saw what happened, didn't they?*

It's just a shame the ref didn't have a TV replay with that one.

So I was back in again and the local press described it as *'not so much coming in from the cold - more like the deep freeze'.*

There was also the old line about 'more comebacks than Frank Sinatra', but I'm only 32! I'm just hoping I can stay in and around the first team and help the club get in the play-offs at the very least, no matter what happens this season.

Whether it's this year or the next, our goal is the Premier League and there's no reason at all why we can't achieve that.

We're a good side, a good group, at a good club with a good young manager.

When you look around the leagues, so many people would love to be in that position, but they aren't.

On a personal level, my short-term target is to get in the side and win the next game. Beyond that, at the time of writing, I'm closing in on 280-odd appearances for the club and my dream is to get to 300.

I have this image in my mind of a North End shirt with 'Huntington 300' on the back and I'm absolutely desperate to make it a reality.

Everyone has a goal to aim for and that's mine.

North End is the only team I care about and, as an adopted Lilywhite, I think I'd be the proudest player on the planet if I could achieve that.

I don't expect to get picked on sentiment - and I know that's not going to happen - so I have to keep my standards up and take every chance I can to get on the pitch and stay in the side. I'm in my eighth year with the club and it would be a dream to get to ten and hopefully even longer.

After I finish playing, I'm not sure coaching is for me, but maybe the mentoring side of things is more up my street - making sure young players are on the right track, giving them the support they need to make the most of their potential.

Again, the dream would be doing something like that at North End, helping players through and bringing more success down the line.

The more you're at a club, the more you care about the surroundings, the fans, the people you live among and the city that you represent.

I'm not saying the lads who have just got here don't care - of course they do - it's just that those feelings inevitably deepen as the years go by.

And I know that in football you can't look too far ahead, so for now I'm just happy and proud to be part of this great club.

I love the club and I just hope that shows when I play.

I've put a lot in and I've had a lot back that I'll always, always be grateful for.

It feels like home and it feels like part of me.

To sum it all up in one word, well . . . *it's magic, you know?*

Chapter 6

BRIAN MOONEY: RETURN OF THE KING

Like most lads I knew, I grew up kicking a ball around the streets of Dublin from as young an age as I can remember. That was our summer, our winter, our weekends, our school holidays - just playing street football the whole time.

There would be dozens of us in games, all battling to get hold of the one ball and all different ages too.

So to keep the ball off the big fellas, you'd have to work out a trick or two and be sure to control it well.

Trust me, if you let it get too far out of your feet, it was gone in a flash - so it was a good learning curve, let's put it that way.

Most of all, it was great fun - the joy of football as it should be. I don't want to come across as an old fogey, but I wouldn't swap it for a PlayStation for a second.

I was football daft, playing whenever and wherever I could. You still see it a bit these days, but not the huge numbers that we used to get *(maybe there are too many PlayStations around now)*.

I was a big Liverpool fan and later on when I was training there, there were a lot of five-a-sides - back in the day in Dublin it was like 25-a-side! But I loved those days and my dad, Gerry, was a big influence on me, always giving good advice.

I'd been spotted at an early age and went across to England for quite a few trials - Manchester United a few times, Everton, Arsenal. They all offered me contracts, so that was quite a boost and knowing there were clubs interested gave me the confidence to bide my time, rather than dive in at the first opportunity.

My dad had played League of Ireland football - he was a goalkeeper and got a schoolboy cap in the same team as Johnny Giles against England one time.

It was a fair way back, but he knew about football and always said I should finish my education in Ireland and get my Leaving Certificate, the Irish equivalent of A-Levels, before starting a career in England. It was good advice and I'm still grateful for it now.

So I turned down a couple of things and played for the local team Elm Mount FC when I was younger, as well as being a schoolboy international, which was always a great honour.

I then joined Home Farm for a year prior to going away to England in 1983 at the ripe old age of 17. And who was I joining after all those trials?

Only Liverpool - my boyhood heroes and probably the best team on the planet over those past ten years.

Joe Fagan was the manager and the squad was just a roll call of football greats: Dalglish, Souness, Rush, Lawrenson, Hansen, Grobbelaar - all just unbelievable players. *No pressure!*

The thing was, from the age of about 14, I'd known I was going to go over to England so I'd mentally prepared myself for it, but there's no doubt it was a little bit intimidating to be in there with all these players who I'd only seen on television before then. Especially as I was going there straight from school.

Luckily, I was going over with another Home Farm youngster, Ken DeMange, so it was good to have a familiar face alongside me. Ken was a very good player who went on to play quite a few games in England for Leeds, Hull and Cardiff City.

Together we were part of the Liverpool reserve team that won the Central League in 1984 and 1985, but it was very hard to force your way into the Liverpool first team.

They were winning domestic titles and European trophies every year and then every close season, they would buy more top players.

I was in the first team squad quite a few times, but, like I say, if you look at the names, it was very hard to get picked in front of those lads.

Not only that, but everyone was playing for their own place and it was very competitive so it was up to you to settle down quickly and make your own way.

Ronnie Whelan was there and had broken into the first team and he was a Dubliner who'd played for Home Farm too, so he gave us some advice which was great. But largely, it was a case of 'show us what you can do'. That was the Liverpool way at the time and judging by what they won - it was a successful way, so you can't knock it.

I was there four years and made one appearance in the first team - away at Fulham in the League Cup in 1986.

Liverpool had scraped the first leg 9-0 (!) so Kenny Dalglish took the opportunity to blood a few youngsters and I'll always be grateful for that chance.

Kenny was the best player I ever played against - even if only in training - and he was a great coach, too. His manner, his ability and everything about him just instilled instant respect. For anyone too young to remember him, just call up some of the old videos online to see how good he was.

I came on for Jim Beglin with half an hour to go in a 3-2 win and it was just fantastic to pull on the shirt and get on the pitch, even if it was only once. I was out there with Ian Rush, Mark Lawrenson, Jan Molby, so it was just great to be a part of it - albeit a small one.

I was in the reserves with some lads who did break through eventually; Mike Marsh, Jim Beglin, Steve Staunton and Gary Ablett, who sadly died a few years back.

So it was possible, but it was hard.

On the bright side, I'd signed a three-year contract and that kept getting extended, so I must have been doing something right.

I kept thinking that my time would come, but as the years went by I was naturally getting frustrated a bit - even though it was great to be part of such a huge club.

In 1986, I went out on loan to Wrexham under Joey Jones, the old Liverpool stalwart, and I enjoyed a taste of first team football there.

They were in the old Fourth Division and it was a great experience to play 'proper' league football in front of a crowd, as opposed to the reserves at Liverpool. It went well, but my aim was to get back and challenge for a first team place at Anfield.

By that time, I was coming into my fifth season with the reds, with just the one first team appearance to show for it. I was around 21 and I suppose I was languishing in the reserves, as they say. It didn't look like I was going to break through and I had to get my head around that a little bit.

Almost out of the blue, John McGrath came in for me to go on loan to North End. They'd been promoted from the Fourth Division the year before and I knew they were on an upward curve, getting some decent crowds for the level they were playing at.

It was another chance to get some league football under my belt and I thought it would all help my football education, so I said yes straight away.

I knew Alan Kelly Junior - and his brother Gary - through the youth and under-21 set-ups with the Republic of Ireland and always got on well with both of them, so it was great to have a familiar face there when I arrived.

I think maybe the team was making that transition to the higher level and John signed me on loan and Tony Ellis from Oldham in the same week in October 1987.

The two of us made our debuts against Port Vale at Deepdale and, as it turned out, the game was an absolute cracker.

It's a bit of a blur, but I remember it went one way then the other and then Tony scored a 90th-minute winner right in front of the home end.

It was great to hear a real roar from that Deepdale crowd and - hey - who doesn't love a last-minute winner?

Coming in at the same time, Tony and I formed a bond and we always played well together. He was a fantastic striker and his movement was brilliant for a winger like me - he could always find space and was a very clever player.

He also had a brilliant natural touch and a shot like a rocket - so he was a great acquisition for Preston by John McGrath at that time.

Warren Joyce came in the following week I think and the three of us went on to have good careers with Preston, so it was a good time to be joining the club.

I got on well with John, he was a good manager and a really funny guy - always with a story or two up his sleeve. He made a great team with Les Chapman, who could also tell a great tale and was a good go-between between the lads and the manager.

John was keen on a brand of attacking football that suited me and sort of gave me a free rein in the team and a lot of the play came through me, which suited me perfectly.

I think these days, managers would have me doing a lot more tracking back, but John just wanted me to get at the opposition. I got a lot of the ball and I always felt that I could create things for the team through dribbling and crossing so I enjoyed the way things were set up on the pitch as well as off it.

I think you need that bit of luck to find a manager who believes in you and I felt I had that with John.

There are plenty of examples of good players not being as successful as they should because the manager didn't fancy them or play to their strengths, but I always thought John knew how to get the best out of me. I think results and performances bear that out over my time with North End.

Also, it was quite near to Liverpool, where I had family, so the whole loan was a good proposition for me. Initially, I lived in Fulwood in digs in the week (run by a lovely landlady called Jenny) and went back to Liverpool, where I had family, after the games on a weekend, so it all worked out great.

That initial spell went well so when North End came on to make the deal permanent, I was happy to sign - I think the fee was around £40,000.

I'd seen the potential of the club and knew it was one of the bigger teams in the area. I was getting frustrated at Liverpool - were was still no real sign of me breaking into the first team - and I suppose it was a step down to move up again.

But I never regretted joining Preston - it was the happiest time of my career in England, without a doubt.

I'd really enjoyed the loan and was going to be getting regular football at a club that I thought was going places, so I looked on it as a good career move. I'd got to know the lads by then and it was a great dressing room to come into.

I'd say Sam Allardyce was probably the leader in the dressing room and obviously he's gone on to have a great managerial career. You could see back then that he was a natural leader of men and a big voice with some great ideas that he wasn't afraid to put forward.

He was a great influence on me and all the younger lads, taking time out to pass things on and give us advice. He was always very encouraging and it was a bit like: *'Well, if Big Sam thinks I can do this . . .'*

As well as Sam, I was always a great fan of Frank Worthington - *I mean, c'mon, who wasn't?* - and it was just great to see him up close with his style and his touch. He was also definitely a character as well, shall we say.

Frank was coming to the end of his career, but was probably the most skilful player of all my time at Preston. He just oozed quality - people would ping balls at him and he'd just take them all down in one movement like he was shelling peas. Incredible skill.

It's still great for me to look back and say that I played with Frank and Sam Allardyce - I'm very proud that I shared the same pitch with them, playing for the same team.

Mick Rathbone was another senior pro and a great guy to have around, while there were people like Gary Swann and little Ronnie Hildersley, who had been a big part of the promotion team.

So no, there weren't many shrinking violets in the dressing room!

Gary Brazil was a very, very good player who was another attacker thriving under John as well at that time and again, his touch and his close control was incredible. It needed to be really, because we were playing on the old plastic pitch at Deepdale and in some respects that was a big advantage for us.

There weren't many artificial surfaces around back then so on match days it was good for us because we were used to it. In retrospect, however, it didn't do anything for your joints in older age, I can tell you!

The other thing was, back in the day, teams were a lot more settled; at Liverpool, you could probably name the same team days in advance every week unless someone was injured and it was fairly similar at Preston.

Squads weren't as big, so there wasn't really much 'squad rotation'; the team was the team unless someone had a real loss of form or something and so we played every week and the line-up was fairly consistent.

I played nearly every game that season after arriving and we trained hard every day on the plastic pitch.

All those hours on that surface definitely came back to haunt me as I've had a number of operations on my knees and I think a lot of the lads from that era are probably the same and subsequently suffered for it.

It was an unforgiving pitch, just plastic rolled over concrete really; there was no 'give' at all.

A lot of the fans from that time will remember it, because the club used to rent it out in the evenings, so people will know what I'm talking about - especially if they tried any sliding tackles too!

It was a world away from the 4G surfaces of today where they're even playing rugby and things on them.

But it was something I think the club had had to do and, like I say, it gave us a bit of an advantage in games and fed into the style of play John wanted; passes to feet, quick movement of the ball and plenty of skill.

The other thing to remember is that grass pitches in the 1980s weren't anywhere near as good as they are now. Come mid-winter you could be playing on a really bobbly surface in away games and the ball wouldn't run true, so knowing a pass was going to go where you intended it at home was always a good thing.

Having said that, if the ball got past you and you had to run for it, it would often just zip out of play. Forget chasing it - you had no chance.

So your passing had to be spot on and I think again that helped us with our movement - you had to be in the right position to receive the ball, because you probably wouldn't catch up with it if it was played beyond you most times.

I know some people in Preston nicknamed me *'The King of the Plastic'* and I don't mind that at all - even though I felt I was a decent player on grass, too.

The pitch undoubtedly suited my style and gave a true run and bounce of the ball, which is probably a lot more common in the modern era.

You look at the surface at Deepdale now and it's like a bowling green - absolutely spot on and I would have loved to have been out there on that every week.

We didn't have the video analysis and things like players get now and there wasn't the same emphasis on diets and things. But it was the same for both sides in a game and we used to enjoy going toe-to-toe with teams under John and Les at that time.

Our league form in that first season was OK for a team that had just come up, Tony and Nigel Jemson were getting a few goals between them, and we finished 16th in the league.

It was respectable but, really, we should have had the bonus of a trip to Wembley that year, which would have been the first time for PNE since 1964.

We got to the two-legged Northern Final of the Associate Members Cup, which became all sorts of things down the years; the Freight Rover Trophy, etc.

It was basically a league cup for the bottom two divisions and we ended playing Burnley in the northern final.

We drew 0-0 at Turf Moor, which I thought was a good result, and we were pretty confident to bring them back to Deepdale for the second leg.

There were more than 17,500 packed into Deepdale, but although Burnley were in the division below us, they had a decent side that year.

George Oghani put them in front early on and that unsettled us for a while but I remember the crowd getting right behind us and Gary Brazil getting an equaliser towards the end of normal time that nearly lifted the roof off.

Being at home, we fancied ourselves and pushed for a winner, but the little lad Ashley Hoskin got a scrappy second and, again as we pushed forward, we got caught on the break and ended up losing 3-1.

It was a real disappointment for everyone, as playing at Wembley would have been a dream - especially as 80,000 turned up for the final, which Burnley lost to Wolves.

But I think it showed we were heading in the right direction and the following year, with a few smart additions, John took us into the play-offs.

Mark Patterson came in - what a battler he was and a really skilful player, too - definitely someone you want on your side.

Tony had scored a brilliant overhead kick against Notts County at the end of the previous season and his confidence going into the new season was up. We both scored quite early on in a 3-0 win away at Chesterfield and Tony's strike from outside the area nearly took the net off - an unbelievable strike.

Things were going well for us by the time Mansfield arrived at Deepdale on Bonfire Night in 1988 and it turned out to be one of my most memorable games in a white shirt.

I went up for a header and one of their guys caught me with a beauty of an elbow, right on the side of the head. Blood was going everywhere and the trainer had to whisk me off to go and get stitched up.

It hurt but I just remember being a bit angry more than anything else, which wasn't normally like me!

I was just like 'Don't sub me! Stitch me up and get me back on!'

In the end, I had about eight stitches before I got back out there and there was a big roar as I came out of the tunnel, all bandaged up.

I remember getting the ball just in front of the old paddock, beating a couple of guys - almost out of temper than anything else - then sticking it in the top corner from about 30 yards out. It was such a great feeling to see it fly in.

I got a few similar to that with my right foot but that was a left footer and has to be one of my favourite goals.

There was definitely a bit of payback in the shot and the celebrations.

It was a case of: *'Crack me in the head will you? Right, we'll see about that...'*

People in Preston still talk to me about it to this day and it's great to be remembered for scoring a goal like that.

We had a great team spirit and everyone piled in to celebrate. John really harvested that and built on it - you really need that togetherness if you're going to succeed.

We were going well again, but took a bit of a knock mid-season when Gary Brazil left to go to Newcastle. I think that was a big blow and affected the team's momentum, although it took a while for the full effect to be felt.

Ian Bogie came in as part of the deal and at the time, there had been talk about him being the next Gazza - which was huge pressure to put on a young player.

Jeff Wrightson had also come in from Newcastle and was doing well for us, but losing a player of Gary's quality was a blow.

I was pushed forward a little bit more and I think John appreciated that I could beat a few players, wasn't a bad passer, I could slot people in and maybe score a few goals too. So he always put the emphasis on me getting forward much more than some managers I played under, who wanted more focus on defensive duties. I took them responsibly as well, but my strength was always going forward, beating players and creating chances. Tackling back wasn't exactly my forte.

As I mentioned earlier, John played to my strengths and gave me a freedom I'm not sure I'd get if I was playing in the more modern era.

Don't get me wrong, we were fit lads - professional footballers who trained hard. But there wasn't the emphasis on physique and tactics and positional discipline that you see in the English game now.

I think there's a great drive for all players to be big athletes who can get up and down the pitch and be physically strong, whereas when they get to the very top level of international competitions with England, that lack of something different - *be it technique, inspiration, individuality or whatever* - holds the team back.

There's no doubt the Premier League is one of the best leagues to watch - and I hope North End can get up there at some point - but the England team itself should probably do better than it does right now. Maybe playing with a bit more freedom might pay off.

I think that emphasis on letting technically good attacking players just go out and play has been lost a bit in the English game and it's a shame.

I was lucky enough to have that backing from John McGrath and, with Tony Philliskirk coming in to provide the goals we'd lost in Gary Brazil, we made it to the play-offs against Port Vale that year.

There had been a steady progression with the team and we were on an upward curve, with a lot of belief, heading into those play-off games.

We'd lost to them on the opening day of the season - I didn't play and we had a few lads missing - but we'd drawn with them at their place towards the end of the campaign and with a full side out we were a decent proposition.

They had people like Robbie Earle, Ron Futcher and Darren Beckford in their side, as well as a classy midfielder called Ray Walker, who was a good player.

The first leg at Deepdale ended 1-1 and wasn't the greatest game - I can't recall too much about it, other than thinking we were still in the tie.

At their place, Beckford scored early on, but I managed to set up Mark Patterson for an equaliser right in front of the North End fans before half-time.

I never thought we were comfortable though and I don't think I had a great game that night, if I'm honest. As a team, we didn't really do ourselves justice.

They missed a penalty before half-time - David Brown saving it - but Beckford scored two more in the second half and we were out.

The funny thing is, the play-offs had only just been introduced and it wasn't a Wembley final in those days; we'd have ended up playing Bristol Rovers in the final over two legs, home and away and I'd have fancied us.

Instead, Vale went through and eventually went up.

But on the night, we just didn't click and we never really got going. It was really disappointing. It was a bad way to end what had been a good season overall.

On a positive note, I was named Player of the Year, something I'm hugely proud of, especially considering some of the other players who were around at that time, too.

I've still got the award on display at home - it's a treasured possession in the house.

I also made the PFA team of the year for the division that season, named alongside people like Nigel Martyn, Steve Bull, Chris Coleman and Phil Brown - so it was a good standard.

The following year, I don't know what happened, but we had a bad start - we lost four and drew one of our first five league games. It wasn't until we beat Chester 5-0 at Deepdale in late September before we got going.

I scored a hat-trick that day and the goalkeeper was a guy called Billy Stewart, who had started out with me at Liverpool in the early 1980s and went on to have a good career for Chester.

It was a very slow start to the season - *maybe it was the dreaded play-off hangover* - but we just couldn't seem to get going until that game.

Steve Harper scored the other two - he was the only guy to have a bigger mullet than me back in those days. He was a forerunner to David Luiz in the hairstyle stakes, but a lovely player and a really funny lad in the changing rooms, too.

People still talk about my old mullet and, err, it's long gone these days!

But, hey, it was the 80s and was very fashionable at the time. Half the crowd had the same trim *(c'mon, don't deny it!)* and it all went with the 'short' silky shorts that we wore in those days, too.

I used to love those old North End kits - the Garratts Insurance one is surely a retro classic these days. I kept mine all these years and it's over at my mum and dad's for safekeeping even today.

The following week, I got my first taste of a North End versus Blackpool derby game. *Wow.*

I remember it was a very fraught atmosphere on and off the pitch.

The fans were absolutely howling at each other and the players were well aware of the expectations on the day. I ended up getting a really bad gash on my leg in a challenge. It was full-on, that game, no quarter asked or given.

It was like going into battle and it was good to have people like Bob Atkins, Gary Swann and Warren Joyce alongside you - we came out 2-1 winners with Skilful Bob getting the winner, which was great and made the pain of my injury worth it.

But overall, for whatever reason, we just couldn't recapture the momentum of the previous season.

We lost Tony Ellis to Stoke for quite a big fee in December and that was a blow to us - as it would be to any team. He was a hell of a player for North End.

No disrespect to anyone, but I felt the people we started to bring in to replace those leaving for bigger clubs weren't of the same quality.

That was the underlying issue, I think, and we started to fall away.

We hadn't had a great start to the season, we'd lost a bit of team spirit and it was hard for new players to come into a team that wasn't doing so well all of a sudden. It's hard to put your finger on it, but you just got the feeling that we were starting to lose our way.

To cap it off, we ended up on the wrong side of an FA Cup giant killing when we lost 2-0 up at Whitley Bay.

I'd had a dose of the flu and probably shouldn't have played that day, but I always wanted to play in every game and so I said I was OK. Some players would probably have looked after themselves a bit more than I did and stepped aside, but I always wanted a game. Perhaps the team would have been better if I'd stayed in bed!

It wasn't a good performance. At all.

We had a good side out on paper and maybe we went out with the wrong attitude; we were expected to win and thought maybe we could just stroll it against these non-league lads.

Well, we've all seen what happens when you think that in the FA Cup and it was just such a poor performance. We felt like we'd let everyone down - and we had.

John wasn't a happy camper after the game and the result just deflated everyone a little bit more. To make it worse, it was on Match of the Day.

These days, almost all games or highlights are on TV, but back then it was a big thing and there we were - embarrassed in front of the entire nation on a Saturday night. It was a real sickener.

Not long after that came another blow - we sold Mark Patterson, almost out of the blue.

I wasn't aware of any major financial worries at the club at that point, so it just struck me as a very strange move. I think a lot of people thought the same.

He was a very good player who had scored better than one goal every three games and went on to have a great career with the likes of Bury, Bolton and Sheffield United.

So it was disappointing that a lot of our best players seemed to be being moved on and the players we were bringing in didn't seem to be as good.

No matter what was happening, results didn't improve and it was a heartbreaker on Valentine's Day when John McGrath was sacked by the club, especially given everything he had done for North End.

Les became the manager and it must have been difficult for him, not just because he was a big pal of John's. He'd previously been the go-between between the manager and the players and now he had to step up to being the Boss himself.

He had been one of the lads and now he had to distance himself a little bit.

Everyone had respect for Les and liked him, but it was a tough situation for him to step into. The team wasn't doing well and it felt like the club was selling its best players, so he was up against it from the start.

He brought back John Thomas, who was a great guy and a proper fans' hero, so that was a good move for the supporters and lifted spirits on the terraces.

Personally, I felt I was still doing OK. I was on the periphery of the Republic of Ireland team and got called into a 'B' international in Cork against England.

They had a lot of big players for them - Seaman in goal, Tony Adams, Matt Le Tissier, people like that - while we had Niall Quinn up front and Dennis Irwin at the back. Gary Kelly was in goal, my old mate Ken DeMange played, Owen Coyle and Pat Scully, too, who had spent time on loan at Preston from Arsenal.

It was a great night and we ended up beating them 4-1, which was a great result, as most of the England team were playing at a much higher level than the likes of us.

Jack Charlton made a few substitutions during the game, but I played the full 90 minutes and felt I did well.

With Italia '90 just on the horizon, I then got called into the full squad for a friendly against Russia. I was really proud, as you can imagine, but the game in Dublin was the day after a really important league game for North End away at Wigan.

In those days, there were no postponements for international call-ups or anything, so Les asked me if I would stay and play for Preston instead.

I really liked Les and didn't want to let my teammates or the supporters down, so I told Jack that I was going to stay to play in the Wigan game.

To be honest, given the season we'd had the year before, I couldn't believe we were in that position but I wanted to make sure that a bad situation in the league didn't get any worse. I wanted to do my bit.

So I played the game away at Wigan and thankfully we won 1-0, with John Thomas scoring, which was the result that really kept us up that year. It was a huge night for North End, but it probably didn't do me or my international career any favours.

Gary Waddock was in the Ireland squad and, although he was a very different player to me, he came in and did well against Russia and that was that really.

I don't know if I'd have made the final squad for the World Cup, but Ireland went on to have a great tournament without me. It's a bit of a regret but it was a decision I made at the time and I can't change it.

Ironically, I did get out to Italy later that summer - but things didn't go too well for me. Sheffield Wednesday had come in for me with a decent offer and, the way things were financially, North End were happy to accept it at that time.

The Owls were managed by Big Ron Atkinson, who had been at Manchester United and remembered me from years earlier when I was there on trial. They did a deal with PNE whereby they paid money to take me on a pre-season trip to Italy to have a look at me, with a fee agreed for a permanent transfer as long as everything went well.

Unfortunately, when we got out on the trip my cartilage went almost before I'd kicked a ball for them.

I ended up having surgery with Sheffield Wednesday which set me back a bit. I was out for three or four months, missing pre-season and missing a huge chunk of the following season.

That put paid to the move to Wednesday and it was very frustrating, because Ron Atkinson clearly fancied me and I thought it would be a good move for all concerned.

Again, it was disappointing and another knock to my career. I did some rehab at Wednesday and some back at Preston, but didn't play my first league game for PNE that season until December.

By that point, I'd got the impression that the club was definitely trying to sell me, no doubt about it.

The deal with Wednesday had been set up months earlier and now that was off, it was a case of finding a new buyer, I think. The way things were back then, I was actually out of contract at that point and the club offered me a new one.

When I saw it, I was quite shocked.

It was really poor - a worse deal than the one I was already on.

I'm sure it wasn't down to Les - his hands were tied - but it was disappointing to say the least, given the way I'd played for the club.

It wasn't like I was angling for a move - I loved being at Preston; I liked Les, had a great relationship with the supporters. I couldn't really understand it, other than the club was looking to get some money in.

I tried just to concentrate on playing and helping the team, as again the season wasn't going too well. I scored a couple of goals and it was great to be back, but we were on a run of four straight defeats before my last league game, at home to Southend, which we won 2-1.

At the time, I didn't know that was going to be my last game for North End at Deepdale, but whatever, it was good to sign off with a win.

My actual last appearance was in a Freight Rover Trophy game away against Scunthorpe where we won 4-1 and I got a couple of goals.

I remember playing well that night, so I'm glad I finished with a couple of good performances.

Lee Ashcroft made his debut in that Scunthorpe game and I remember him as a cheeky young fella - always trying to grab the Number 7 shirt from me when he started getting into the first team squad.

I was always like: *'Woah, hold on there you cheeky little sod, that's my shirt and I'm keeping hold of it!'* He was a great lad though Ashy, a good player and a real character who went on to have a decent career with Preston and elsewhere. (Also, he had that rare thing . . . a bigger mullet than mine!)

After that Scunthorpe game, a deal was finally done and I was on my way to Sunderland in the old First Division. I think the fee was around £225,000 and I have to be honest, I was disappointed to be leaving.

I'd had a great time at Preston, got on with the manager and all my teammates and I had a great bond with the fans. All the old *'Mooney, Mooney'* chants were just amazing and always gave me a boost in confidence.

I felt they were with me and even if things didn't come off that time, they knew they would work more often than not, for us to do well as a team.

I think they appreciated how much the club meant to me and how proud I was to pull on the shirt. The club had given me an opportunity and I was always grateful for that. I still am, to this day.

Yes, I was very disappointed with the way the hierarchy at the club were towards me in the end, but that's individuals and you have to separate that from your feelings towards the club itself.

Like I say, the contract offer was just bizarre really when you think about it. It made no sense to me; why offer less than I'd been on, when I was an established player?

Football is a business, I know, but the way things were done wasn't good. If you need the money from a sale, just come out and say it.

I'm not the first footballer to say that and I won't be the last, but there you go. It happens to a lot of players. So I was sad and disappointed to leave the club, but you have to move on - even with a heavy heart.

And I moved on to Sunderland, under Denis Smith in that February of 1991.

They were in the top flight at the time, but were struggling. We won our first game - at home to Brian Clough's Nottingham Forest in the era when he had Roy Keane and Stuart Pearce in the side.

But largely we were down at the wrong end of the table in a relegation battle. Things just didn't work out for me. I didn't like living up there and I just never really settled. Not that long after I joined, I went over on Luton's infamous plastic pitch and broke my metatarsal.

Unfortunately, the injury was misdiagnosed and so they kept rushing me back to try and get me fit, but I knew the injury wasn't right and kept breaking down.

I ended up breaking it four or five times, so to say it was 'frustrating' was an understatement - I was annoyed with the situation.

Sunderland got relegated that first season and Denis Smith left at the end of the year. I got back the following season but never really pinned down a decent run in the side, due to injuries really.

Ironically, I was fit by the end of that season and available for the FA Cup Final against Liverpool. But this was the days when there were only two substitutes and I wasn't picked for the 2-0 defeat at Wembley against my boyhood heroes.

Again . . . *'frustrating'* doesn't really cover it!

The following year I was back at Deepdale. During a brief loan spell at Burnley, I played for the Clarets against North End.

I remember getting a good reception from the PNE fans, which was great considering I was playing for one of their local rivals, but I had a quiet game.

I was always professional in my outlook and I did OK overall at Burnley, but by that time my heart just wasn't in it. I was still a bit disillusioned because of the way I'd left Preston and I hadn't settled in Sunderland on or off the pitch really.

So I'd kind of fallen out of love with the game and was looking to go back home.

I was 27 and realised that I wasn't really going to crack it at the top level in England, so I started to think about my long-term future.

I had a couple of contract offers in England - not with North End, sadly - but my mind was made up to go back to Ireland, where I could play in the League of Ireland and work towards a career outside football at the same time.

I had ten years playing back home and had some great experiences for Shelbourne, Bohemians, UCD (University College Dublin) and Monaghan United. In fact there were a few times when I was in the League of Ireland when North End fans would come over to watch games I was playing in. I'd meet them in the players' lounge afterwards and it was always great to have a chat about my time at Preston.

I scored goals in the Champions League and the Cup Winners Cup and had a successful career, while studying at college. I was happy with my move and, in hindsight, I'm happy that I made the decision to come home - my life has turned out OK. These days I work for a state agency in the education sector in Ireland that deals with school attendance.

But I still look back on my time at North End as the happiest of my career and I was honoured a few years back when Gavin Willacy, a huge Preston fan, put together a book on my career at Deepdale. He did a great job and it was quite humbling to know people still remember me.

Obviously, as time goes on you forget about any negative things that happened and just focus on all the great days we had as a team with John and Les and the fans.

There are always things that you look back on and think 'what if?'; What if I hadn't had injuries at certain times? What if I'd have moved to other clubs who came in for me? But overall I look back on things positively and with great affection for PNE.

I really love the club and I always look out for the results now and make sure I tune in if they're on TV. I've been invited back a few times to do the half-time draw and things on the pitch and I've always been touched by the reception I've had.

It's quite moving to go back and get such a warm welcome many years after I played for the club.

They've done a great job with the stadium and the pitch is always immaculate. It's all geared up for the Premier League and I just hope we can get promoted soon because I think we've gone close a few times over the years and the fans definitely deserve to see the club in the top flight.

Some of the people still going on today will have been around since my time and that loyalty deserves success. They're fantastic people and I look forward to coming over to watch North End up in the Premier League soon.

Come on you whites!

Chapter 7

ERIC JONES: LUCKY MAN

Lucky? Me? Well, have a read of this and see what you think. I played for Preston North End at a time when the club was pushing for league titles, the FA Cup and was known all over the world.

The team was packed with internationals, the crowds were huge and we had the greatest player on the planet on the wing.

Obviously, that wasn't me!

I was Tom Finney's understudy and I went from watching from the packed terraces to becoming life-long friends with the Great Man himself. (See what I mean about lucky?)

There aren't many people still around who can tell you what it was like back then, but I'm 88 years old now and after a lifetime of following the whites, I hope I can give you a flavour of life at Deepdale in the 1950s - the glory days, as people often call them.

They were glorious for me, that's for sure.

To start at the beginning, my father was a master cobbler up in Barrow, who moved down to Preston looking for work when I was two, around 1933.

We were in lodgings opposite Moor Park, just near Deepdale and while he was waiting to get a job, he somehow managed to find a rubber ball and used to take me for a kick about on the park every day. He was a keen football man and because I was right-footed he said to me: 'Son, you're not going to use your right foot at all.'

And that made me a natural two-footed player from a young age. He took me on that park, day-in and day-out while he was waiting for work and after a while, it became natural for me to use either foot.

Over time, I developed into a fairly decent winger, able to cross from both sides and with a decent shot on me - even though those old balls used to weigh a ton.

Eventually, my father found work (he went on to have a very successful career) and we moved to Kingfisher Street, within sight of the ground, just behind the Town End.

I played in the amateur leagues when I was younger and enjoyed it, but because the war was on, it wasn't as well organised as it would have been otherwise.

Half the time, our biggest challenge was finding a ball. The war effort was still being compensated for and proper balls were expensive. I remember my mate getting one for Christmas and we kicked so much hell out of it that his mum came round to complain!

During the war, crowds were limited to 15,000 by the Government in case there were any air raids, but on the plus side, we got to see all the greats; Stanley Matthews, Wilf Mannion, Stan Mortensen.

Players used to guest for different clubs, depending where they were based with the forces and when these great players came out at Deepdale, well . . . the hairs on the back of your neck stood up.

Blackpool used to get a lot of guests because people were seconded there with the RAF. Stan Mortensen even had a plate in his head after his plane crashed and was told he'd never play football again. Typical of those days, he was back playing within three weeks.

I remember one time, North End played Middlesbrough in a replayed FA Cup tie at Deepdale, a midweek afternoon kick-off, so no floodlights and about six inches of snow and ice on the ground.

These days it would have been called off in the blink of an eye, but back then it was going to be a full-house even on a week day, so y'know, the club's not daft . . . they wanted it on!

So did I, especially as I'd skived off work with the old 'dental appointment' routine that afternoon to get to the game.

Wilf Mannion was playing for Boro and he was a beautiful footballer, quite slight for the time, but oh so skilful. He had blond hair, played for England and was nicknamed 'The Golden Boy' - a sort of David Beckham of the time.

I remember George Hardwick, another Boro great who played for England, firing this ball 60 yards across Deepdale to him at about head height.

I was in the front row of the crowd and Wilf was just in front of me.

Well, he put his foot up and took this ball down as if he was catching it in his hand.

Then in one movement, he switched feet and sent a 40-yard pass out to the other flank, all in the blink of an eye.

I thought: 'By God, that's a proper footballer.'

It almost took my breath away and I remembered it for years - I can still see it today. Wow.

Anyway, many years later, I was playing for Lancaster City and we came up against a team called Earlestown and Wilf Mannion was playing for them.

He wasn't treated very well by Middlesbrough and despite playing for them for 18 years, they hadn't given him a testimonial, so he was still turning out at quite an old age.

As we were walking off the Giant Axe at half-time, I happened to be near him and mentioned my memory of him all those years earlier at that snowy Deepdale.

'By heck,' he said, 'You've got a good memory. But I remember that game too and I'll give you my side of the story.

'I remember George kept sending me these great passes and each time Bill flippin' Shankly would come sliding in straight through me, sending me flying into these mounds of ice and snow with him ending up on top of me.

'In the end, I could hear him coming like an express train - so my only thought when I got the ball was to get rid of it before he arrived!'

I must admit, it punctured my memory a bit, but I like to think he was just being modest.

Mind you, Shanks couldn't half put a tackle on someone, so . . . maybe not.

One of the other things that sticks in my mind was when the Ministry of War took Deepdale over just before D-Day and all sorts of American tanks and aircraft appeared on the car park.

They all came down the A6 in this convoy that went on for miles and the Americans used to give us oranges and a bit of chewing gum. Proper treats!

Some of the more frivolous Preston ladies, shall we say, got silk stockings and I remember watching the GI's playing baseball on the Deepdale pitch before heading down for the invasion.

I sometimes wonder what became of those lads.

About a year later, there was a big stockade built on Moor Park, just opposite the Sir Tom Finney stand now and they put about 1,000 Italian prisoners of war in there.

We used to go up and see them and they used to carve things from wood and give them to us kids - I think they were just glad to be out of the war.

There were air raid sirens every now and again, but I don't remember any bombing raids specifically on the town - they were mainly looking for Liverpool or the air base at Warton.

You'd hear the ominous throb of these bombers going overhead and because we didn't have an air raid shelter at the house, we just used to go under a big oak table in the kitchen and hope for the best.

There was a tragic incident where a lone German plane bombed Lostock Hall and 25 people were killed, but really, the town escaped the worst of it, which is surprising when you consider how many factories there were in Preston at that time and, of course, the docks.

North End had a really good side during the war and who knows how many titles they would have won if it hadn't happened.

Tom, who later served under Montgomery in North Africa, actually made his North End debut at Leyland Motors' ground - but, of course, only after his father pushed him into getting a proper trade.

He said that a one-year contract to play football was too dicey and insisted his son get a 'genuine' profession.

So he would sometimes turn up with his boots in his wheelbarrow full of his plumbing kit while he was serving his time and getting a trade under his belt. That was the way it was back then and I tell you what, he was a cracking plumber too.

Personally, I was working for a wire goods manufacturer in Preston. It was quite good fun but, well, it wasn't for me.

So I was overjoyed when there was a knock on the door at home one day and this chap said he was a scout for Blackburn Rovers - would I fancy a trial?

Would I ever!

I got the train over to Ewood and discovered Rovers wanted me to sign as a part-time professional to play in the A team alongside Ronnie Clayton and Brian Douglas - two great players.

There was another young lad in the Blackburn A team at that time, a certain Trevor Hemmings. Good player, but as a young lad he broke his leg and that was him finished.

We all know what happened next!

But just as things were about to take off for me, I was called up to the RAF to do my National Service as an armament mechanic. It was a setback for my footballing career, but really, they were the two best years of my formative life.

The training made us so strong and really physically developed me. I played for the RAF and was in fantastic shape when I was demobbed a couple of years later.

I remember coming home and my father asking me what I was going to do for work. I said: 'Well, I'm not going back to the factory, that's for sure.'

And with that, he took out a letter and put it on the kitchen table, saying: 'Well, you'd better read that then.'

PRESTON NORTH END FC

Dear Mr Jones,

Thank you for your letter concerning your son Eric.

We have been monitoring him closely during his time in the RAF.

Can you ask him to come and see me at 10.30am on Monday.

Yours sincerely,

Will Scott,
Manager

Well, I was flabbergasted, over the moon and, most of all, a bag of nerves.

I walked down to Deepdale on the Monday and there were all these players buzzing around as I tried to compose myself to see the manager. Eventually, I went in and there he was; very formal, very proper, quite brusque, overall . . . a bit intimidating!

'Come in son, sit down, how was your time in the RAF?'

'Fantastic Mr Scott, best two years of my life.'

'So you're ready for action then. Well you'll get that here. This is a football club.'

Then he pushed this piece of paper in front of me: £6-a-week in the summer, £8-a-week in the winter and a £10 signing-on fee and a one-year contract.

That was it. Well, I couldn't wait to sign. Get paid for playing football?

Blimey! Yes, please! Especially as I was on £2.50-a-week in the factory.

The North End wage was equal to a decent tradesman's salary at the time - and I was only a young lad, so it was great for me.

When I turned up for training I couldn't believe it. We were all in together, young players and senior professionals - I was two pegs away from the Great Man himself.

I had to pinch myself and just kept thinking: *'I shouldn't really be here.'*

I was quite naive but I wish I had had the feelings I have now, back then, just to savour it all, take it all in - the significance of it all. At the time, you don't think like that - you think day-to-day and just want to show what you can do.

Of course, one of the best things about it was getting to know the Great Man. He was so down to earth and humble, and he took me under his wing right from the start.

Any doubt I had about being there was eased quite a bit when he said he'd heard about me and that I must be a good player, because Preston had signed me.

That boosted my confidence and I set about trying to learn everything I possibly could from that master of the football trade.

Not long afterwards, my great friend Peter Higham arrived from Bolton, where Nat Lofthouse had been keeping him out of the team. Pete was over six feet tall, a proper colossus and with this deep brown sun tan. I remember Tommy Docherty saying: *'Blimey, we've signed a black fella!'*

He was a great addition and the pair of us played in the Central League side. It was a really good team and we used to beat the first XI quite regularly - they all feared for their places. Well, all bar one, obviously!

The issue we had was that the North End first team at that time picked itself and was in the top three in the world.

That's no exaggeration, Preston was known around the planet and was always up around the top of the First Division. The ground was always packed and if you weren't there by about 1pm, you might well not get on at all.

Training was pretty basic, but effective for the time. The idea was not to put muscles on frames that didn't need them. We were all pretty fit, without becoming muscle-bound.

I was only 10st 7lbs, so if they had tried to put extra muscles on me, I would have just been carrying weight I didn't need.

I think today, they sometimes try to make athletes into footballers or vice versa. Back then, it was all about turning footballers into better footballers.

Training started at 10am and went through to 12 noon when we might head up to the snooker room upstairs for a bit of relaxation.

It was fairly basic, but not without innovation of a sort; Will Scott used to like to get you under a sun lamp, with these big, thick goggles on every now and then, for a massage. The rays were supposed to help you recover from injury. I'm not sure if they ever did - they certainly didn't give you a sun tan.

On a Tuesday, Peter and I would come back in the afternoons with George Thompson, the goalkeeper. I'd put these balls in and Pete would charge in for them while George had to decide whether to come for the cross or not.

That's the biggest test of a keeper, he can be the best shot-stopper in the world, but knowing when to come for a cross is as important today as it was back then. It's part of the game that hasn't changed down the years.

This was on Deepdale and while it was good for George, I'm not sure the groundsman would have appreciated it.

Our boots in those days were just about two steps up from the clogs people used to wear in the mills. There was no adidas or Puma, let's put it that way.

They weighed a ton, with thick hard leather up to your ankles, had proper toe-caps on them and once they got wet in a game, well, it was like dragging lead weights around on your feet.

It took three weeks to break them in, soaking them in a bucket of cold water, followed by a bucket of hot, over and over again. Then when you first wore them, you still came off with a foot load of blisters!

And after three months, they were worn out and falling apart, so you were back to the start all over again. It was awful, really. What we would have given to have boots like the lads have now.

Our shin pads were about four inches thick. They had bamboo canes stuck in the middle of them for protection and once your sock got wet and muddy, you were carrying an extra two or three pounds around with you on each leg.

Same with our shirts. Modern material disperses the water and gets rid of it. Back then, it just absorbed it and weighed you down something rotten.

If it was raining you'd be carrying pounds and pounds of extra weight, with these big thick shin pads, sodden shirt and boots dragging you down all the time.

People might say the game was slower back then? Aye, there's a good reason for that!

One time though, Tom had been away with England and came back with this South American pair. They were amazing; like nothing we'd ever seen. Low cut, no toe-caps, like leather slippers to our eyes.

A few weeks later, everyone had gone for the day and I spotted these boots on the shelf, near mine. Tom was the same size as me so I couldn't resist.

I slipped them on and went out to run up and down the Deepdale pitch two or three times, just to feel what they were like.

Well, as you can imagine, they were amazing - worlds apart from the clunkers that I was lugging around in.

But within a few minutes, I was overcome with guilt and rushed back inside to get them spotless and back on the shelf before anyone noticed they'd gone.

Many years later, I confessed my 'crime' to Sir Tom and he just smiled, saying: *'Don't be daft Eric, we're teammates - you could have borrowed them at any time. No problem.'*

What a man - and what a pair of boots.

Later on, Tom was one of the first players to have his own sponsorship boot deal at a time when such things were virtually unheard of. That's how big a player he was.

Still, that was for the future and it was a long way off for us lads in the Central League. Not that it was a poor league though; I remember we played Manchester United's reserves when they had a lot of the Busby Babes playing and there were 19,000 on Deepdale.

Same when we played Wolves, we'd be getting 17,000 on a Monday night.

You used to get first team players coming back from injury or loss of form in the Central League so the standard was very high.

Peter and I had a telepathic relationship on the pitch and we both enjoyed successful times for North End at that level. It's strange to explain, because they don't really have that set-up beyond the first team now, but back then it was a big thing.

And we'd have Preston's first-teamers come in with us quite often.

Tommy Docherty wasn't the most educated person in the club; he'd had a tough upbringing in the Gorbals up in Glasgow.

He was notorious for hiding with the hose they used for cleaning out the bath, then jumping out and blasting this powerful jet of cold water into your nether regions as you tried to get dressed. Shoes would disappear, laces would get tied together and clothes would get mixed up - and you knew it was most likely Tommy who was the culprit. It was no surprise to see him go on to manage Chelsea, Manchester United and, of course, North End, through the sheer force of his personality.

But he was a great player and a really funny man to have around.

Whenever I played with him, Tommy used to get hold of me before the game and say: 'OK Jonesy, when we're out there, just listen to me, don't give the ball away in our half and just play your natural game.'

Then, with a little nod and a wink, he'd add: 'Oh, and if anyone whacks you, I'll sort them out for you, don't you worry about that.'

Crikey, he meant it too! You wouldn't want to be on the receiving end of some of Tommy's challenges, I can tell you.

Unsurprisingly, I had a lot of trouble getting in the first team as I was competing with Tom Finney, so you could say opportunities were few and far between! Talk about big shoes to fill, but every now and then, I got my chance.

It's a well-known story, but whenever the Great Man wasn't fit to play, the club would always keep it quiet for fear of reducing the attendance.

They'd always tell the Lancashire Evening Post that he was having a late fitness test, but I'd know on the Thursday that he wasn't going to play.

Mainly it was down to a long-standing groin injury that just required rest, so there was no way he'd be risked in case it meant he was out for a long period.

There were literally thousands of people who would come down from Lancaster, the Lake District, all over the place, just to see him play. And if he wasn't fit, it was some unknown local lad who they'd never heard of!

I'd walk to the ground with the crowd, knowing I was going to play, but they were expecting Tom. I'd be in the dressing room, hearing the buzz outside getting louder and the adrenaline starting to pump.

Then out into the tunnel and it would happen . . . an announcement over the tannoy: 'Change to the North End team in the programme, Number 7 *Jones* replaces *Finney*.'

Well, that was it.

Straight away, they started booing.

I was thinking: 'Oh come on! Give me a chance, we haven't even kicked off yet!'

But people had come to see Tom Finney, not some snotty-nosed kid from round the corner.

The Doc was normally behind me in the tunnel and he'd often crack a gag: 'They love you really Jonesy!'

Thankfully, I always managed to play well and have a decent game, so the club was happy to have me as a back up to the Great Man.

And that Great Man was great with me. He took me under his wing and always tried to develop me as a player, passing on tips and advice to make me be as good as I could possibly be.

He was the same with everyone, Tom, unlike a trainer we had called Jimmy Milne - a really dour Scotsman who never took to Peter or me for some reason. He always seemed to favour Scottish players and I can never remember him saying I'd ever had a good game.

Of course, the role of trainers and managers was very different in those days. The team itself was trusted to know what they had to do.

When I first signed, Will Scott was the manager, but the team used to virtually pick itself and run itself. We didn't have team meetings or anything. Even for the biggest games, we rarely talked tactics. The manager might have said a few words before we went out, but it wasn't a big motivational speech or a tactical analysis or anything.

It was more a *'good luck today lads'*, type of thing. It was a totally different role to the modern manager.

No-one told us what to do when the game started, we just worked it out for ourselves.

Everyone had their own rules; for me it was 'don't do a silly dribble and lose the ball'. That was Number One.

It was a different mindset from modern football, where they play so much football in their own half. All we wanted to do was *attack, attack, attack* and try to score goals.

When we got the first goal, we carried on as if it was still 0-0 and we always pushed on to try to make it 2-0.

You knew that once we went two up, their heads would drop and we'd be able to see the game out because we were so strong in defence.

As I've mentioned, I had the impossible task of trying to dislodge Tom Finney from the team, so over five years I was a regular in the Central League, but only made 13 appearances in the first team.

I didn't really play many games unless Tom was injured, because let's put it this way . . . he was never struggling for form!

In the run-up to the 1954 FA Cup Final however, the Great Man was having trouble with his groin again and I managed to get a few games in.

I'd been playing well in the reserves and the manager Scot Symon called me in about a month before the final for a league game away at West Brom.

It was one of those days when everything went right and I gave their captain the runaround that day. We lost 3-2 but the Sunday Express said: 'If Finney isn't fit for the final, Jones is a ready-made deputy in a similar mould'.

My family had a real laugh about that; me! In a similar mould to Tom Finney!

It was probably the only mention I ever got in the papers. Unlike Tom.

Whenever we went to London, the hotel lobbies would be full of press people taking pictures of him and shouting questions, just like you see on the TV. A proper scrum, all to see him and he was always the calm in the middle of the storm.

I remember one time at a hotel when I was twelfth man - there were no substitutes in those days, but they'd take a spare player in case anyone got a last-minute injury.

They read out who was sharing rooms with who and there I was, in the same room as Tom. I was dreading it; *What if I snored? What if I kept him awake in the night?*

In the end, I was so nervous about it that I couldn't get to sleep - so thankfully he slept like a log.

Anyway, in the build-up to the cup final, the manager told me if Tom didn't recover, I was going to be in the team, because I'd done so well in the league game.

Of course, it didn't work out like that.

By the time it came around, Tom played, we lost 3-2 and the bottom line is . . . he was not fit.

In later years, he said to me that he knew he wasn't right, but had been forced to play by the club hierarchy. He was upset, thinking he'd let the whole of Preston down.

It was a terrible situation and Scot Symon eventually resigned over the issue - they'd over-ruled him and he was very unhappy about it. Who wouldn't be?

I ended up watching the game from the stands just in front of the Royal Box. To make matters worse, I'd dressed up for the day and someone behind was dropping cigarette ash onto my best suit.

Eventually, I turned round to say something - only to find it was Princess Margaret, the Queen's sister and guest of honour at the game!

Not wanting to ruin my chances of a knighthood, I faced the front and said nowt.

Back at Deepdale, one day after training, Tom said he wanted a word with me. He was sat at this desk behind a mountain of letters and fan mail - he used to get sackloads of it all the time.

He said: 'You're playing really well at the moment Eric and there's a good career for you here at Preston. I want you to train with me for a month.'

So we paired up and did everything together; running, dribbling, drills, the lot. By heck it was hard work, but I was trying to learn everything I could from the master.

I remember him telling me that full-backs always wanted you to go to the corner, so you had to let him think that was where you were going. Then at the last minute, switch feet and swerve inside - he either had to foul you or you go past him.

It was all great advice and saved me from getting boxed in and clogged in the corners a fair bit after that.

On Friday it was 'sprint day' on the cinders surrounding the pitch. They came from a local colliery and the idea was they gave way so you'd not pull a muscle - very scientific. The plan was that we'd get warmed up with a jog along the touchline and then sprint the goal sides.

Are you ready? We're off!

Well, Tom was into stride three while I was still on one-and-a-half! Such powerful legs he had.

And all of a sudden as he disappeared in front of me, this big block of blue cinder popped up and caught me right in the nether regions. *Blimey, it hurt, I can tell you.*

Overall though, I was just so grateful that he'd taken the time to pass things on to me and try to develop me as a player. It was great, but on the other hand, it left me a bit disillusioned because I really saw the gap between us.

I went home and said: *'That's it Dad, I'm going to have to get a job. There's no way I can match that standard.'*

I didn't realise I wasn't up against any old player - it was one of the greatest players the world has ever seen. But I kept my head up and did OK when I got in the first team, laying on quite a few goals.

I remember setting one up for Charlie Wayman to tap in when we beat Burnley and he came over laughing his head off saying: 'Blimey Jonesy - I don't get that kind of service when Tom's playing!'

I said: *'Give over! Of course you do!'* Cheeky bugger.

Time went on with me getting the odd game, but just as things were going well, I was told by the club that I was not going to be a regular first team player until I was 25 years old. When I asked why, they just said they liked Preston North End players to be mature and that was the age they'd settled on.

I was a bit nonplussed by it, because although I was behind the Great Man, I could play other positions along the front line and was hoping for a decent run before then.

I'd been at the club a few years, done well and age shouldn't really come into it, I thought. I was probably around 23 at the time - these days they see that as a good age for a player. But at the time, I was facing another couple of years before getting a proper chance by the looks of it.

When Scot Symon left, the club got a new manager - Frank Hill - but the thinking didn't change. In fact, things went downhill for me.

He was a bit full of himself and I was only a young lad. I played away at Burnley and the pitch was a quagmire that day - it should have been called No Turf Moor.

I was struggling to stay on my feet and at half-time, the manager had a right go at me. Tommy Doc stepped in and said: *'Hey, you leave the lad alone - he's a good player!'*

He really backed me up but the second half was just as bad, I was all over the place. I found out later that my boots didn't have the right studs in - the trainer looked after them in those days and decided the length of studs and such like. Our boots were packed away before games, so I only realised afterwards.

Something fishy was going on for quite a while there I think, because the boots we had weren't the best. We asked time and time again if we could have different ones, but I think the trainer had a deal with the wholesalers where he got a little bit of, err, *commission* shall we say?

Anyway, Frank Hill had a go at me again at the end of the game.

I said I knew I'd not played well and asked him to leave it at that. Doc piled in again to back me up and the manager took umbrage with that I think; a senior player was standing up to him and I was the cause of it.

He was fairly new to the job, so it didn't look good for me.

On the Tuesday, he called me in and said: 'Now then Jones, Nottingham Forest have been on the phone asking about you. We have agreed a fee and they want you to play on Saturday for them.'

That was that. Cold as you like - I was out.

It hurt me really, because I'm a huge Preston fan and growing up I had only ever wanted to play for North End.

I had no agent of course, they didn't exist in those days, so my dad took me over to Nottingham - no motorways, so it was a bit of a drive - and I was reunited with my great pal Peter Higham who had joined them a little bit earlier.

I played for Forest for a while, then Doncaster Rovers, Accrington Stanley, Southport and Lancaster City, before forging a successful career in the motor trade with Audi/Volkswagen around the Preston area.

I've got a season ticket now and in all the years I've been watching, I struggle to think of a better central defence than Patrick Bauer and Ben Davies. Young Ben in particular is one of the most outstanding talents I've seen come through the ranks at Deepdale for many, many years.

But, for me, there are certain players who would have been brilliant in any era and Paul Gallagher has everything; skill, vision and he plays with his head. He is a proper footballer, Gally.

Thankfully, the training and facilities now are leaps and bounds ahead of what they were in our day and it's good that the safety of players has become more of a priority.

So many people from my era have succumbed to dementia and it's little wonder when you consider the weight of the balls in the 1950s and 60s - it must have been several pounds on a bad day.

I remember one time, a big, high goal kick coming down on me in a game when it was wet and - *much as I was trying to get out of the way of heading it* - the defender pushed me at the last minute and it cracked me right on the head.

I was out like a light and when I came round, I was seeing stars and checking where my teeth were. That's how hard and heavy they were. And, of course, not only did I not go off (still no substitutes in those days) I played another game two days later.

That was the way things were. Crazy, when you think about it now.

Luckily, I was never a great header of the ball, so didn't have that regular impact during games, but it's no surprise that people like Jeff Astle were terribly affected in later life.

Obviously, Sir Tom himself suffered from dementia towards the end of his life and I remember discussing the Astle case with him a few years earlier. I asked whether he thought there might be a link between heading those heavy balls and the onset of dementia.

He looked at me very seriously and said: 'I don't think so Eric . . . I bloody know so.'

Now, Sir Tom never swore. So I think he really wanted to emphasise his answer to me that day and it was heartbreaking to see the Great Man affected by that illness himself a few years later.

Through it all though, my love for the club has always stayed strong and I've seen some real highs and serious lows over the decades.

Preston North End is my club and will be to the day I die.

I'm proud to be part of the PNE Former Players Association and to have had the sheer honour of pulling on that famous white shirt. It may not have been as many times as I wanted, but every single game, I was filled with pride.

I was wearing the shirt that I loved, for the club that I loved and mixing with some of the best players in the world.

When I look at that crest, I'm sometimes lost for words.

And as anyone who knows me will tell you . . . that's very unlike me!

Since I stopped playing, I've enjoyed decades of watching from the stands and been fortunate to see some great North End teams down the years.

I sit in the Sir Tom Finney Stand and, while it was sad to see the old terraces go, the new surroundings do justice to Deepdale - it's still the same ground to me. It's never lost its magic. Same place, different era, that's all.

Obviously, the game has moved on and the money around nowadays has put a whole new perspective on things.

I think it plays too big a part, if I'm honest, but that's probably because it wasn't really a consideration in my playing days.

We played for our town, our club, our pals and, largely, for the love of the game.

I'm not saying those things have gone entirely, but certainly money plays a bigger part than it used to. I never made a financial fortune from football, but it never mattered to me - I consider myself a rich man for the memories I've got.

With all due respect to the players today, I wouldn't swap places with them for all the money in the world.

I played with my best pal, for the best club in the world, with the best player in the world. It doesn't get any better than that, so I'm happy and proud in equal measure.

But most of all, when I look back at the great times we had, I think to myself: *'Lucky? By God . . . I was lucky.'*

One of the all-time greats - Alex Bruce at Deepdale, 2020

'It's magic, y'know?' Paul Huntington in Preston and celebrating victory at Deepdale (right)

Battered and bloody - Gareth Ainsworth in classic North End mode, 2002

Still The King - Brian Mooney meeting fans in 2019 and (above) in action at Deepdale 1988

Lost in the moment - Sean St Ledger sends PNE into the play-offs, 2009

Not changed a bit: Gary Peters in 1996 and 2020 - still in love with North End

Who put the ball in the Blackpool net? Tom Clarke celebrates on a special night in 2013

Andy Saville forming 'an emotional bond' in 1996 (left) and keeping up with his reading in 2019

Jon Macken celebrates with Sean Gregan, Mark Rankine, Chris Lucketti and David Healy

Brian O'Neil - midfield general

Champions - A glorious day in 2000

Ryan the Lion - Ryan Kidd at Deepdale, one of the most popular players of his generation

Unbelievable but true - Peter Higham scores while wearing a boxing glove

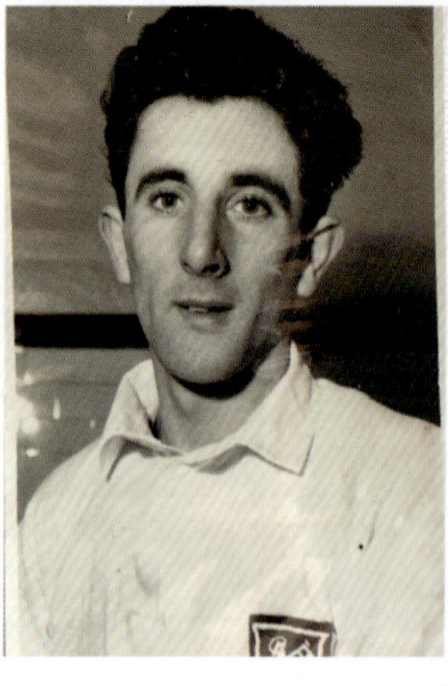

Best pals - Peter Higham (left) and Eric Jones.
Right - Eric in his North End years

Pure relief - Paul McKenna moments after the winning penalty against Birmingham, 2000

Mike Elwiss in action for North End against Shrewsbury in 1978 and with the author, 2019

Tony Ellis (complete with shiner) celebrates THAT hat-trick against Blackpool in 1992 and (right) sharing memories in Manchester, 2020

Chapter 8

SEAN ST LEDGER: ALL TOGETHER NOW

If anyone had told me when I was starting out that I'd score for my country in a major tournament, play with some of the world's biggest talents and make more than 350 senior appearances, I'd have taken it. Who wouldn't?

Like every single player out there, I've had highs and lows - but without a doubt, the happiest time of my career came at Preston North End.

I'd first come to prominence at Peterborough United at a time when they didn't have loads of money to throw around.

To bring in a bit of extra cash, the club signed up for a 'fly-on-the-wall' documentary series, with Ron Atkinson coming in to offer advice to the manager Steve Bleasdale.

I'll be honest, I was very young at the time and didn't come across too well - I don't think many people did, to be honest, apart from Big Ron - but I'm sure it made good TV.

The thing is that I was just starting out in my career and some people who saw the show formed an opinion that stuck, long after I'd matured and moved on. I hope I've proved them wrong over the years.

The good thing that came out of it for Peterborough was that it brought Darragh MacAnthony into the club and he's done a great job there over many years now.

To get some experience, they sent me out on loan to Stevenage at one point, where I spent six months under future PNE boss Graham Westley.

I got on OK with him, but only played one FA Trophy game there in the end. I was still a teenager and it was a good experience to be fair - I'm all in favour of young lads going out on loan. You see the benefits of it with people like Ben Davies at Preston now, who's been out and got loads of games under his belt.

If nothing else, it gave me a taste of being at the sharp end of the football world, where there was even less money than there was at Peterborough.

One of my early tasks was cleaning Jimmy Bullard's boots and he was exactly as he comes across on TV now - a really funny guy and an unbelievable player.

I'll always be grateful to Posh for giving me a chance though and I'd played more than 80 games for them by the time I left at the ripe old age of 21.

If you've ever heard me talk, you might be able to tell I'm a Brummie (!) and I grew up as an Aston Villa fan. But when I was leaving Peterborough United, it came down to a choice between North End and . . . Birmingham City.

Well, come on, there was only one choice to make wasn't there?

Joking apart, it was purely a football decision to come to Deepdale. *Honest!* I'd been training at the Blues, who had just been relegated from the Premier League, and

Steve Bruce was keen to sign me. But they already had players like Matthew Upson there at the back and I wasn't sure I'd get many games.

When Preston heard I was available, Paul Simpson came in for me and was straight up - he said I'd be behind Youl Mawene, but would get my chance at some point.

Simmo had not long arrived at the club, having replaced Billy Davies. The team had lost out to Leeds in the play-offs the year before and I knew they were a good outfit.

I was impressed by Paul and thought my opportunities would be greater at Deepdale, even if I might have to bide my time. I got a really good vibe from him and he came across as an intelligent manager. He'd done really well at Carlisle over the past couple of seasons and there seemed no reason that wouldn't continue.

Throughout my career, I always looked to work with people who could improve my game and I think that happened at Preston definitely.

Training-wise, Springfields maybe wasn't the best facility I ever had, but it gave you a sort of daily spirit and togetherness that can carry you through at times.

The Northern lads were really friendly and down to earth and I enjoyed it right from the start, so settling in was no bother at all. On top of that, the people in the town were lovely and welcoming and I loved living in Fulwood, getting out and meeting people.

Not long after I arrived, the club also signed Liam Chilvers, who had a bit more experience than me and was also a really good defender. So I was probably a back-up, third choice behind Youl and Liam, and I had no real problem with that.

Chilvs was doing well and there was never any shame being behind Youl - what a player he was. It was a case of coming in, working hard and earning my stripes.

My first game was Paul McKenna's testimonial against Everton in pre-season and I felt I did well against a good Premier League side.

There were more than 9,000 on for a pre-season game and I was thinking: *'Wow, this is a step up!'*

Just before the season started, we played Manchester United at Deepdale in front of another big crowd and unfortunately that was the game Youl did his cruciate ligament injury that ruled him out for the entire season. It was a big blow because everyone knew the quality he had - *let's be honest, he was a fantastic defender* - and I loved playing with him. He was a top guy around the club.

Obviously, it gave me an opportunity to start games but I knew they were pretty big shoes to fill. Luckily, me and Liam struck up a good partnership straight away.

He used to love those long diagonal passes from the back out to Simon Whaley on the left wing and his distribution was just brilliant.

Overall, it was a really experienced changing room. Players like Brian O'Neil, Callum Davidson and Paul McKenna were all big influences and one of the differences I noticed straight away were the demands in training.

These players had winning mentalities and the culture was all about that - winning.

Whether it was a five-a-side in training or a league game on a Saturday, that was the the all-important aspect. Coming from Peterborough, where things had maybe been a bit less organised at times, it was a *very* different environment. You looked at someone like Brian and the career that he'd had and you knew the standards being set.

You had to be fully focused in training and *on it* every single day. If you weren't then those lads would let you know - Kenna would be straight into you for sure.

There were plenty of things we'd have a joke about, but when it came to training and the games themselves, it was all deadly serious. No messing about.

I remember making my debut against Sheffield Wednesday, a big club with good support, so I was a bit nervous to be honest. The game was at Deepdale on a brilliant sunny afternoon and it was a great feeling to come out onto the pitch in front of probably the biggest crowd I'd played in front of at that time.

Wednesday had brought a good following and the North End fans were in good voice so it was a great atmosphere. Don't underestimate the difference fans can make - I'll be honest, I was absolutely loving it.

It was exactly what I'd signed up for; big games, big crowds, big clubs. Fantastic.

Our team was a really good blend of youth and experience, with Danny Dichio up front, Graham Alexander at the back and the young legs of David Nugent and Simon Whaley to give us a burst of pace.

Obviously, I'm not saying Dich wasn't quick, but . . !

I think I got Man of the Match on the day, but more importantly for the lads at the back, we kept a clean sheet in a 0-0 draw.

A win would have been better, of course, but from a personal view, it gave me a bit of confidence that I could play in the Championship. I thought: 'Yeah, OK I'm here now - I'm stepping up. Let's do it.'

I think, tactics-wise, Paul had looked at what Billy Davies had achieved and took it on a bit in that first half of the season; we were tight at the back and flying up front.

Some people might say we were lucky that me and Chilvs took to that level and formed a good partnership so quickly, but we were playing without fear and, like I've mentioned, a big part of it was the culture at the time and the players that we had around us.

Callum, Brian, Graham, Carlo Nash behind - when you've got that much experience around you, it makes the transition a lot easier.

It wasn't all smooth sailing though and Paul Simpson was probably the first manager to give me a proper rollocking. We were 2-0 down away at Luton and he went right through me at half-time. I thought: *'Wow, this is a big one.'*

But, fair play, he got the right reaction from me and I think he understood me as a person. There's that old saying about knowing when to put your arm around someone and when to give them a rollocking and he always seemed to get that right with me.

We had great momentum under the new boss and topped the league in the first half of the season. I think we just needed a bit of extra help in January to keep us right up there challenging, but for whatever reason, it didn't materialise.

At the time, you keep your head in the right place and just keep working hard, but looking back, we finished one point and one place outside the play-offs and, looking back, it feels like a missed opportunity for sure.

I think we were 2-1 up against Southend at Deepdale in March with two minutes to go and they somehow beat us 3-2. If we'd have just held on, we'd have been in the play-offs. Painful.

But I suppose everyone has these tales of 'ifs and buts' don't they?

We beat Birmingham on the last day of the season *(which is always nice)* but other results went against us and we just missed out. Still, I was happy on a personal note with how things had gone and confident we could have a real go next time out.

The following season, one of the biggest differences was that we had Neil Mellor available more often. Mells was an unbelievable finisher and if you gave him the service, you always knew that he would score.

It was just a case of trying to keep him fit, because you could see every day the reason why he'd been at Liverpool - he was so calm in front of goal, it just came naturally to him.

On top of that, the club started to spend some relatively big money.

Darren Carter came in from West Brom and later on that season Richard Chaplow arrived, both for decent fees. The pair of them had Premier League pedigree and were a signal of intent by the club.

Up front Nuge was coming into his prime and personified the work ethic of the team. He put defenders under pressure all the time and was a nightmare to play against in training. On top of that, he was deadly in front of goal and always played the game with a smile on his face - he still does, doesn't he?

Every time he played back then it was like a child in the playground; everything was so natural to him and he loves scoring goals.

The fans absolutely loved him and you can see why people were so glad to welcome him back to Deepdale under Alex Neil. *I don't think he's changed a bit!*

Sadly, in that second season under Simmo, results weren't going our way and you could sense things getting a little bit restless about the place.

It was especially difficult for me because Paul had brought me into the club. Whenever someone gives you such an opportunity, you're always really thankful and grateful to that person. So it was hard to see him under pressure.

Like I said, I think he understood me as a person and a footballer and brought my game on significantly over that period.

It was sad for me to see him leave in the end, but by that time, I understood *'this is football'* y'know? It's all about results and it can be a hard, hard business.

Luckily, Paul's replacement was Alan Irvine and he was unbelievable - I learned so much from him. His training was some of the best I've ever had and his preparations were spot on.

Some of the team meetings were pretty long, but the detail was superb - you felt like you knew absolutely everything about every one of the opposition team, right down to their pre-match meal almost!

We soon climbed up into mid-table, finishing 15th in 2007/08 and on a personal level, I was honoured to win the Player of the Year award, which is something I'm really proud of. When you look at the players who have won the award before and since, it's great company to be in and it means a hell of a lot to me.

Alan really gelled the squad together, but the only thing was . . . *pre-season.*

Now, I didn't mind a hard pre-season - most of the lads are the same; get in, get it done, get cracking.

But Alan's?

Blimey, I'm telling you now . . . they were TOUGH.

You worked and worked and worked but at the end of it, you KNEW that you were strong physically, strong mentally and you were absolutely straining at the leash for the games to start.

We went away on the first day down to Ipswich who were a really strong side about that time but we beat them 2-1 at Portman Road.

Obviously, Youl was back by then and Billy Jones had come in as a fantastic full-back to replace Grezza. Mells was fit up front and Paul McKenna was bossing the midfield. Simon Whaley got the winner that day and the potential he had was incredible. I think Liverpool were monitoring him at one point but, for whatever reason, he never achieved that top level and his career fell away after he left Preston. It's sad to see, but football can be an unforgiving business if you take a wrong turn.

Overall, Alan knew what he wanted and was forging a team that could make a decent stab at the play-offs. Jon Parkin had come in and was just a huge character in the dressing room in every sense.

I remember he signed on a Friday and I remember him stepping through the dressing room door - I couldn't believe the size of the guy!

The next day he made probably the best debut I've ever seen, against Charlton at Deepdale. He was just unplayable; big and strong, but also with great feet and technique.

Defenders sometimes got so hooked up on his size, they underestimated how good a player he was with the ball - and paid the price.

As you might know (!) he's also a really funny guy and was a great addition to the changing room, always there with a proper Yorkshire one-liner.

He slotted into the team straight away and I think the football we played that season was probably the most enjoyable of my career.

I'll always remember we beat Wolves 3-1 at Molineux in January and Alan Irvine said I was *'superb'*. Me and Youl played at the back and I also scored that night.

But to get praise like that from a manager as demanding as Alan meant a lot to me.

As the season went on, we were chasing Cardiff down and everyone remembers the game when we beat them 6-0 at Deepdale to wipe out their goal difference advantage.

What a great day that was - it gave us real belief going into the next game away at Birmingham. For me as a Brummie and a Villa fan, that was always one of the biggest games of the season.

I always had loads of family and friends there and, to be fair, they had a good side around that time with Lee Bowyer in midfield and Kevin Phillips up front. They were on the verge of going up and I think they saw our game as maybe a formality that day.

As is often the case with Preston, we were under the radar a bit, but two screamers from Kenna and Ross Wallace made people sit up and take notice - especially as the game was live on TV.

On top of that, it ruined the Blues' promotion party, which was a real shame for me as you can imagine. Yeah, yeah, 'keep right on' for a few more games fellas!

It set us up for the QPR game at Deepdale where we knew a win would put us in the play-offs - but only if Cardiff slipped up at Sheffield Wednesday.

Going into it, I was a bit worried if I'm honest, because they had Patrick Agyemang up front. Anyone who's seen Pat play knows his pace was absolutely frightening and when a player goes back to his old club, you always get that fear that they're going to score. Lo and behold, Parky put us 1-0 up, but Pat got an equaliser in the second half. (Had to happen, didn't it?)

As the game wore on, the fans obviously heard that Cardiff were losing and this great noise went around the stadium . . . we just needed one more goal. Deepdale was buzzing but we knew time was running out: *'Come on lads! Let's not blow it!*

We got a throw-in at the Fulwood End and I remember shouting over to the manager to ask if I could go up. We had to win the game and had nothing to lose, so he said yes and I legged it forward.

It was a fair way out but - *out of the blue* - Jon Parkin delivered the perfect long throw into their box. I think it surprised everyone, us and them!

Chris Brown got a good header on it as their keeper came out and I managed to get above their defender Peter Ramage at the back post.

Net bulging, crowd roaring, and I'm off: *Get in!*

It's hard to explain but as soon as the ball hit the back of the net, euphoria kicked in and I celebrating like a madman - just like the fans all round the ground. Absolutely brilliant. I know I just went crazy - instinctively; *big game, big goal for your club, big celebration!*

Forget money - you can't put a price on that, it's a reward football gives you. They are feelings that live with you forever and I still get them when I think about that game. The atmosphere at Deepdale that day was electric and the noise when it went in was off the scale.

When I look back on it now, it makes you realise how VAR might put an end to those crazy first few seconds after you score. You're lost in the moment.

These days, you'd have this doubt at the back of your mind, worrying if the goal was going to be ruled out. *That can't be right, can it?*

You wouldn't want to be waiting for some approval from a a guy sat 100 miles away - it takes all the fun out of it.

QPR weren't giving in though and I remember right at the end they put us under real pressure at the Town End, with their keeper coming up and everything. It was absolute bedlam with three corners, one after the other, in injury time before Darren Carter cleared one off the line with the last kick of the game. Drama? *Unbelievable.*

The scenes at the final whistle though . . . wow!

Fans piling on the pitch, players being carried off shoulder high, everyone jumping around and singing - it was just the best feeling being in among it all. Again, things you are so lucky to experience and that you will never forget.

We were up against Sheffield United in the play-offs and I knew they would be two tough games. They had a good side and I remember Kyle Walker was playing for them, who was absolutely flying.

The first leg was at Deepdale and, for me, there was always something special about night games at home. I used to live near the Asda in Fulwood and the view you get as you came down Watling Street Road there when the floodlights were on - it looked like a shrine almost.

There was this glow in the night sky and it got you pumped up just seeing it. It's still the same now when I come up and see it from the motorway if the lights are on at night. I still get that same feeling. The floodlights are quite iconic and there's not many other stadiums in the country that you can see from so far away like that. Fair play to the designers because it's a fantastic sight.

Anyway, it was getting a bit lighter when we played Sheff United on the following Friday night. The lights were still on though, the crowd were up for it and we believed we could do this.

We started well and after about 20 minutes, we got a free-kick just inside their half.

Billy Jones floated a long ball in, it flicked off one of their lads' heads and suddenly I was all alone in the six-yard box with the ball at my feet. Paddy Kenny dived the wrong way and I just tucked it in to put us one up.

I thought it was quite a good finish and Paddy was a teammate of mine with Ireland, so it was special to put one past him. I think I might have mentioned it to him once or twice since!

No great celebration this time though, obviously there was a long way to go and we had to stay focused, keep our minds on the job.

I think we were in control of the game at that point and were unlucky to be only 1-0 up at half-time. In the second half, they came out and scored virtually straight from the kick-off. Inevitably, that took a bit of wind out of our sails and it was a different game from then on.

It gave them something to defend and the game petered out a bit really, leaving us with a tough task at Bramall Lane, where the atmosphere was always intense.

In that second leg, Alan changed things around a little bit, maybe to freshen us up, but they grabbed a goal, clung onto it and just about saw us off.

It just wasn't to be and the feeling afterwards was just . . . *gutted.*

I know people always say that but we were. All of us, really disappointed and down.

Everyone knows losing in the play-offs is one of the worst things in football and, trust me, the players feel it as much as the fans.

I don't think we played our best in the second leg and deep down we realised it, so that was a big blow. Maybe we missed our best chance when we only drew at Deepdale. Going into the second leg with a lead to defend puts a whole new spin on the way both teams approach it.

Maybe though, they were a better side than us that year and sometimes you've just got to take your hat off to the opposition and say, fair enough, they deserved it.

Even so, it was a tough one to take.

But we were still in a good position and I don't think anyone would have foreseen the problems the club was going to have over the next two years at that point.

We had a good, settled squad, great manager, had just been in the play-offs - no-one would have predicted we'd be relegated a couple of seasons later.

On a personal level, things were going really well for me and I made my Republic of Ireland debut in May 2009 against Nigeria, then played again in a World Cup qualifier against Bulgaria. I'd been in the squad before, but Alan Kelly was involved with Giovanni Trappattoni's backroom team and obviously saw a lot of Preston matches and gave good reports on my progress.

I was always really proud to play for my country and had some great times in green - scoring against Italy in Dublin in another World Cup qualifier . . . unforgettable.

Just don't mention the play-off against France and Thierry Henry's handball goal!

Back in Preston, West Brom came in for Alan that summer, but to their credit North End stuck to their guns and kept hold of him. The transfer window passed and we brought a few lads in, but lost Paul McKenna to Forest - a big loss to any team.

Kenna was probably the most underrated guy in the league around that time; he was an unbelievable player, but he kept everything real and always had a low profile, even when he was winning national awards.

Anyone who played with him or against him will tell you how good he was, but I don't think the North End fans need to be told. They already know and it was a real loss to the club when he left.

As for me, there was nothing to suggest I'd be leaving at all as the transfer window came and went.

I was getting my head down for another crack at promotion with Preston when, out of the blue, Middlesbrough came in for me.

They could get round the deadline by taking me on loan and then making the move permanent for around £4 million in January.

It wasn't something I'd been pushing for or even heard about, but Boro had just come down from the Premier League and Gareth Southgate was the manager there.

He was already carving out a reputation as a great coach and because he was a centre back, I thought it would be a good opportunity to develop my game under him.

The fact he'd played for Villa wasn't the major factor, but it was a bonus and all in all it was Gareth's presence that swayed me. When I met him, he was great with me and I thought it would be a chance to learn from him, develop my game and get in the Premier League.

Still, it was a tough call because I was enjoying it so much at Deepdale and deep down, I didn't want to leave. I remember we were at a hotel before a game at Scunthorpe the following day when I eventually told Alan Irvine I was going to go.

I was crying as I was saying the words to him - so that's probably a sign: if you've got tears in your eyes, then maybe it's not such a good decision!

That was in September 2009 and Boro had started the season well. Not long after I arrived, I actually played against North End at Deepdale and that was such a strange feeling.

I'd always had a great relationship with the Preston fans; I think they'd seen that I gave my all in every game and always tried my hardest for the club, so I was chuffed to get a good reception from both sets of supporters that day.

That meant a lot to me and showed that I'd not burned my bridges at Deepdale. I had to mark Jon Parkin and the game ended in a 2-2 draw so no-one went home too unhappy.

In October, Boro were one point off the top of the league when, out of nowhere, Gareth Southgate was sacked and Gordon Strachan came in. I've got to be honest, I'd signed on the premise that Gareth was going to be the manager, so it was a blow to me personally. I had no problem with Mr Strachan's sessions or anything but, without Gareth, my heart wasn't in it. It wasn't what I'd signed up for.

Also, I'm my own biggest critic and I don't think I'd played my best football there. I was quite poor, to be honest. I didn't really settle in the area and if I had my time again, I would have stayed at North End. I knew that I was only on loan and in the end, when the time came I asked if I could go back.

I'm not sure it went down too well with everyone involved, but for me it was a case of getting back to work under Alan Irvine and a club that I loved playing for.

I wanted to pick up from where I'd left off with him and continue to grow and develop as a player.

Financially, if I'd signed permanently at Boro, the wages would have been around double my PNE contract, but that wasn't important to me.

It was a football decision, pure and simple.

The way I saw it, if I was good enough, I'd get a chance in the Premier League and ideally that would be with Preston.

If not, maybe another opportunity would come up further down the line.

When I got back, I still thought we had a decent squad and weren't far off the standards of the year before.

In my first game, we played Sheffield United away and although we lost late on 1-0, we matched them for most of the game.

We hadn't become a bad side over a few months.

So it was a real shock when Alan was sacked after that game. I couldn't believe it really - I'd come back to play under him and now he was gone.

He was so popular with the players and we all thought he was a great coach who had really improved us.

The club wasn't in any relegation trouble or anything so it was a strange decision and a blow to me personally, as a huge part of the reason for coming back was to work with him again.

I was massively disappointed, a lot of us were, but we understood that when you're a player, these decisions are taken and you've just got to carry on, not lose focus and do your best for the club, whoever the boss is.

I hadn't known Darren Ferguson from my Peterborough days, but when he came in I thought he was a really good man manager.

Whether it was all the Middlesbrough situation, the change of managers at Preston, I don't know but, I'll be honest, I didn't play that well for the rest of that season.

The previous year had all gone smoothly, but when you're disrupted a bit with all these changes, I struggled to get back into the same rhythm I'd had before.

Maybe everyone did, because we struggled a bit in Darren's first season, finishing 17th and going into the next season, I was also struggling with injury really.

When I did get in, I probably didn't play as well as I had done in the past and it was just a frustrating time for everyone at the club. We seemed to lose momentum.

We knew we still had quality in the squad, it was just turning it into results.

Probably the game that summed it up for us was when we went to Leeds and won 6-4 at Elland Road. That showed that, on our day, we were still capable of beating anyone.

I've got to be honest, we conceded four so it wasn't the best game I've ever had, but I just remember Parky being absolutely unplayable. As defenders you could loft it, chip it, play it along the floor and he would always get on the end of it.

It sounds daft, but he was so big, he was difficult to mark and his movement was underrated at times because his positioning was so good. He'd always find space somewhere. It was a crazy game - one of those that people talk about for years.

To be 4-1 down and beat Leeds 6-4 at their place was just unbelievable.

In the dressing room afterwards, quite a few of us were just sat in stunned silence but Parky was laughing his head off and joking that he could do that to Leeds every week. *Has he ever mentioned he's from Yorkshire, by the way??*

Sadly, that game was a blip and overall, results were going against us. For the previous five or six years, North End had been very successful with various pushes and play-offs and now we were struggling. It hurt everyone, including the players.

Darren ended up being sacked and Phil Brown came in, who was really positive and lifted things around the squad, even if results didn't pick up enough.

My final game was a 2-1 win against Coventry. I didn't realise it would be my last appearance, but I got a medial ligament injury that I knew was going to take quite a while to recover from.

That was painful, but having to watch from the sidelines as we were struggling was worse.

I felt helpless as we were relegated; it was just an absolutely terrible feeling. It still hurts to think about it now. I know no-one has a divine right to be in the Championship, but it was a fairly dramatic fall from grace given the squad we'd had a few short years before.

When you go down, the club obviously has to look at the finances and inevitably quite a few of us left that summer.

It was a really sad time, as I had some fantastic days at Preston and played with some great players. I also had a great relationship with the fans and am always touched by the welcome I get whenever I go back to Deepdale now.

But at the time, I had to move on.

Under the circumstances, the club knew it and I knew it.

I signed for Leicester under Sven Goran Eriksson, who had spoken to Trappattoni about me, as they knew each other from the Italian league. I liked Sven - he was very gentlemanly and calm about things, no matter what.

Bizarrely, my debut was against Real Madrid in a pre-season friendly and maybe it was a sign of things to come.

I'd bought a new car and on the way to the stadium I kept hearing this funny noise. I was just about to pull over and have a look when a wheel fell off and I went skidding into an island.

Obviously I was a bit shook up, so I only got to the ground at about ten to three, but as I was only on the bench I thought I'd be OK. About 40 minutes in, someone got injured and I had to go on.

I was a bit light-headed after all the drama so, not surprisingly, Karim Benzema gave me a bit of a runaround!

Speaking of top class players, Paul Gallagher was at the King Power at that time and I think he spoke well of me to Sven too, after his time on loan at Deepdale a few years earlier. What a player Gally is; so much ability and a fantastic attitude - a model professional. When I go back to Deepdale, you can see his influence on younger players. It was great to see him get Player of the Decade recently, because I know he has been unbelievable for Preston and the fans absolutely love him.

I spent three years at Leicester, but injuries disrupted me and it was around the time they got new owners in who were investing heavily in the squad. If you were ruled out by injury, it was very hard to get back in.

In my third year there I started the season in the team, but suffered another knee injury similar to the one I'd had at Deepdale and ended up not playing that much.

The club got promoted to the Premier League that year, but my contract was up and I briefly joined Ipswich before embarking on a career in the USA.

I was 30 by this point and just wanted to play games. I'd not played as much as I would have liked since leaving Preston and saw it as an opportunity to try something different. DC United had been in touch, but I ended up signing for Orlando City, which was a great experience.

The Brazilian great Kaka was a teammate there and was just unbelievable to play alongside. Anyone who thinks he might have been taking it easy in America should have seen the work he put into training.

I spent a year there and then had another season at Colorado Rapids. It was a great chance to see the States and be part of the MLS at a time when the league was really expanding with players like David Villa, Frank Lampard and Andrea Pirlo signing up.

It was also the scene of one of the more bizarre rumours I've had, when I was pictured with Taylor Swift. (*There's nothing to this, honestly.)*

I was with some friends and we went to an after-show party that she was at in New York and I had my picture taken with her. That's the entire story. It didn't stop all these mad tabloid rumours coming out over the next few weeks, but that's how people can get the wrong idea about things very quickly.

Sorry, it just didn't happen. We were never, ever, ever together.

I came back home, I had a taste of non-league football with Guiseley for a while and then took charge for a few months. Nowadays, I am part of the first team recruitment set-up at Leicester and love my work there.

The owners have been fantastic and it's a real team effort at the King Power - I think you can see the results of that on the pitch.

I also help coach the Ireland Under-15s and really enjoy bringing young players through and passing on the benefit of my experience.

But, as I said earlier, my playing time at Preston was the happiest of my career and I never regretted joining North End - it's a club very close to my heart.

They gave me fantastic opportunities, developed me as a player and helped me represent my country. In an ideal world, we'd have made it into the Premier League and been together for years.

I think the club has the potential to get there one day for sure, and I hope it's sooner rather than later.

I always look out for North End's results and often think back to some of the great days at Deepdale with a brilliant set of lads.

We had a togetherness like no other and those memories will stay with me forever.

Chapter 9

ANDY SAVILLE: HEAVEN AND HULL

I had a funny start to my career as a professional footballer - I actually played for Hull City while still working in a local factory. I'm not sure people do that type of thing these days!

In fact, I had to take a pay cut to sign for my boyhood heroes, who were offering £130-a-week . . . '*take it or leave it, son'*. I took it and never looked back.

Of course, everyone thinks you're on a fortune playing footy and my Mrs, who still worked in the factory, used to get ribbed by people saying: 'You're only with him for the money!'

She'd hit back: 'You're joking aren't you? I'm on more than him!'

That factory gave me a great grounding though and made sure that I always kept my feet on the floor, not that I was ever one for airs and graces. I always knew how lucky I was and appreciated every minute making a living playing football.

I'd been a Hull fan all my life and I still am; my local team, my city, my club.

I always got the impression Preston fans were like that, too. There's a lot of big clubs in the North West and it would be easy to go glory hunting, but I think there's still that bond with North End, stretching back to the days of Sir Tom Finney and beyond.

I don't get it when people support teams from elsewhere, unless there's a family connection or something. Support your local team and you'll get the rewards. You'll feel it more. You'll appreciate it more. You'll have that bond with those around you.

I've got quite a few mates who are 'Dirty Leeds' fans, just because they were successful when they were growing up. It's pathetic, quite frankly, as I remind them all the time!

I used to love going to Boothferry Park with my dad. It was a proper old ground, decent-sized and with a great atmosphere. You were standing in those days - *well, we were at least* - and when Hull scored we'd jump around and get towards the away fans. It might sound a bit off these days, but we weren't after any aggro.

Back then everyone did it when we scored and it was part of going to the game - for both sets of fans. Of course, when they scored they'd surge at the fences too and it was proper atmosphere, more freedom than now.

Don't get me wrong, Hull's new stadium is fantastic and the facilities are amazing, but . . . we've definitely lost something from the game I knew growing up.

Maybe it is better now. Maybe it's rose-tinted spectacles. Maybe not.

I don't miss the old toilets, that's for sure.

Anyway, as a young lad I made it into their youth teams and as the years went by, I worked my way up to the reserves and - like I mentioned - played four games in the first team before eventually being signed on a proper contract.

Brian Horton, who was assistant manager later on at PNE, was the manager at the time and I liked him; no nonsense, straight to the point. Great guy.

Steve McClaren was on the books as a player and Big Billy Whitehurst was just coming to the end at Hull as I came through. Anyone - and I mean *anyone* - who was around in the 1980s will remember him. Certainly everyone who played against him.

Talk about hard as nails! Blimey - he'd leave a dent in the hammer, Billy.

Perhaps people saw me as a bit of a replacement for him at first, but I decided that I wasn't going to be the next Billy Whitehurst - I was going to be the one and only Andy Saville; try as hard as I could in every game and see where it took me. Maybe fans looked at us as similar players as I was big and aggressive, but I'd like to think I could play a bit too. *(I'm not saying Billy couldn't - he might read this one day!)*

Anyway, I did OK at Hull, playing over 100 games and scoring around one-in-five, which wasn't bad as a young player getting into the game.

To be honest, all I'd ever wanted to do was play for the Tigers and to score goals for them was every lad's dream come true round our way. So it was a real wrench when they sold me to Walsall for £100,000.

It was a decent fee, but it didn't go quite so well down there and that was the start of a fairly nomadic spell where I went to Barnsley *(I did a bit better there, goals-wise)* and Hartlepool *(again, I did OK)* before joining Birmingham City under Terry Cooper. All the glamour spots, eh!

Coops was a no-nonsense manager again and by this time I was used to playing as a bit of a target man, chipping in with goals, but also setting up other players around me. I was a bit more than a battering ram, but at times you had to take some stick, physically.

It's a man's game, you're playing up front, you've got to take a bit haven't you?

It was during my time with the Blues that I lost my two front teeth, thanks to none other than future North End boss Simon Grayson.

He was playing for Leicester and as I went up for a ball he accidentally caught me with his elbow. *Smack!* Right in the mouth. I lost one tooth straight away but the other was embedded in my gum at a funny angle - absolute agony. I couldn't eat properly for a couple of weeks but after lots of visits to the dentist I got my perfect smile back, eventually!

I'd joined Birmingham quite late on in the 1992/93 season and we just about stayed up - winning on the last day to survive.

David Sullivan had taken over and put 23-year-old Karren Brady in charge a few months before they signed me, so when we had a bad start to the following season, Terry was out and Barry Fry came in.

Barry is exactly as he appears with all that *'cor blimey guvnor'* business - a complete one-off. He'd think nothing of putting on three subs at the same time if things weren't going well, complete with clear instructions - *normally starting with 'f'* - about what he wanted them to do. As for the lads who got the hook, it was off-f-f-f (that's 'off', followed by several more 'f's as you made your way to the bench!).

And the one thing Barry loved to do was sign players. I think we ended up with 40 lads on the books in my last season there and about 14 of us were strikers.

He brought in the likes of big Kevin Francis and quite a few he'd had at Barnet and Southend but, to be fair, he played me quite a bit and we ended up winning promotion from the third tier back into what is now the Championship.

North End had wanted me in the 1994/95 season when David Beckham was there, but I don't think they could afford a permanent deal and Blues wouldn't let me go on loan. But games were getting rarer and at the end of the season, it was clear Barry wasn't going out of his way to keep me.

Thankfully, Preston came in again and I shot up to see Gary Peters, even though I was playing for a Championship team and they were in what is now League 2.

I was 28 and had no agent or anything (not many people did outside the top flight in those days) so I just drove up, met Gary and felt at home straight away.

I just wanted to play a big part in something. I didn't want to be a bit-part guy. I wanted to be at the centre of things, scoring goals - that was what drove me on and I thought I'd get that at Deepdale.

Gary had a vision of how he wanted the team to play and how I would fit into it with a lad he was signing from Mansfield - Steve Wilkinson.

I knew North End had just been beaten in the play-offs, so they must have had the nucleus of a good side, especially when you looked at some of the lads on their books; the likes of Ian Bryson and David Moyes. They were people who you respected as they had been about and were known as good players.

When I looked at it, I thought that squad was probably playing a division below what it should have been at, even then. I fancied us to go up right from the start - and so did Gary. It was infectious and I couldn't wait to get going.

The new Tom Finney Stand was taking shape, the top men from Baxi were driving things behind the scenes and you got the impression that the whole place was about to move forward.

The crowds were already too big for that division and the away support was always lively, so I knew the fanbase was there - it was all set up.

It was a £200-a-week pay cut, with bonuses built in for promotion and things like that, but to be honest, I never played for the money.

Don't get me wrong, it was always good to get paid for doing something you loved, but it wasn't my driving force - and I don't think it was for any of the lads back then.

You were on decent wages, but it wasn't a fortune. It wasn't going to set you up for life, even in the Premier League back then.

You wanted to play and win things, so you could look back with pride on what you had achieved in your career.

These days I think some of these lads will look back and see how much money they've got in the bank. It's a totally different outlook.

Of course, I'd have been much better off financially if I'd played in the modern era and - hey - it would have been great, thanks very much. But would I have swapped?

You know what . . . probably not.

Back then, if you played well and the team won, you played every game and clocked up hundreds of appearances. Now, with squad rotation, players will probably play far fewer games but end up much wealthier at the end of it.

I work as a postman now and am quite happy with my lot, but if I was playing now, I might not have to work again once my career ended.

I'm not bitter - good luck to people. That's just the way it is and, happily, the move to Preston turned out to be priceless. You can have all the money in the world, but you can't buy the times we had that season.

When I arrived, I knew Graeme Atkinson from way back in Hull - I even knew his mum and dad - so he helped me settle in straight away. Graeme's a great guy who used to clean my boots when he was a young lad - we still keep in touch now, especially as he's still involved at Deepdale working with young players.

Back then it was good to see a familiar face and get cracking on the training pitch. We had a good pre-season and straight away I could feel things clicking with Steve Wilkinson on the pitch and off it.

Wilks was such an unselfish player and always one of the most intelligent people on the pitch; a really clever footballer and our partnership worked all season.

The way he found space was almost instinctive and he had such a lovely touch that the ball was under control straight away. He always had his head up as soon as he received it, looking for what pass was on - and thankfully, it was normally to me.

In all honesty, I think Gary had expected me to do the heavy-lifting and Steve to get the goals, but it turned out that I scored more than him.

Again, part of that was down to his unselfish nature. If he had the chance to score, but thought you were in a better position, he would always try to set you up - and that season, it worked time after time.

It was just one of those years when everything seemed to go right; goals flying in the top corner, tap-ins, long shots, volleys - bouncing off my backside!

Everything seemed to lead to a goal and when you get that confidence, you can't wait for the games to come about.

I started well with a goal on my home debut on the first game of the season. Sounds great, but after going in front, we got beat 2-1 at Deepdale by Lincoln.

It was a setback and a signal that, even though we had a great squad, nothing was going to be given to us on a plate. This was the bottom tier of the Football League, lads battling for their living with non-league just around the corner if they went down.

We wanted to play good football, but we'd have to work hard to do it, too.

There was no panic from Gary and with good reason - we then went on an unbeaten run in the league that lasted until the new year.

He was such a hard-working manager and ahead of his time in many respects. He would study videos of opposing teams, long before it was fashionable and would always be able to tell you about your direct opponent; which side to go on, what he was like with the ball at his feet, really useful stuff.

Every player in the team was well-informed and well-drilled about the game ahead. We had a clear plan about how to tackle each team we faced and, most times that season, it worked.

Obviously, it helps when you've got good players and we had almost the perfect squad that year. We had good young lads like Kevin Kilbane and Lee Cartwright, both quick as lightning and fit as fiddles, flying down the wings and whipping great crosses in - perfect for me in the air.

Then there were the technicians, people like Brys and Graeme in midfield, alongside Simon Davey.

At the back, there was Ryan Kidd, another solid player who gave his all in every game, Moyesie and Russ Wilcox, a big mate of mine and hard as granite. He'd been around the block - and back again - so he knew that league inside out.

All three were 'no nonsense', as the saying goes. As a striker, you wouldn't want to play against them every week, I can tell you.

Russ came from my part of the world and we used to share the driving over to Preston. Gary used to joke that he'd only signed Russ so he could give me a lift into training. No-one believed it for a second.

Russ and David were both were really sharp footballers too, with great positional sense after years of learning their trade. They'd both seen everything down the years and knew exactly how to handle situations.

The team didn't really change that much from week to week unless someone was injured or suspended and again, I'm not sure you'd get that these days.

The benefit for us was that we worked almost like a machine going through the gears because we were so familiar with each other. I'd just instinctively know where Wilks or Brys was going to put the ball and get on the end of it.

Moyesie was doing a fair bit of the training at that point, as he was doubling up as Gary's assistant, as well as playing. It started to take a bit of a toll on his form after a while and Steve Harrison came in.

Even then, Moyesie was one of the best coaches I've ever worked with but Steve took things on to a new level. He'd been with the England set-up under Graham Taylor and his sessions were just fantastic.

Strangely enough though, our form took a bit of a drop when he first arrived and I remember some of the PNE fans giving him some stick.

If so, it was unfair as it was the players who were responsible for any bad results, and most teams - even in title-winning seasons - have a blip at some point. It was surprising because I always found the North End crowd to be an intelligent bunch.

Genuinely, I'm not just saying that. Obviously, it helps when you're having a good season, but even at the start, they were always patient and saw the bigger picture.

It was the same the following season when we hit the higher level and things got tougher; the fans were really good with us and I don't recall them ever getting on our backs at all - it was just proper support and all the players appreciated it.

(I remember when I played at Walsall and if you had a bad result there, the fans would be trying to dismantle the tunnel at the end of the game. *At Walsall.* Crazy.)

Back at Deepdale, we were doing OK but drawing quite a few games. In fact, we'd drawn four out of five before beating Chester 2-0 at the end of September.

Before that, I'd got three goals in 11 games but from there our momentum grew and we started to turn teams over. We beat Scarborough at home and I got a couple at Torquay in a 4-0 away win before we faced Mansfield at Deepdale in one of the most memorable games of my career.

Both me and Wilks grabbed hat-tricks in a 6-0 win and it was the first time that had happened in a PNE team since the 1960s, I think.

To say we destroyed them is an understatement - come on, it was 6-0 after all!

But the way we played was as near to perfect as you're going to get. A clean sheet, great goals and a result that gave us a real boost.

I was chuffed for Steve as it was against his old club and it's a sign of the belief we had that for my last goal I went round the keeper and slotted it in at the Town End.

There's no better feeling for a striker than putting a goalie on his backside just before you put the ball in the back of the net. It's holding your nerve long enough for a little dummy or a shimmy. Then he's down and it's just a dink over him. I love those goals - the ones you've had to think about and win a mind game.

Sometimes it's just instinct; here's the ball, hit it or head it. But those that you've got time to think about are sometimes the toughest ones, which makes it all the better when they go in.

I also love a late winner - *who doesn't?* - and I got that in our next game away at Northampton. The North End fans went crazy behind the goal and I just ripped my shirt off and started wheeling it around my head in celebration.

It's hard to describe that feeling - you just lose yourself for a few moments as all the noise and the emotion takes over. It's like no other feeling in the world.

These days I'd probably be booked for that celebration, which is ridiculous. The people who come up with these rules have probably never played the game.

And they've definitely never scored a late winner for PNE away at Northampton.

Back at Deepdale for our next game, I got another hat-trick - two in two consecutive home games as we beat Orient 4-0. All three came in the second half at the Town End again and the second was one of my favourite goals of the season.

I was slipped in about eight yards out and again managed to sit the keeper down before just dinking it over him at the near post. It still makes me smile even now, 20-odd years later.

If you're wondering how I can remember all these goals, well, some do live in the memory. And for others, there's always YouTube, where I sometimes log on and proudly show my grandson what grandad did when he was a bit younger!

My next goal wasn't quite so clever - an OG in a 1-1 draw away at Exeter. It was one of those that just hit me and went in. You can't let things like that bother you.

It certainly didn't dent my confidence and that's a key thing for any striker.

The following week we saw off my old club Hartlepool at Deepdale and maybe my trick of going round the keeper was getting too well known. I went round him once but, fair play, he got up before I could shoot.

I had to go round him again before eventually scoring in front of the Kop.

We then had a few dull draws before thrashing Cardiff on New Year's Day. I got two, with Simon Davey, Graeme Atkinson and Mickey Brown getting the others.

It was a result that summed up the strength of the team, especially in midfield, where we had players who could chip in goals if it wasn't happening for the strikers.

Simon had been captain up at Carlisle before joining PNE and was just one of several on-field leaders we had in the team. Think about people like Russ and Moyesie at the back - really vocal and top organisers - but the captain was Brys and, to this day, he was the main man. For me, the best player in the squad.

He had everything; skill, workrate, goals - he was just a huge presence on and off the pitch. I still keep in touch with him and it's good that he still has connections with North End on the corporate side of things.

Just think what he would be worth in today's transfer market.

He was a great joker too, but probably the biggest 'character' in the dressing room was his fellow Scot, Ray Sharp. Ray was always bouncing around and full of life. Whenever we scored, he would run as fast as he could to try to be the first to pile on top of you. He loved every minute of it, Ray, and was a really funny bloke.

I don't think he ever scored for North End which is a shame as I'd have loved to have seen his celebration - he'd probably still be running round the pitch now!

Just after Christmas, Barnet popped our bubble after 22 games with a 1-0 defeat on their sloping pitch at Underhill, but we were back in the groove in January with three wins out of four, including away at Darlington, where the North End fans popped a few snowballs at the keeper as I ran up to score a penalty. Again, I'm not sure they'd have played that game in the modern era - health and safety would probably have called it off and there'd be CCTV appeals to find the snowballers!

Then flaming Barnet beat us again (at Deepdale!) before we got on a run that really set us up for the title.

We beat Colchester 2-0 with my goal coming from a great corner set-piece that had been around since John Beck's days; a short touch to the edge of the box, a reverse pass and a near post cross that I flicked in. It was a testament to work on the training ground and the players always loved it when one of those paid off.

The following week we went over to Scunthorpe and I was lucky enough to score one of the best - if not ***the*** best - goals of my career.

Simon Davey whipped a corner in, the keeper got a bit of a touch before it was headed out towards the edge of the box.

It was just instinct really, but I launched myself at it for an overhead volley and it flew into the top corner - right in front of the North End fans. It was just one of those moments where in a split second I hooked my foot around it and - *bang!* - it's in the back of the net. It was my right foot, too, so my celebration was almost as much in surprise as anything else!

I think confidence plays a huge part with goals like that; a season where you've scored plenty of goals, everyone is right behind you and the team's doing well . . . you just go for it and it paid off.

Even now, when my grandson is talking about great goals in the Premier League or whatever, I just give him a little nod and say: *'Scunny, away.'*

There was still work to be done though and our next two games gave us just one point from a draw against Hereford and a 2-1 defeat to Rochdale. Like I say, teams like that aren't going to roll over and beating Preston at Deepdale in front of a big crowd was a good scalp for them. A couple of weeks later, we beat Rochdale 3-0 at their place as we set about another long unbeaten run with some tough games in it.

We beat Cardiff 1-0 at Ninian Park and it was one of those late goals where I celebrated by pulling my shirt over my head in a trademark celebration.

Only trouble was, I couldn't get it back off again!

I ended up running down the touchline with the shirt over my eyes, the lads mobbing me and then scrambling to get myself sorted out just in time for the restart.

(At the time, I tried to be cool about it, obviously!)

We then got tanked 3-0 at home to Northampton before another 2-1 defeat at Cambridge. We were gutted as we could have sealed promotion that day and it was the first time we'd lost two in a row all season, I think.

Next time out, we were away at Orient and determined there would be no mistakes - we were going up that day and that was that.

It was a beautiful sunny day and it was fitting that Steve Wilkinson put the cross in for me to open the scoring after good work by Kev Kilbane.

I remember pulling my shirt over my head and running almost the length of the pitch to celebrate with the North End fans - there were thousands of them in London that day and they were going mad with celebration.

I think I might have outpaced Kev for a bit *(only a bit!)* in my sprint to the away end - that's how keen I was to get to the travelling fans.

In the second half, the Orient keeper had a bit of a nightmare and fluffed a clearance straight to me about 25 yards out.

Again, it was one where I had a moment or two to think about it but I made up my mind quickly and lobbed it back over him into the empty net.

That made it 28 goals for the season and I couldn't have been happier, not just for me, for everyone. The lads behind the goal were going crazy again - no seating, everyone bouncing about. It was just perfect.

We were up and at the final whistle the North End fans came pouring on the pitch.

Like I say, forget money - you can't buy moments or memories like that.

They were still up in the stand about half an hour later as we came back out and it was just pure celebration, as one; fans, players, staff - everyone all together. Exactly as it should be and absolutely brilliant.

The following week we clinched the title, with a 2-0 away win at Hartlepool and again, there seemed to be PNE in every stand. At the final whistle it was party time once more - so we felt like we had two bites at the cherry with it!

The only downside was that Russ Wilcox and me were getting dropped off as we lived over that way and had gone before the team coach stopped off in Scotch Corner.

Of course, the place was rammed with North End fans and it turned into another big party as the journey home was seriously held up by some celebrations in the local pubs. When we found out, Russ and me were gutted.

The good news was we still had another home game to go and we knew we'd have a chance to celebrate a bit more.

Exeter City came to Deepdale for the last game of the season and by now, the Tom Finney Stand was fully open.

Not only was it packed to the rafters, with just shy of 19,000 on - *in the bottom division don't forget* - but there was probably another 3,000 who were locked out that day. That's how much the people of Preston came out to support us - and it was without doubt one of the best days of my life.

At first, I thought Exeter had brought loads of fans, but then I realised the 'away' section was full of North Enders who had nipped in there, too - but, as ever, with PNE, there was never any trouble. The singing never stopped from start to finish and I managed to put us in front early on with a volley at the Kop end.

Fittingly, Steve Wilkinson grabbed the other goal as we ran out 2-0 winners on a glorious sunny day. It was the perfect end to a perfect season and I'd loved every minute of it. We went off the pitch, then were introduced back out with our names read out to unbelievable noise and it was just . . . incredible.

They are moments that will live with me forever. Goosebumps, every time.

I'd waited a long while to be properly successful and be a big part of winning something and now here it was - with a club I'd grown to love and supporters I'd run through a brick wall for. I just wanted to savour every minute - and I did.

The pictures from that day still have pride of place in my house and I carry them with me on my phone - I'll never get tired of looking at them and remembering what we achieved. It was without a doubt the highlight and the happiest time of my career.

We were able to go out celebrating with the fans and, to be fair, that's something that Gary had encouraged all season; no barriers between team and supporters.

We used to go out as a group to The Sumners after games and talk with fans about the match. It was a great bonding exercise, not just for the players but for everyone who cared about Preston North End. I don't want to keep saying *'these days it's not like that,'* but it really isn't and that's sad.

Sometimes you see players coming in with big headphones on, blanking fans, and that's just wrong in my opinion. At the top, they get wafted in while fans are held back and that link has been lost a bit. I'm not saying it's all modern players, plenty are good lads, but the culture has changed. They're inevitably more removed now from the people who pay their wages and who follow the team through thick and thin.

Obviously, the money in the modern game has contributed to it but, at the heart of things, the players should have a bond with the fans and I'm not sure they've all got that relationship we had with the supporters at Preston. If not, they're missing out.

For me, there was one more highlight to come - the open top bus parade through the town to the Flag Market.

You'll have to forgive me as parts of the day are a bit vague (!) but it was just incredible; so many people, a beautiful day in every sense.

The laughs we had on the bus and the faces of all the fans who turned out to see us - you should be able to bottle it - just pure happiness.

When we got to the Harris Library and then came out onto the steps . . . *well, it just took my breath away.*

There were thousands and thousands of North End fans there - absolutely packed in as far as you could see. It was the first time the club had won the league for about 25 years and you could see what it meant to people.

I know what it meant to me . . . absolutely everything.

To step out into that sunshine and hear the fans singing 'There's Only One Andy Saville' . . . I just filled up with pride. It was probably only a few seconds, but it was almost like time stood still for me at that moment. Just *'wow!'*.

Talking about it now brings it all back like it was yesterday. Totally unforgettable.

The best moment of my football life, without a doubt.

Before I knew it, I was joining in the singing and toasting the fans for their support before we set off round a few - *well, OK, a lot* - of the town's pubs to celebrate.

My missus was driving and when I was handed a bottle of Champagne I made sure I shared it with as many North End fans as possible. I think everyone had a good time that day - to put it mildly.

We all went away for the summer but I couldn't wait to get back to training and get at the higher level - what is now League 1.

Gary signed Micky Holt on a free in the close season but there was no big money arrival up front and when we got going, I was starting every game again.

Unfortunately, it was the complete opposite to the season that had gone before - the goals just weren't coming. I still felt I was contributing to the team but I just wasn't hitting the back of the net. We played Spurs in the League Cup over two legs when I was up against Sol Campbell - a tough game for anyone - but by the end of September we'd only won two games in the league.

Finally, against Millwall on September 30, I got my first goal of the season. Kev Kilbane got down the left and pulled over a cross that I instinctively cracked back into the far corner.

It was a relief and, working on the principle that once you've got one, the goals start to flow, I hoped it would be the start of a decent run.

Sadly, it turned out to be my last goal for North End.

The one thing I can take from it is that it was a great way to sign off - a good strike in a home win at the Town End. I played at a few clubs, but I have to say that was the best home end I ever played in front of.

There were times I'd look at the fans jumping around in there and think: *'God, I wish I was with them!'*

The atmosphere was special and it's something that's very hard to recreate once the terracing has gone and there's a new all-seater stand in its place. I understand the need for progress and - same as Hull - the facilities at Deepdale now are top drawer.

But that old Town End was something special when it was bouncing. The noise, the ticker tape, the scarves, the flags, the games under the old floodlights - it's hard to explain it to people who are too young to be part of it, but if you know . . . you know.

And this is from someone who only played in front of it. Being part of it must have been amazing, what being a proper fan supporting your home town team is all about.

Anyway, a week or so after I ended my goal drought, the club splashed out £300,000 on David Reeves from Carlisle. I've no problem with that, anything that makes us stronger is a good thing.

But it was a shock a couple of weeks later when I was told Wigan had come in for me and the club had accepted a bid. I had a couple of years or so left on my contract and I wanted to see out my career at PNE. That was all I wanted to do.

It had been the scene of my happiest days just a few months earlier and I'd just got 30 goals in the previous season, so I backed myself to come good, even though I'd had a slow start.

To be honest, it was a real kick in the balls.

I almost couldn't believe it when I took the phone call. I know people say *'that's football'* and it's tough, but it still hurt. There wasn't a lot I could do, really.

I didn't want to go to Wigan but the club had agreed a fee and that was that. I ended up winning promotion there that season but didn't score anywhere near the same number of goals as I had done at PNE. It meant though that I'd won promotion at three clubs in consecutive seasons, Birmingham, North End and Wigan.

It's a great achievement, but of those three, the PNE one stands out by a mile.

I wasn't there for as long as I wanted to be, but it left a massive mark on me - I'd seen what an emotional attachment you could have with a club as a player.

And that lasts to this day.

Obviously, I'm a Hull fan, but I'd like to think I'm an honorary North Ender, too.

I'm chuffed that one of the boxes in the Pavilion Stand is named after me and I always check the North End scores and see how they're doing. My dream in a season would be for Hull and PNE to be promoted automatically - that would be just perfect.

I played for quite a few clubs throughout my career but my time at Deepdale is *'The One'*. I feel proud to have been a part of the club's history and to help win a title with a great set of lads, a top manager and incredible fans.

If I could sum it all up in one word it would be . . . *'amazing'*.

And, of course, I'd do it all over again in a heartbeat.

Chapter 10

MIKE ELWISS: WRITTEN IN THE STARS

I suppose it was written in the stars for me and North End - because the first time I ever saw them play was the 1964 FA Cup Final. I wasn't a Preston fan at the time, we were from Doncaster and used to go and watch Donny.

But my dad was able to get Cup Final tickets through his work and he took me down to Wembley as a starry-eyed 10-year-old for the biggest game I'd ever seen.

It was a massive thing and as we were standing near the PNE end, we were cheering them on.

I'll always remember the noise when the teams came out; this great roar that made the hairs on the back of my neck stand up. There were home-made banners everywhere and I'll always remember some guy running on the pitch; he had a white boiler suit on with 'PNE' scrawled all over it in blue.

The less said about the result the better I suppose, but I remember North End had some great players out that day; Alex Dawson, Alan Spavin and the young Howard Kendall. I would never have thought that a few years later, I'd be pulling on that famous shirt and lining up alongside Spav.

Back in Yorkshire, I was gearing up for my 11-plus, which I passed to get into Danum Grammar. It was a fantastic childhood really; I loved football, my family were very supportive and things couldn't have been better.

Donny had a player called Alick Jeffrey who was a brilliant player, who had battled back from two broken legs. *By God, he could ping a ball.*

I can still see him now, getting these balls on a terrible surface, just catching them perfectly on the half-volley. I remember thinking: 'Wow, look at that!' It's those moments of wonder that stay with you forever; perfect technique and just sheer natural ability.

As I got older, I was all geared up to stop on at school and get some qualifications, but I was doing well in the youth teams and clubs were starting to take an interest in me. I could have gone to Manchester City or Sheffield United as an apprentice, but someone suggested going to see Maurice Setters who had just taken over at Doncaster Rovers, who were in the Fourth Division at that time.

I thought: *'Are you crazy? Why would I want to go there when I could go to one of these much bigger clubs?'*

But anyway, I went along to see him and I was really impressed. He said: 'Before you make your mind up, why not come down and train with us for a while?'

They were on my doorstep, so that's what I did and after a fairly brief period, he said: 'Right, don't sign anywhere as an apprentice - we'll take you straight on as a professional.'

Well, not only would this get me out of cleaning a lot of boots and sweeping a lot of floors, I thought the chances of getting in the first team at Doncaster were a bit higher than at Man City (!).

So I packed in my A-Levels and signed on for the tidy sum of £20-a-week - a good wage for a 17-year-old lad.

The thing is, people looking from the outside might say it was *'only Doncaster Rovers'*, but when they're your team and you've spent your childhood watching them, it was a big thing. It meant a lot to me.

Steve Uzelac, who later joined North End, was there too and had come through the school teams and junior ranks with me, so it was good to have a familiar face there at the same time.

Maurice was true to his word and with the season only about 11 games old, I went into the first team for a game against Newport County.

Somehow, I tripped over two chances on the goal-line and they credited me with both of them so I made a scoring start to my career in my first-ever game.

I managed to score a few goals in my first couple of seasons and I remember we played Liverpool in the third round of the FA Cup at Anfield - it's not something you forget really, is it?

Anyway, raggy-arsed Doncaster Rovers got a 2-2 draw against Bill Shankly's champions. We were actually winning 2-1 at half-time before Kevin Keegan - *a Doncaster lad and big Donny fan* - equalised.

The replay was on the following Tuesday afternoon, and had to kick off at 3pm as we couldn't use the floodlights because of the miners' strike. That's the way it was in the 1970s. We lost 2-0, but it was a great experience and I got a call back to the ground on the Friday afternoon where I was asked straight up: 'Now lad, do you want to sign for Liverpool?'

Me: *'Errr, yes please!'*

So that should have been that. I was told we were going over to Anfield the following Tuesday to sign and . . . I never heard any more.

What had happened was the deal should have gone through for £50,000 before I even knew about it. Then it was £70,000 when they told me. Then by the time I was due to sign it had gone up to £80,000.

By that point, Liverpool got fed up of being messed about and pulled the plug.

It was disappointing, but I just got my head down and carried on.

Luckily, Maurice Setters was big pals with Bobby Charlton who was in charge at Deepdale and recommended me to him not long after that. I was still only 19 and at that age, at that time, you didn't know a lot about the world. These days, 19-year-olds are a lot more worldly-wise and have agents and all the rest of it.

In 1974, when I was told I was to get over to North End and sign for them I was a bit like: *'Preston? Where's that?'*

Obviously, I knew all about Bobby Charlton - I'd had his picture on my bedroom wall and everything. So it was a big thing to come over and sign for him, especially as the £60,000 fee was a record at that time.

I look back now and think how amazing it was to have played alongside him and Nobby Stiles. To think that there's me, a scruffy little kid from Doncaster, in the same team photographs as two World Cup winners is just mind-blowing, really.

You're aware of it at the time, of course, but you don't quite take it in until after you've finished playing. The older you get, the more you appreciate it.

And, really, it was brilliant.

Him and Nobby were excellent, really nice people. The only two Englishmen to have won the World Cup and the European Cup, but no airs and graces - especially Nobby, as you can imagine. You couldn't meet a more down to earth fella.

Like a lot of people have said though, I'm not sure Bobby was cut out to be a manager. I remember before my debut against Carlisle at Deepdale, I was very, very, very nervous. I'd come from the Fourth Division to what is now the Championship and I don't think I slept a wink the night before. I was up at about 4am and that was it, pacing around for hours before setting off to the ground as early as I could.

The funny thing is, Bobby was reading out the team in the dressing room and I noticed his hand was shaking like a leaf.

I was gobsmacked, thinking: 'Blimey, if a great man like Bobby Charlton is nervous, what chance have I got?'

However, as soon as the game starts, you forget all the nerves and you're OK. Luckily, I managed to get two goals on my North End debut to earn us a 2-2 draw so that helped me settle in quite quickly. Blimey! The relief that night . . .

One of the things I remember thinking about the squad was that there were a lot more players than we'd had at Doncaster. And there seemed to be a lot of older pros coming to the end of their careers.

One of the younger lads was Mel Holden, who I used to knock around with quite a bit. He was a great lad - *daft as a brush* - and it was absolutely tragic when he died from Motor Neurone Disease at the young age of 26.

The club had put me up in the Tickled Trout for six weeks with Ray Treacy and then after that I went to live with a Mrs Hall in digs on Blackpool Road.

We trained in the mornings and I spent the afternoons exploring the area; going off to Lytham or up Beacon Fell. There was always something for you to do if you looked hard enough for it.

The beauty of playing for Bobby and Nobby was that they just let you get on with it. You went out and you played your own game. Later on, when Harry Catterick took over, he'd say to me: *'Michael, I want you to do this, that and the other.'*

And I'd be on the pitch, during the game, thinking: 'Hang on, where am I supposed to be now?'

I wasn't playing my natural game and by the time I'd thought about the instructions, the ball had gone and sometimes the game had gone too.

I couldn't really play like that, so after about six games I thought: 'Blow this, I'm just going to play my way; off the cuff, play what I see, go where the game takes me.'

I'm not sure he even noticed!

I don't think my style would have fitted in with the modern game as players are a lot more regimented these days. Players have a lot less freedom.

You see subs coming on and they're being given instruction after instruction. Very rarely do you see someone given free rein to just go out and play, like we used to do. It's a lot more tactical these days and it's sad that some of that free spirit has been lost.

Don't get me wrong, I understand the game's moved on and managers have had to move with it, but I think it's lost a bit of character, a bit of its magic, along the way.

That's progress, I suppose.

Anyway, back in my first season, it was really disappointing to be relegated within a couple of months of arriving, but I never regretted the move.

The club was always a nice place to be around; good people, very friendly and a good atmosphere. When we went down, it was just a case of: 'Right, let's get on with it and get back up as soon as possible.'

Obviously, it was a blow, but there was no great panic. On a personal note, I always wanted to go to the top, which in those days was the First Division.

I was still a young player and knew the only way I'd get there was by working hard and doing well for my club.

I was never motivated by money - I don't think anyone was back then. The motivation was a sporting ambition to be the best and to compete with the best.

We weren't paid a fortune and I would have gladly taken a pay cut if it meant getting into the top flight, because that's where I wanted to be.

Yes, North End had taken a step backwards, but I still thought we had a good squad and sooner or later we'd be back up and aiming for the First Division. It was just two steps now, instead of one.

On the pitch, Bobby came out of retirement as a player in Division Three and just oozed class every time the ball came near him - we're talking about one of the world's all-time greatest players here, no matter how old he was by then.

As for Nobby, you'd look at him and jokingly think: 'Seriously - how did you win the World Cup?'

He was never your typical player and by that time he was probably the most unlikely-looking footballer you'd ever seen.

It wasn't just on the pitch either; he wasn't the most stylish bloke. I remember one day he came in for training with one brown shoe on and one black shoe - and he hadn't noticed.

But, in all seriousness, I absolutely loved him and what a player he was; ahead of his time in that defensive midfielder role and with an engine that just kept going and going. I was always glad he was on our side, not theirs, let's put it that way.

And as managers, the pair of them were just totally genuine people - no agendas. They would always tell you what was going on or if someone had come in for you.

A lot of people have said that Bobby in particular, was too nice to be a manager and I think that's right. Deep down, he just wanted to be one of the lads and play football.

I don't think he enjoyed the side of it where you have to be hard with people or maybe make decisions that people aren't going to like.

But I certainly enjoyed working with them and it was a real honour to have been on the pitch with them, too.

I used to play all across the forward line and - *how can I put this?* - defenders in that era weren't shy in letting you know they were there.

To me, if someone came through the back of me in the first five minutes, it spurred me on. I wanted to be the best and I hated getting beat - I still do.

I'm a very bad loser, so no matter how hard or how often I got kicked, I always tried to use it as a positive to drive me on in the game.

We finished ninth in that first season back in Division Three and I was very proud to be named Player of the Year. I can remember receiving the award like it was yesterday, up in the old Supporters' Club and it's something I look back on with great pride - I was really, really touched to get the award.

That summer, Bobby left amid a bit of a transfer row, but to be honest, as players in those days, we didn't know too much about the background - there was no internet or anything. I was sad to see him go, because he was a good man, but when you're a player, you just get your head down and carry on.

Harry Catterick came in and was a big name, because he'd managed Everton. He'd say things and even if I wasn't sure about it, I'd be thinking: *'Well, it must be right - it's Harry Catterick.'*

But players soon work people out and, for me, it was clear his heart wasn't really in it when he came to Preston.

Nobby and Alan Kelly used to take all the training and the only time we'd see Harry in his tracksuit was if the press were coming down.

And that tracksuit was always immaculate - because he'd hardly had it on.

One time, he came in and he'd had his hair dyed black, not a spot of grey anywhere, just jet black all over. What he'd forgotten though was that the pen pics we'd had taken at the start of the season were already published and in circulation, showing Harry with a more realistic swathe of grey.

One of these pictures found its way onto the changing room wall of course, where Tunksy took out a black pen and coloured it in - *a bit like Harry had done, really!*

Sometimes if he'd come up to the training ground at Willow Farm, we'd joke that he was there to do a bit of bird-watching.

I don't want to be too harsh, because he was alright really, but players aren't daft and it didn't take a lot to weigh him up. He wasn't the most committed manager I ever had, let's put it that way. He was always happy to be interviewed by the press though - especially if we'd won.

One time, there was a story that went about that he said he wouldn't be at our game on Saturday because he was supposedly going to look at a player. Rumour was that he went golfing at Southport instead! I don't know if it was true or not, but stranger things have happened.

With Bobby and Nobby, you wanted to get into training because it was fun. But when they said 'right, now it's time to work' - then we really did work. There was no messing about, because we had total respect for them.

We respected Harry too, he was a good manager when all is said and done, but I'm not sure he ever really put in the same dedication as someone like Nobby - and the players knew it.

On the plus side, a certain Alex Bruce came back from Newcastle and straight away, things fell into place for the pair of us.

I loved playing with Brucie and we struck up a great partnership. He was so quick over the first few yards and his movement was just fantastic; he was just so difficult to mark and he was also very strong on the ball, a lot stronger than people realised.

Alex just wanted to score goals and that was it. I wanted to do what I did and it was just a coming together of two working parts that complemented each other almost perfectly. It wasn't something we ever really worked at, there was something instinctive about it really and it was just a really natural football partnership.

We were two people who could read the game reasonably well and bounce off each other. I always say *'you play what you see'* and if you've got any sense about you, you get your head up and you can spot a pass. Movement is the key and Brucie could go from a standing start with a defender on him, to being in space on his own in the blink of an eye. By the time they'd seen where he went - the ball was in the back of the net.

Maybe it was easier in our day, because we weren't weighed down with tactics and instructions - it was just 'go out and play'.

One of the key differences between now and then is the condition of the pitches.

It was always a big thing when we were playing to get on Deepdale at the start of the season. You couldn't wait to see it, all lush and perfect, like a carpet in August and September. Then the weather turned and it just went downhill from there. To be honest, home games weren't so bad - but some of the away pitches . . .

I remember one time, we played at Brentford in the last game of the season and there wasn't a blade of grass on it - it was just dried mud with great big cracks in.

Even at Deepdale though, I remember if you came out of the tunnel and ran towards the Town End, it was sometimes that boggy in places that your foot went right into the pitch and the water came over your boot. We just got on with it, but I wouldn't have minded playing on the pitches they've got today - immaculate all year round.

The other thing I think is different from my era is how much quicker the players are today. I always remember Alan Kelly telling me how much faster things were in our day from Sir Tom Finney's era and I think it's the same again now.

The game just gets faster and faster and the way the North End lads pass the ball around now, I'm not sure we'd be able to keep up.

You look at how good Manchester City were when we played them in the League Cup recently - it really changed my opinion of them as a team. They absolutely worked their socks off and had a gameplan that few teams can live with.

Anyway, back in 1975/76, I managed all 46 league games that season and Brucie wasn't far behind as we were joint top scorers with 15 goals each.

I think that's what you need as a team - strikers who you know can give you that solid foundation of goals up front, then other lads can chip in too. It takes the pressure off when your forwards are scoring and I think that's what we've missed in recent seasons under Alex Neil - a solid 20-goals-a-season man up top who can shoulder that responsibility.

I'm surprised that when North End have been in good positions recently, they haven't gone out and spent big on a striker just to get us over the line. OK, if we don't then go up, we might have to sell a couple of our other better players, but we'd still be in a good position and we'd be able to recoup some money. Over the years we seem to get close, but then don't make that final push. Always so near, yet so far.

It surprises me because Trevor Hemmings is a man who normally gets what he wants and I thought they'd have gone for it a bit more when the opportunity has arisen.

At the same time, I understand the need for financial stability and you always want a healthy club. We've seen what's happened at Bolton, Blackpool and Bury in recent times and everyone knows the normal rules of business don't really apply to football.

So it's good to see North End in a stable financial position compared to so many clubs out there. It's just a shame that they've always been a selling club, going back decades now. Back in 1976, for example, we were doing OK, but we sold Tony Morley to Burnley in January.

They doubled their money on him when he went to Aston Villa, where he won the European Cup and played for England.

Same with Mark Lawrenson and Gary Williams going to Brighton a couple of years later. Lawro was a great player and I remember coming up against him when he'd left - those long gangly legs that just always seemed to nick the ball away.

He started off as a winger before Nobby moved him into defence, where he was brilliant - and he was another one who went on to win the European Cup - so again, it's just sad that the club sold him so early.

Obviously, when you're a player, the finances are nothing to do with you, but it just seemed back then that we always had to sell someone each year to tide us over, which was a real shame.

Lawro played every game in 1976/77 and we only used about 17 players throughout the entire season. It sounds odd these days, but back then you had a nucleus of players and used them every week. There was only one substitute allowed and quite often, they didn't get on.

If you've got the right players, with the right attitude, that want to get out there and play then that's what they'll do. They wouldn't care about going out with a bit of a knock, they just wanted to play.

We weren't interested in 'squad rotation' - you wanted to be out there every week.

You kept things under wraps and said you were fine, unless it was something that was really going to hold you back.

Anyway, we finished sixth that second season under Harry which would have got us in the play-offs these days, but to be honest, I've still got mixed feelings about them.

I think it should be over the long-haul and, let's face it, the play-offs have hardly been kind to North End down the years.

I know they're exciting and they keep the season alive and all that, but if you've just missed promotion by a point and end up losing out to a team that maybe finished 12 points below you, I think you've got every right to be aggrieved.

Back in 1977, despite a reasonable record, over the summer North End decided to dispense with Harry and put Nobby in charge.

I think it was a move that went down well with the players, to be honest. He wasn't a bad bloke, but from a football perspective a lot of people were relieved that he'd gone; we needed more drive, more commitment and Harry just didn't seem to have it.

On the other hand, Nobby was determined to take his chance and we just wanted to get on with it. I think it gave us new impetus.

The whole place lifted and we went on to have a great season, winning promotion and having some wonderful times.

The funny thing is, if people ask me about games and goals and things from those years, I've never been good at remembering them. Some things - goals and incidents - stick in my mind, but overall, I'm useless at recalling things from when I played.

I know I scored about one goal every three games, but I'm not one of those players who has an encyclopaedic knowledge of everything they did. When you're playing, they're just games, one after another. Go out, do your best, hope for a win.

I do remember that season we went up under Nobby as being a brilliant time, playing up alongside Brucie and the pair of us getting 40-odd goals between us, but individual games are lost on me, generally.

Someone told me I played all 46 games in the league and the only other player who managed that was Roy Tunks.

I've got to be careful what I say about Tunksy, because he's a big mate of mine and if I praise him too much it might go to his head *(just kidding, Roy!)*. But he was a great goalkeeper, a real presence, and he's also a fantastic guy.

The funny thing was the opposition always used to get his name wrong when they were reading the teams out on the PA.

It's almost as if when they came round asking for the team before kick-off, someone would deliberately give them a comedy name. (Who would do such a thing??)

Even now, in my phone, he's not down as Roy Tunks . . . it's Ray Turps.

What was a shock for me that season was to go the full season without suspension - I'm quite proud of that, especially as I'd got 18 points by October and if you got 20 you got suspended.

So to go all that way without getting booked again was a near-miracle for me.

I normally got booked for, *errr*, over-exuberance, but quite often I was yapping in the ref's ear all game too and eventually they get sick of it. I watch Ben Pearson now and I know where he's coming from, but I think we could talk to referees a bit more back then.

It was the era of Clive Thomas, Jack Taylor and a guy called Roger Kirkpatrick; look him up if you can, he was an absolute one-off.

So, on best behaviour, I managed to play all season right to the last game against Shrewsbury at Deepdale, when we got a 2-2 draw that wasn't quite enough to send us up straight away.

Some people were on the pitch - they might have thought it was all over, but we still had to wait a couple of days to see whether Peterborough would pip us at the post by beating Wrexham in a re-arranged game.

Some of the directors - and quite a few fans - went over to The Racecourse Ground for the game but I'm not sure my nerves could have taken that. Instead, us players went to the old Guild Club upstairs at Deepdale.

It was either going to be a party . . . or a wake.

Of course, it wasn't on the TV in those days - so it was a case of just waiting, waiting, waiting for the result to come through. Blimey, talk about tense.

And finally - the final score came in: Wrexham 0 . . . *Peterborough . . . 0.*

We'd done it - on goal difference. Yes! Get in!

A fantastic moment and then, almost straight away . . . I just went as flat as a pancake. I was shattered emotionally I think; we'd been so high and had all the waiting and the anticipation and then when it came through, after the initial *'Yes! We've done it!'* it was just a bit of an anti-climax. I'd expected to be jumping around the room, but in reality, it wasn't like that and I don't really know why.

Don't get me wrong, I was absolutely chuffed but I just felt drained. I wasn't bothered about going out and hitting the town, so just went home after a while.

I settled for a big smile and a bigger sense of relief: *'Phew! Thank God for that!'*

Over the next couple of days, people started saying: 'Hey, we're having an open-top bus parade!'

Me: *'Give over, are we heck.'*

But then word came through that it was true and I thought: 'Well, I don't think many people will turn up to see us riding about on a bus.'

Of course, come the day itself - well, it was *absolutely incredible.*

We set off and all along the route there were people on roofs, in trees, on bus shelters, cheering and waving scarves and banners - I'd never, *ever* seen anything like it. It looked like the whole town had come out and I didn't think there'd be anyone left by the time we got to the Flag Market.

But when we arrived . . . it was absolutely rammed - people everywhere.

The noise was incredible. I managed to speak over the microphone, but I'm not sure if anyone could hear me and I'm even less sure I would have found the words to say how I was feeling - *it was just fantastic.*

There's a picture of me with Nobby standing on the Harris steps with this huge crowd behind and even looking at it now, it almost doesn't seem real. The stuff of dreams, really.

To get Player of the Year again that season was just the icing on the cake and again something that I'm very proud of.

It was the perfect end to the perfect season and I was just so pleased to have played a part with such a great bunch of lads and with a manager that we all really liked and respected.

I was looking forward to a new season back in Division Two with North End, but I also knew that there were some big clubs who had been monitoring me. Leeds United were interested, while Aston Villa and Norwich had watched me all season.

It was a chance to play in the top flight and, in all honesty, I thought I was going to Villa - a massive First Division team at the time.

But then I got a phone call from my old boss Maurice Setters who told me Crystal Palace were interested. They were still in the Second Division, but he said: *'Look Mike, they're really going places. They've got this great young manager called Terry Venables, some really good players and they're an up-and-coming club for sure.'*

My mind was spinning with it all, so I went on holiday with my brother, while I pondered what to do next.

I don't know how he found us, but out of nowhere, Terry Venables turned up to our hotel in Spain - he brought a physio and all the trappings for me to sign. I thought: 'Blimey, he's keen!'

Obviously, I was really impressed with him and I knew the crowds that Palace were getting in those days were really good - around 25-30,000, compared to 10-12,000 at Deepdale.

What probably swung it was that he said: 'Sign now and if you change your mind and don't want to do it when you get home, we'll just rip everything up, no problem.'

He was pretty persuasive and there was something about Terry - *the way he spoke, his vision* - that you could just tell he was going to be successful.

So away I went to London. I had mixed feelings, because I'd had such a great time at Preston and it was such a good club, but at the time there was this big thing about Palace being the *'Team of the 80s'*.

They had people like Vince Hilaire and Kenny Sansom coming through and I thought they'd have a really good stab at promotion.

As it turns out, I wasn't wrong - but sadly, things didn't work out so well for me personally.

Terry was a lot more tactical than I'd been used to, but I played up front with a lad called Dave Swindlehurst and he just used to let us get on with it.

In team meetings, he'd go right through the team discussing things, then he'd get to us two and say: 'Oh, I'm not asking you pair - you'd only say the ball doesn't come up fast enough!'

And he was right, that's exactly what we'd have said.

It was all very well this nice passing in midfield, but when you're up top you just wanted it quick before you got closed down again.

He was a great manager though and I think if Palace had kept hold of him for a few more years, they would have achieved great things. As it was, we went up as Champions under Terry that season, but I only managed 20 games for them.

On the plus side, I did have the pleasure of living with John 'Budgie' Burridge for a while and just thinking about those days makes me laugh out loud.

What a character he was - and still is, actually. Completely bonkers.

For those who may not remember him, Budgie once climbed up and sat on his own crossbar during a game when Palace were beating Ipswich 4-0 - that's the kind of guy he was. I'd come home some nights and be sat watching the TV when Budgie would come in with a big carrier bag full of goalkeeping gloves.

'Try these on Mike,' he said, *'What are they like?'*

And he'd be launching balls, bits of fruit, whatever he could get his hands on to throw at me across the lounge.

I'd be like: 'Yes, Budge - they're grand.'

'OK, cheers Mike. Now, try these - what are they like?'

Same again, stuff going all over the place. Then he'd be asking me to throw things for him to catch, diving around in the living room, furniture going everywhere.

And this would go on for ages - when all I wanted to do was watch the telly!

He was a total one-off, John, but a great guy and a fantastic keeper who played until he was 46.

Funnily enough, quite soon after I arrived at Palace, I was back at Deepdale for a league game against North End.

I ended up scoring the winner in a 3-2 victory and, while it was strange to be back at Deepdale with the opposition, my attitude was that I was a Palace player - so you just have to do your job. I can't remember how I celebrated when I scored, but I don't get this thing about not celebrating that some players do these days. I think some of them are patently false anyway, but for me when you score a goal, you celebrate.

Of course, I wanted North End to do well, I always looked for their results and I was really pleased they had a good season - but, in that moment, the ball hits the back of the net and you're chuffed.

Especially as it was past Ray Turps (!).

Things were going well, but everything changed for me in an instant in a game away at Burnley. I was just chasing down a lousy ball that Steve Kember put through, there was nothing on it really.

But as I put my left leg down, the full-back hit me from the back and the side on that standing leg.

Well . . . that was it.

My foot stayed in the ground, my body twisted round and I knew there and then that I'd done something serious.

My ligaments had just been shattered; it was the anterior cruciate ligament, the medial ligament and the cartilage - as bad as it could get.

It was a mess. I remember Barry Case, who used to be the surgeon for North End, having a look at it and he just shook his head.

The experts can manipulate it by putting their hands behind your leg and pulling it forward to see how loose it is - mine nearly hit him in the face.

I went to see three surgeons; one in Manchester, one in London and one in Cambridge and they all said they could fix it. So I went for an op and they said: *'Oh yes, you'll be right now.'*

I worked hard to get back into training, but as soon as I did a five-a-side it just gave way again. I went for another operation, then another - *my knee is just a criss-cross of scars now* - but none of them worked.

The bottom line is, they just didn't know what they were doing at that time.

I could run straight, but I couldn't turn and twist, it would just give way.

Despite this, I somehow made it back into the Palace first team and managed to score one of my most memorable goals - a header against Newcastle from outside the 18-yard box. Any header I scored would be pretty memorable, but that one just flew in and I remember the Newcastle keeper saying: 'That's one of the best goals I've ever had put past me!'

I hadn't been scoring before that, but suddenly I was bagging a few goals, even though I wasn't really involved in the games, because I knew I couldn't do what I wanted to - the knee wouldn't let me.

I started trying to keep out of trouble in games and I think defenders thought: 'Well, we don't need to worry about him.' But then I'd be in space and manage to knock one in. It was a strange, strange situation. Eventually though, it got to the point where I thought: 'No, I can't carry on like this.'

Palace went up to the First Division as Champions, but I never managed to play for them in the top flight.

The following season, I came back to North End on loan, but I was useless.

It was great to be back at Deepdale and I scored a few goals - three in eight starts - but I couldn't do what I wanted to do. I'm told I scored in my last-ever appearance - a 3-2 defeat at Cambridge - but in all honesty, I can't remember it.

I couldn't compete and, really, I was a waste of time. I hadn't come back as the player that I had been before. I wasn't contributing properly.

I always liked to be involved in games, going in where it hurt, but I just couldn't do that any more.

I wasn't in a good place mentally because I knew deep down, it was over - I was done, finished.

I've never got over that and I never will do.

I was only 27. I had a lot more to do, a lot more to achieve and I wanted to do the best I could and see where it took me. It was very hard to come to terms with and I was just lost for a while. Everything had been taken away from me and I was now looking at a very different future from the one I'd anticipated.

There was no big insurance pay-out or anything in those days, I think I got about £1,500 and that was it. Any money I'd made from transfers or whatever, I'd put into my pension pot for when I was older, so I had to wait for that.

Anyway, I'll put my violin down now . . !

It was time to get a 'proper job' so I came back to Preston and bought a milk round.

I did that for three years, but to be honest, I hated it.

It wasn't the early mornings or the deliveries - I quite enjoyed those bits. But it was a seven-day-a-week job, collecting money was a pain and in the end I knocked it on the head and started working in the dairy where I got the milk from.

I ended up running the place for many years and then stayed in the dairy industry right up until retirement. So I can't complain and I've had a good career after football - I just had to start a few years earlier than I'd hoped for.

I also had the good fortune to marry the daughter of former PNE chairman Keith Leeming - Olive and I have been together for nearly 40 happy years now. Keith was a real stalwart for North End through some tough times in the 1980s and he was a brilliant bloke, sadly missed.

These days, I really enjoy being part of the PNE Former Players Association and I still go to every home game now to cheer the lads on.

Like everyone else, I'm just desperate for us to have even one season up in the Premier League - I think that would whet people's appetite's and set the club up financially for many years ahead.

Once you've been up there, I think it's much more likely that we'd be able to get back up even if we came down straight away at first.

Deepdale is a fantastic stadium that would grace the Premier League and you just know that promotion would really get the people of Preston back supporting their team.

With the budget we've got, I think we've have done a good job of keeping up with the pace of developments on and off the pitch. It's frustrating that we've not been up in the Premier League yet, but if we keep battling away, I'm sure our time will come.

As for my playing career, North End was just a brilliant time for me and everyone who was there will never forget those golden days.

I'm really, really proud to have played for such a great club.

I have so many fond memories of running out of the tunnel, Nobby in the old dug-out, the Fulwood End in the sunshine, wearing that famous white shirt and playing with Brucie and the lads.

If I could press pause and rewind, I'd just spend my life doing it over and over again.

But I'll settle for doing it once - and I wouldn't have missed it for the world.

Chapter 11

BRIAN O'NEIL: ON SONG

Ever since I was young, I always wanted to be . . . a singer. What? You were expecting me to say 'footballer'? Aye, well that as well, obviously.

But I've never needed to be asked twice to get up and sing.

There's a reason for it, that I'll come on to later, but let me say this right at the top - if you ever need *'Sittin' on the dock of the bay'* with a wee Scottish twang . . . I'm your man.

Hairbrush/microphone in hand, I grew up in a big family, the youngest of five children in Erskine near the mouth of the Clyde in Glasgow - all big Celtic fans.

My dad Robert was in the scaffolding business and ran one of the local football teams that my brother John played in. He was four years older than me and I was the pain-in-the-backside little bro who'd tag along for training.

Our John was a good player, who had a particular knack for getting in fights and being sent off, so it was always interesting to watch him in matches and see whether he'd last the full 90 minutes!

When I was around 10, I played for Erskine Boys Club and we had a good side (Derek Lilley, who went on to play for Leeds and Dundee United played for us, too).

After a couple of years, I was asked to join Celtic Boys Club at Under-12 level, which was a big commitment, because it was a fair old trek from where we lived to Celtic Park.

My dad was brilliant though; he made sure I always got to the training sessions if he was around. If not, it was two bus journeys - Erskine to Glasgow, Glasgow to the East End - twice a week. Matches were on a Sunday, so my mum and dad were always around then, but I was always grateful - and lucky - to have such a supportive family.

Things took off from there really and after a while I made it into the Scotland Schoolboys team, which was a good side - we won the old Home Internationals and beat England 3-1 at Tannadice. Just thought I'd drop that in!

Then in 1989, the Under-16 World Cup was held in Scotland and Craig Brown picked me for the squad. It started off low-key, but as we progressed, crowds started getting bigger and bigger.

By the time we played East Germany in the Quarter Final at Pittodrie, there was virtually a full-house - around 20,000 people for a youth game - so it was a fantastic experience.

We then played Portugal in the semi-final at Tynecastle in front of another big 29,000 crowd - they had to delay the kick-off because so many people turned up.

Of course, you don't know anything about the opposition at the time, but looking back they had people like Luis Figo and Abel Xavier playing for them. Luckily, I managed to get the goal in a 1-0 win to send us to the final, so that was another great night, because they'd been favourites to win the tournament.

It's funny because although it was a big thing to be playing in front of these crowds at such a young age, I was just loving it. I wasn't fazed or anything, it was a case of 'just get on with it'.

By the time the final came around - *Scotland in a World Cup final in Glasgow* - you can imagine the buzz about the place.

Around 51,000 turned up at Hampden to see us against Saudi Arabia, so we were carried along by this incredible wave of support, 2-0 up and absolutely flying at half-time.

Early in the second half, they got one back and - *uh, oh!* - things got a little bit edgy.

But then we got a penalty - a big chance to make it 3-1 and probably game over.

The only thing was . . . it was me to take it. I swear I wasn't nervous at all, that wasn't the problem.

The problem was, I wasn't very good at penalties.

To be fair, it was actually a good effort, hard to the keeper's right . . . but he went the right way and saved it. *Agh!* What can you do? I kept my head up but they got it back to 2-2, then extra time and then . . . penalties.

Paul Dickov missed our first kick and one of their lads missed too, so it came down to sudden death - proper squeaky bum time. Craig looked around and asked who wanted to take it.

Of course, stupid me, I put my hand up.

Having missed one in the game, old Broon was probably thinking: *'Oh God, Brian, no . . .'*

But to be fair no-one else was rushing forward, so I stepped up.

And . . . it was a TERRIBLE penalty. Awful.

Low to the keeper's left, but not hit hard enough and nowhere near the corner. Gut-wrenching agony in that moment - that's all I can describe it as.

They scored theirs and that was that. That's football, one kick - all over. Brutal. I was absolutely gutted, *but hey*, that's the game.

It would have been amazing to win it, but it was a great experience and I looked at all the positives I could take from it all.

On top of everything else, I'll never forget getting some kind words from the great Pele at the end. He was one of the guests at the tournament and when the organisers asked him to pick out five players for the future he named me as one to watch out for.

Praise doesn't get much higher than that for a young lad, really!

Pele knew *my* name.

I'm not sure if he remembers me now *(!)* but he did at the time, so I'll take that all day long.

After that, I got my head down and worked hard at Celtic, who I'd joined after leaving school at the tender age of 15. Blimey, the stuff we used to have to do; all the kit, all the boots, sweeping up, everything.

When I think about the grounding that we had - it just wouldn't happen nowadays.

The stick we used to get off the first team players was unbelievable, but it was all part of growing up. You knew you were going to get it and you had to stand up to it.

When you eventually got round to playing, there was just the first team and the reserves. That was it.

So you were maybe 16 or 17, in with guys in their early 20s and above, which was a tough task, but it didn't half help prepare you for the 'real' thing.

It may not look it on a flipchart, but it was so much better than the academy set-up that is around now.

You look at lads playing Under-18 football against other Under-18 sides and you just think: *'What's the point of this?'*

It's pointless. It's all very well getting lads looking good in an academy, but the aim has to be to prepare people for the first team and being in with lads their own age every week is not going to help when they're thrown in against real men who've been around the game a long time.

You look at people like Ethan Walker and he's got all the talent in the world, but he needs experience of that horrible, nitty-gritty, real-world environment of mixing it with men to help him bridge the gap to the first team.

Playing among lads your own age in an academy only takes you so far; it's all very pretty, but the real thing is an ugly old beast that you need to be prepared for.

Luckily, Celtic have always had a great reputation for bringing through young players and the legendary Billy McNeil put me in the team when I'd just turned 19. Billy was a great, great man, a Celtic legend and a brilliant manager.

Again as an example of what things were like, if you saw Billy coming along the corridor towards you, you had to tense up your stomach muscles because you knew what would happen next.

He'd give you a dig in the stomach every time and if you took it well he'd say: *'Good lad!'*

That was one of his wee tests. If you got a *'good lad!'* from the boss, you came away and you felt great. You puffed your chest out, y'know?

It's just the way things were and I wouldn't have had it any different, to be honest.

Liam Brady took over after Billy and he was brilliant in training even then - just oozing class even when he was around 40 years old.

When I got in the team I had some great times on the pitch; I'll be honest, scoring a last-minute winner against Rangers at Ibrox right in front of the Celtic fans takes some beating.

It's the kind of stuff you dream of, isn't it? Like a North End fan scoring against Blackpool at Bloomfield Road - you never, ever forget that feeling.

We had Paolo Di Canio there too and he was an incredible guy, what a player and what a presence. One time we had our Christmas party in this big fancy hotel, and someone came round and said Paolo would like to see us all with our wives in this room he'd got set up.

So we all trooped in and he's there, all tanned, hair slicked back, looking a million dollars. In pidgin English, he makes this speech, thanking all his teammates and saying how much everyone means to him.

Then he invites all the wives up, gives them a peck on the cheek and presents them with a little silver trinket each - what a guy, an absolute class act.

Anyway, by 1994/95, Tommy Burns had taken over as manager and I was playing in virtually every game. We got to the Scottish Cup final, but in the build-up, I was marking Paul McStay in a practice session.

Paul was my hero growing up, an unbelievable player and a lovely guy. That day, he did this little shimmy and as I tried to move, I felt something go in my knee.

At that time, they didn't do scans straight away, but it turned out I'd done my cruciate ligament - as everyone knows, that's a serious injury.

But back then, I was sent to a general orthopaedic surgeon to have the operation, not a knee specialist. I'll be honest, my knee has never really been right since. I was never able to get the quad muscles back to how they had been and I always had a problem with it.

I don't understand why clubs - even in those days - don't look to protect their investments in players by getting them the best treatment available.

Footballers are assets to clubs, why don't they look after them properly?

Years later at Preston, I had an operation with a top guy and he could tell straight away that the surgery I had while I was at Celtic had not been very good.

But I played with it for the next 10 years, so yes, that rankles me a bit.

After that op, it took me a long time to get back to full fitness and in March 1997 I joined Nottingham Forest on loan at the same time as Pierre Van Hooijdonk signed for them permanently.

Stuart Pearce was manager at the time with Dave Bassett helping him out.

I'm not sure Pierre was Dave's type of player; he was always trying to get the big man to chase balls down the channels.

Pierre would just say: *'Why do I need to run out there? Just give it to my feet.'*

A lot of people had the wrong idea about him at the time, but he was a fantastic player - and he was only saying what everyone else thought.

That was the year Forest got relegated from the Premier League, but I really enjoyed it there and wanted to go back permanently.

They came in for me at the end of that season, but Aberdeen wanted me in Scotland and outbid Forest.

I was still saying *'no'* to the Dons but in the end, I said to Roy Aitken, the manager there at the time: *'If you get 'X' in wages then I'll sign.'*

It was the only time I ever did that and, in truth, it was because I didn't think he'd be able to do it. When he came back and said that he'd sorted out the money, I said: *'Oh, er, great - that's fantastic.'*

But inside I was like: 'Oh, bugger. What do I do now?'

So I ended up going there for all the wrong reasons and I learned a lesson from it.

From then on, my moves were all about football reasons and developing my career - the money was a side issue.

I was 24/25, married by this point and we'd just had our first child, so it was a big thing to move the family up there and, in truth, I never settled and maybe took my eye off the ball, football-wise.

I played a lot of games for them, but Roy left as manager and a year later I was on the move again. It was a good contract to walk away from, but I wasn't bothered by that - I wasn't enjoying my football. That was the important thing.

I got invited to go on trial at Kaiserslautern, who were looking for a back-up centre half. I did OK and off the back of that trial the great Otto Rehhagel recommended me to one of his old players, Wolfgang Wolf, who was managing Wolfsburg.

Yes, the manager of 'Die Wolfe' was called Wolfgang Wolf - and the general manager was a guy called Peter Panda. I'm not making this up, honestly.

So I went to train with them for three days, during which time they kicked the crap out of me, before we played a local team in a pre-season friendly.

We won 10-1 and I scored a hat-trick, including a header, a tap-in and one from about 35 yards. They must have been thinking: 'Blimey - who's this guy? Does he do this every week?'

By the time they discovered the truth the deal was done, for about £450,000 danke very much. No regrets at all, I loved my time over there.

Off the pitch, it was a real culture shock because this was about 1998 and there was no internet, no mobile phones, no British TV or anything - it was a different world and a different culture. Wolfsburg is based on the Volkswagen plant and it was a very working-class club, a bit like North End - right up my street.

I was playing at the back there as a libero, the games were more technical and everyone knew their jobs.

If you didn't do it, there were no excuses, people dug each other out quite openly and there was none of this hiding behind things - they let you know.

That's exactly as it should be - it toughens you up mentally and makes sure no-one gets a big ego or anything.

You don't see that plain-speaking attitude so much these days - players giving each other rollockings on the pitch. It's something we're losing from the game and it's a shame. You can't be biting your lip if someone's not doing their job and it's letting the team down - you've got to let them know about it.

If it upsets them - tough - they should do their job properly next time, y'know?

Our first game was against Bayern Munich at home - Stefan Effenberg, Giovane Elber - all the big players. We lost 1-0 but it was a full house and fantastic to be a part of. Perhaps the biggest thing was the training; the quality and intensity was spot on.

And, blimey, it was aggressive.

I'd like to say Wolfgang Wolf's bark was worse than his bite, but he was hard as nails and used to kick the hell out of everyone in training.

He didn't speak English but if I thought I could get away with swearing at him in training, I was wrong. He brought in an interpreter and fined me anyway!

I had a really good time out there and in our first season we qualified for the UEFA Cup, where we had a good run the following year before getting knocked out by Atletico Madrid.

I feel I grew up in Germany and as my contract came to the end, I was talking to the club about renewing, while Hertha Berlin were also showing an interest.

However, Stefan Schnoor was looking to come back to Germany from Derby and Jim Smith had already spoken to me a couple of times about going there.

Wolfsburg were interested in him and in the end an exchange deal was sorted out.

I was on my travels again - swapping one manager who barely spoke English for another! Jim was a great guy - you could have the biggest barney with him in the world and then it was all forgotten about. He was a proper football man.

My debut for Derby was against Manchester United at Pride Park and, looking back, it turned out to have a big impact on my career.

In the very first minute, Roy Keane - *who else?* - came in with a really high tackle on my knee.

It was a terrible, *ridiculous* challenge, but he didn't even get a yellow card for it. It was unbelievable, really.

I knew he'd done some damage but because it was my debut, I thought: 'Well, I can't go off - I'll stay on until half-time.'

At the break, the physio looked at it and just said: *'Woah, sorry Brian, we'll have to get a sub on.'*

He could tell it was bad straight away. I went for a scan and had a third degree tear in my medial ligament - out for 12 weeks.

That Roy Keane tackle probably had more impact on my career than tearing my cruciate, because of everything else that came from it down the years. So many later problems were down to it.

I can look myself in the eye and say I've never gone in to hurt anybody, but I'm not sure he can do the same thing. He probably thought he was just doing his job, *but . . .*

Anyway, I had to keep myself as fit as I could, but the training at Derby was just so bad, it was unreal.

To be fair, Jim wasn't a coach, so he'd leave it to others and it really wasn't up to standard. Even in the warm-ups, the application was so slack-arsed; people laughing and joking, it was really poor.

Steve McClaren had left just before that and they'd not replaced him - you could see why they were struggling at the bottom of the Premier League.

They weren't lacking good players; Stefanio Eranio was there and he was fantastic, different class and always worked hard, too - a great guy. On the other hand, Georgi Kinkladze had all the talent in the world, but he didn't want to run, even in training.

What's the point of being that good if you're not going to work?

I'd rather have less talented players who are going to run their balls off every day and give everything for the shirt.

As for me, the knee injury hadn't really gone away and, with one or two other problems, I ended up having eight operations over two years there. It's always bad when it's like that and you know people are doubting you behind the scenes.

During that time, the club got relegated, Colin Todd took over, then John Gregory came in.

Jim and Colin had been good guys, but John Gregory wasn't my kind of fella at all; he's a bit like Marmite, to be fair - some people love him, but it's a *'no'* from me.

The only thing I can say for him is that the training improved.

Derby is a great club but around that time, they started to have financial troubles and one day, as about six of us were having lunch, the Chief Executive came down and just handed us all these letters.

There was me, Craig Burley and a few others and the letter said they wanted to come to an agreement for the remainder of our contracts - they wanted to pay us off.

That was bad enough, but the terms were just ludicrous. No-one would have accepted it in any line of work.

When I said no, they stopped my wages (!) which was a ridiculous thing to do. They were doing it to all the lads though - I've never known anything like it.

Rather than go to the PFA, I called in a specialist contract lawyer and we ended up issuing a winding up order against the club unless they paid me. Unsurprisingly, that upped the ante a fair bit and got things moving.

While it was being sorted out, I was training on my own and somehow Craig Brown heard about it and invited me up to Preston. It was obvious I was leaving Derby, but I couldn't sign because of the transfer window.

Harry Redknapp was keen to take me to Portsmouth, but I'd had enough of moving about and wanted to put down some roots.

North End were having a bit of a tough time under Craig, but as soon as I got into training I could see what a great set of lads they were.

The ITV Digital deal had just collapsed so Derek Shaw was playing on that a bit, as you can imagine. In the end I said: *'Look, I don't care about the money, I just want a bit of security. I'll gladly take less money if you give me a longer contract.'*

So I signed for two-and-a-half years, moved my family up to Lancashire and never looked back.

Jonny Gould signed around that time and I'd been in a few Scotland squads with him, so we became big pals - he's a really clever guy, but daft as a brush too and great company. It's fantastic to see him back on the staff now at Deepdale, because he's got so much to offer.

I'm not sure how many people know this, but Gouldy was a right-back up until he was 19. Then he had such a nightmare in one game, they put him in goals and the rest is history.

I still can't imagine him as a full-back personally - not with those legs!

We used to have some great rows, but there was never anything personal in it. It was maybe something that I picked up in Germany, but I was never one to shy away from telling someone if I thought they were doing something wrong.

One time in a game at Deepdale, the ball kept going through and Gouldy was never coming out to collect it. At half-time I said to him: *'Hey, any chance of you coming off your flipping line?'*

He said: 'You what?'

I said: 'They keep passing it through and you're just standing there. Why the flip aren't you coming out and clearing it?'

He paused for a second and then gave me probably the most honest answer I ever heard in a changing room: *'I'm not coming out . . . because I'm not very good at it.'*

Everyone just cracked up, but that was Gouldy; he could be the angriest man in the world, but then 30 seconds later, he'd be laughing and joking again - a great bloke.

Mind you, he still blames me for his departure from North End a few years later.

I used to room with him and could always talk him round when he was getting all het up about things. One time though, I was injured and he was in with Chis Lucketti.

Gouldy had a row with Craig about something or other and ended up pushing a hand-written transfer request under his door.

Twenty minutes later, he got another hand-written piece of paper shoved back from Craig in return.

It just said: *'Request granted!'*

Why is it my fault? Because Gouldy says if I'd have been there, I'd have been able to talk some sense into him! *Oh yeah, right . . .*

Back at the start, the biggest thing that struck me when I arrived was how much the lads wanted to train. They wanted to work hard, do things properly and when you looked around, there were some very, very good players in the squad.

Obviously, Ricardo Fuller was there and I knew all about him from watching Scottish football. As everyone knows, he was a hell of a player - just give him his own ball and watch him go. But there were others too; Eddie Lewis was a phenomenal left winger and in the middle there was Paul McKenna.

I think Kenna is one of the most under-rated players that I've ever seen - such a massive talent.

People maybe look at his height and underestimate him, but he was one of the best in the air that you'll see; he had a fantastic spring and was so, so strong.

I've no idea why someone didn't take him to the Premier League, but he showed great loyalty to Preston right up to the later stages of his career.

I was really surprised that Davie Moyes, knowing how good he was, didn't take him to Everton when he left, because he would have fitted into that team perfectly.

It was North End's gain and I really enjoyed playing with him and still keep in touch with him now. He was a cocky wee sod though - in fact, he still is!

But you need that on the pitch and me and him were always in the referee's ear during the game: *'Ref, what about this? Ref, you're not going to let him do that, are you?'*

All the way through, but we did it cleverly. If we could see him getting naffed off with one of us, the other one would have a go for the next 10 minutes.

There's a difference between chipping away at the officials and bawling in their faces - that just doesn't work.

And we looked after each other; if someone did something to one of you on the pitch the other one would give a little nod and go get the fella back.

So straight away, I could tell this was going to be one of the happiest times in my career because the changing room was so good. I'd known Craig since I was 15 and he hadn't changed a bit. OK, there were things he thought were important that maybe drove some lads mad, but he stuck to them and had that air of discipline about him.

He had some odd habits though. He'd sometimes just wander across a pitch while a game was taking place, just pottering about.

After training one time, Grezza, Cressy and Kenna were practising penalties - smashing them in.

And all of a sudden, I just saw Craig wander over and start chatting to a fella who was watching training.

Craig was sort of leaning with his arm on the goalpost, back to the pitch, casual as you like, while the lads were trying to take these kicks.

I was thinking: *'What's he doing? He really shouldn't be standing there.'*

Well, of course, Kenna swears to this day he didn't mean it . . . but he stepped up and leathered one right on the back of Craig's head.

Bam! He went absolutely flying, face first amid a volley of effs and jeffs: *'Ooh ya wee bugger! Who was that? Kenna? Kenna?!'*

Obviously, Paul was protesting his innocence and trying to keep a straight face: 'Sorry boss! It was an accident.'

The lads were all creasing up as Craig picked himself up and shouted: *'I know you didn't flipping mean it, ya wee sod ye . . . or else you'd have flaming missed!'*

Or words to that effect - even cuddly Craig Brown could break out the swear words at times. Especially if he'd just been smacked on the back of the head by Kenna.

But he had an amazing eye for a player - just look at some of the people Craig brought in. Riccy, Eddie, Claude Davis, Youl Mawene, Callum Davidson - some of the best recruitment I've ever seen over a short space of time.

Callum was like me, he'd had a few injuries and just wanted to settle down somewhere and play, but what a top, top professional he was.

Getting Youl in was another piece of classic Craig business and what can you say about Youl?

Not only is he one of the best players I ever played with, but he's the nicest guy you could meet. He's one of my best friends and like family to me. The fact that the fans still sing his name more than 10 years after he left says everything.

And he was on a free transfer don't forget - what a signing and what a top, top man.

But despite all the talent, when I arrived, the team was having a bad run.

In my first game, I was on the bench for a home defeat by Rochdale in the FA Cup where we got beat 2-1 and Paul Simpson, of all people, scored the winner.

I didn't come on and, to be honest, I was thinking: 'Thank God for that.'

I got in for the following game and after that things picked up and we ended up finishing mid-table. I think Ricardo had started that season on fire, but did his knee just before I joined. If we'd had him all season, we'd probably have done a lot better in that campaign, but who knows?

I got injured myself towards the end of my first season there and was laid up after an operation. While I was recovering, I decided to tackle something I'd had all my life - a stammer.

The way I played, people are maybe surprised to learn about it, but there's no shamc in it or anything.

When I was at North End and not playing in games, they'd ask me to do the commentaries sometimes, but I always said no because I knew my stammer would come out. That summer, when I was recovering from an operation, I went up to Scotland to do a course to try to tackle it.

It's called the McGuire Programme and it's one of the best things I've ever done - but also one of the weirdest; we spent two days just focusing on our breathing, which was actually a really interesting thing to do. I remember when I was at Celtic, we used to go to supporters' events and things and I'd always get out of speaking by breaking into song: 'Altogether now, *Sittin' on the dock of the bay . . .'*

To be fair, it always went down a lot better than anything I'd have had to say anyway!

The stammer hadn't really affected my life - one or two people had made jokes about it early on, but I was big enough and ugly enough to laugh it off. However, I was with people who had been really hard hit by it and seeing the changes the sessions made for them was incredible. It really was quite emotional.

One of the tasks we were set was to go out at 3pm on a Saturday afternoon and talk to people. Well, I was getting better with the talking - but I was way more happy to sing, so if anyone remembers seeing a good-looking crooner in the middle of Stirling in 2003, yes, that was me.

'Thistles Shopping Centre . . . you were a great audience, thank you very much!'

Back at Deepdale, maybe the one thing we were lacking under Craig was the intensity in training; if you get that, it carries over into games. If things are a bit lax, it spreads and people start to drop off things a bit. You need to be on it all day, every day. There's no doubt when we clicked, we were a very good side though.

The game people probably remember from that period is when we beat Burnley 5-3 at Deepdale just before Christmas, the season after I joined.

I know Blackpool is THE derby but Burnley are still Lancashire rivals and the atmosphere that day was just fantastic.

The weather was all over the place, they had a good side and it was a case of: 'Right, let's get at it and may the best team win - no prisoners taken.'

Mike Dean was the ref and it was a cracking game, wasn't it? Everyone got stuck in and Riccy was virtually unplayable that day, it showed he was back to his absolute best. I remember Gouldy made a great save from Glen Little at 3-3, we went straight down the other end and Riccy got his third, before Dave Healy finished it off.

I loved those days; proper games of football between two sides going for it. It was brilliant - but it's always a lot easier to say that when you've won!

That game showed how good we could be under Craig, but we never really clicked with the consistency you need and that was really disappointing.

I think the team got changed about a lot and by the build-up to the following season, the atmosphere around the squad had gone downhill a bit.

Ricardo was on his way out in a big money move and, don't get me wrong, none of the lads begrudged him that at all.

But it dragged on and on and started to have an effect on the changing room. It wasn't Ricardo's fault, he's a great lad, but the deal should just have been done and everyone could have moved on.

Instead, there were problems, delays and everything was in limbo.

Riccy started to come in late once or twice maybe and people like me, Grezza and Chris Lucketti were picking him up on it: *'Hey, what's going on? You can't be late, you know that.'*

'Ahh, well . . .'

'Never mind 'ah well'. If you've got a problem with your move, it's not our flipping problem. That's your problem with the club, not this changing room. You've still got to do your job. Sort yourself out.'

Then Claude came in late too and again us older lads were like: 'What? We can understand Ricardo to a degree, but what's it got to do with you? You can't come in late. We're not having it.'

So it wasn't a good atmosphere around the club at all at that point.

You don't need it - especially at the start of a season when everyone should be at the freshest and pulling together. It just felt wrong.

We went down to Gillingham and Riccy played, but it was almost as if he just wanted to show he was fit. Not long after that, the move finally went through, but the atmosphere still wasn't great. I don't think Craig was happy with the way things had been done, we'd not started too well and it wasn't a great time.

We got beat at home in a TV game when Grezza, of all people, missed a penalty and it just felt like things were conspiring against us. Everything seemed like hard work and nothing was going for us.

The following game Craig got sent off away at Brighton, which shows how things must have been getting to him, because it was so out of character. When when we got back . . . he had gone. It was a shame because everyone liked him, but there were obviously things that had been going on that he wasn't happy about.

When Billy Davies took over, the first thing he said was that he was only going to be in charge temporarily while the club found a new manager. He said he would be going with Craig as soon as it was sorted out. But then he put on his own training sessions and - *wow* - the intensity just went up tenfold.

I don't think I've come across any better in my entire career.

It was back to being like it was at Wolfsburg, or Celtic under Tommy Burns; very uptempo, big demands on you, very strict, no messing about.

When that happens, it's no coincidence that teams improve and results pick up, so it was no surprise when he got the job full time. You get your training right, people start demanding more of each other and you were really pushing people, digging teammates out if they weren't working hard enough.

They'd start chipping back, but Billy would step in and say: *'Hey, what are you moaning for? He's flaming right! Shut the hell up and work harder.'*

People knew exactly where they stood and it simplified everything: just do your job. He didn't indulge anyone, everyone got it exactly the same - older pros or young lads - he didn't care if he upset anyone: *'Just do your job.'*

It was fantastic. The demands were high, but so were the rewards.

We used to start games like a house on fire and just blow teams away before they even knew what had hit them sometimes.

Kick-off. Bang. We're on it. Can you cope with us? No? Right, move over. Job done.

I remember Sunderland coming to Deepdale under Roy Keane and they were right at the top of the league on a long unbeaten run. We just couldn't wait to get at them; Cressy got a hat-trick in the first half and that was that - 3-0 up at half-time. We weren't getting beat from there, even if they did make a game of it in the second half.

I think they were absolutely shell-shocked in that first half, but we just had this belief that we were going to go out and beat everybody. Listen, Carlo Nash was great for us, but it must have been a dream to be a goalkeeper in that team.

The entire focus was on getting at the opposition, going forward all the time, pressing them with incredible intensity - never giving them time to think or get a minute's peace. Bang - we're on you.

Obviously, people remember that we beat West Ham home and away, but going down to Upton Park was no problem to us. We were like: 'Right, where are we this week? Oh, West Ham eh? OK, bring them on.'

When you've got that mindset, that confidence, it's disciplined but it also frees you up to be aggressive in games, put the opposition on the back foot - say to them: 'Come on then, deal with us.'

You soon find out who can cope and once you see cracks in the opposition during a game, people starting bitching at teammates, you know you're on a winner.

Not that we were averse to having a pop at each other ourselves - but we used it as a good thing. One of the great things about that team was that we drove each other on in games. And if that meant having a go at someone, then so be it.

But it was a positive thing for us. Look, me and Grezza are big pals and he was a phenomenal player - no-one needs to be told that.

However, there were times when I'd be saying to him during games: *'Hey, what the hell are you doing? You're the right-back - not the play maker. That's my job. You give the flipping ball to me then get back to doing your job.'*

Fair do's, he'd be chipping back, telling me to sod off and whatnot - but he would start giving me the ball.

(Of course, he then goes to Burnley, becomes a brilliant play maker and I'm sure he was saying exactly the same to the right-back over there.)

It says a lot about the team that the relationships are strong enough to have those type of rows on the pitch and no-one minds; it's not about bringing anyone down or getting on their case for the sake of it, it's for the good of the team.

There have been times when I've come across players who DO want to have a go at you just to bring you down, but at Deepdale it wasn't like that.

We all had the best of intentions, to be as good as we could possibly be - as a team.

There were lots of leaders but I have to say the big man at the back, Chris Lucketti, was a superb captain. I still call him *'Skip'* to this day - all the lads do.

He was a cracking guy and someone you could trust all day long, on and off the pitch. Everyone respected him and he respected us back. When you've got that type of culture it creates a bond that still exists to this day.

People say it's hard to explain but it really isn't: you've got a group of people with the right work ethic, the right character, people who you respect and like working with, at a really good football club.

For a footballer, that's the kind of situation you dream about and that's what we had at North End. We all cared about each other, we cared about the club and the supporters and, I'm telling you now, we cared about winning - top priority.

The way the club brought players in kept this going, too.

New recruits were either lads stepping up, looking to 'get there', or guys who had been there and knew how to do things properly.

You probably get sick of hearing this, but there were no 'Big Time Charlies' at all.

People like Nuge came in and you won't find a more well-liked lad in football. He's such a great character, just a lovely, bubbly personality who always has a smile on his face. But he also had that desire to get better, to work hard and his attitude was absolutely spot on. The older players loved him because he was just a bundle of positive energy - on and off the pitch.

I was always proud to play for Scotland and got seven caps over nine years, starting off in 1996 against Australia after I'd recovered from my cruciate injury.

I always seemed to be in the squads and I've been all over the world courtesy of the SFA, but I had some top players in front of me. My best period was when I was playing at the back in Germany, but Colin Hendry and Colin Calderwood were the first choice partnership and I was behind them.

Nevertheless, it was fantastic to be involved and I always treasure the times I did get on to represent my country.

Probably my best game was against Ireland in Dublin and we beat them 2-1 when I played at the back with Matt Elliott and Christian Dailly, while they had Niall Quinn and Robbie Keane up front.

Craig was in charge at first but by the time I finished, Walter Smith was manager and I was really, really impressed with him.

As I was older and been around I appreciated how good he was even more. I had some great times when I did play and I remember playing at Hampden when we beat Lithuania 3-0 in a World Cup qualifier. As you can imagine, that was a special night.

Of course, when you're in so many squads, there's a frustration as well about games that I didn't manage to get on for.

For example, I'd have loved to have played in those European Championship play-off games against England.

Mind you . . . so would about six million other Scots, too!

Billy also brought in Chris Sedgwick, another top man, very down to earth and hard-working, to give us balance on the right while Eddie Lewis was doing his stuff on the left. I knew that if I got the chance to play it out wide, Eddie would be on his bike, making a run and giving you the chance to get a good pass into space for him.

But it wasn't just him, all over the park there were people running their legs off for the team; Tyrone Mears and Dickson Etuhu - look at the great careers those two had.

At the back we had Carlo Nash and Andy Lonergan and when Lonners came through, he was just on fire. We were all looking at each other saying: 'Who the hell's this kid?' He was unbelievable.

But then he did his cruciate and, incredibly, the club didn't sort the operation out properly - there was a problem with it and he ended up being out for about 18 months.

Again, I just can't understand clubs not looking after players properly, but thankfully Andy has gone on to have the great career he deserves.

It's no coincidence that talented people who work hard go on to be successful.

And so when you put all that together, it's easy to see why a team of these people would be successful too.

That was what we had under Billy in 2004/05 - and really, well, THAT was our year. That was the season we really HAD to do it. And we came *very, very* close.

What was brilliant was seeing the ground get fuller and fuller as the weeks went on. We played Wigan in the last home game of the season (I scored as we drew 1-1) and there were 20,000-plus on.

The atmosphere was just brilliant and it gave you a glimpse of what it would be like every week if we could just take that next step; people would flock to the games and it would be packed out every week.

You talk about motivation and it's things like that that drive you on as a player - not money. No way.

You can't put a price on the feelings you get from being part of something special like we had at North End and everyone was busting a gut to get us over the finishing line in the play-offs.

I remember we'd played Derby in the season and beat them 3-0 at Deepdale - Marlon Broomes had an absolute stormer. So when we knew we were facing them, I don't recall anyone being too worried at all.

We knew we were better than them and if everyone did their jobs we'd be OK.

Again, that first leg at Deepdale, with the crowd bouncing and packed out again - the belief we had was tangible. You looked around at your teammates and you thought: *'Yes, these lads aren't going to let us down - I've got to make sure I don't let them down either.'*

I think that was the same for everyone. Nuge and Cressy scored and, while we weren't complacent, we were confident we'd see them off at their place - and we did. So that was it, down to Cardiff for the final against West Ham; one more game to go.

Our preparations were good and there were no problems for me at all - right up to the night before the game.

All was going smooth as a few of us older lads sat down for a hot chocolate before bed, but as we sat there just talking, David Kelly came in and asked for a quick word.

He said something had happened to my wee son at the hotel he was staying in and he was in an ambulance on the way to hospital.

What had happened was the players were staying at Celtic Manor, but my wife had come down with our three children and was staying at another hotel with the other wives. My son Oscar, who was four or five at that point, had been sliding around on the dancefloor, as kids do.

He slid against the wall, but the 'wall' turned out to be a big stage which had then toppled on top of him, catching him in the face and making a right mess.

It was about 10.30pm and Julian Darby drove me through the city to get to the hospital. It was about half an hour away and it was so weird, because the city was absolutely packed with North End fans, West Ham fans, fans of the other play-off teams who'd played that day - and there was me and Julian going through them with our PNE tracksuits on.

When I got to see Oscar, he looked like Buzz Lightyear with his jaw all stuck out and coming through his skin. The doctors said he'd dislocated his jaw, broke this, done that and it was all a lot to take in.

They said they had to do an operation the following morning, so understandably my wife was really upset, and then I had to go and see my other two children at their hotel to check they were OK. What I probably should have done is just stay there with them but in the end, I left at about 1.30am and then drove back to Celtic Manor.

When I got there, Billy and 'Ned' Kelly were waiting up for me, which was really good of them, and I filled them in on what had happened.

The upshot of it all is that I never slept a wink that night.

I was sharing with Eddie Lewis and thankfully, he slept right through, no problem. It wasn't the best preparation but the question of me not playing in the game never came up. If Billy had thought it was the right thing to do, he'd have said so and I'd have had to accept it. But I think we both knew that once the final got started, it wouldn't have any effect on me.

My focus would be 100 per cent on the game for those 90 minutes - and it was.

But, my God . . . *it was a terrible game.*

Neither side could get going and it never really took off.

Whether it was because it was a really hot day, I don't know, but as a showpiece final, it was dreadful. One thing's for sure, the pitch was absolutely horrendous - they'd watered it and watered it and there had been a game on it the day before, too.

People were sliding about all over the place so it was no surprise that the goal came from a slip. One scrappy, bobbly cross, a slip and a goal - it summed that game up really. Terrible.

It should have been two teams having a right go at each other, but we never got into our stride. It was so unlike us. I don't think it was anything West Ham deliberately set out to do but we just didn't play our normal game, like we did do in the season.

I got a nasty gash in the first half that needed seven stitches, so that didn't help, but none of this is excuses - we just didn't get going.

The one thing I think they did do, which was clever, was Alan Pardew brought in a few younger players with fresher legs than they'd used against us in the other games; Nigel Reo-Coker started, Mark Noble came on.

They had more energy than when we'd played them previously and then once they went in front, their experienced players took over to slow things down, break the game up, all that sort of annoying stuff that makes it hard when you're chasing a game.

But the frustrating thing is . . . we were better than them.

Over that year we were the better team.

We just didn't do it on that day and, as I've said before, football is a brutal business.

After the game I was feeling really down and crappy - everyone was the same. It was a tough, tough defeat to take, especially as we knew we could have played better.

But the operation on my son had gone well and seeing him afterwards in hospital made me realise that, yes, it was a big game for the club, a really disappointing day for everyone . . . but my wee boy was going to be OK.

For me, when all is said and done, that was the important thing. Priorities, isn't it?

Looking back, what made the West Ham defeat harder to swallow was what happened afterwards. We had a good team and all we needed to do was add a couple more good players to strengthen it and go again - just that wee bit of extra quality.

Billy always had it in his mind to get a target man and that summer we got Danny Dichio in. He'd been at Millwall the season before and gave me, Claude and Skip a real battering down at their place - we just couldn't get to grips with him.

So getting him was a great move and everyone was pleased.

But then, *ridiculously*, we lost Eddie Lewis to Leeds - and he was a big, big player for us.

He had real quality and was brilliant at whipping crosses and free-kicks in. Yet the club let him go on a free transfer, because they wouldn't give him a pay rise.

It made no sense whatsoever. If he left, the club was going to have to go and buy a replacement, who may well not be as good - *so why not just give Eddie the money?*

I know for a fact he wasn't asking for a fortune and the view of the changing room was that if he wanted a bit more money, just pay it - because he had earned it with his performances on the pitch.

He was out of contract, you won't find anyone better, he's happy here - so just give him his due. It was crazy that they let him leave the club, especially on a free transfer.

If it was five or six million to a Premier League club or something you couldn't turn down then, maybe, OK. But it wasn't like that. I'll never understand what the club was thinking at that point.

So that was bad enough, but then we lost Cressy for just over a million - another one to Leeds.

Again, I think North End could have kept him if they'd pushed the boat out just a wee bit, because he wasn't looking to move, or asking for a fortune either.

You speculate to accumulate, but with those two there wasn't much speculation - because everyone knew how good they were.

Two key men, who had just started the play-off final for us, gone for a relatively small amount of money to a rival team in the same division. Crazy.

We shouldn't have been losing those lads and, of course, who lined up against us in the play-offs that next season? Cressy and Eddie, who swung the entire tie with a brilliant free-kick.

I'm not saying blow the bank, but when you've had a year like we had, you keep it together and build on it - you don't let key people walk out the door.

It was so frustrating. That was the most disappointing period of my time at Deepdale.

We replaced them with good players, but not the same as those two. So the hangover at the start of the following season wasn't just down to the West Ham defeat. I think losing two big players in the way that we did knocked everyone sideways a bit and the players were thinking: *'What the hell's going on here? Are they serious about going up or not?'*

Up until November time, we were on a terrible run but then something just clicked, we finally shrugged off the disappointment and collectively snapped out of it.

We were like: *'OK, enough. Let's go.'* But it just shows you how big an effect things can have at a football club, without people realising it consciously.

Personally, I'm a big advocate of clubs strengthening in the January window; if you're having a good season, back the manager when he needs it.

Give him what it takes to get over the line and if you're worried about money, you can say to him: 'Right, you can have these players now, but don't come calling in the summer if things don't work out.'

Don't wait to the end of the season when the chance is gone and other clubs start picking off your best players - strengthen when you're up there.

I think we've maybe seen that at Preston once or twice down the years and it hasn't really happened in the January window, when if there had been a bit more thrown at it . . . who knows?

It would be great to see the club really seize that opportunity one time and see where it takes them. If you never do that, you get stuck on the same cycle.

It was the same in 2006 when we came to January. If we'd have gone out and made a couple of big signings, I think it would have maybe made the difference.

I'm not talking about going out and spending millions, because obviously North End can't and won't do that.

But when the team has an opportunity in a season, you know what's needed in January and I can never understand why clubs shy away from it. Even if you push the boat out for a couple of good loans - the rewards on offer outweigh the risk.

I know it's frustrating for the supporters when it doesn't happen - and, believe me, the players feel it too. At the end of the day, we all want to be successful. No-one cares that the loan centre forward was getting paid *'X'* or *'Y'* when you're running round the pitch celebrating promotion.

As it was, when we got going again that season, the boys did great - we really pulled it together. People had almost written us off but our attitude was: 'Right, we'll show you.'

Billy was at his motivational best; like a man possessed at times, driving us on with sheer ferocity coupled with tactical know-how in the changing room.

I'd got injured at Norwich towards the end of the season and been out for about four weeks, so I wasn't expecting to feature in the play-off first leg at Elland Road.

But Billy rang me up on the Wednesday and said: 'I need you on Friday night at Leeds.'

I told him I was technically fit, but maybe not match fit and he was happy with that.

In the end, I lasted about 60 minutes and we played really well; Nuge scored and we were doing great . . . *but then who scored a worldie free-kick?*

Eddie Lewis - and that was where the tie was won and lost. People talk about *'job done'* and all this other stuff, but all that is unimportant - it's just talk.

To me, it was lost in that moment when Eddie put that free-kick in the top corner.

So then you look back to the decision to let him go on a free the previous summer and think: *'Oh aye, how much has that cost us now then?'* Absolutely stupid.

There was something else that went on that caused a bit of grief - the theory that Leeds knew our team in advance.

And they did. Even though I'd been out for four weeks, they knew I was going to be playing and what that meant for our shape and things on the night.

I've no idea how they knew, but they did. It came from somewhere, but to this day, I don't know where.

That really got Billy's back up and maybe affected his thinking for the second leg at Deepdale. He was furious about it in the build-up and certainly threw them a few curveballs in the line-up for the game.

Marcus Stewart, a great lad a good player, came in and we went with a really attacking line-up, with Dich, Nuge and Brett Ormerod all starting, too.

People can question it, but if you look back, he used to spring surprises quite a lot in the season anyway and one of the big things about Billy is that he trusted players. There was discipline, but he trusted you to go out and, *yes,* get the job done.

The funny thing is, we started the game really well and were just getting a foothold when Brett got his leg broken in a ridiculous challenge.

The referee was terrible and didn't even issue a yellow card. We couldn't believe it *- the lad had his leg broken and no card (!).*

So that set a bit of a marker for what he was going to be like.

As I've said before, we were always great at the start of games, but when the injury happens - the momentum goes.

Marcus gets injured and has to go off at half-time - more momentum goes.

Then the floodlights fail - the momentum goes again.

It was like everything was conspiring against us getting going.

Then they got the first goal and all the momentum swung over to them. It's such a massive, massive thing and it's hard then when the clock is running down.

The other thing was, by then we'd lost Chris Lucketti, Callum was out injured, Cressy and Eddie had gone - I'm not knocking anyone, but that's a lot of experience that you need in situations like that.

On top of everything else, the ref was having a nightmare. There were so many ridiculous things going on out there that night and in the end it was almost like he was making up for it by sending two of their lads off - including, ironically, Cressy.

I think he issued about eight yellow cards to Leeds, but it was no good trying to get a grip on things when they were 2-0 up and time-wasting - the damage was done.

We never minded a physical battle, but we needed a strong referee from the start and we just didn't get one. Leaving the pitch after losing that night was a real sickener, an absolute downer and I just felt crap. It was awful.

Don't give me this *'so near, so far'* business. We hadn't achieved what we had set out to do and it was another big chance gone. I've had some lows in football and that was a real sickener.

I'd have felt even worse if I'd realised that would be my last league game in a PNE shirt.

So it was a momentous night all round. I think everyone knew that if we didn't go up, Billy was coming to the end with the club. Other opportunities were being put in front of him and it was clear he wasn't going to get what he wanted at North End.

They weren't going to bring in the level of player he wanted and he'd seen them let Cressy, Eddie, Skip and Dickson Etuhu all leave. Claude Davis and Tyrone Mears left a month or so after the Leeds game, too. That's a lot of quality going out of the door and if you're not reinvesting, it's hard to replace.

So I think Billy had seen enough and realised the challenge was just too big at Preston. If they could have kept everyone together and backed him a bit more, I'm sure he would probably have stayed around and then who knows? My bet is he would have got us into the Premier League.

Luckily, I got another chance to wear the famous white shirt when we had Paul McKenna's testimonial against Everton that summer. It was a good turnout and a fitting tribute to Kenna.

So I'd rather count that as my last appearance, especially as we played well and it was honouring one of the club's best players over the past 20 years.

When Billy went, Paul Simpson came in and . . . well, it just wasn't happening for me. He brought in his own coaching staff and totally changed everything around.

Everything suddenly became very relaxed straight away, but then weirdly some little things were really rigid.

We were doing a lot of squats in the gym and were told everyone had to do them.

Exercises like that didn't really suit me and in the past, there would have been a bit more flexibility if it was having a detrimental effect. Billy or Craig would probably have looked at things differently, but with Paul it was *'everyone has to do it'*.

So I did it - a long session - then went outside and my hamstring had gone. It was ironic because the intensity of the training sessions had really dropped off, but to be fair, he had a great start and the lads were flying at the start of the season.

I missed a couple of games out injured but then wasn't getting in when I was fit. The team was playing with a lot of attacking freedom, but there was still a lot of Billy's hallmarks and good habits stamped on the team.

Those habits don't happen by accident - they are drilled into you in training and if it's not at the right intensity then they start to fall away. People start thinking: 'I don't need to track my guy, I don't need to get back there, etc.'

And it spreads through the team, almost subconsciously.

On top of that, I had a run-in with one of the coaches, who wasn't really involved with the outfield players.

He'd been going behind my back, telling people I couldn't get around the pitch any more, couldn't do this, couldn't do that - he was totally out of order.

So I asked for a meeting with him and Paul Simpson to have it out in the open.

I said to the fella: *'What right have you got to question what I do on the pitch?'*

He gave me some guff about something Blackburn Rovers were doing and I said: *'I don't give two stuffs what they're doing. You don't go round bad-mouthing me to people who I've worked with for years. And if you DO have anything to say, you can say it to my face.'*

Simmo sat there and didn't really say much one way or the other, let's put it that way. I suppose deep down I'd already known pretty quickly that this new regime wasn't for me, but that was just about it.

I'd been getting a few injuries anyway and now some sciatica was flaring up too, so I went to see Derek Shaw and reached an agreement on my contract. It was a sad day, but the way I saw it, it was the right thing to do.

I've no axe to grind with Paul Simpson, in fact I bumped into him when Grezza took Salford City to Wembley a couple of years ago and we had a good chat.

It wasn't how I wanted things to end and at 34 I'd hoped to be playing longer.

But I'd had 15 operations in my career and over time, that had taken its toll.

I didn't want to linger around behind the scenes, either injured or not playing, and I didn't want to do anything to sour my time with the club where I'd had so many good times.

However sad I was about ending, I wanted to leave with my head held high - and that's what I did.

These days, I still manage the odd five-a-side game in a team with Colin Hendry, Gavin McCann, Scott and David McNiven and Youl, when his knees allow.

Career-wise, I keep myself busy in the property business and when I stopped playing I went into sports management where I've represented a few ex-North Enders - Kenna, Chris Sedgwick, Youl, Kelvin Wilson - and one or two others, including Wes Morgan at Leicester. Really, it's about people putting their trust in you and I enjoy helping people and doing the right thing for their careers.

There's no doubt North End is a good club and very well run these days; if someone was to ask me about going there, I'd say it's a positive move, especially with the manager and the strength of the squad at the moment. Alex Neil is doing a great job, but the club has been here before under David Moyes, Billy Davies and Alan Irvine - another guy who did a great job with the squad he had. All of them got the maximum out of the players they had without having the resources of other teams around them.

The question is: Will North End have that push, that ambition, to finally get up in this period? Will they be able to keep everyone together?

Or will they lose players and see the cycle start all over again?

I understand the financial model they're working to and there may be an offer they can't refuse at some point. I get that.

But for me, the key would be to take those funds and reinvest in the squad. Be pro-active, go and get two or three players for decent money and see where it takes you.

I certainly hope they can do it because it's a club very close to my heart.

I'm a big-time Celtic fan and am fortunate to have had some great times in my career, but being at Preston was one of the happiest times I had, because it was such a great set of lads.

We were like a family; we'd argue, fight, have a go at each other - and then laugh about it because we had an incredible bond.

Getting promotion to the Premier League with that group would have been the absolute dream for me.

We didn't quite make it, but it wasn't for the lack of trying.

I think it can still happen for Preston though and the fans deserve it, because they're so loyal and were absolutely brilliant in all the time I was there.

I'll never forget some of those games at Deepdale - fans, management, players all together as one. It was a hell of a thing to be a part of and I'll always be proud and grateful to have experienced it.

Even now when someone introduces themselves as a PNE fan, I always feel that instant connection, y'know? They're proper football fans.

We went on a brilliant journey together and hopefully North End go that one step further in the years ahead. It can be done.

Keep the faith.

Chapter 12

PETER HIGHAM: WHAT A LIFE

I may be a bit out of kilter with most of the people in this book (with one notable exception) in that I played for Preston North End in the 1950s. Of course, things were very different then, but as I approach my 90th birthday I hope I can pass on a bit of what it was like to play in that era.

And at the same time, I'll try not to sound like an old fart!

But when I say things were very different, what I mean is . . . it was a different world. I was born in 1930 and was just a young lad when war broke out. I come from the village of Haigh just outside Wigan and I had a typical upbringing for the time.

We made our own entertainment and I remember during blackouts we used to climb up a little hill near our house to watch the searchlights over Liverpool during air raids.

We could hear the drone of the bombers overhead then see flashes from the anti-aircraft fire and sometimes you'd see a plane get hit and everyone would cheer: 'We've got one!'

Haigh never got bombed really, apart from one time a bomber jettisoned its load in a field and killed the farmer's cow. The next day all us lads were all piling into the crater to collect bits of shrapnel - and cow.

There was a brewery at the end of the road with big cellars you could shelter in, but sometimes when the sirens went off, my mum would just say *'we'll take our chances'* and we'd all crouch under the kitchen table. I'm not sure it was actually bomb-proof and, thankfully, we never found out.

Of course, there was rationing at the time and I remember one day my mum coming back from town with this yellow thing for me and my two brothers.

She said: *'Have a look at this - I've bought you a banana.'*

Well, we looked at each other, then looked at this thing - we had no idea what it was. We'd never seen one before: 'It's a *what*?'

They used to come in from the docks at Preston, but you didn't see many in the shops and goodness knows how much she paid for it. But there we were, an actual banana with milk and a bit of sugar and that was a proper treat. Happy days.

(Hey, how am I doing at not sounding like an old fart? What?? You cheeky sods!)

Anyway, as everyone knows, it's Rugby League country round Wigan and my eldest brother played for Warrington. I was a bit of a rugby player myself too for the local youth club, St John's. We made it to two finals at the old Central Park stadium and Wigan said they wanted to sign me when I'd finished my National Service, which was coming up. I was tempted, but I had a mate who was a couple of years older than me who had been playing for them around that time.

In his first game he broke his collar bone and then not long after that he smashed his arm up - it just seemed like one injury after another.

At the same time, I was making a bit of a name for myself as a centre forward at football and Wigan Athletic had asked me to sign for them. That seemed a bit of a safer option, so I said I'd stick to that from thereon.

Everything had to be put on hold for a couple of years though, as I got an early call to join the Royal Marines.

My God, it was tough. Speed marches, training exercises with live bullets whizzing over your head, really hard physical exercise all the time . . . *I loved it.*

I thought that I was a fit lad going into it, but - *by heck* - I was even fitter when I came out.

After Commando training, I was based in Portsmouth and was playing football for the Royal Marines when this fellow came in the dressing room and said he was a scout for Portsmouth. He said: 'We'd like you to play for us while you're based here.'

I couldn't sign professionally because I was still in the forces. So they didn't pay me, or even give me a bus fare, but I went along Tuesdays and Thursdays and started scoring a few goals in the reserves.

The manager, a chap called Bob Jackson, was from Morecambe and Portsmouth at the time were First Division champions - a really good team in the late 1940s.

Not that long after I arrived, he called me in and said I was playing in the first team on the Saturday.

Imagine that, today; I was still a full-time Royal Marine, but I was being put in the team for the League champions!

To be fair, the Navy loved that and had no problem with it, so that Saturday afternoon, I made my way to the ground and played for Portsmouth against Birmingham City in front of nearly 40,000 at a packed Fratton Park.

We won 2-0 and I must have had a good game because after the game the manager called me in and said he wanted to sign me when I was demobbed in about six weeks' time.

I thought it was a great chance, but I'll be honest, I hadn't been home in months and it might sound daft - but I was missing my mother's cooking.

Genuinely, she was a fantastic cook, so I wasn't sure about staying down south. Lo and behold, a couple of days later, a scout from Bolton Wanderers turned up at the barracks and said they'd like to sign me too.

I thought: 'Well, Bolton's only a few miles from my mum's kitchen . . . it's no contest!'

I was there two years and scored loads of goals for the reserves, but I was up against Nat Lofthouse for a place in the first team - one of the greatest centre forwards England has ever seen. So no matter how well I did, I was always going to struggle to get in the team.

I remember one time we played Morecambe and I scored seven goals in the game. I knew I'd been on a decent run, but this chap came up to me after the game and pointed out that in my last four games, I'd scored 28 goals. And I still couldn't get in the first team . . !

That was how tough it was in those days. To be fair, Nat Lofthouse was brilliant with me. I was only 19 and he was at his peak, a smashing fellow and despite his physical reputation on the pitch, he was nice as pie.

Wages-wise, I was getting £7-a-week during the season with £2 for a win and £1 for a draw. In the summer, I'd get £5 a week. I was quite happy with that, but it was always a one-year contract and you never knew until around April whether you were being kept on for the following season.

You were just hoping to be retained and sometimes a lot of it came down to luck; *were you in form when the decision was made? Were you fit or were you injured?*

It was a sad time for a lot of players and there was no great financial safety net if you were out.

At the end of my second season, Bolton had a new manager and they let me go, which was a bit of a surprise as I'd scored loads of goals in the reserves.

Years later, I heard that the new man didn't like Catholics. I'll never know for sure, but there was a fair bit of that going on back in those days.

Either way, back in 1952, a couple of days later, a chap called George Barge from North End came to our house in Haigh and asked me to sign for Preston.

It was a great move and one of the best things I gained was my friendship with Eric Jones - not only were we great teammates on the pitch, we were great pals off it too and remain best mates 68 years later.

Eric and I had a telepathic relationship on the pitch and he used to put over these brilliant crosses for me to get my head on - goodness knows how many goals he set up for me.

So I was very happy to be at Deepdale; it was a good club, with some legendary players - obviously, Tom Finney being the absolute finest.

He had this aura about him and - I know everyone says this, but it's true - he was a lovely man. He was one of the best - if not THE best - players in the world, but he always had time for us younger lads and was always complimentary if you had a good game or whatever.

I remember him telling me to respect on the pitch, respect the officials and respect your opponents. He said: 'Everyone's human, we all make mistakes but do not retaliate in words or actions particularly with the officials.'

That always stuck in my mind.

When I got older, I used to tell younger players what Tom had said and to be honest, I think some of the lads today could learn from it, too. Tom used to get kicked from pillar to post, but I never once heard him swear or saw him retaliate.

He just used to say to me: *'If they're kicking you, they are frightened of you.'*

He would never say anything to the full-back, he would just leave them on their backsides with his skill. It must have driven them mad.

And when I eventually got in the first team, well, I was a centre forward and TOM FINNEY was putting the ball in to me.

You know, when you think about that . . . what can you say? In the history of football, you can't ask for anything more.

Of course, my best mate Eric was his stand-in and he was a very good player too. In fact, the whole team was one of the best in the country, with the ground packed out every week and pushing for titles and the FA Cup. It was a brilliant time to be at Preston, I'm not sure there's ever been better.

I don't think the coaching methods were always spot-on though. I remember one time, a coach came to us before the game and had these little white tablets. He said: 'These are what they give night-fighter pilots to keep them awake. I want you to take two each.'

I wasn't having any of that. I said: 'What are you talking about? *Keep awake? It's three o'clock in the afternoon and we're just about to kick-off. Who the hell is falling asleep?* No thanks.'

I'm sure they weren't drugs, but I do know some of the lads couldn't get to sleep that night.

So it was certainly an education at that time at North End. We had this coach, Jimmy Milne, who later became manager but he never really took to me - and I never took to him. In training, we used to always run round the pitch anti-clockwise and his idea of *'doing something different'* was having us go round in the other direction.

We had to laugh - what was the point of that?

One time in winter, he had about 12 of us in for extra training behind the old Town End - even though there was snow on the ground.

As I was hitting the ball, my left foot slipped on the ice and I felt a real pain in my right thigh. I said: 'Jim, I think I've pulled a thigh muscle.'

Straight away he shot back: *'Don't be so soft!'*

That was his answer to most things; he was always going on about how he played at Wembley with a broken collar bone.

Anyway, he said: 'Right, this will cure it. Take this bag of balls and volley them against the back of the stand over there. That will loosen it up.'

Well, daft me, I took the balls and started doing what he said. After a couple of minutes I thought, this is making it worse, so I asked him if I could stop.

Instead he just shouted: *'Don't be so soft! Carry on! You'll feel the benefit in a bit!'*

Finally, I hit this one ball and I felt like a red hot knife had sliced my leg from my knee all the way up my thigh. It was agony and straight away this lump the size of an ostrich egg came up on my thigh. The pain was horrendous. I hit the ground and shouted over to him: 'Jim, you'd better have a look at this.'

By now he was getting worried, so he sent me inside to see Des Coupe.

Des was physio at the time, but he was very unusual - because he was blind.

The club had taken pity on him a bit because he'd had his optic nerve severed during the war but, to his credit, he had come back and done all the physio courses.

Because he was blind, I think the club thought he had a magic touch.

And had he?

Had he buggery! He was absolutely useless.

It was all very sad. Nice enough fellow, but come on . . . *the man was blind.*

Still, I hobbled off to see him but, bless him, he didn't know what to do.

Thankfully, my brother Ted knew the Wigan Rugby League trainer and arranged for me to see him. When I told him the story, he took one look and said I should go straight back and sue North End. I'd ruptured one of my quadriceps and he said it could have finished my career there and then.

Of course, I'd never sue North End and fortunately, he was able to work on it. Unbeknownst to the club - I went to see him three times a week at night over the next year to get back to being right. That's how serious it was - and how easy it was for careers to be lost on so-called medical advice in those days.

'You'll feel the benefit in a bit'? Absolute nonsense!

Thankfully I recovered, but despite scoring 90 goals in 88 appearances in the Central League, chances in the first team were hard to come by.

I didn't get a look-in as North End were pushing for the league title and lost out on goal average to Arsenal in my first season, 1952/53. Eventually though in 1954/55, Charlie Wayman was having a rough time in the first team. Great player Charlie, but everyone goes through a tough patch every now and again.

I got called in against Sheffield Wednesday at Deepdale and scored a hat-trick as we won 6-0. I kept my place against Manchester United in the next game at Old Trafford, but we lost 2-1 and I didn't score.

Then, however came probably my favourite North End goal, against Wolves at Deepdale. The ground was packed to the rafters - these were the days where if you weren't there by 1pm you couldn't get on.

The crowd was all packed tightly together, people having a smoke, a lot of chaps in flat caps and the kids being passed over heads to sit at the front. There was barely a policeman in sight - and those that were there were watching the match!

Anyway, I was up against Billy Wright, England captain and an absolute legend of the game. But I'll be honest, it was one of the easiest matches I ever played.

He was too much of a footballer at centre half - he wasn't very big and he never kicked you, like most of them did all the time. He was too much of a gentleman.

They had a brilliant team at that time and were 3-0 up at half-time. Now, half-times in those days were not like they are today.

You might have a squeeze of an orange, but one or two would nip in the toilets for a crafty fag, or even a tot of whisky if it was cold.

There was no great team talk by the manager, that just didn't happen in those days. No tactics - and no substitutes back then either.

That day, it was just that we felt we were letting the people of Preston down, so we were determined to give it absolutely everything in that second half.

I was fouled in the area and Jimmy Baxter scored the penalty to put us back in it before Bobby Foster got another to make it 3-2.

With just a few minutes to go, Billy Wright had the ball just outside the penalty area. He was dawdling a bit, so I nipped in and robbed him of the ball and just let fly.

Well, I've never hit a ball better - it flew into the back of the net!

The cheers were fantastic and people still come up and talk to me about that game - even though it was more than 60 years ago.

I ended up scoring 10 goals in 15 games and my last game was a 3-1 win against Aston Villa down in Birmingham when I scored two goals.

That was the Saturday and on the Monday after training, the manager had me in the office and told me I wasn't playing the following Saturday.

I'd scored 10 goals in 15 games and got two in the previous match. I couldn't believe it. I'd scored more than a goal a game in the reserves, waited patiently for a couple of years for my chance and then scored loads of goals in the first team.

I was taken aback, really. Very disappointed. So I said: *'I'm very sorry, but I'm not happy with this. I'd like to go on the transfer list.'*

It was a big thing because I was set on playing for Preston, but I knew Tommy Thompson was coming in around that time and I thought: 'No matter how well I do, they're never going to play me here.'

Luckily, three clubs came in for me and the first one was Nottingham Forest.

They played a similar footballing style to North End and I went down to see their manager Billy Walker who offered me a deal for £11-a-week - £4 more than I was getting at Deepdale.

(Don't forget, even Tom Finney was only on £12 in those days, so it was a good wage for me.)

When I put pen to paper, I always remember, he pulled out a tenner from his back pocket and said: 'There you go Pete, there's your signing on fee - £10.' I never found out how much they paid for me, but I framed that tenner - never spent it!

They were in the Second Division at the time, but paying better money than Preston and we soon got promoted into the top tier again.

Not long afterwards, the manager asked me if I knew of any decent left-sided players, so I put him in touch with North End about my great friend Eric Jones, who was still not getting a regular game.

He signed for Forest too and the pair of us ended up sharing these digs right next to the City Ground. Long before Morecambe and Wise - *Eric and Ernie* - Eric and Peter shared the same bed.

No funny business of course, top and tails. We were just trying to keep warm!

The house was lovely, but it was bitterly cold and run by a lady called Mrs Fletcher, whose husband had left her.

We soon realised why! She never used to cook for us and - *blimey!* - it was freezing in that house in winter. There was frost on the inside of the windows.

The mice were jumping on the traps just to get out of there!

I ended up writing to my mum asking her to knit us two long-sleeved, high-necked jumpers that we could wear in bed, along with our football socks, the lot.

And we were First Division professional footballers! Talk about a different world.

When we played, things went on that would never be heard of these days.

The pitches, for example, were mud baths for much of the season; we played games in all weathers, snow, hail, frost - clear the lines and it was 'game on'. No problem for players or supporters, it was expected that you'd play so we just got on with it.

And I swear I scored a goal like no-one else has ever managed in British football, or the world probably.

I was playing for Forest in a local derby against Notts County at Meadow Lane when we got a corner and the ball was swung in.

As I went to head it, I got a violent push in my back that sent me flying towards the goalpost - which of course was square in those days.

Instinctively, I put my hand out to stop myself and cracked straight into it. *Whack!* I broke and dislocated my little finger on my left hand and I still can't use it to this day. It's been at a funny angle ever since.

This was in the first half and the pain was absolutely creasing me - it was excruciating - and my hand was all swollen up.

At half-time, the trainer Tommy Graham came up to me and said: 'Don't worry Pete, I've had a word with the referee and he says you can play the second half with a covering on your left hand.'

I said: 'Covering? What sort of covering?'

And he pulled out a boxing glove!

Well, I looked at it and thought he was mad, but I was in that much pain, I'd have said yes to anything.

I've no idea where he got it from but, no pain killers or anything, he just pushed this huge glove on me and tied it up: 'There you go son, now, get on with it!'

That's the way it was.

So I went out second half and the crowd were all giving me funny looks and having a bit of a laugh, but unbelievably, I went out and scored!

I've got a photograph of me scoring with this boxing glove on and show it to people now to see if they spot it.

If I hadn't got that picture, people might not believe it was true - that I scored a goal while wearing a boxing glove!

No-one's ever done that before or since. Talk about 'It's a knockout'!

While I was at Nottingham, we were promoted and we all received a special watch as a memento. Many years later, we had a burglary and the watch was stolen.

My son-in-law, a big Forest fan, wrote to the club and got a reply back from Brian Clough, saying how sorry he was to hear about it. And he sent a specially-commissioned plate that the club had had made after they won the European Cup to replace the stolen watch - I've always thought that was a lovely touch.

I played more than 60 games for Forest and scored 20 goals before moving on to Doncaster (where my old pal Eric was playing), Wigan and Morecambe, as well as a few other teams.

After football, I went on to be a school teacher and - *get this* - a male model.

You might laugh at that looking at me now at 89. Then again ladies, you might not!

I did a few catalogue shoots and things for mail order firms; looking into the distance, all brooding and thoughtful. Normally, I was just thinking: *'What am I having for tea tonight?'*

I did everything from Wellington boots to cruise ships to looking a bit like James Bond. The good thing was that not only did I get paid, but I got to keep the stuff. Not the cruise ship though, sadly!

So it's been an interesting life - *Royal Marine Commando, professional footballer, male model, teacher* - and I definitely wouldn't swap my time for the game today.

Of course, there's a lot of money in it these days, but you can't buy the memories we made.

I still come back to Deepdale for the odd game and have been in the Invincibles Lounge when North End play Forest.

You look around the stadium now and think how much it's changed, but the pitch is still the same.

Yes, it's in much better condition, but when you look out on it . . . this is where it all happened.

That's where I robbed Billy Wright and scored against Wolves.

This is where Tom Finney destroyed teams.

Here's where me and my best pal Eric got to live out our dreams.

What a time we had - I wouldn't have missed it for the world.

Chapter 13

RYAN KIDD: NOT A BAD TRIP

Wow, it's like Wembley! That's what I remember thinking when I first laid eyes on Deepdale. That probably says more about the state of our national stadium in the 1980s than it did about Deepdale, with the curving terrace of the Kop and the old (very old) West Stand.

I was about 14, all wide-eyed, fresh-faced and innocent-ish, up for a trial after being spotted on the youth circuit.

I'm not sure how it happened, but my 'trial' ended up in a session with first team players like Sam Allardyce and Skilful Bob Atkins on the plastic pitch.

At the time, I thought it was brilliant, but it didn't go as well as I hoped and I got a *'no'* from the club.

Out of the blue, Port Vale came in and offered me a scholarship, so that gave me a foot in the door and away I went. I travelled the first three months by train every day from Bolton, so that was fun (!).

But it was worth it to get to Vale and the delights of Burslem, which everyone knows is a beautiful part of the Potteries. It's like Blackpool, without the tower.

Once I got used to the surroundings, I ended up doing two years there on a YTS and then another two years as a pro.

My debut came away at Liverpool in the League Cup with the simple task of coming on as sub and marking Steve McMahon.

We had Mike Pejic as a coach, who was hard as nails, and I was just a kid. I remember he said to me: 'Just make sure you stick tight to that McMahon guy.'

Message received.

I got on and straight away '*that McMahon guy*' (title-winner, England regular, World Cup player, etc) played a pass and the ball was gone before I even knew it had been there.

It was all a bit too quick for me - so I just leathered him right across his shins.

Well, the look he gave me . . . and then the mouthful of abuse!

I legged it before he could kick me back.

We got a 2-2 draw that night at Anfield though and as the season went on I thought I'd done enough, so it was a bit of a surprise when I was released.

Not long after that, I had a call from Walter Joyce at North End who said they wanted to sign me. Les Chapman was the manager and I think they'd remembered me from trials and reserve games they'd seen so I jumped at it really.

There had been interest from Kenny Hibbitt at Walsall, but for me Preston was always a better option - plus it was a chance for me to move back to Bolton *(a big upgrade on Burslem, which tells you all you need to know).*

They offered me a year's contract on very little money, about £125-a-week, but I didn't care really. I just wanted the chance to play football.

Les only did about the first couple of months that season though before he got the sack, which was a shame because he was a good bloke.

There were some decent players in the first team - Mike Flynn and Aaron Callaghan were centre halves - and I was playing mainly in the reserves before Les went.

Then Sam Allardyce took over as caretaker boss and I knew he quite liked me as a player, because I'd been in the reserves with him.

He had me on the bench against Blackpool on the day we beat them 3-2 with Tony Ellis getting a hat-trick.

Blimey! That was lively, wasn't it?

I remember warming up behind the dug-outs and getting hit with chips, bits of pies, everything. And the abuse! It was like Steve McMahon all over again.

I'd heard it was feisty, but for a young lad, it was a proper baptism of fire that one.

It was my type of game though and I couldn't wait to get on - I think I replaced Tony after he got a knock on the head.

He was immense as a player, I remember as a teammate just looking up to him and thinking: *'Wow - this guy can do everything.'*

To be on the pitch in a big local derby like that was just brilliant and the scenes at the end with the North End fans going crazy just whetted my appetite to become a big part of the club. I'd got a taste and I wanted more.

It was a great day and then not long after that, Sam played me from the start in a night match against Reading at Deepdale that we won 2-0.

That's where my career took off from really.

Dave Flitcroft and Lee Ashcroft got the goals and Lee Cartwright also played, so you can see there were a lot of us young lads getting a chance around then.

I think the crowd was about 3,500, so there wasn't much money around for anything other than giving youth a go, really - I think it was 'needs must'.

I played four or five games but then got my first bad injury, when I did my ligaments in a game against Bolton where I went over on my ankle on the plastic and ended up out for a while.

At the time, we all thought Sam was going to get the job. He was a great bloke who lived round the corner from me and I used to give him a lift home now and then, picking his brains and talking football all the way.

Results had picked up, the fans loved him and we all thought he was nailed on to be manager full-time. But then one morning, we walked in and there he was . . . *John Beck was waiting at the top of the players tunnel.*

It was one of those situations where you were trying to be normal like: *'Oh aye, err, yes, good morning.'*

And inside you were thinking: *'Oh noooo! He's here . . . here we go now.'*

We'd all heard a lot about him and we were like: 'Jeez, this is going to be fun.'

From that moment on, the turnaround was huge in terms of playing style, training, pros leaving, different lads coming in, I've never seen anything like it in my life. It was like a whirlwind and I think that's just how John liked it.

I was out injured for about three months and during that time, results weren't good. What had worked for him at Cambridge wasn't going to plan here at all.

I was just getting back and I was called into a meeting between John and the senior pros. He asked: 'Who doesn't want to play this kind of football then?'

Quite openly, a lot of people put their hands up.

And that was the end of them, really. They had no future under John Beck.

Lads like Colin Greenall, Mike Flynn, Mark Leonard - good players who knew the game inside out . . . for them that was it.

We seemed to be signing a lot of lads from non-league, who were good players in their own right, but with the situation they were coming into, it was a tough ask.

Same with the young lads, we had people like Martin James, who had done well in the first team, was a really good footballer and could pick a pass. But suddenly, he was being told to hit it as high as he could into the corners.

The strange thing is, despite what people might think, John was actually a good coach. I'm a coach myself now over at Blackburn Rovers and looking back, you can see how good he was with his sessions. You might not agree with his philosophy and his tactics but in terms of getting a team to understand exactly what you wanted them to do, he was very good. As a bloke, he was alright with me and I think he quite liked me.

In my first game back, we won 5-2 against Rotherham and I think he liked what he saw.

I was a young pro who would give everything on the pitch, I didn't question his tactics or anything. I thought: 'Well, he's playing me, I'm getting first team football so I'll just get on with it.'

You just had to try to take it all on board, keep listening and keep learning. If the manager says there's a science behind how high you need to hit the ball, how you need to put backspin on it and stuff, it might sound daft, but you go along with it - he's been in the game a lot longer than me. But it was unusual, no doubt about that. There were names for areas all over the pitch: Paradise Alley, Quality Street, the Ghetto.

('Kiddo, not Quality Street - get it in Paradise Alley!')

Hang on, where's that? Down the wing behind the full-back? OK, boss.

It was a bit bizarre, but it had worked for John before and he was sticking to it. I remember one time later on, Paul Raynor and Ian Bryson did a one-two in their own half. They were both good footballers, so no danger, they didn't lose it or anything.

But that wasn't in John's rules, so he brought them both off - and, arguably, they were our best two players (!). He was just black and white, you did it his way or you suffered the consequences. In that first season, the consequence for the club was that we were relegated, which was absolutely horrible.

It all came down to the last game away at Bolton where I played at the back with Colin Greenall - a fantastic professional and a great guy. I remember they got a dodgy penalty right near the end when the ball hit Simon Burton's arm.

Big John McGinlay scored and that was that.

I think even if we'd won that day, we wouldn't have stayed up because we were on something like minus 30 goal difference and needed a bit of a miracle.

Being a Bolton lad, I had a lot of my old schoolmates there supporting them and I ended up walking home in among them, wearing my North End gear.

They'd gone up. We'd gone down. So you can imagine what that walk was like that day with my old mates. Talk about low - I was absolutely gutted. A terrible day.

There were no split-loyalties or anything for me; I was a Bury fan anyway, as that was nearest to where I grew up and my dad used to take me there. So I just had to suck it up, get in, shut the door, flop onto the settee and wonder where we went from there.

Thankfully, John Beck had seen something in me and - at a time when players were coming and going like crazy - I was sticking around at Deepdale.

The funny thing with John was that he was ahead of his time in many ways. He worked a lot on statistics and he had two fitness guys coming in to work with us. These days every club has sports scientists, but back then specifically working on stuff like that was unusual.

There were things like massages after games - sometimes John would be hands-on, doing them himself and talking you through the game you'd just played, while he pummelled your muscles.

So people can have a go at him, but there's no doubt he was a deep thinker with some good ideas, a good coach and he was one of the first to head down that scientific approach. Big Sam gave me a shot in the game, but John Beck stood by me too, so I've a lot to be grateful to him for.

Of course, I didn't think that when we were having buckets of cold water thrown over us before games.

I remember one time down at Barnet, we were in one of the worst changing rooms you've ever seen; solid concrete, like an igloo and it was about -3 degrees in there already.

Then you had to get starkers in the shower at about quarter to three and here it comes: *'Bang! Have that!'*

Whooooosh. Flaming hell, it was cold.

Then you'd look up and he'd say: 'Right saan . . . now you're *READY*!'

I was thinking: 'Well, I was *READY* before mate. Now I'm just flipping freezing!'

So some of those those things were all a bit madcap, to say the least.

People also think he always signed a certain type of player; big, physical, strong and there's no doubt we had a few. Lads like Gavin Nebbeling - what an unbelievable senior pro he was, absolutely top class. I looked up to him a lot and he mentored us young pros really, a great guy.

Obviously, Moyesie came in and he was a natural leader; he had the presence, the voice and he took it on himself to be a spokesman for the players, along with Ian Bryson, who was another top, top man. Those senior pros made sure that players performed and standards were maintained, no matter what you thought of the tactics.

As a young lad, I knew that not only did I have to please John and Gary Peters, I had to please Moyesie and Brys as well - because those lads were winners and they'd come to the club to win things, not see out their careers mid-table in the bottom division.

Also though, when you look at a lot of the lads John signed - Mike Conroy, Brys, Rayns - there was a lot of skilful lads in there too.

In that second season, with his own players in, results improved and it looked like we'd turned a corner. What was strange is that although we'd been relegated, attendances actually went up.

You just wouldn't get that in modern football, but off the pitch John was really sparking the town into life.

He was a character for sure and did so much to get fans excited again. Putting home fans in the Town End was a masterstroke - we loved kicking towards that end. At times it was like it was sucking the ball in and you could just see teams crumbling.

With us bombing forward in front of them and the noise coming from behind them, Deepdale was a hell of a place to come to. When we put them under siege it must have seemed inevitable that we were going to score.

Of course though, there was still John's tactics.

Straight from the kick-off we had to put the ball as high as possible onto the opposition left-back's head. The height was to keep the ball in the air long enough for Gareth Ainsworth to get there.

And when he did . . . his job was just to *batter* the defender.

At the start of every game, we'd do this and I used to feel sorry for their poor soul, thinking he's got all the time in the world to head this high ball away and then - *whack!*

Gareth would run through a brick wall, so you've got the worst person you could ever wish for, pelting it down the wing straight at you . . . *bang!*

Time and again, you'd see Gareth with stitches in his head and the full-back all bandaged up straight from the kick-off, thinking: 'What the hell?'

Welcome to Preston, mate - you've got another 89 minutes of this!

Crazy times, but I think we won five games on the trot at the start of the season so that gave us a good foundation and we went from there.

Things carried on going well and by April, we were pushing for promotion when we played Carlisle at Deepdale in our last home game of the season.

They were up around the play-offs too so it was a big crowd with a good away following down from Cumbria. The ground was bouncing even before kick-off with a massive roar even as we came out for the warm-up.

That got the adrenaline going and you start to feel pumped up - you know this is a big game. The Town End was packed, bags of noise . . . if it wasn't for the plastic pitch, you'd say it was the perfect setting for a football match.

Now, in those days, you could get away with a nice early tackle - or so I thought.

David Reeves did and he fouled me in the build-up to their first goal; early on and right in front of the Town End.

Reevesy being Reevesy, he scored and then wound the North End fans up as he ran away to celebrate. I was fuming. He'd fouled me and the ref had let it go.

I told him what I thought about it. In fact, I might have called him a flipping joke and - *surprise, surprise* - he gave me a yellow card.

I remember they had a lad called Ian Arnold who was playing up front too, a really tricky player. In other words, annoying.

A few minutes later, he was getting the ball under control, doing his stuff, and I just thought: 'I'm going to hit him hard here.' I swear I could see a tackle when I set off - and I thought I got a bit of the ball at the time.

But actually . . . when I look at the replay, it was a naughty challenge and unfortunately, he ended up going about four feet up in the air.

To make matters worse, it was right in front of the Carlisle fans and they were all going crazy, climbing the fences and calling me all sorts.

With all this going on, my mate the ref took his time (I think he just wanted me to suffer a bit more abuse) then gave me the red card.

It was a strange one, because the Preston fans were applauding me as I went off. I don't know, but maybe they thought Arnold deserved it *(if so, they're good judges those North Enders!)*.

It was the first time I'd had been sent off and I didn't know you were supposed to go down the tunnel, so I just went and sat on the bench.

Things went from bad to worse as they went 3-0 up, so everyone was in a foul mood and later on, there was a right flare-up right in front of the dug-out.

All sorts of things were going on and I just thought: *'I'm having a piece of this.'*

So I went for that Ian Arnold again, mainly because I thought he'd milked it a bit to get me sent off.

After that, I can't fully remember what happened *(honest!)*. I didn't thump anyone, I just sort of grabbed hold of him and had a word. I recall getting dragged away by some of our lads and pushed back into the dug-out before the ref realised what had happened and got me in even more trouble.

I was sat there, trying to look like a choirboy, while it all calmed down.

('What, me ref? Noooo, I've been sat here all along!')

Afterwards though, in the changing room, John pasted me for getting sent off - he absolutely ripped into me in front of all the lads.

Probably rightly so, I suppose.

He called me a *'deserter'* and all sorts and it got to the point where I was thinking: *'You're going a bit strong here, boss!'*

But I was in the wrong so that was that - I had to take it. And no matter how much it hurt, the 3-0 home defeat was worse.

That night, there was a supporters' event up in the Pavilion doing the Player of the Year awards *(I didn't win)* and I was sat there, pretty down in the dumps, when I saw John coming over. I thought: *'Oh my God, here we go again.'*

Instead he just said in his Cockney accent: 'I've seen that tackle again, saaan. You might have got the ball, you might not.

'But either way . . . I'm flipping proud of you. That's the type of fight I'm looking for!' He'd done a complete 180 and was now patting me on the back and saying how much he loved that I battled for the team, etc. I couldn't believe it, but that was John.

To be honest, I'd always get involved if there was any trouble on the pitch. In a flare-up, I'd be the first one in, but if the punches started flying, I'd be the first one out. I never wanted to hit anyone, I just wanted to look after my mates.

And that team thing was important; if someone wanted to play football against us, then fine. If they wanted to kick us, we'd kick them back . . . and a bit harder, probably.

The following week, we were away at Wycombe and I scored my first goal for North End. I didn't get many and I've probably got the world's best collection of *The Most Dreadful Goals You've Ever Seen In Your Life.*

I'd make them into a DVD, but it would be a pretty short one!

For that Wycombe one, I think the ball hit my knee, then my shin, then bounced off my foot and went in from about three yards out before I knew anything about it really.

A classic of its kind.

I wasn't a big one for scoring goals - *which is a good job when you look at my record* - for me it was all about keeping clean sheets. Us lads at the back would celebrate them as much as goals.

Later on, Michael Jackson used to come up with me for corners and one season he got a ridiculous amount of goals, with me doing all the dirty work and blocks for him to get a clear run.

I was Beardsley to his Lineker. No-one ever mentions that, do they Jacko?

The way I looked at it, I was there to defend and we had enough good players who could put the ball in the back of the net - a lot cleaner than any of my strikes too.

Obviously, that season under John we got to the play-offs and I was suspended for the first Torquay game, but drove down to watch it with my wife on the day.

John had told me that I was starting the second leg, no matter what, so I wanted to watch their winger, a lad called Gregory Goodridge, who was a really good player that I'd be up against.

We lost 2-0 down there, but for the return game we stayed at a hotel in Southport the night before the game. I remember that Moyesie called us all into his room and gave us a talk about how important it was that we were all focused on our game and how massive it was. He really psyched everyone up brilliantly and I thought that was an amazing thing to do.

At that moment, you could see the manager in him and it was plain to see he was going to be brilliant when the time came because he was such a natural leader.

On the night itself - well, what an atmosphere. You could almost feel the crowd straining at the leash even in the warm-up.

We went 1-0 up, but then Goodridge did me on a long ball and got in behind me.

So much for my scouting trip!

I just thought: 'Bugger.' It was now 3-1 on aggregate and I felt terrible. I was furious with myself and was then carrying this burden: 'I've cost us a goal there.'

But the big thing was . . . the fans stayed with us.

There was no grumbling. In fact, if anything, the noise got louder.

That helped me shake myself out of it and I thought: 'Look, there's loads of time left - the way we play, we're going to get plenty of corners and free-kicks and we're going to get back into this.'

It turned out to be an amazing night of football and one of the most incredible turnarounds I've ever been involved in. We were like a team possessed and it was a real privilege to be out there that night. I can't remember whether John Beck gave a team talk at half-time or not, it didn't really matter. He knew that we knew the task, we had good leaders and we would do what we had to do.

You probably know the rest. We won - thank God - and I've never seen celebrations like it. Fans poured onto the pitch and the funny thing was, everyone was taking home these big clumps of astroturf. There were lads rolling it up by the metre and putting it over their shoulders - hilarious. Half of Preston must have got a new plastic lawn.

Fair play to them; I don't think the club wanted to keep it - and the players definitely didn't!

We went out after the game, but I don't think I slept when I got in. I just lay there.

When it all sank in . . . well, I'm not sure it did for days. I'd always dreamed of playing at Wembley, so to get there was just surreal.

Wembley was the place where massive teams went for the FA Cup Final, where European Cups were won, where England won the World Cup - so to be playing for Preston in League 2 and get there was just unbelievable.

The club did everything right in terms of preparation - we went down to a hotel a couple of days before, we knew the team two days in advance and had worked on everything over and over again.

I was left-back, with Stuart Hicks and Moyesie in the middle with Andy Fensome on the other side. All sorted, good to go.

When the big day came, we got to the stadium and had a look around - it was everything I'd expected it to be, absolutely huge, massive pitch, overlooked by those famous towers. Incredible.

But when I got back to the changing rooms, I could see Hicksy, head in his hands, crying floods of tears.

I was like: 'What's going on mate? We're going out in a minute, what's happening?'

Well, John Beck had dropped him, just like that, not only on the day of the game but with about an hour to go before kick-off.

Jamie Squires, a young lad who was only about 18, was coming in instead and I was just like: *'What the hell has he done that for?'*

It was just crazy; we'd worked on the team for ages and now he was switching a centre half just before kick-off - everyone was shell-shocked. The whole mood of the dressing room was on the floor and the timing was disastrous.

It wasn't Jamie's fault - he was a good young lad. It was just a really poor decision, but John was like that. Quite often, he'd call people over in training late in the week and drop them because: 'I've got a funny feeling in my water son.'

What can you do? You suck it up and get on with it as best you can.

We went out at Wembley and Ian Bryson scored a brilliant goal to put us 1-0 up. In fact, we were ahead twice after Paul Raynor scored, but I never felt we were in full control of that game.

I was up against a lad called Dave Carroll and he was the hardest player to mark that I ever came up against. No matter what league I faced him in, he always gave me a bit of a chasing throughout my career.

I could never work him out; he was like a Chris Waddle-type of player - but he had spaghetti legs. They went one way and his body went the other - a nightmare to play against. He could go both sides of you and ended up scoring two in that final.

In all honesty, I had a terrible game, I just didn't play well whatsoever, I think the occasion got to me massively. I don't think the team played particularly well either and Wycombe deserved to go up, no question about that.

The coach going home was miserable as hell and Hicksy was still inconsolable. John Beck stopped off and brought a load of beers on and whatnot, but we all knew he'd made a major mistake with his selection.

Whether he'd ever admit that himself is a different matter, of course. I was keeping my head down at the back of the bus, but when he spotted me he announced: 'Flipping hell, saaan - you had an absolute stinker.'

Cheers, boss, I know.

It's hard for me when I talk about John, because you tell these stories and people must think he was a nutter. But he was a good coach and he did an awful lot of good for the club and for me as a player.

Obviously, he wasn't everyone's cup to tea and that summer we lost Tony Ellis, which was a big blow, as he was almost guaranteed to give you 20-plus goals a season at that point.

However, Tony was a great footballer and you can understand why lads like that got a bit peeved with the way we were playing under the manager. Flair players like Tony were a bit too regimented in the system and I think it was harder on them than us lads at the back.

We didn't have the best start to the following season and we lost seven league games on the trot from late September into October.

The pressure was mounting a bit and John was desperate for me to play in the FA Cup against Blackpool in November that season. I was keen to play too, but there was no way my ankle would let me.

The passion of those games against Blackpool was always unbelievable as a player. Mike Conroy scored the winner that night and the fans sang about if for years afterwards - literally years.

Everyone knows that if you're in a North End team that beats them, it's something special - and if you score the winning goal, well, you're almost like a god.

Funnily enough, it was only a couple of games after that derby win that John was sacked.

I don't know what went on with all that at board level, but the transition to Gary Peters was smooth.

We all knew him and he knew the issues we were having with the style of play. We had good footballers like Brys and Paul Raynor and we just wanted to play a little more football really.

Gary was always a bit more relaxed than John and was a great coach too. But the thing that sticks with me was that he was outstanding in terms of his recruitment - the quality of player we started bringing in just went up a notch when he took over.

I don't know if he was looking for a striker (!) but I managed to get the winner against Barnet in one of his first games.

It was another in my *'Terrible Goals'* collection - it just trickled over the line at the Town End. A shocking attempt and how it went in I'll never know. But - *hey* - a goal's a goal and it won us the game. I was on a roll at that point and scored again against Rochdale next time out too, by which time Allan Smart was settling in up front, so my goalscoring duties could take a back seat again for a while.

Of course, it was Gary who brought David Beckham into the club on loan that season - and what a great lad he was. I always remember in his first session we were just about to practise corners and Rayns started jogging over to take them.

Gary was like: '*Woah, woah, woah!* David's going to be taking all the set pieces while he's with us.'

There were a few funny looks, but the gaffer said: 'Look lads, he takes them ahead of Denis Irwin at Man United.'

We all thought: 'Yeah, right. What a load of balls.'

But then, of course, he started whipping these corners in and we were going: 'Wow, blimey, great ball son, etc.'

Everyone apart from Rayns, who was a bit sniffy with it all, muttering: 'Yeah, whatever. That one went out of play . . .'

We all loved Rayns, but it was hilarious to see him chuntering away. In the end, even he had to admit that the kid was a bit special.

Becks himself was quite quiet but a great lad to have around, not 'big-time' at all and he really mixed in with the lads.

He scored straight from a corner in his first game and then banged in a cracking free-kick in the next one. I remember sitting next to him on a long journey down to Exeter and he was interviewed in Match magazine, after he'd played in a Champions League game alongside Eric Cantona.

Our nutcase of a left-back Raymond Sharp got hold of this magazine and he was reading it out loud like it was a romantic novel or something: *'After the goal, I jumped into Eric's arms . . . ooooh Eric!'*

He just annihilated him, but fair play to David, he just took it and had a laugh with the lads. Even at that age, you could see he was going to be a big, big star.

Unbelievable talent and it was a shame we couldn't keep hold of him longer. If we had, I think we might have finished better than fifth, but as it was we were in the play-offs - against my boyhood team Bury.

It's a measure of the fella that Becks turned up to the game and was in our changing room beforehand, willing us on to win. I said: 'We'd have a better chance if you put your boots on mate!'

As it was, we fancied ourselves as we'd beat them 5-0 at Deepdale only a month or so before. Instead, we got done 1-0 at home - massively against the run of play - so we were really up against it for the second leg.

I'd dreamed of playing at Gigg Lane as a young lad so it was a big night for me. But at that stage of the season, the pitch there was shocking, more mud on it than grass.

There wasn't much in that game and I was up against their winger Tony Kelly, who did me right down the back of my leg quite early on.

I thought: 'OK mate, I'll have you back for that when the time comes.'

Anyway, they scored a second goal late on, so it was clear we weren't going through and I got a chance to tackle him straight from the kick-off after the goal.

I thought I'd just leave a bit of a marker on him, but looking back, I actually caught him with my studs right in his groin.

Purely by accident, obviously, I was going for the ball - *not his balls.*

But I've seen a replay and it was a right naughty one, no doubt about that.

Next thing, he went all Sugar Ray Leonard on me, bopping around and throwing punches - the lad completely lost it. The ref missed the worst of the tackle, but saw the aftermath and gave him a straight red.

Unfortunately, that meant he missed the play-off final and Bury got beat by Chesterfield. I feel a bit bad about that now, but he did rake his studs down me and then punch me, so y'know . . . don't do it.

We did know that we didn't want to risk the play-offs the following season - we wanted to go straight up, no messing about.

Luckily, Gary brought in some top lads that summer to get us set up right. I'd played against Steve Wilkinson when he was at Mansfield and thought he was an alright player, maybe not as physical as we needed, but skilful.

I didn't know much about Andy Saville; he looked OK in training and pre-season and obviously knew his way about.

But once they started in the league . . . they were just an unbelievable partnership.

Steve was an intelligent player who could see a pass and drop into positions where defenders couldn't find him, while Sav was the cutting edge when the balls came in.

He was physical, but he could play too. They were both going to score goals, all they needed was service and for us to keep the door shut at the back.

Two more great signings - Russ Wilcox and Dean Barrick - arrived as Gary really balanced the squad brilliantly, so that there were no weak spots in the starting line-up and plenty of cover in all positions.

In goal, we had John Vaughan and we all lived in fear of him because he was hard as nails. If he said something, you just did it, no messing - he was a proper enforcer.

The only lad brave/daft enough to mess about with Vaughany was Kevin Magee, our flying Scottish winger.

His nickname among the lads was Shifty - say no more (!).

One time, Vaughany was having treatment with one of those electronic machines that twitches your muscles to help recovery, when Kev sneaked in and turned the machine up to full power sending a proper charge through John's leg. Shocking, really. Next thing, he's ripped all the patches off and is chasing Shifty all over the place - I'd never seen him run so fast. I swear if Vaughany had caught him, it would have been the end of Kev - and not just in a football sense!

But John was a top keeper - more than just a shot-stopper. He played the game for you, very loud, always shouting and was a really good guy to have on your team.

Gary was massive on that team ethic and knew how to bond the lads together. We were built on togetherness and would all socialise together on a Saturday night after games - going out round Preston in the pubs. You don't get that much these days, but back then it was a different outlook and I think it brought us much closer to the fans who we were playing for.

Also, if there were any club fines for being late or anything, you paid them in cans of beer.

So there were times on away trips when we'd be loading up crates of beer for the journey back and people might be thinking: 'How many fines have this lot had?'

The camaraderie went back to the days of John Beck, to be fair. I remember one time we had a stopover down south as we played Fulham on a Saturday and Gillingham on the Tuesday night.

We won 1-0 at Craven Cottage and John arranged a pub for us to have a night out in Maidstone - *as you do.*

Well, of course, the beer starts flowing and eventually I end up walking back to the hotel with Terry Fleming at about 2.30am and we've both had a few. Suddenly, Terry's in an argument with some local lads, the police step in and he gets arrested.

They take him to the police station and straight away, all our lads are in there: *'Come on officers, let him out - free the Preston one!'*

The coppers are having none of it and insist he has to stay overnight to dry out. And all the time we can hear Terry shouting from the cells: *'You've got to let me out . . . I'm the new Ryan Giggs!'*

Typically, on the Tuesday night, we went to Gillingham, won 1-0 and who got the goal? Norman Stanley - *sorry!* - Terence Maurice Fleming.

Maybe he was going to be the new Giggsy after all. Or maybe not.

Either way, you can't out a price on that camaraderie between us at North End. There were times when we felt unstoppable and I know from talking to other lads who came in, it wasn't always like that at other clubs. We had a special bond.

Around the time that Gary took over, Baxi had got involved in the club and you could just feel momentum growing off the pitch as well as on it. There just seemed to be a more professional approach taking hold and investment coming in.

With Bryan Gray as chairman there was positive change and a clear vision for the future. Training facilities improved and we moved into Springfields, so we had a permanent base instead of having three of four different places we might go.

You could just see things progressing and getting better and better. So as a player, you really wanted to be a part of it.

When you saw the frame of the Tom Finney stand going up, it was 'lump in your throat' time - it looked absolutely massive compared to what had been there before. I just couldn't wait to play in front of it and it gave me another incentive to step up my game.

I played 30 games that season as I was still having a bit of trouble with my ankle, but I'll never forget the celebrations down at Orient and the scenes on the last day of the season against Exeter with the new stand absolutely packed. What a day that was.

The thing that really sticks with me is the open-top bus parade.

All the way through that season, you'd meet fans and they'd be telling you how mental the town would go if we went up and how the Flag Market would be packed with all these people.

But you don't quite believe it until you see it.

And then . . . wow. Just amazing.

There were so many people lining the streets on the route, I just thought, well there can't be many in the town square now. So when we got there and saw this sea of people . . . it just hit you that this is a really big club.

This is what a proper football town looks like.

All the lads had the same reaction. We just looked at each other and knew that we'd started something here and if we could keep it going, there was no limit to what we could achieve.

It was just a fantastic season and I was chuffed that I'd played a major part.

Deep down though, I felt there was more to come from me and I knew I'd have to improve to stay in the team at the next level.

I'd been at left-back and centre half, but I could feel better players coming in around me and knew that I'd have to step up again to nail down a spot.

I had to battle harder, train harder and apply myself harder, which wasn't going to be easy because I felt like I was giving it everything I had already.

I was brutal with myself and knew I had to improve physically at centre half and I had to better on the ball at left-back.

I just gave it everything I'd got and in our first season back up, I think I played more games than anyone apart from Russ Wilcox.

I knew Gary liked me and what I brought to the team, but the competition was so strong, I knew I couldn't relax; I had to keep pushing on.

Good players were coming in and good players were going out. We were all really sad to see Andy Saville leave, but you had to trust Gary and he clearly knew what he was doing.

Dave Reeves came in and later on Gary Bennett arrived. Reevesy was great for us, and Benno had got the Golden Boot at Wrexham before joining us.

He certainly had a golden smile - his gnashers always looked too big for his mouth - but he was a lovely lad. He was always there to tell us a funny story first thing in the morning, standing stark naked most of the time. *Don't ask!*

Gary also brought back Lee Ashcroft who I think was underrated at the time. When I look back at my ten years with the club, Ashy would be up there when it came to forwards definitely He also had a temper on him for sure and he could two-foot you in training and not even think about it. I loved him though, he was a really good competitor when he channelled his talent the right way.

He was a local lad too, just like Lee Cartwright, who I used to room with. What an engine Carts had; if you were ever playing with him in front of you, you always felt safe because he'd be back helping you out in defence, then the next minute he'd be on the edge of their box, whipping balls in. He'd just do that all game without breaking sweat.

He's a great lad, really unassuming, and when I look at other lads with me, like Carts and Paul McKenna, Dave Lucas - to go from where we started out to being 90 minutes from the Premier League in front of 88,000 at Cardiff was just unbelievable really. If we'd have managed it there would have been several of us who'd been with the club right through the leagues *(but let's not go there just yet!)*.

It wasn't always a smooth ride for young players, however. I remember Kevin Kilbane bursting onto the scene when we were in the bottom tier and he was a brilliant player; big long legs, ate the ground up, bags of skill, great crosser, could score goals, the lot. But when we went up and we weren't doing so well, I remember playing left-back with him just in front of me and some idiots in the Tom Finney Stand were giving him pelters.

I remember it because it was so unusual for North End fans - they're not normally like that. Despite what anyone tells you, players hear these stupid shouts, even if they pretend they don't.

To make it worse, he's a local lad, a North End boy.

I really wanted to shout back: *'Oi! Leave off him - he's a kid.'*

But you can't shout at an entire stand when the vast majority of the people in there are fine, so you have to bite your tongue. I think that negativity maybe affected him a bit, but he had so much talent and desire he was always going to have a great career - it's just a shame he didn't stay longer.

I wasn't immune to the odd bit of stick, either.

You can't please all the people all the time though and I remember one time I'd leathered someone in front of the Tom Finney stand.

The ref came sprinting over reaching for his cards and as he pulled out a yellow, this wag shouted out from the home crowd: *'Do us a favour and send him off, ref!'*

I had to laugh myself, to be honest.

Cheers mate!

Meanwhile, Gary brought in a bright-eyed, bushy-haired, gentle lad from Darlington that season - a young Sean Gregan.

Some lads coming into a new dressing room might be a bit quiet at the start. But Greegs? Quiet? *Never!*

He was an unbelievable character, huge presence and a great player. He came in as a centre half so I was thinking, yet again: 'Here we go - another lad being bought for my position!'

They'd splashed out £350,000 on him, a lot of money in those days, and you could see his talent from the start.

I think he was so good on the ball though, it was only a matter of time before he moved into that midfield enforcer role with his technique, his size and, of course, his giant backside.

It was an outstanding signing by Gary - probably the best of the lot - and, for me, the best player I played alongside, just because of the impact he had. He definitely had the best debut of anyone I can remember; beating Blackpool 3-0 at Deepdale.

To be honest, debut or not, it doesn't get much better than that for anyone, does it?

Gary Bennett came off the bench and put us one up with about 20 minutes to go before Reevesy got a second.

What sticks in my mind though was the third goal, as I'd gone up for a corner.

Reevesy flicked it on at the near post and I could see this ball coming to me; unmarked, back stick.

In that split second I swear I thought: *'Oh my God! It's coming to me, I'm going to score against Blackpool at the Town End - it doesn't get any better than this . . .'*

And at that very moment . . . Benno popped up in front of me to make it 3-0. The little sod! I've never forgiven him!

I was marking Tony Ellis that night and it was weird because I obviously knew him really well and even though I'd been his teammate, I idolised him a bit because he was that good. Not surprisingly, he was getting dogs' abuse from the crowd and I was just thinking: 'Whatever I do, I can't let this bugger score. They'll flipping lynch me!'

Another big game we played that season was away at Tottenham in the League Cup.

I was centre half that night, so missed out on marking Darren Anderton or Ruel Fox. Instead, I had the easy option in the middle . . . Teddy Sheringham.

What a player. I think I had a decent game that night and, to be fair, he was talking to me all game, saying *'well played son'* and whatnot.

I remember thinking: 'Blimey, what a nice guy.'

Of course, they were beating us 3-0 at the time, so he could afford to be friendly.

I think the result flattered them and it was a great experience for us all. You just try and learn from nights like that and carry the lessons over for next time. We drew 1-1 with them in the second leg at Deepdale, so for a League 1 team, we did really well.

Overall, after the drama of Wembley and then going up, that season was more of a consolidation, as we brought new lads in and got used to the higher level.

Moyesie was doing a bit more coaching and growing into the role as assistant manager and you could see him developing all the time.

Gary was still the boss though and everyone thought highly of him, especially the way he coped with losing Kev Kilbane by bringing in three hot prospects from Man Utd; Michael Appleton, Jon Macken and Colin Murdock.

Yep, another left-sided centre half for me to worry about. Cheers, boss.

When someone comes in, you're always watching them and I thought: 'Yeah, he's good on the ball, technically sound, good passer, mmmm.'

Then you start thinking: 'Yeah, but he's not as aggressive as me. Can he play left-back too?' You're trying to reassure yourself - and checking the length of your contract!

I'd heard of Michael Appleton - always a tidy player - but knew nothing about Jon.

In one of his first training sessions, he was all over the place; shots going high and wide, kicking the ground, you name it - a nightmare. I remember thinking: *'Blimey, this kid's terrible!'*

Of course, he just needed a bit of time and patience and then - *wow!* - you saw how much it paid off.

When he got going, his transformation was unbelievable; his shots were flying in, he was getting headers, tap-ins, screamers, everything. Hell of a player.

That 1997/98 season didn't start great and you started to feel this shift among the mood and the mindset of the players.

As I said, Gary's recruitment was outstanding and he had brought in some really, really good players; Michael Jackson, David Eyres and Gary Parkinson, for example.

I think the feeling was we could play better football than we were doing and we needed to progress a bit more tactically.

Don't get me wrong, we played some really good stuff under Gary, but there were times when we were focused on just clearing our lines when I thought we could be using Greegs more in midfield to spring us forward and build attacks.

We felt we could play out from the back a bit more and change the dynamics of our approach. We were a young group and Moyesie was having more of an influence, so there was just this seamless slide into him taking over from Gary.

Everyone liked and respected Gary and there was no animosity or anything when the change came.

I think he was looking forward to working on the youth side and did a really good job in there for many years. His reputation and standing is absolutely top notch.

But there's no doubt this was the opportunity Moyesie had been waiting for.

Just as Gary had done when he took over from John Beck, David got us playing more football and set about pushing us more. He was always quite serious, so he took the change from being player to coach and then manager all in his stride.

He'd made no secret of his ambitions and he was determined to make it work.

It was a bit weird for me, as we'd been teammates for about five or six years, but now he was in charge. It wasn't just a case of having an idea we could work with between ourselves - now it was *'what he says goes'*.

It didn't happen straight away though and he started with a terrible run or results. It was strange, because even though we were losing, we all still felt confident in him and that we were moving forward as a team. He was very direct, very clear, very steely in his determination to prove that he could be a good manager.

He signed good players and he improved the players that were already there.

Mark Rankine had taken a bit of stick when he first arrived, but he worked so hard to turn things round and his partnership with Greegs in midfield was just legendary.

We had Ranks covering every blade of grass, Sean as the enforcer and then someone like Paul McKenna who had so much guile and craft on the ball.

Kenna would tuck in to make a three in the middle, then we'd play with one proper wide man - Eyresy or Iain Anderson later on, who could carry the ball.

So, over time, we became this unit that worked so well together - no big stars, but lots of good players with a proper work ethic.

Moyesie would drill into us where everyone should be depending on where the ball was on the pitch.

Not just when we had the ball, it was just as important to know where you need to be without it too - even more so as a defender.

You knew: 'Right the ball's *there*, I need to be *here* and you'd look around and know exactly where your teammate was going to be, because we were so well trained.'

I loved playing behind Eyresy, what a player he was - especially as he was about 51 when we signed him. He must have been about 60 when he left, or maybe he just looked that way!

He was just so consistent, so clever. I still play with him now and again at charity games for the Gary Parky Trust and he looks like he could still get a game now - absolutely ageless and a class act.

One of the games everyone remembers from around that time was when we played Arsenal in the FA Cup, live on Sky at a sold-out Deepdale.

We set off like a house on fire and we really took it to them in the opening stages, going 2-0 up with goals from Kurt Nogan. We caused them some real problems early on, but then we conceded right on half-time, a deflected shot that just clipped someone's leg and that changed the complexion entirely.

At 2-0 we could have got in, regrouped and had a proper plan - 2-1 is an entirely different situation. We'd played so well but we were a bit dejected at half-time because they'd got this scrappy goal.

Of course, in the second half, Eyresy got in a chase with Marc Overmars and there was only ever going to be one winner there.

The ref sent Dave off and Emmanuel Petit scored straight from the free-kick - as World Cup winners do, y'know? After that we were up against it and as they piled forward I found myself in our box, with Fabian Caballero just about to nip in front of me. I put my arm out to pull him back a bit and he swung his elbow right at me - *smack!* - right in the chops, a proper hit.

I was sure the ref or the linesman would have seen it so I went down, thinking they'd stop play, maybe send him off and we'd be back to ten-a-side.

Unbeknown to me though, the officials somehow missed it, the game carried on, Petit nipped in to score again and I was left in this heap - with the ball in the back of the net.

The North End crowd were going mad and these days it would have been one of those situations where they automatically stop play for a head injury.

I think VAR would have seen the elbow for sure - but then again, they might have seen me tug him back in the first place . . !

The main thing I remember from that night was marking Ray Parlour. Before the game, I'd looked at him and thought he was nothing special, not cracking any pots, that lad. And by this time, I'd been around a bit, playing against some really tough lads in the lower leagues, proper hard cases.

So I thought I'd give him a welcome tackle early on, the sort of thing you used to get away with. *Bang!*

Oh my God . . . it was like I'd run into a block of marble. He was just solid, absolutely rock hard and I thought: 'Blimey, I wasn't expecting that.'

Not only was he tough, his movement was different to anything I'd ever come up against, he was dropping off into pockets, pushing on, he was just incredible and afterwards I looked at him in a whole new light.

That's why he was at that level, those top drawer players have everything, but sometimes you don't realise it until you come up against them. We lost 4-2 in the end, but we played well and the season was going great, overall.

I was still having trouble with my long-term left ankle injury though, so missed another big chunk of the season as we pushed into the play-offs.

Some days I'd have injections to play - I had various operations and treatment but it used to flare up regularly, lots of arthritis and was just a right pain.

I was just coming back from an operation when we were away at Fulham in the last game of the season. I was due to be on the bench, as I hadn't really done enough training to play the full game, with Dominic Ludden starting. Somehow, Dom got injured on the bus on the way to the ground so Moyesie asked if I would do a job.

I really shouldn't have played, but me being me, I said yes.

It wasn't my best decision as I was nowhere near right and spent the last 20 minutes limping as we got pumped 3-0. I should have asked to come off, but I was never one for doing that - I'd just keep going.

It was stupid of me really and playing in that Fulham game ruled me out of the play-offs against Gillingham, so I was gutted by that.

We ended up staying down that season but by that time Moyesie was really in his stride and the next season we were flying. We set off with four wins out of five before Wigan came to Deepdale for a match that was memorable for all the wrong reasons.

We were 1-0 up through Steve Basham when a long ball came over the top just before half-time. I thought I'd just lay it back to Dave Lucas, but I hadn't seen one of their lads nipping in between us. I didn't get the best contact on it and suddenly the lad's gone round Lukes who tripped him up a bit.

Stuart Barlow nipped in from behind me and had an open goal. I was getting back at him but he got a shot off . . . and put it wide.

I thought: 'Blimey, we've got away with that!'

But then the ref has not only given them a penalty - he's sent Lukes off.

Crazy, talk about double jeopardy. I was fuming, but not half as much as Dave. He still goes on about it to me now, with good reason - because he never got back into the team all season . . . and we went on to win the league. I played the next game and poor old Lukes was out of the team for almost a year and it was all my fault.

I've apologised to him a thousand times, but I'll say it again - *sorry, Dave!*

The other thing I recall from that game is that we lost 4-1 and Barlow got a hat-trick. Towards the end, he was doing keepy-ups in front of the Wigan fans and showboating a bit.

No-one likes that and afterwards, Moyesie showed us a video of him doing it. He said: *'Just remember that, lads. Just remember that . . .'*

He knew that when we went to their place for that magical night towards the end of the season, we would be properly fired up.

Before that, we had another game against Arsenal, in the League Cup this time, down at their brilliant old Highbury stadium.

Normally we'd have a go at every team, but that night Moyesie told us to sit off a bit more and try to catch them on the break. So we spent the first part of the game just watching the ball being pinged around this immaculate surface and we were all getting a bit agitated.

The next thing, this blur just went past me down the right hand side and I thought: *'Blimey, what the hell was that?'*

I turned round and Thierry Henry was about ten yards behind me - he'd just gone before I even knew he was in front of me.

I thought *'I'm going to have to do something about this'* so a few minutes later, I hit him with a great hard tackle on the halfway line.

It was one of the best tackles I've ever done; I got the ball no problem, but unfortunately he went about six feet up in the air and it started a full-scale push-and-shove with him and half their team. Henry was mouthing off at me and out of nowhere I just shouted: *'Aww shut up you, what have you ever won?'*

A couple of our lads looked at me a bit funny and then I remembered . . . oh crap, he won the World Cup with France last year!

You've got to laugh about it now, but at the time these things just come out. After about half an hour, I remember chasing back to catch up with Kanu who'd beaten our offside trap and got in down the left-hand side. I was absolutely pelting it back and thinking he was going to shoot with his left foot. That's what anyone in the lower leagues would do.

Not that lad though. I slid in to tackle him, but he just stopped dead in his tracks, from 60 to nought in one second. It was one of them where he could have waved to me as I went sliding past - *whoosh!* - thinking: *'Oh my God. He's absolutely done me, there!'*

Then, cool as you like, he pulled it onto his right foot and put it in the back of the net. Job done while I was still on my backside. It was just so effortless and again, another example of those top players and what they could do to you.

To be fair, Jon Macken equalised for us and we put in a decent performance despite losing 2-1.

We were on a charge in the league though and beat the old enemy Blackpool 3-0 at Deepdale in late December, so as the song goes, *Merry Xmas Everybody.*

We just fancied our chances and our class and superiority showed in the end. Eyresy got two and Michael Appleton got the other on a brilliant night. Blackpool had one of the poorest teams out that night I've ever seen them have, but who cares? It's always nice to beat them, isn't it?

It wasn't all smooth though and if ever we lost a game we always had a video inquest with Moyesie to see where we could put things right.

I remember we lost 3-2 to Colchester and Lomana Lua Lua scored an absolute corker for them, which he could probably do about one game in ten.

Maybe we were getting a little bit jittery around then, but you get that over a season, you're bound to get a dip, you've just got to respond in the right way.

I was playing left-back some games and centre half in others and in all honesty I couldn't tell you which was my favourite position. I liked getting forward from left-back, getting up and down the pitch and maybe setting goals up.

But I also liked the physicality of being centre half and having a battle. I didn't mind either and played them both pretty much equally well, so I suppose I was a bit unusual in that respect.

Sometimes though, that versatility went against me. I'd be having a decent run in the middle but when the left-back would get injured I was put out there for a couple of games and shifted about.

I never complained, obviously, I was just glad to be in the team and I'd do the job wherever I was asked. I wasn't precious about anything, me.

We were back on track in the league by early April when we went to Wigan, backed by one of the biggest North End followings I've ever seen.

There must have been eight or nine thousand there as they took over a full side of the DW Stadium.

The fans knew as well as we did that THIS was a massive game. Again, it was one of those where you could feel the anticipation in the warm-up. We got back in the dressing room and were so focused it was like: *'Right lads, let's go to work here.'*

It was just a phenomenal night. Jacko got the goal early on with a great flick over his shoulder and we just played them off the park for long spells.

I remember Greegs got a bad injury early on - *he actually broke a bone in his back* - but just carried on playing until right near the end. He put have been in agony, but he wouldn't go off. Jacko was all blood-spattered and doing his best Terry Butcher impression at the end, but the whole thing was just everyone together; players, manager, coaches and that army of fans.

It was great to win for them and avenge that Deepdale defeat, eleven against eleven this time - a fair fight. Oh, and Mr Keepy-Uppy Barlow? *He didn't play . . .*

After that night, we just felt unstoppable and I think we knew then that was it - we were going up. We just had to hold it together for a few more games.

Of course, we eventually went up on the back of one of our worst performances of the season. We lost 2-0 at Cambridge where they had big Trevor Benjamin up front for them and the ref was letting him get away with murder.

They'd only just avoided relegation and now they were playing like world beaters against us, really putting a lot of effort in. I kept thinking: 'What a load of cheats this lot are - they've been rubbish all year and now they're bringing this out of the bag.'

We were two down at half-time and in the dressing room there was a right ding-dong between the forwards and defenders about whose fault it was. They were 'good' arguments, though - for the right reasons. Even though we were about to go up, we were still pushing each other on and making sure standards were maintained.

In the second half, I was getting more and more wound up as the game went on and chipping away at the ref constantly. In the end, I think he was so fed up of all the moaning, he sent Jacko off for something or nothing in the last minute.

Thankfully, results elsewhere went for us and we'd gone up anyway.

Cue massive celebrations, Moyesie running onto the pitch spraying Champagne about - just beautiful pandemonium all around.

And in the middle of it all Jacko was still saying: 'Flaming hell, Kiddo, that's your fault I got sent off, you didn't shut up all flipping game!' *Sorry mate!*

We had a great night journey back and there were fans waiting back at Deepdale for us, so it was just an amazing experience. We had a great night out round the town when we got back, I can't remember much about it but those times don't come around very often.

You're like 'king for the night' with everyone singing, cheering and celebrating everywhere you looked; players with fans and everyone in together, just as it should be. Don't ask me for specifics though, it's all a bit hazy - as I'm sure it is for everyone who was out that night . . .

We had one home game against Millwall where we were getting the trophy afterwards and, while it was a brilliant occasion and we won 3-2, I was beating myself up a bit as I gave one of the goals away.

It was a sign of Moyesie's focus that I knew he wouldn't let it slide and even in the midst of all this celebration, he sidled up to me and said: *'Got done for the goal there, son.'*

I'd stepped up my levels that season massively, but that was a signal that I'd have to get even better in the Championship. Moyesie didn't need to say it - I just knew.

For now though, I was celebrating again with the fans, the backroom staff, the players - it was just magical.

It was the second time I'd won the league with North End and I remember trying to savour every moment and thinking how lucky I was; not many players get to win a league once in their careers but to get two titles with the same club was just unbelievable.

Me and Lee Cartwright were able to tell the lads what the bus parade a few days later was going to be like, but I don't think they believed us until they saw it with their own eyes.

It was just amazing - every bit as good as the first time and those type of days stay with you for the rest of your life. Even people that had come in for big fees and been around a bit were like: 'Wow - look at this!'

It really impressed a lot of players and again we felt like we were on this journey with the club that could maybe - *maybe* - take us right to the very top league. Everything at the club was on the up, so they were great times to be involved in.

But, for me, there was a dark cloud on the horizon.

Prior to the Cambridge game, I remember sitting with Mick Rathbone in his physio room, just chewing the fat with a few of the lads and having a laugh with Baz because he's such a great guy - he's almost like a comedian.

He was just strapping up my ankle as usual and I almost casually mentioned to him that every now and again throughout the season, I'd been getting the odd feeling of pins and needles when I headed the ball.

He suddenly looked very serious as I said that the feeling was like a spasm that goes right down through my body, along my arms and right down to my toes.

I said it was only every now and then when the ball caught me wrong on the top of my head but he said straight away: 'I don't like the sound of that, Kiddo.'

I could tell by the look on his face he was worried. I thought: *'Blimey! What have I said here?'*

From the off, he said he didn't want me to play at Cambridge, but I wasn't having any of that. I said: 'You're kidding Baz! We're going for promotion and you want me to drop out? No way - I'm not missing that.'

We compromised and agreed that I'd have a scan as soon as possible, which I did a couple of days after the game. The results were bad news for me - I needed an urgent operation on my neck.

A disc in my neck had severely crumbled and was hitting my spinal cord. If I caught another header wrong, it could sever my spine and leave me paralysed for life.

I was absolutely taken aback by the seriousness of it all and the medical opinions were scary, quite honestly. I missed the last game of the season away at Bristol City but the beauty of being at a good club like North End is that they don't mess about with stuff like that and within a week, I was having the surgery.

Until the day of the op, I didn't realise how big it was going to be. It was a major operation, life support, the whole works, with the best neuro-surgeons out there, so I was really lucky and grateful for that.

The recovery time was listed as six months and I was in a neck brace for three solid months - I could never take it off. Talk about a pain in the neck . . .

We'd gone up to the Championship and I was gutted to be missing out on that, but mainly I was thinking: 'Am I ever going to play again?'

It was that serious and there were some very dark times as the months dragged on. Your livelihood is at risk, you worry about the future and obviously, I love football, I love the club and the thought of never pulling the North End shirt on again was a really, really frightening prospect.

You're thinking: *'Is that it? Am I done?'* All those emotions drive you on and I was desperate to get back.

Eventually, I got that flipping brace off and couldn't wait to get back training. It was a massive relief that things had gone well and again, me being me, I probably came back a bit too soon, playing a couple of games in November, which amazed a few people - *me too, I think!*

I'd only done a bit of running but someone dropped out and it was a case of 'Kiddo, can you play?'

Of course I could. I wasn't 100 per cent right, but I'd never say no. After that I was in and out a bit as I had to err on the side of caution and take things a bit more steadily. I got a run properly around New Year and stayed in the team right through to the Play-off final after that.

The higher level was another challenge, but I looked round my teammates and knew how well they'd been doing in the league. I thought that if I could hold my own with them in training, I was confident of stepping up when the time came.

It was great that there were a few of us; me, Carts, Paul McKenna, Dave Lucas, who'd been with the club back in the old fourth division days and we'd now progressed to knocking on the door of the Premier League.

We'd talked about it among ourselves and said to each other: *'Imagine going all the way through the leagues, wouldn't that be unbelievable . . .'*

And suddenly, it was possible.

We all knew we had to keep improving though - the manager drilled that into us every single day. No-one was allowed to rest on their laurels.

On top of that, I'd become more experienced both at left-back and centre half. I think centre half is not a position you really nail until you're about 26 and have got a lot of games under your belt.

I was in my late twenties by then and felt confident I could handle Championship football, so I just threw myself into it as per normal really and we went on another great run. It wasn't enough to go up straight away, but we had real momentum as we went into the top six.

We all knew the play-offs hadn't been great for us in the past, but I thought the key thing was that the second leg would be back at Deepdale and that was a massive thing for us. With a big crowd on and our fans right behind us, I knew Birmingham would have a job on their hands unless they got a decent lead in the first game.

For me, losing 1-0 at their place was like a 0-0 in all honesty - I think they needed more and we got away with it a bit. We were all quite happy coming away with that result, knowing we could get right at them at Deepdale.

And the second leg? What . . a . . . night . . . that . . . was!

Possibly my best night in football ever; the excitement, the emotion, the adrenaline and the drama . . . you just couldn't write that script.

It's what makes people fall in love with football and football clubs. Dave Healy scored a great goal, but then Geoff Horsfield equalised. The ball was whipped in, in front of me, it looks like I might have been able to reach it but I couldn't, I swear. It was just too far for me to get to it. He nipped between me and Rob Edwards and I was left thinking *'Bugger! Now we need another goal.'*

Then Grezza misses a penalty for like the first time ever, but there was no time to feel sorry for ourselves. While you're playing and the ref hasn't blown, the game's never over.

So of course we're going to keep going right to the end because that was in our nature as a team - it's what we did in every single game.

We were still pushing forward when Stan Lazaridis went through right in injury time and you just think *'here we go, that's it, game over'*. He should score, but it just rolled across the goal-line and Lukes managed to grab it. Incredible.

We were still in it.

We've given it everything for 90 minutes, the tank's empty, we're absolutely drained and then that miss gave us one last blast of energy.

You can see now when you watch it back that people are playing it forward fairly calmly in the circumstances - but I just think we were shattered!

And when Ranks scored . . . well, . . . *there are no words, no words.*

If you were there, you'll know.

What's that famous Sir Alex Ferguson quote? 'Football, bloody hell!'

I don't think I've ever had a bigger adrenaline surge in my life.

And suddenly, we went from almost out on our feet to full of energy again. We were like: 'We've got 'em here now. We're doing these lads! Come on!'

The switch flipped totally in our favour, so when the penalties came around and Trevor Francis got rattled it was just crazy.

You need to keep your focus and your manager is flipping out over which end to take the kicks at? It was just *bonkers*. I've no idea what it did for their lads' state of mind, but it won't have been good.

We already knew who was taking our penalties - me and Jacko were looking at each other, both thinking *'I hope it doesn't get to us'*. He was ninth and I was tenth!

Obviously Lukes does brilliantly and they missed the first two. We were thinking: 'Oh my God - we've done it!'

Then Rob Edwards misses his and it all comes down to Kenna.

I would NOT have liked to have been in his shoes for that kick. I've watched the video loads of times and you can see the look on his face . . .

Fair play to Paul though. Bottle? *Never in doubt.*

Brilliant penalty; right on the floor, plenty of power and - *bang!* - we're going to the Millennium Stadium for the final. Come on!

The fans piled on the pitch, the flags came out, the scenes will live with me forever. Everyone just swamped by a sea of ecstatic faces - what a feeling to have!

God, it was emotional - and a long night too. I think by the time Kenna scored that penalty at the end it was about half past one in the morning!

We went out into Squires after the game but I'll be honest, it was one of the quietest celebrations I can remember. Lads were just sitting around, totally drained by the emotion of everything that had gone on.

Well, I was anyway. I had nothing left, that night.

And the enormity of it - one game from the Premier League, when we were in League 1 just over a year ago.

We were just gone. Done. Body empty. Drained physically and mentally. I remember I was totally shattered, but couldn't sleep that night. That's what the emotion did to me.

Eventually, we recovered and prepared for the final well, but if I'm honest, we just didn't perform as well as we could have done.

Unlike the '94 final, I look at my own performance and thought I played quite well. Personally, after what had happened at Wembley, I was determined to enjoy it and was able to cope with the pressure better.

Because there's a hell of a lot to think about, if you let it get to you. Imagine making the mistake that costs the club promotion, kills your teammates' dreams, kills the supporters' dreams, costs the club tens of millions. You've got to block that out and by that point in my career, I was able to do that, thank God.

I don't think anyone had what you'd call a bad game. It was just that, as a unit, we didn't find our rhythm, we couldn't get going.

We had a couple of chances in the first half, but nothing you'd say was a sitter or a bad miss. In the second half, their keeper made a couple of decent saves, but on the day, no matter how hard we tried, it just didn't happen.

I think they probably had too much experience for us once they got in front; Colin Hendry, Gudni Bergsson, loads of their team had been in big games before and with Sam Allardyce there as well, they had a lot of know-how on their side.

We can't complain - no matter how much it hurts, they were better than us on the day, even though 3-0 flatters them, because obviously we were chasing the game at the end and got caught up the pitch.

I still see Sam regularly and he's always got good things to say about Preston North End; his grandson was with us for a time at Bury and Sam always talks about the old days at Deepdale.

He took Bolton up and they stayed in the Premier League for many years after that, as did Fulham and Blackburn who also went up that year, so we'd come up against a particularly strong Championship and done well.

At the start of the next season, Chris Lucketti arrived. I knew he was a really strong defender, but by now, it was par for the course in my career at Deepdale - the club bringing in other defenders and me having to meet the challenge.

Quite right, too. The club has to move forward and the more good players we had the better, as far as I was concerned. I'd had a couple of opportunities to leave over the years, but I loved North End and never, ever wanted to go.

I thought I was over my injury problems, was part of a good team with a good manager at a great club and I had a fantastic relationship with the supporters.

If you're a footballer, it doesn't get much better than that.

I didn't have any worries and I was looking forward to clocking up 10 years at Deepdale; the money was getting better, everything was going well.

Moyesie wasn't one for giving you extra time off if you'd been in the play-offs, so we only had a few weeks over the summer before we were back running on the sand dunes. Me and Graham Alexander both did our cartilages, so I missed the start of the season but was back by September.

I had a run in the team and we'd just beaten Stockport 6-0 before we came up against Barnsley at Deepdale on a Thursday night TV game.

When I'd had my neck operation, I'd been warned that the discs above and below had been slightly corroded, even though the surgery had fused together the disc that was causing the initial problem. I'd been back for nearly a year and had no problem with my neck at all, so I thought everything was fine. But then in that Barnsley game, the ball came towards me from a goal kick and as I headed it back, that dreaded reaction was suddenly on me again . . . pins and needles.

In that instant I thought: 'Oh my God.'

I went down and Baz came sprinting over to me: 'What's up Kiddo son? You alright?'

As soon as I told him I could see the look in his eye and straight away he said I'd have to go off. Obviously, he was really concerned, but for both of us there was a sadness and a real fear that it was something serious again.

There and then, I knew something wasn't right. I can't really describe the emotions as I came off: disappointment, disbelief, dejection. I suppose it's what footballers really mean when they say 'gutted', but a hundred times worse.

We eventually drew the game 2-2 (after a certain Alex Neil scored for them) but in the aftermath, there was something more important for me to think about.

Baz fixed up for me to have a scan and I had a few days off beforehand.

I think deep down we both feared the worst and he'd prepped me a bit, saying: 'Look Ryan, you might have to prepare yourself for some bad news.'

In the meantime, I saw Moyesie and he was saying: 'We need you to be OK for Saturday Kiddo, you're in the team away at Forest.'

I had to tell him: *'Dave, I've got to see the consultant this afternoon and I'm not sure it's going to be good . . .'*

So I went to see Professor Charles Davis at Fulwood Hall Hospital and had various scans and X-rays done - the full works.

I was trying to keep my emotions in check, but I was just wracked by fear - I can't really put it into words. And at the end of it the consultant looked at the results over and over, while I just had to wait for my fate. Then he said it, straight out: 'Sorry, but you are not allowed to play football ever again.'

I couldn't believe it - everything just went blank for me.

I think I might have said: *'You what? No!'*

I don't think I could take it in. It was brutal, but it had to be I suppose and he was adamant. What can you say in a moment like that? He's a top surgeon with the medical evidence staring him in the face. There's no argument to be had.

The discs above and below were seriously corroded and the main disc couldn't be fused any further. One more knock and I might have no movement in my neck for the rest of my life, be paralysed, everything.

I just broke down in tears.

My career was over, my livelihood had gone, everything had changed in an instant. I'd played for North End on the Thursday night and four days later, I was finished.

Baz was great and tried to comfort me, but I rang my dad straight away.

He'd watched every game I played when I was a kid, driven me everywhere, watched me for years at Preston and given me every support you could wish for.

I was an emotional wreck and it hadn't quite sunk in.

The next day I drove in for training as normal, not believing what had happened. The lads were all great, but obviously, I couldn't be involved. The most frustrating thing was that I could do everything apart from head the ball - I was physically fit apart from that, I could do the running, kicking, no problem.

That made it worse I think and I didn't handle it mentally very well at first.

I was almost in a trance, like it hadn't happened.

And every game you miss, you become further detached from the lads.

There was a mini-break to Spain and Moyesie asked if I wanted to go, but I said no. I knew everyone was doing their best for me, but I was struggling to get my head around it.

And no matter what I felt about things, life carries on. The team moves on, the club has to go and get a replacement and your chapter is done.

It's a lot easier to say that now - even though it still hurts - than it was at the time.

I was just about to sign a new contract for another two-and-a-half years, but obviously that wasn't going to happen now.

It was just heartbreaking.

I didn't really know what to do with myself, but as it was my testimonial year, I got stuck into that and some of the events lined up.

I'd just got to the stage where the money was coming into the game more, wages were getting better, but now that was all gone.

Because the injury was ruled as 'wear and tear' I didn't get a big insurance pay-out or anything, either. I got some support from the PFA but it wasn't a huge amount, so it was a case of putting everything into my testimonial events and trying to use that to get some funds in, really.

Luckily, I always got on great with the fans and I think they appreciated that I was giving everything for the cause. And the response to my testimonial game blew me away quite honestly, it was proper *'lump in the throat'* time.

All the events were great, but to have more than 13,000 at Deepdale against Manchester City in pre-season was just, well . . . amazing.

That night holds a special place in my heart, to think that so many people were there to say their farewells. To say I was touched and grateful is putting it mildly.

But whenever I played, the fans were always brilliant with me and they still are when I go back. I didn't have a high profile beyond the club, but I didn't care.

North End gave me a chance and I wanted to pay them back every single day.

It's such a special club to me and - *I'm not just saying this* - I think the fanbase is very educated in football terms. It's very rare they get on the team's back or an individual player's back. I always feel, even now when I go back to watch games, they're always with the team.

Of course you're going to get the odd moan and groan in games, especially if you're losing, but you know they really just want you to do well and give your all for the shirt. *That's not much to ask, is it?*

I went back with the Youth Team when I was with Bury and the welcome I got from everyone was just really touching - it meant a lot to me.

I'd been back with Simon Davey when we were at Barnsley and will always remember the big cheer we got from the Town End when we came out of the tunnel - and we were in charge of the away team!

It's great to be held in such high esteem when I don't think I did a lot to deserve it - other than doing my job to the best of my ability.

Simon's a big pal of mine and had eased me into coaching at Deepdale after I had to retire. I'd not really thought of it when I was playing, but I'd been lucky to have good forward-thinking coaches throughout my career.

One night, I was watching a session when I saw that I could help a couple of the lads out defensively, just pass a few things on to them. I saw how I could have a positive effect again and things snowballed from there really.

I threw myself into it, got my qualifications and saw how rewarding it can be to help players reach their full potential. With hindsight, I took something from every coach I played under and now use it to help young players make the most of their potential. I was part of a successful team bringing 25 young players through to their debuts at Bury and generating £2.5 million in transfers over five years.

But what happened to the club was just terrible beyond words. I think football needs to do whatever it takes to make sure that can never happen again.

I'm now at Blackburn Rovers working with the Under-18s with Mike Sheron and hopefully bringing through some more good players in the future.

But I'd never swap my years at North End for anything else.

We were always chasing things, nearly every season I was there.

I was so lucky to be there at a time when I could grow with the club on a brilliant journey on and off the pitch.

To be part of it, to be in two championship-winning teams and three other play-off campaigns, to get within a whisker of the Premier League, to play at Wembley and the Millennium Stadium, to take on the world's best players in the cup competitions, to play with brilliant teammates and great managers in front of fantastic supporters . . . *well, it wasn't a bad trip was it?*

Chapter 14

TOM CLARKE: LIVING THE DREAM

Sitting in the dressing room after we lost to Rotherham in the 2014 play-offs, everyone was cut up, gutted, devastated.

One match, one defeat, one more season in League 1.

We'd gone in front through Gally, but they'd got back at us fairly quickly and seen us off to reach Wembley.

I thought we'd deserved to go up after the season we'd had, but it was probably the right result on the night.

That never dulls the pain though, especially in the play-offs. And especially for me.

If we'd won, we'd have been facing Leyton Orient, who were captained by my elder brother Nathan.

Two Clarke lads would have been leading the teams out under that giant arch in one of the showpiece games of the season.

So you can imagine how low I was after that game. I ended up sitting in the toilet, just trying to hold it together and not break down. It would have been amazing and it would have been such a proud occasion for the entire family.

It would also have been a chance for both of us to pay back a little of the incredible support we had from our parents growing up, when they were working full time but still making sure the pair of us always got to where we needed to be.

Growing up in Sowerby Bridge, Halifax, I'd been spotted by Huddersfield Town from a young age and actually joined them aged just eight, same as Nathan, who was five years older than me. We have another brother, Jay, who wasn't really into football. He was much more interested in animation, beavering away in his bedroom, while we were kicking lumps out of each other in the street.

It turned out to be a good career move for him as he went on to become an animator at Nick Park's Aardman Studios, working on things like Shaun the Sheep, and later the Isle of Dogs and The Grand Budapest Hotel films.

I know Nick Park is a Preston fan - I keep telling Jay to bring him up to a game *(or at least do a plasticine version of the lads!).*

None of us brothers would have been able to achieve what we have without the support of our parents and we're all grateful for that - they're certainly the biggest influence on my career and I'll always be thankful to them.

I was actually a ball boy at Huddersfield when our Nathan was in the first team, so it was a great chance to get a close-up view of the action - and see just how physical it was in the 'man's game'.

I'm not sure I qualified as a 'man' when I made my debut as I'd only just turned 17.

But Peter Jackson and Terry Yorath were the coaching staff and if they said I was ready, then I wasn't going to argue.

They were real characters those two, tough as old boots and a bit old school, but fantastic to work with and they gave you massive belief as a player starting out.

There wasn't a lot of money to spend, so there were quite a few young lads coming through from the academy and players got their opportunities early on.

I played left-back in that first game, with my brother at centre half, so again that was a really proud day for all the family. It wasn't really my natural position but the club had a few injuries and I was just champing at the bit to get out there - I'd have done a Gally and played in goal if they'd asked me!

It was a bit daunting, but having Nathan there was a great help - not a lot of players get to make their debut alongside their brother, guiding me and talking me through it.

We ended up playing 40-odd games together over our time at Huddersfield, sometimes the pair of us as centre halves, which was a dream come true really.

Around that time, I got a call up to the England scene, playing a few games for the Under-19s.

I managed to score against Belgium in one game and I remember being shown around the set-up by Lee Holmes, who was a good lad and later came to North End.

Kyel Reid was also involved and one time, I roomed with this wiry kid from Newcastle United; quiet lad, terrible little mullet haircut.

No idea what became of him. *Paul something . . . from Cumbria. Huntington??*

Theo Walcott was with us sometimes, playing a couple of years above his age group, while Aaron Lennon was there too, so we had plenty of pace on the wings for sure.

Back at Huddersfield, the downside of coming through at such a young age was that I was still physically developing, while trying to cope with the 'man's game.'

I was up against big strikers like Wayne 'The Chief' Allison at Sheffield United and I remember going to mark him at the first corner, with all the crowd going: *'Chief! Chief! Chief!'*

What's that phrase? Character-building. You can say that again.

But, you know me, I'm all-in or nothing, so I was always throwing myself into tackles and challenges - it's just the way I've always been.

Looking back, at times it's probably been detrimental to my body, but I'd clocked up 60 games or so before it caught up with me back then.

I tore my cruciate ligament and damaged other parts of the knee too, probably because I tried to carry on when I should really have come straight off.

It took a long while to get back from and I had a couple of loans at Bradford and Orient to get fit, but I played a lot of games in League 1 in the season we got promoted via the play-offs under Simon Grayson.

Once we went up, Huddersfield signed a lot of players, sometimes for big money, and I felt like I was always fighting against that a little bit, because I had the 'local boy' tag. Sometimes, when you've come up through the academy it can go against you, because you've not cost anything and you're up against players who the club has paid money for. There's probably a bit of pressure to justify it, rather than put in a lad who's come up through the ranks.

Coming into my last year I was a bit-part player really, at a time when I really wanted to be playing in as many games as I could. I felt like I was training well, but just not getting a chance and it felt like a losing battle.

Simon left and Mark Robins came in, but it just didn't work for me under him.

I understand it - some managers click better with certain players, but I didn't feel it with Mark unfortunately and, as my contract was running down, it became clear I'd be moving on. I had a bit of time to get my head round it, but it was still disappointing. I'd been there 17 years 'man and boy' and knew a lot of people behind the scenes, forged good friendships and had a real feeling for the club.

If I'd have played there my entire career I would have been happy, but instead I knew it was the right time for me to go.

In fact, my only appearance in that 2012/13 season was as a sub in a 2-0 defeat in a League Cup game at Deepdale against Graham Westley's North End.

So you can see why I had to move on and get playing regularly again.

It's strange when you get to that point, not really knowing what's coming next, but pretty quickly I got a call from Simon Grayson, who had taken over from Westley midway through that season. He asked me to come over to Preston for a chat and a look round the training ground.

There were a couple of other clubs interested as well, but even though I didn't play as much as I would have liked under him at Huddersfield, I always enjoyed working with him.

Maybe it's because we could understand each other's accents.

Once we had a chat and looked round the ground, coming to North End was a no-brainer for me. The thing about Simon is, it's always enjoyable - lads always like working with him. Whether you're playing or not, he always makes you feel involved and part of things and he's a great man manager.

He never gets too high when things are going well, or too low when you hit a bad run. He's calm and level-headed at all times and that rubs off on the lads.

He's also got the right staff around him, so it's not just all about the manager, there's a team of people all looking out for you, pushing you when needs be, but putting an arm round your shoulder at times too.

His training is good. He gets a good group of lads together and he knows how to get out of leagues - especially League 1, which is where Preston were when I joined.

Right from the off, they were a good set of lads, Holmesy was there who I knew, Iain Hume, Hunts, quite a lot of people Westley had brought in from Stevenage; good, honest lads who would work all day long and give everything for the cause.

Scott Laird probably epitomised that; he had a fantastic attitude, great work ethic and obviously he could play a bit too *(has he ever told you he once scored against Man United?).*

Obviously, Simon wanted to bring his own players in but I could see it was definitely a squad that could compete. Joe Garner was there and I knew him from a loan he'd had at Huddersfield, so I was familiar with the full Garns experience (!).

I looked at what we'd got, looked at the other teams in the league and thought we had a good chance.

The first game was a fairly dull 0-0 against Wolves at Deepdale. Not much to report, other than we held our own against a team fancied to win the league. It was one of those classic 'first game of the season' encounters where no-one wants to get beat; all safe and steady. Not a lot of drama.

The second game? Well, that was a totally different kettle of fish - the type of game you dream about; North End versus Blackpool at Deepdale. *Oh, what a night, eh?*

It was the League Cup, but it could have been tiddly-winks and I think the entire city would have been up for it.

Before the game, you hear rumblings about how big it is, especially as Blackpool were in the Championship at that time.

But come the day, you could just feel it everywhere, and when we walked out . . . this wave of noise just hit me and I thought: *'Flipping hell, this is a big one, isn't it?'*

Normally you get a big cheer when you come out, nice applause all around the ground. *But this?* This was like a gladiator walking into the arena.

It wasn't the normal cheer, it was like a roar: *'Come on! Get at 'em!'*

You see people in the seats near the tunnel, who wouldn't normally say boo to a goose, and they were shouting at the top of their voice and I thought: 'Blimey, we'd better not lose this!'

The stadium was full, it was loud, a night game, the floodlights, TV cameras buzzing about - just a fantastic atmosphere, absolutely electric.

Obviously the game itself was tight but the way it all panned out, the timing of everything, the release of emotions, you couldn't really write the script - but I'll always be grateful that I managed to score THAT goal.

I can remember everything about it - probably because I've watched it back so many times!

Holmesy floated it in and I'd got myself in the position I always look to get in; just at the middle to back post area where you get a good run on the defenders. I managed to lose my marker and as the ball - *a great ball* - was coming in, I saw the flight of it and, in a split second, thought: 'All I've got to do is get my head on this and it's in.'

You just know sometimes when you see it coming, you think: 'Yes, we're in here.'

It's one of those where you've just got to keep your eye on the ball and if the keeper clatters you, well, who cares? I'm getting a header in here.

So when it came all the way, the keeper didn't come, it was just a case of nodding it down and then . . . *whoosh!*

The rest is a blur for the next 30 seconds or so. Bedlam.

You can tell when it's a BIG goal, because the noise is different.

And the fans? Absolutely crazy. The entire Town End just seemed to be bouncing up and down.

I ran over to the corner near the tunnel where I knew my dad was sitting (that's who I was pointing to in the celebrations), so it couldn't have been more perfect for me to share that moment with him.

I'd been through a lot at Huddersfield, with the injuries, being frozen out a bit and I think that goal was something I'd worked hard for - the start of a new chapter.

Through it all, my family had been with me, so I couldn't have been happier for them, the lads and the supporters.

A few minutes later, it was all over and they piled on the pitch like we'd won the league. Lads everywhere, jumping all over us in celebration, they knew what it meant and so did I now.

When we finally got back into the dressing room, Simon hugged me and said: 'You do know what you've just done don't you?'

I said: *'Not really, but I'm starting to understand a bit more!'*

He said: 'You'll go down in folklore for this. They'll be singing your name for years!'

I thought he was joking, but brilliantly, the North End fans have lived up to that and it always makes me proud to have scored such an important goal.

The mural in the city centre is fantastic and I've been down and signed it and I know people are always taking pictures of it, so it's just amazing really. I tell people back home about it all the time and they can't believe it: 'What? There's a life-size painting of you in the city centre?'

I'm like: 'Yep, beat that.'

The bits on road signs and whatnot too, where fans have put the score in, always makes me smile. I was on a Zoom chat with Bailey Wright and he was on about still seeing all the stickers everywhere.

I said: *'Yeah, it's been a few years . . . I suppose I should stop putting them up now!'*

Those games don't come round too often and it's brilliant for the supporters to have that one-upmanship and be able to shout it from the streets.

In terms of starting well and getting the fans on your side, it was perfect really, not just for me, but for the team in general; I might have scored the goal, but the lads were brilliant that night and it set the tone for the season ahead.

I was 25, playing regularly and in League 1 the games come thick and fast.

I wanted to be a big part of things and that year I ended up playing more than 50 games - so no complaints there at all. It's a tough league, you're playing Saturday and Tuesday nights, lots of cup games, lots of travelling - but I loved it.

The team was winning and there was never a moment where I wasn't enjoying it.

We had some great wins along the way - I remember us beating Carlisle 6-1 at Deepdale near the end and going into the play-offs against Rotherham, I think we were all confident.

The first leg of the semi-final was at Deepdale and, while we may not have won, it was a game that will always be remembered for one world-class moment.

Joe Garner scored one of the greatest goals I've ever seen and not only that, I can claim the assist - even from 50 yards away.

In fact, I always tell Garns that I made his mind up for him about what to do (!).

I remember it getting cleared out and Bailey squeezing it across to me, I looked up and knew that Joe was brilliant at those little diagonal runs across the box - his movement was fantastic.

I also knew how good he was at taking it on his chest, so I thought I'd just clip it forward to him and there was a good chance he'd get on the end of it.

I know Garns loves a battle, so in all honesty, I thought he'd just get on it, hold it up and look to play someone else in.

Of course, what he did instead was just unbelievable.

He got his chest on it and when he flicked it over the second guy, genuinely, I already thought: *'This is in here!'*

It was just perfectly set for the volley and I knew how well Joe could strike it.

It just dropped nicely and when he hit it . . . well, it was one of the best goals I've ever seen.

It wasn't just goal of the season. It was goal of ANY season.

To do it in such an important game, says everything about Joe though - what a character and what a player for North End.

Unfortunately, we couldn't get the winner and a 1-1 draw left us with a tough task at their place, but we never felt out of it.

As I said at the beginning, I was devastated at the end; all their fans running on and us, gutted as anything, having to get back to the changing rooms through them all.

All I could do was get over it as quickly as possible and go down to Wembley to support Nathan, where, of course, they lost to Rotherham too. (The Millers weren't exactly popular in our family that year, I can tell you.)

So we were back in League 1, but Simon was strengthening the squad all the time and bringing in experienced players like Kevin Davies and Jermaine Beckford.

As the season got into its stride, he pulled me to one side and said he would like me to be captain.

It was a massive moment for me, a huge honour and I was just overjoyed.

I'd always given everything I had, but I think we had a team of leaders on the pitch and off it, so to be asked to be captain was just amazing.

To still be leading the team out six years later is just magnificent. It's not something I ever take for granted and I'm so proud every single time.

Not just to be leading out such a good set of lads over those years, but to be doing it for such a good club; solid, well-thought of everywhere you go, with great support - I couldn't ask for anything more as a footballer.

Our away support in particular is amazing and there are times when we run out at midweek games miles away from Preston and think: *'Blimey - that's impressive!'*

Don't ever think the lads don't appreciate it, because I know they always do.

People give up their time, spend money, maybe get back in the early hours and are knackered the next day - it's just top support and we're grateful to everyone who follows us, home or away.

It's great when you can get a good cup draw and can bring some top players to Deepdale and we managed that that season by drawing Manchester United in the FA Cup. We'd worked hard in the earlier stages and beat Sheffield United at Bramall Lane to reach the fourth round, after Gally scored a worldie free-kick.

So it was a just reward for everyone - players and fans - to get such a great tie.

As captain, I had to go to the referee's room beforehand with Wayne Rooney and it was interesting to see the interaction between him and the officials.

He was sound with me, chatting away about how things were going and asking if we were going to swap shirts at the end. I said I'd have his, but I didn't really offer mine up (he didn't seem too upset about that, to be honest!).

It was good to be able to have a chat with him for ten minutes or so though, just to pick his brains and see how those top, top players operate up close.

When we came out for kick-off, it was similar to walking out against Blackpool; the ground was full, really loud - just a great game to be involved in. I don't think anyone expected us to win, but we thrived on that, puffed our chests out and played without fear.

They had Falcao up front, with Rooney sitting a little bit deeper and they played a really strong team, which was a compliment to us in a way. They knew they had to take us seriously and I think we gave a good account of ourselves overall.

Louis van Gaal will have done his preparation of course, but I think even he might have been surprised on the night that this team from the third tier of English football could get 21,000 on and have such a great stadium.

When Lairdy scored his goal - *what a strike it was* - I genuinely thought we could pull off a shock and beat them.

Obviously, things didn't work out like that and one or two things went against us in the second half, not least a dubious penalty for United towards the end.

One thing I remember is that the ref was from the Premier League and throughout the game, it was hard to have any real dialogue with him. As captain, I wanted to raise things as normal, but he wasn't having any of it from me or any of our lads.

The way he was looking at us, he was almost saying: 'Who are you??' The United players though? He was on first name terms with them, so that jarred a bit, to say the least. Overall, I think we were really unlucky in the end, but we took them all the way and showed we were a good side.

We took that into our league form and had a great unbeaten run to the end of the season - I think in any other year, we'd have probably gone straight up automatically.

But we always knew MK Dons were close on our heels.

When we got in after games, it was always a bit of a downer if they'd matched our result - we were just hoping they'd slip up, but they never did, to be fair.

We were getting good results, but they were often 1-0 or 2-1, and I felt when I looked at the MK Dons' results, they seemed to be beating people 3-0 or 4-0.

I could see they were coming strong and winning by a lot of goals, so that was always in the back of our minds, having that pressure of being hunted, rather than doing the hunting.

When it came down to the Colchester game on the last day of the season, it was one of those days when we couldn't get going. They were battling for their lives, but we should still have had enough to win it and go up there and then.

If I could tell you why it didn't happen, I would . . . but it's one of those you can't put your finger on in games. You're doing all the usual things, but it's just not happening.

Of course, it was just when we needed it most and we were all devastated afterwards. We'd had a brilliant season and to fall just short was really, really painful.

You could see it on the lads' faces - it was all so raw.

But you can't go back and play the game again. You can only look forward. People like me, Hunts and Gally had to swallow hard and try to lift the lads.

Simon told us to remember the feeling of disappointment, but put it away for now, get focused and concentrate on putting things right. We'd got a second chance and it was a case of getting our heads right and making sure we made no more mistakes.

It was great that he did that and it reset everyone for the task ahead - three tough games, but if we played as well as we knew we were capable of, we could still go up.

When you look at the team we were lucky that we had such strong characters; Welshy, Garns, Jermaine - these lads had been around the block and knew what was required. Never for a moment did I think they would fold.

In fact, I could see the determination in everyone - players and staff - and I fancied us, even if people were always going on about the so-called 'play-off hoodoo' at Preston. I didn't believe in that stuff and the way I looked at it was we were a different team, we'd got lads who had been promoted elsewhere and we couldn't affect what had gone on before. We could only deal with what was in front of us now, so that's what we set out to do.

It was a quick turnaround into the Chesterfield game and they were a decent side; a good ball-playing team, good manager and they had a lot of players who went on to bigger clubs in the Championship and beyond.

So they were two really tough games and I knew we'd have to be resolute. But I looked at us and I knew we were hard to beat, hard to play against, because we were so hard-working and had individual talents that could win us games.

We didn't concede many and with Becks and Garns up front and DJ and Gally creating stuff, we were a good side.

To get a 1-0 win at their place was a great result - I watched the full thing back recently and it reminded me how tough a game it was. They had a lot of the ball, but we knew we had a threat on the break.

Becks was on fire at the time, even though he had a toe injury and was hardly training - he was on a spin bike most of the week, but on game days, he was unplayable.

The goal he scored in the second leg from near the halfway line was almost typical of him in that period - everything he hit seemed to go in. At the end, the North End fans poured on the Deepdale pitch and I was so, so delighted for everyone - after Rotherham and Colchester, now it was our crowd piling on and you could see the joy everywhere.

For me, it was pure relief!

I was chaired up by some lads who must have had strong backs (!) and it was just one of those perfect days in football. I thought we deserved it and I was just glad we'd got the chance to put everything right at Wembley.

Fired up as we were, when we got in the dressing room, we knew the job wasn't done. Instead, the mood was: *'Right - let's finish this now.'* The overriding emotion was one of relief, but we knew there was still one game to go.

Obviously Simon had been there and done it before - I'd been on the bench in 2012 when we beat Sheffield United and, believe me, it was tense. *(How tense? It came down to a penalty shoot-out and we missed our first three kicks. In the end, it went all the way to the keepers - and we eventually won it 8-7. So, yep . . . tense!).*

So I was expecting a big occasion and a tough game against Swindon.

We'd been to watch Plymouth against Wycombe the day before our game and Wycombe were 3-0 up at one point, before getting pegged back to 3-2, so maybe that was in the back of our minds - no matter what happens, we can't get carried away.

Finals are normally tight affairs, but going into the game I felt confident.

You come out and there's the flames going off and the noise - and then seeing the North End fans in such numbers . . . just amazing.

It was one of the proudest moments of my life - a great feeling and what you've worked for all season. You're just desperate to do well and not let anyone down, y'know? Don't come off that pitch without leaving everything out there.

Obviously, I had nerves but I looked at the lads lining up with me and thought: 'We're OK here.' I'm not saying it was easy, but the way it panned out . . . we couldn't have wished for anything better.

One-nil early on was a great start, then Hunts scored like the coolest centre forward in the world *(has he stopped running in celebration yet?)* and then Jermaine gets another worldie from outside the box.

We got in at half-time and the main thing was to not get too excited by it, we still had another 45 minutes to go and obviously Swindon weren't a bad side. Again, they had a lot of the ball, but our tactics were spot on and we just kept catching them on the break. Once it got to four, their heads dropped a bit and it gave us extra energy to see it through with a clean sheet.

I know people reading this will be grafters and football maybe isn't seen as a tough profession, but I'd always worked hard in my career; training, playing, dedicating myself to the game and days like those are the reward - that's when it all pays off.

No matter what job you do, everyone gets paid. But, in every walk of life, people want to achieve things. That is the biggest reward you can get because ultimately, that's what you are measured on.

Simon told us that we could be the team that gets remembered years down the line and I hope we will be.

I tried not to think about lifting the trophy too much beforehand, but one thing I knew for sure was that I wanted Welshy there with me and we'd do it together if we won. I was captain but John was still a massive influence on and off the pitch. He'd welcomed me in with open arms and if you're going to war in a game, you want him with you. He'd worked so hard, had a great season and had a brilliant game in the final so it was never a question in my mind.

I remember him coming up to me on the bus to thank me, but I was like: 'Don't be daft, you deserved it.'

The cheer when we lifted the trophy though - *what a moment, what a feeling*. Indescribable, really, but when you watch it back (as I do) you can see the pure emotion of it all.

I think as a team we had a real bond with the supporters and that's carried on through all my years at the club. Walking round the Wembley pitch with the trophy and seeing all the fans' faces, was just something I'll never forget - it wasn't an 'us and them' situation, we were all celebrating together.

Proper 'one and only North End', wasn't it? Just a perfect, perfect day.

Following on from that, I had another proud moment when I was named in the PFA Team of the Year with Garns. To get voted by fellow professionals from other clubs was a real honour and again, something I'm really proud of.

When we went up, North End didn't go out and splash the cash on a load of new players. Instead we brought in quality, rather than quantity, with Greg Cunningham signing and Adam Reach arriving on loan.

Greg is a quality defender and a really great lad and Reachy could get up and down that line in a flash - so quick and with such skill to match, perfect as a wing-back that season. On top of that, we brought in Jordan Pickford from Sunderland at a time when he was virtually unknown. What a keeper he's turned out to be - and a great lad off the pitch too.

I think when you go up, clubs sometimes look just to stay up and the careful ones make sure that if they do drop back down again, they've covered themselves.

It's a tough league and if you go throwing money at players who don't always do well, that's when you get in trouble. I think North End have always had that sensible outlook, bringing in players who fit the hard-working team ethic and also have the right personalities to fit in with what we're trying to achieve.

Everyone has to be hungry for success, it's as simple as that, really.

Simon and the club put a lot of faith in the lads and it paid off as we consolidated with a decent season at that higher level. Hunts was superb again and I don't think we looked out of place against anyone.

Jordan Hugill was starting to get his chance and the transformation in him as a player was incredible as time went on. When he first came in, he was quite raw and, if anything, maybe trying a bit too hard. You could see in his physical attributes that he had everything to be successful; quick, strong, really powerful.

There's not many big lads who are fast like Jordan is.

He took on board everything the coaching staff were saying to him and it was great for everyone to see him get the rewards for that as time went by.

These days he's an absolute beast; throwing centre halves around and bullying people non-stop - a nightmare to play against. He's a real workhorse, can hold it up and score brilliant goals. Top man.

For me, a game I was looking forward to that season was on Boxing Day - away at Huddersfield. It was a bit strange and most of the players had changed, but it was nice to see a lot of the staff behind the scenes. On the pitch, I got a good reception from the home fans, so again, that was a nice touch and I was really pleased. The less said about the result though, the better.

A happier day came in April when we went to Blackburn and Rovers allocated an entire end to the Preston fans.

Of course, our supporters packed it out with more than 7,000 there and the sight was just incredible. When you've got your support packed in like that, the noise gives you a real lift and we ended up beating them 2-1.

Joe scored a penalty then did his classic chicken celebration, while Gally picked out Jordan and he showed a lovely touch to put it into the top corner. It was just a great day and I remember giving my shirt to a young lad in the celebrations at the end.

For some reason, I think we've tended to do well in those derby games over the years and it's always great to know the fans are going to be going home happy with the local bragging rights, etc.

We had a few great results that season actually, beating Wolves at Molineux, beating Bolton at their place - it was a solid return to the Championship.

Hunts and me played loads of games together at the back and you know what you're going to get with him; he's a defender who loves to defend.

The other thing he loves is his pre-match superstitions - I don't know how he remembers them all. He's got so many, you just see him talking to himself or nodding away all day. People who didn't know him would think he's a bit weird - and they'd be right!

I love him to bits though and from rooming together as young lads with England to playing regularly in the Championship, the pair of us have come a long way - it's great to have that type of bond.

I think North End have done well over my time, in that they've had lots of lads who love the club and will put their bodies on the line for it. You don't get that everywhere. You can see it sometimes in the opposition and you think: 'These lads aren't putting it in here.' You can just tell.

I don't think we've ever been like that - certainly not in my time at the club. Fair enough, we might not win every game, but no-one would ever accuse us of not giving everything we've got. It's just not in our nature.

But back in the Championship, we weren't just about effort, we had people like DJ stroking the ball about, Gally giving a passing masterclass every week and young Callum Robinson bursting onto the scene.

On top of that, as we went into the following season, Simon brought in Aiden McGeady. What a player he is; some of the fastest feet I've ever seen. He was an absolute genius on the ball. The stuff he did in training was a joke - no-one wanted to mark him. You'd always try to stay as far away from him as possible.

He was the type of player where if the game was tight, he could always pull something out of nothing and it was a masterstroke by Simon to get him in and get him playing as well as he did for us.

You think you've got him going one way and then, whoosh, he's gone past you on the other side, whipped it in or stuck one in the top corner.

He was amazing for us that season, probably none more so than against Arsenal in the FA Cup. We went in front again and we were unlucky not to get a replay at least, but again I thought we showed up well. I was up against Olivier Giroud who was captaining them that night and remember thinking how big he was up close.

It was a good battle with him down the middle though and I enjoyed it - apart from the result, obviously.

Throughout my career, I've always been a centre half but I've played elsewhere if needs be. I'd played right-back at Huddersfield and if someone was out, I could slot in all over the place. But, by trade, I'm a centre half.

I've played full-back on and off throughout my career really, filling in and using my defender's instincts. However, I think the position has changed over the years; it used to be all about stopping the opposition and then giving it to the winger in front.

These days, you pretty much need to be a winger yourself, up and down, overlapping, getting assists, so I've had to adapt.

There are some games where the manager will want me in there for extra height at set pieces and I'll always give 100 per cent wherever I play.

But I think everyone has their favourite position and, for me, I'm happier down the middle - I don't think anyone will be surprised to hear that.

One lad I wouldn't fancy coming up against out wide is Tom Barkhuizen. He's like lightning and you know that if teams have to come at us, Tom will be straight into the gaps that they leave. Again, it was a great bit of business by Simon and the club to bring him in and Barky is a key member of the team these days - he's done brilliantly.

Towards the end of that second season, we were away at Huddersfield ironically when someone absolutely clattered me from behind.

I was looking around to see who'd done it, wanting to have a word with them, but there was no-one nearby. I even said to Barky: *'Who's done me there?'*

But he looked at me like I was mad and said: 'Tom, there was no-one near you mate.' By this point, I knew it was a serious injury. When a player goes down with no-one near him, it's always a bad sign.

The funny thing is, at first the pain subsided quite quickly. I tried to carry on, but soon had to go off and the following day it was confirmed - I'd snapped my achilles tendon.

It was devastating. I'd had another good season, played nearly every game, got voted Players' Player of the Year by the lads, but now I was looking at a long spell out injured. I was just massively disappointed and I knew it was a long road ahead.

We finished 11th again and I think that's great credit to Simon, the coaches and all the lads. To come up and have two top half finishes in two seasons, without breaking the bank shows how good we were as a group and I think we were all ready to kick on the following season and get in the Championship play-offs.

So it was a massive shock when I came in for the first day of pre-season training to find that Simon was leaving. We were just having breakfast and I could see him mulling about and shaking people's hands, then I just saw him get in his car and vanish. He never really mentioned anything to the lads and it was Peter Ridsdale who came in and explained the situation.

Simon was going to speak to Sunderland and, as it turned out, that was that. Steve Thompson took over training and we just really cracked on.

We were sad to see him go, but we were professional about it and had to focus on North End, nothing else.

It would have been great to talk to Simon before he went off, but I think there were a lot of things happening and he texted me a couple of days later to thank me for everything while he'd been with us.

When Alex Neil came in, straight away we all thought it was a good appointment. Declan Rudd had just arrived from Norwich and had worked with him there, so we'd heard a bit about what he was like, training etc, and it was all good stuff.

The Gaffer came in and met us in the changing room and right from the start, he was assertive and clear about what he expected. He was in charge, we were going to work hard - and we were going to be successful.

I was still recovering from the injury, but he was brilliant with me. He called me in and said he'd spoken to a lot of people about me and they'd all told him what kind of lad I was.

Thankfully, they must all have said good things because Alex Neil is really close to his captains and he was more than happy for me to stay on and lead the lads.

I was absolutely chuffed because it's a role I'm really proud of, on and off the pitch.

You're the go-between for the manager and players and you're dealing with all sorts of things; from something about training to arranging a little night out.

Alex and I meet daily and he always wants to get a feel for how the lads are and if everything is all smooth.

Obviously, when he first arrived, I was out injured and it's always difficult when that happens, to still be that leader when you're not able to get out on the pitch.

The frustration gets to you and I found that really hard to deal with at times, but Alex was brilliant with me, as were all the lads, and it's support like that that helps get you through some dark times.

Even though we've got people who've been round for a few years now, we're actually quite a young group, but the culture is spot on. No-one tries to pull a fast one and the standards are first-class. People like Alan Browne are just consummate professionals; never late, always focused, just a top man.

It's the same with all the younger lads, not just because it's in their nature, but because of the culture at the club.

Again, you hear stories and it's not like that at every club, so you can never take it for granted. It's about keeping on top of things and making sure nothing slips.

When I did get back, I managed to score in my second game back, away at Burton on a freezing cold day.

I'd scored against them before, so while I might not get many . . . I'm prolific against Burton.

It was right in front of the North End fans and I think they could see in my celebration how good it felt - not just back in the team but scoring too. When you've been out for so long, that release of emotion just comes out and again it's a reward for all the hard work you put in.

We just missed out on the play-offs that year after a bad result at home against Derby cost us in the run-in. That was massively disappointing, but from personal perspective, it was good to get back and get some games under my belt, especially at centre half, which I really enjoyed.

Ben Davies was establishing himself in the team and is just an incredible talent; he's been away on couple of good loans and getting that experience of playing 'man's football' at a young age was exactly what he needed.

He's so calm on the pitch and he's a model for any young lads looking to make their way in the game. I remember Alex Neil telling me he'd watched him when he was on loan at Fleetwood and knew as soon as he came to North End that Ben was going to be an important player for us.

In that first season, Alex really put his mark on the team and took us on again from where we'd been with Simon.

I think it was an unusual situation for him to come into, because normally you take over when a manager has been sacked. But it wasn't like that. We were doing OK, we just needed to step up to that next level and I think that's what we've achieved.

The intensity in training, the preparation, the tactical analysis, the detailed gameplans, everything is just spot-on. The demands are huge every day and his attention to detail both in games and in training is second to none.

In matches, he sees things and counteracts them straight away, both defensively and going forward. He's taken things to a whole new level and you can see the experience he had at Norwich has helped shape the way he is today.

I know he kicks every ball on the sideline sometimes, but he's just so passionate about winning - absolutely driven to achieve success and that's something that rubs off on the team. He's brilliant with the lads and, yes, you can have a laugh and a joke with him *(honest!)* although it's best to pick your moment obviously, just to be on the safe side. He is Scottish after all!

In his second season, I was in at the start and had some decent spells in the side, but picked up another injury down at Millwall in February that really did me for the season again sadly. I'd actually scored early on but then I remember getting caught between Declan and one of their big lads up front. I just got absolutely clattered on my knee and straight away I could feel the medial ligament wasn't right.

We'd made all our substitutions by then and there were still 10 minutes to go, so there was no way I was coming off. I'd crack on, go again and sort it out when the final whistle went.

They were piling the pressure on and I was hopping about trying to get in the way of things and help us see it out for a 3-1 win.

Afterwards, it was confirmed that I'd damaged the ligament and the recovery was a lot longer than I expected. I don't know why, but it's been a really difficult one.

I've come back from it, thought I was fine and then felt it again, so it's been a real pain in the backside and a frustrating thing to properly shake off.

Ironically, I got back for the first game of the new season - away at Millwall, where they got revenge with a 1-0 win on the opening day, with me at full-back this time.

I played the first few games, but then had issues with the knee again and haven't played as much as I would have liked, as the lads have been doing brilliantly.

Sometimes, I'm probably my own worst enemy in terms of how I play, throwing myself into things and picking up little niggles that put me back a bit. But I'm not going to change now, it's just not in my nature.

My contract is up at the end of the season but I would love to stay for as long as possible - if I saw out my career at Deepdale I'd be the happiest man in the world.

I love the club, I've been here a long time and it means an awful lot to me.

The decision is out of my hands but whatever happens, nothing will ever take away the pride I've felt every single time I've pulled on the Preston shirt.

I'll have played the majority of my career captaining a great club, under top coaches, with brilliant groups of lads and fantastic fans.

I hope the journey can go on for a while longer yet and I've loved recalling all these great memories here; the big cup games, Joe's goal, Chesterfield, Wembley, beating Rovers.

It's been brilliant and I've thoroughly enjoyed every moment of it.

Even if it all ends tomorrow, I'll always be immensely proud of my time at North End - it's been fantastic.

And on top of all that, I'll always have the answer to one of football's greatest questions . . .

Who put the ball in the Blackpool net?

Super Tommy Clarke, cha!

Chapter 15

OOH . . . TONY ELLIS

Don't get too excited, because I'll say this right at the outset - there is no controversy as far as I'm concerned. I had five good seasons over two spells at North End, was top scorer and Player of the Year twice and helped the club to two play-off campaigns and a Wembley final.

So I haven't got a bad word to say about Preston, really. I'll always have a great affinity with the club and no-one - *no-one* - will ever take that away from me.

I remember the good times I had there with managers, players and the fans so, yes, I'm happy with my contribution. My only regret is not being able to explain my departure at the time.

That was out of my control.

Just like some people's reactions to it are out of my control. I just shrug my shoulders and don't let it affect me - it is what it is.

Maybe I can clear a few things up for some people here, so if you want the full story, I'll start at the beginning.

Like most young lads, I always wanted to be a footballer, but at the age when people are getting picked up at trials and things, I know I wasn't good enough.

I can see that now. I was decent, but more of a late developer in football terms. In fact, when I left school, I probably spent more than a year not playing properly at all.

Then I joined my mates in a Sunday league team called Poets Corner FC.

Trust me, I think some of the lads thought they were poets but there weren't any wordsmiths in the side, it was just the name of our local pub.

The same lads would play on a Saturday, too, for a team called Magnesium in Salford, so we were a really close group; I'd gone to school with some of them and we went back years.

We'd play on a Saturday, go out for a drink after the game, go back home at 9pm and meet at the Poets Corner the next morning to play again - that was our weekend.

It was the first time I saw what the right environment, proper team spirit could do in terms of results and performances - everyone battled for each other. It's a basic principle and it should be obvious, but teams that don't have that togetherness will always be lacking.

Work-wise, I was training as a painter and decorator and working for FADS, the old decorating and wallpaper firm, setting up the displays and going to college to get the qualifications. They had a flagship shop in Deansgate in Manchester city centre - where all the posh bars are now.

It gave me a great grounding about the real world, as people call it, and it also meant I was playing men's football at the weekend as a young lad.

The Salford Sunday League at that time was physical - I imagine it still is - so it was a useful toughening up process for sure, though I'm not sure my ankles always appreciated that.

Anyway, I remember I was up a ladder one day when someone gave me a shout and there was a call for me. A man called Dave Russell, who I didn't know, wanted a word. He was assistant manager at Horwich RMI *(which is now Leigh RMI)*, and I have to thank him for getting me on the path to playing at Football League level.

He said he'd seen me a few times on a Sunday and thought that I'd got something that would take me to a decent standard in the Northern Premier League, if I was prepared to work at it. He offered me the chance to get paid playing for them and he would pick me up and drop me off.

It was a great opportunity - and £25 a week - so it was a no-brainer for me.

I didn't play that many games for them, probably only around 15, but I scored a few goals and clubs started to come in for me.

Bolton were interested and I went for trials at Man City, who were under Billy McNeil at the time. I thought I had a better chance of signing for Bolton, to be honest, but in the end nothing came of it and I ended up leaving Horwich that year to sign for Northwich Victoria instead.

They were managed by Stuart Pearson, the old Manchester United midfielder, but I actually only played two games for them in pre-season. I played against Halifax and Joe Royle, the Oldham boss, was there watching one of their lads.

Gordon Hill, another ex-United and England star, was in the Northwich team that day and he probably made me look better than I was at the time.

Obviously, he was coming to the end of his career but he looked after me on the pitch; everything detailed, everything was safe side, his passes into me were just superb, so it was easy for me to play - he was just a top quality player.

That night, Stuart came in and said Mr Royle wants you to go for a week at Oldham. So I did three days there and ended up signing on the Saturday morning.

It all happened fast, but obviously to be in the game full time was a dream come true. I was just determined to work as hard as I could to make a success of it.

Whatever happened, I was going to give myself every chance. I made my debut quite early in my time at Oldham, but coming out of non-league I sort of plateaued for a while and ended up playing a lot of Central League games for the reserves.

That was a strong league at the time - clubs would have first team regulars playing and the standard was high. I told myself that if I could stay with it and progress during that first season, I'd end up having a career in the game. I did OK and as time went on they offered me another contract which I was happy to sign.

I wasn't starting first team games regularly though and half way through the next season, I got a call from Mr Royle who said Preston had come in for me, the club had accepted an offer and John McGrath wanted to have a chat.

I wasn't too sure at the time, because I was still fairly new to football so I spoke to Willie Donachie, a wise old head.

He said that when a club accepts a bid for you, it's a sign that you're leaving. So the fee was around £25,000 I think and that was that.

John McGrath actually came to my house and made a big impression on me straight away - *as I'm sure he did with most people!*

Looking back, I should have asked for more money really, because he agreed to the first thing I asked for. But that was John, very shrewd, very sharp, and a really good manager.

He told me I was his 'rough diamond' and he was going to polish me into a gem.

At that time, I was still young and sometimes had that mentality that 'I knew best' when I definitely didn't - which I soon came to realise working under him and Les Chapman. They managed me well and, true to Mr McGrath's word, they polished me up at Preston.

When I got there, there were some big names around: Frank Worthington - *I don't think anyone can add anything to how good a player he was* - Sam Allardyce, Bob Atkins, Oshor Williams, so bags of experience and know-how.

And there was me - a bit loose, if I can put it that way.

Sometimes I spoke when I shouldn't have spoken and I just played my type of football - I didn't really have any other way to play. If I wanted shoot from outside the box or cut inside or whatever, I'd just do it. *(That's one of the reasons I didn't fit in with John Beck, but more of that later.)*

As you get older and you learn more, get more experienced, you see that you're part of a team and you have to do stuff to help that team more. But at the time, I was still being polished up.

I'd signed at Deepdale in the same week as Brian Mooney and we both made our debuts at home against Port Vale.

The Central League was a decent level, but it wasn't at the pace of the first team. A proper league game in front of a big crowd was a different proposition. People were on you really quick - you had to think faster, act faster. Do everything quick.

It wasn't easy and I didn't play all that well in the game.

In fact, probably the only thing I did was tap in a last minute winner at the Fulwood End to seal a 3-2 comeback win - so not such a bad start, after all!

That was a great feeling and if they'd brought me in to score goals, well, I'd done what they asked. But, in the main, with the step up in standard from the reserves, it did take me a bit of time to settle in that first season.

It does with most young players and people have to be given time. It doesn't just happen in the first teams straight away sometimes, no matter how good you are. People have to be patient for players to get up to speed with the higher levels.

It probably took me two or three months to settle in. I was coming to a new club, getting to know the environment, the higher standard, the style of play - it doesn't happen straight away.

As time went on, I got to know all the lads better, knowing their strengths, understanding what they were going to do in a game.

Obviously, that really helps and getting a big chunk of a season at that level under my belt was vital. It's like anything really; the more you do something, the more you understand it and know what to expect, so the easier it gets.

For example, the first time I walked in the door and saw Frank Worthington, was I overawed? Most probably. When you see him do things with a ball that you can only dream of doing, you think to yourself: *'What am I doing on the same training pitch as him?'* He was unbelievable.

But over time, you get used to having him there and being in the same team.

To be fair, it was the same with Moons. What he could do with the ball, you just watched and went *'wow'*. Just incredible.

I thought to myself sometimes how privileged I was to play with these people. I was also fortunate that John and Les saw something in me. They had the foresight to understand that what they saw wasn't necessarily for *'now'* but maybe for the future, somewhere down the line. If they showed a bit of patience and I continued to work hard, we'd all get our rewards.

In the time when I wasn't scoring, John never put me under any pressure.

He could have done, but he didn't.

I can't remember any pressure on me at all and that helped me a lot.

Don't get me wrong, there were still times when we'd have disagreements. One time I did something in training that he didn't like. He said something and I answered back, as I sometimes did in those days. He sent me off but we had a chat about it afterwards, apologies were issued and we moved on.

I wasn't getting special treatment. He was the same with me as with everyone; very straight. He liked a laugh and a joke, but you knew where the lines were and what would happen if you crossed them.

But overall, as a management team, John and Les gave me belief. They could see I was getting better and making progress.

Another thing that helped me win a few people over in the crowd was a goal I scored against Notts County at Deepdale in the last game of the 1987/88 season. We lost 2-1 on the day, but I scored an overhead kick at the Kop end which flew in and showed what I was capable of.

It helped that Brian had signed permanently after his loan from Liverpool. His route in the game had been completely different to mine, having been at Anfield with players like Kenny Dalglish from a young age, but we formed a great bond on and off the pitch. We sat next to each other in the dressing room, both loved football, both loved a night out - both had the mullets.

We got on really well - in fact, I got on with most of the lads really well.

A few years ago I got misquoted about having *'acquaintances in football'* rather than friends, which made it sound like I was maybe a bit distant from people I played with. It's not the case at all, nothing could be further from the truth.

But if you think about it - *anyone* - how many really close friends have you got?

Half a dozen, if you're lucky.

Then think about how many people you've worked with or that you know and how often you actually see them.

There have been so many good people that I've come across in football; would I want to meet up with them and chat and catch up? Of course, 100 per cent.

Little Ronnie Hildersley, for example; what a nice lad, a top bloke and a great laugh. Mick Rathbone, whose son Ollie is with us at Rochdale now, where I'm Academy Manager; what a nice man, an absolute top bloke, always worked hard, demanded everything from himself to be the absolute best he could be - just a great fella.

The point I was making is that there's a difference between having a group of friends and then really close friends. It got twisted, but I think most people will understand where I'm coming from.

And back then in my first spell at North End, we were a really tight group.

John made some very good signings around that time; Mark Patterson came in and we also added Mike Flynn, who is also with us here at Rochdale these days.

Those two lads are the type of people you want on your side in any game. Talk about character and 'will to win'. You knew they would fight for you and leave everything out on the football pitch.

A proper pre-season with the lads helped and the following year, I was flying almost from the start. We hit the ground running and I scored a long-ranger from outside the box away against Chesterfield in an early 3-0 win - in off the underside of the bar, they always look good!

My son reminds me about some of these goals because people put them online and it's great to be able to look back and see them flying in, even all these years later.

My favourite goal was probably at Port Vale that season - I started with my back to goal and managed to twist and turn before beating the keeper into the top corner.

Just looking at the fans behind the goal, like a sea of happy faces jumping about and coming towards you - it's almost indescribable, that feeling.

We gathered momentum as the 1988/89 season went on; I was playing every game and scoring regularly as we sat up near the top of the table.

Gary Brazil went out to Newcastle in the February but Ian Bogie came in as part of the deal and formed a good midfield partnership with Warren Joyce - another guy who epitomised the spirit of the team at that time.

Gary had been the main man when I got there and was another very, very good player. He wasn't just a goalscorer, he was very intelligent and had a lot more to his game - a pleasure to play with up front.

Luckily, Ian Bogie was superb; fantastic feet, could see a pass and a nice lad off the pitch too, really funny lad. John also brought in Tony Philliskirk to help replace some of Gary's goals and he did well, too. I've always got on well with Tony - he's a coach now at Burnley - and he helped push us into the play-off positions.

He was a really good foil for me. I could hold the ball up, but Tony was a great target man and fantastic at laying it off just where you'd want it. We both scored goals too, so it was a good partnership.

It was a good season, where the football club kicked on again. We'd consolidated the year before, but now we were moving forward and finished sixth, where we faced Port Vale in the play-offs, which had only just been introduced.

We drew 1-1 with them at Deepdale but went down to a Darren Beckford hat-trick at their place a few days later. We were drawing 1-1 for a time, but they had a good side that year; Beckford, Robbie Earle, people who went on to have top flight careers.

I think we'd progressed though and everyone at the football club was happy with the direction we were going in.

We all expected to kick on again the following season, as we had a fairly young side and players that were getting better as time went on.

John didn't rest on any laurels either; we brought in Graham Shaw from Stoke for some decent money and also grabbed Steve Harper, who was the bearer of another classic curly 1980's hairdo.

People may look back on the mullets and things now, but at the time you don't really think about it; it's just the look of the day at the time, isn't it?

You look at the length of some of the shorts we wore back then and it's entirely different to now, but really, it's just a kit isn't it? It was all just *'of the time'*.

Although Tony Philliskirk left, we'd kept the nucleus of the previous season's team so it was a bit of a shock when we had a bad start to 1989/90 - we didn't win for five games. For whatever reason, we just weren't getting the results on a consistent basis.

Then, just before Christmas, a bombshell was dropped on me - the club had accepted an offer from Stoke City and they wanted me to go down and have a chat with their manager Alan Ball.

I hadn't heard anything about it before then, it was a bolt out of the blue really, but it was clear I'd have to go and talk to them. It was all a bit new to me, so I took an agent in, which was the first time I'd ever dealt with one.

We had a chat on the way down, but when we got there, what we'd agreed in the car was not what he came out with at the meeting.

The agent asked for a figure that wasn't what we'd talked about - it was too much money and I was sat there thinking: *'What's going on here?'*

It's fair to say Bally wasn't impressed so they told the pair of us: 'Off you go.'

I went home and got a call from John McGrath the next morning, asking me what was going on and why had I taken this agent in?

I didn't know what to say to him, but he said he would get me back in there with someone else. He said: *'Son, you're signing for Stoke City this morning.'*

I got the impression the club needed the money, 100 per cent.

Let's face it, John was losing his leading goalscorer. It's not something he'd have wanted to do of his own accord, I'm sure.

After talking to John, the deal was done and it was a good chapter for me, to be fair - I learned a lot, not just about the process of transfers, but about arriving for a decent fee and playing for a big club with an expectant fanbase.

The fee was around £250,000, big money at that time, and you had to perform all the time - there were no days off from it, there was a lot of expectation.

They were at Championship level, Alan was bringing in quite a few players at the time and he was a great manager. We beat Newcastle 2-1 in my first game there and we thought it would be onwards and upwards, but we just couldn't get the results.

It was really disappointing because he was a great manager; passionate, always wore his heart on his sleeve and he taught everyone so much.

Obviously, he'd been such a good player - a World Cup winner - that he wasn't just telling you how to do things, he could show you how to do them.

He'd look at your game and say things like: 'I like the way you peel off the shoulder of the centre back, but we can add this into your game . . .'

Then he'd show you how to do it. I felt I was always learning new things from him.

A few months after I left Deepdale, Preston sacked John McGrath, which was a real sickener. He'd got the club promoted, consolidated, then reached the play-offs - all on a small budget and over a short period of time. He'd then had to sell his leading goalscorer.

After all he had done, I think the club should have shown him more loyalty, but that was the way things were at the time.

I did OK at Stoke, despite a couple of injuries and the sad sacking of Alan Ball. When my contract was up a couple of years later, they offered me a new one but I wasn't really playing regularly and I wanted games.

I was on a decent wage at the Victoria Ground, but I actually came back to Preston for half the money.

Lou Macari was keen for me to stay and go to the Isle of Man on Stoke's pre-season, but I said to him: 'I've got to find myself a club where I can play.'

I could have sat there, picking up a very decent wage and playing reserve team football, but that's not me.

I didn't want to do that. I wanted to play first team football. When I first spoke to Les in that summer of 1992 he said: 'Tony, we can't afford you.'

So I had to make a decision and money was just one aspect of it. Yes, it was a drop in wages, but the way I looked at it, if I had to go down a little bit to come back up then I was prepared to do that for Les and for North End.

I thought I'd play regularly and the club would be successful.

It was a big call and I had to speak to my family about it, because obviously when you go from having a certain amount of money to having a lot less, things would have to change. And things did change for us, but I said to my wife: 'I'll do well, the club will do well and things will change again.'

People may not know about that, but it puts what went on later into a bit of context.

I showed loyalty by coming back to the club for a lot less money than I could have got elsewhere, because I loved the place; loved the manager, the environment.

I wanted nothing more than to be successful with Preston North End and I was prepared to take a step back financially to achieve that. I came back to the club even though I knew the team wasn't as strong as when I left.

Did that bother me? *No.*

I'd had a great time at North End previously, I trusted the manager and he was a big part in me coming back. I liked Les, I liked the fans, I knew some of the players and I knew what the environment was going to be and I was happy with all that.

That was a big selling point for me. It was really nice to *'come home'*, that's how I looked at it, and start enjoying football again. So I was pleased to be back and scored in my first couple of games to hit the ground running.

Les had brought a couple of local lads through the ranks by then; Lee Ashcroft and Lee Cartwright. Carts had a great engine on him and could run all day, while Ashy was a real character I knew from the first spell there. He was a cheeky kid alright, but he wasn't disrespectful.

When he was a really young lad, me and Moons used to hide him in the dressing room under a pile of kit when John McGrath was talking to us and he wasn't supposed to be in there. You'd suddenly just see this little head popping up in the background and John would know something was up: *'He's here again! That little sod's in here again! Ashcroft! Where is he?!'*

Then he'd chase Ashy out of the room with a kick up the backside while me and Brian were cracking up in the corner.

Part of the reason I'd come back was for Les - he was such a top man and a great character. I'm not sure he got a fair crack of the whip when he stepped up after John and by October, he was sacked. I was surprised, to be honest, and after all it was less than a quarter of the way through the season. We weren't really struggling and the fans hadn't turned on him or anything.

Sam Allardyce was still at North End doing some coaching and he stepped up as caretaker boss. He was a ready-made manager, right there.

He had been a manager on the pitch, always very vocal and inspiring people with the way he led by example. It was great to have played alongside him.

Everyone liked and respected Sam and his first away game certainly gave him - *and us* - a test . . . at Bloomfield Road against Blackpool. It turned out to be an incredible match.

I'd played in those local derbies before, but that day when we went for our pre-match food, the place was absolutely bouncing.

You could feel it through the stands, both sets of fans just really, really fired up. Great noise, exactly how it should be.

The atmosphere was just incredible and I don't need to tell anyone here how important those games are - from either side of the divide.

The lads were up for it anyway but, to be honest, it just seemed to go really quick and I don't remember that much of it. I know their keeper made a mess of a long throw from Flynny for the first one and I just stooped to get my head onto it.

The second one, I think Ashy had a shot that he spilled and I got the rebound.

As for the third, I'd been clothes-lined on the halfway line - *absolutely cleaned out by one of their lads* - just a couple of minutes before. There was a bit of a delay in getting me back out and these days they might not have even let me carry on.

But I got back into it and was basically playing on instinct when the third one went in; I just tried to get it out of my feet, twisted to get some space and put in the back of the net.

The fans were going wild, all standing behind on that big open away end they used to have and I could see what it meant to them. It was great at the time, but to be honest I can't remember that much about it after that bang on the head.

I remember the ref coming over as we went back to the centre circle and I thought he might be checking if I was OK - *instead he just told me to hurry up back to my own half so we could kick off again!*

I got taken off just after that and there's a picture of me with the match ball just after the game - with a nice shiner coming already.

I've seen it on YouTube and videos since, but all I can really remember is I scored three - and we won 3-2. It's the result that counts.

When I eventually signed for Blackpool, a lot of the time that was the first thing their fans mentioned, not surprisingly. But they forgot about it once I started scoring goals for them.

That was still some way off though and I was more than happy banging them in for Preston that season, even when John Beck came in.

Sam had done well while he was in charge, so it was a bit of a surprise when the new manager arrived. He had a good track record at Cambridge but everyone had heard stories about his methods.

For me, it's all about creating the right environment for players to prosper. No doubt some of what John Beck did worked for some of the lads and especially some of the lads he brought in.

But not for me, really. I didn't find it very enjoyable. Like I said, it all about creating the right environment and, for me, he didn't do that.

Did I agree with how he spoke to people at times? *No, not at all.*

Did I agree with some of the things that went on behind the scenes? *Absolutely not.*

But that was his philosophy.

He was very strict on the type of football he wanted to play, where the ball was to go, when it was to go there and that wasn't my type of style at all.

I used to like to lay it off or play it out wide then get into the box to get on the end of crosses. There were constant arguments in training because he was totally against the ball being passed backwards.

He wanted everything to be very direct.

But there were times when people like Gareth Ainsworth were so quick he'd be at the byline and whipping it in before the strikers even got there.

Meanwhile, we had great passers in midfield who could put the ball on a sixpence who were just being bypassed.

If they needed a touch before playing it behind, it gave me time to get into position, but he didn't want that. It had to be played quick. I could see flaws in that direct approach, but nevertheless, I tried to make the best of it.

Another thing was that he didn't like you shooting from outside the box.

I remember we played away at Chester one night, really cold, wet night at the Deva Stadium and I hit one from 25 yards that flew over the keeper's head and into the back of the net. We won 4-2 and when we got back into the changing room the first thing he said to me was: *'Fantastic goal son . . . but we don't do that, do we?'*

I thought: 'Yeah, and if I hadn't done that, we might not have got the three points mate!'

Always going outside a defender was another thing. I scored another goal that season after cutting inside and it was the same again: 'We don't go on the inside son - I've told you, always go on the outside.'

I'd just scored a goal!

You were never allowed to think for yourself. As a coach these days, I give the kids freedom within a framework and I give the other coaches that same freedom, all within a framework. It all has to fit within the vision, the values and the philosophy of the club here at Rochdale.

John Beck had his own philosophy and that was up to him. It was all about *'going down Quality Street'*, hitting *'Paradise Alley'*; the word *'bold'* was everywhere '*be* ***bold***, *be* ***bold***'.

But it struck me that *'being bold'* was the last thing we were allowed to do.

Take a player on and stick it in the back of the net - that's what I'd been doing for years by then. Now, I was being told that wasn't what was wanted. We had to score goals *his* way.

So, yes, it was a strange environment.

When he was at Cambridge, where he'd had success, they let the grass grow in the corners. So when the ball got played there, it held up.

At Deepdale, we had the plastic pitch and so the ball just ran away from you. When they put sand on it, it just got even quicker. We could never catch up with play and, like I say . . . it was a difficult environment.

I think it was the players and the fans that kept everything level around that time; kept things on an even keel, despite what was going on. Us players were all mates and we kept things level for each other - we were all in it together and we stuck together.

But it's no secret that I wasn't his type of player, really. I didn't fit in with that direct philosophy.

It didn't mean that I didn't give 100 per cent - of course I did, every game. You're playing for the club, your teammates, the fans, your family, yourself - not just a manager.

I didn't like him much, but that didn't come into it - he was there and I always tried my best.

To be fair, he brought in some good players; he started giving Ryan Kidd some gametime and Kiddo went on to be a great player for Preston for many years. I liked Micky Norbury as a striker and we had lads like Gareth Ainsworth who could fly down the wing and get the ball into the box.

No disrespect to anyone else, but I thought Gareth was the best player I played with at Deepdale - he created so many chances for me. I scored the goals, but I couldn't have done it without those good players around me.

But, like I say, you had to play his way.

He took Ashy off one day for cutting inside and having a shot and - *in the days before fourth officials* - Beck was the one holding up the board with his number on.

He was making a point to Ashy that *'you do it my way, or you're off'*. It wasn't a great surprise when Lee left to go to West Brom that summer, even though he was a big Preston lad and loved North End.

So my first season back at Deepdale was up and down in many ways.

On a personal level, I got 22 goals and was named Player of the Year, something I'm very proud of.

But all that was overshadowed because, much more importantly, we were relegated to the bottom tier again after a last-day defeat at Bolton.

Yes, it was nice to get individual praise, but what the team does is far more important and overall that year, we hadn't been good enough to stay up.

The club stuck with the manager the following season and again, it was the good and bad of John Beck.

Players like David Moyes, Mike Conroy and Ian Bryson came in and were all great additions; experienced heads and good players who knew their way around.

Me? I had a year left on my contract and wasn't looking to leave.

It was disappointing to be in the lowest tier, but I thought we could get out of that league and I wanted to be a part of a successful, promotion-winning PNE side.

Despite relegation, I was happy at North End. I was scoring goals, loved playing with the lads, had a great relationship with the fans and had just been presented with the Player of the Year award by Sir Tom Finney.

What an honour that was. I still carry the picture around with me on my phone of the great man presenting me with the award. Talk about special moments.

We did well in that following season and, of course, ended up in the play-offs against Torquay. That was a magical night at Deepdale; the last on the old plastic pitch and the one that set us up for a play-off final at Wembley - the first time the club had been there for 30 years.

The scenes at the final whistle will stay with me forever. How can they not?

In the end, we came up just short at Wembley against Wycombe in what was - *sadly* - to be my last appearance in a PNE shirt. I didn't want it to be and I didn't realise it at the time. But it was.

It was a really disappointing way to bow out, but I'm not sure anything would have happened differently even if we'd have gone up.

I got the impression John Beck wouldn't have played me even if I'd stayed.

Again, I was leading goalscorer - this time with 26 in the league - and was named Player of the Year for the second season running.

Why would I want to leave? If anything, I wanted to stay as long as possible. I was sure we'd go one better the following year, I loved playing for North End and I was settled at the club. At that point, I'd have probably stayed there for the rest of my career if I had the chance.

My contract was up, but I hadn't heard anything from the club. I thought maybe they were waiting to see what division we'd be in.

After the game at Wembley, I went to see them early the next week because when you're out of contract, you need to sort these things out.

As I said, I'd been top goalscorer and Player of the Year again that season. I wasn't asking for much more money than I was on . . . but I wanted a three-year contract.

It was a matter of principle as much as anything else.

I'd shown the club loyalty in coming back from Stoke on a lot less money than I was being offered to stay. I'd served North End well and now I was looking for a bit of loyalty in return.

And yet . . . the club were adamant they would only offer two years.

It's as simple as that.

I wasn't going to sign a two-year contract - I thought I'd earned a bit more loyalty than that.

I don't know if anyone else was on a three-year deal and it didn't matter to me if they were or they weren't. I was never interested in what other people were getting.

I just felt like I'd earned a three-year deal - and, for whatever reason, they wouldn't give me one.

Even if it had been club policy to only issue two-year contracts - *and no-one ever said that to me* - they could have made an exception if they wanted to.

But they didn't, so it was their decision, out of my control.

They said my age was against me, but I was only 29 - and I went on to play league football until I was 36!

It's still strange now when you think about it; your top scorer is saying he wants to commit the next three years to the football club and the club is saying *'no'*.

I had an agent by then, but I dealt with the negotiations myself so I know exactly what the discussions were.

The people there at the time were firm on it though; they were not going to give me a three-year deal and that was that.

I was dealing with the manager, not the chairman in those days, so I think it was his decision. If it had been Les Chapman, he would have fought for me a lot harder.

If it had been Sam Allardyce or John McGrath, they would have, too.

But I was dealing with John Beck and it was just: *'No.'*

I wasn't happy. I didn't want to go. But there wasn't a lot I could do.

I took a deep breath, shook his hand, wished him all the best and walked out of the old reception onto Lowthorpe Road.

And that was that.

It was disappointing at the time because clearly I wanted to stay, but you're a professional and you move on.

People ask if I was hurt by it, but that didn't really come into it.

I couldn't control the situation. All I could control were my reactions.

At the end of the day, I have a family, they are my priority and I had to support them. I couldn't mope about, that doesn't get you anywhere. I had to move forward.

I knew there were a couple of clubs interested in signing me so that afternoon I started to make some phone calls.

I hadn't had contact with anyone before then, because I really hoped I'd be staying at Preston.

There was a club down south interested and another one fairly local - I spoke to a couple of teams around that time.

But the best move for me and my family at that time was moving to Blackpool.

Whether other people like it or not doesn't bother me.

I didn't really think about other people's reactions. It didn't come into it. You can't run your life around what other people may think.

My family come first and foremost, 110 per cent.

We'd just settled into a nice house in Manchester and it was important that I didn't unsettle them by moving down south or anything.

For the money North End paid for me and the money they later sold me for, with all the goals in between and two years of being Player of the Year, I think I did a good job for Preston. I can hold my head up high.

But they didn't want to commit to me in the same way I wanted to commit to them.

So when the Blackpool deal went on the table, it was a no-brainer.

I couldn't really refuse the money that was being offered. It went far and beyond what I was asking for at Deepdale.

A lot of Blackpool fans were surprised that they were able to sign North End's top scorer, but that's just the way things were.

Of course, I understand the passion and the rivalry between the clubs and knew Preston fans would be disappointed.

I can understand some of it, but not all of it.

I'm a Salford lad. I support Manchester United and professional football was my job. It was how I paid my bills and provided for my family. It still is.

The fee went to a tribunal that summer and probably the only thing I regret is that I wasn't able to talk about what had gone on at the time.

I wanted to come out and tell everyone what had happened, but I wasn't allowed to. Blackpool didn't want me to speak and so what went on didn't come out.

People might not have fully understood, but they would probably have understood things a little bit more.

To be honest, I didn't like speaking to the press anyway. There's talk of a radio interview that I did, but I can't remember it at all. I wasn't one for courting the limelight. I just wanted to play football.

I remember going back to Deepdale to play for Blackpool and the Town End was calling me *'Judas'* and all sorts, but if you let things like that affect you, then you won't be successful as a professional footballer. You just blank it out.

In a way, they're having a go because they know you're going to be a danger.

That game passed by really quickly if I'm honest, and any stick I got probably affected friends and family at the game more than me.

Obviously, it's nicer if they're chanting your name in a good way and if I'd stayed at the club those very same people probably would have been doing that and talking about me like a hero.

But I'd still be the same person I am now.

A couple of years later, there was talk of me going back to Preston again when Gary Peters had taken over. I'm not sure how much there was in it - but Blackpool offered me a new contract straight away and I stayed there again. That's how they dealt with things, no messing about.

The bottom line is, I loved playing for Preston and really enjoyed my time there with the players, John McGrath, Les and the fans.

I might not have enjoyed the style of football under John Beck at times, but I was successful and gave the club good service.

I learned a lot and would I have my time there again? *110 per cent.*

Like I said at the beginning, no-one will ever take that away from me and I'll always have a warm feeling towards the club. People's reactions to where I went after leaving and a bit of name-calling don't hurt me.

You occasionally get the odd idiot popping up on Twitter or something who'll drag something up, but it's water off a duck's back, to be honest.

I went back a few years ago with a bunch of former players for Sir Tom's birthday and we were all introduced onto the pitch. Everyone got a cheer until it came to me . . . when a big *'booo'* went up from the crowd.

That's fine. That's life.

If some people want a pantomime villain then that's up to them. Knock yourselves out. We had a bit of a laugh about it among the lads and that was that.

Whenever I meet North End fans now, people might talk about the Blackpool move but mainly they remember the goals and the good times.

I hope they come to understand the circumstances that led to my departure.

I can't even say I regret leaving, because I went on to play with some great lads and have some great times at Blackpool, Bury, Stockport, Rochdale and Burnley.

So, yes, it was a disappointment Preston didn't show a bit more faith in me at that time, but overall I had a fantastic career at Deepdale.

And when I look back, I focus on the positives.

I'm happy with what I achieved at North End, I'm happy with my career in the game and I'm proud to have played for all my clubs.

Like I said at the beginning, no-one can ever take that away.

Chapter 16

GARY PETERS: HEART AND SOUL

There are moments in your life where it all comes together: *'Right place, right time, right people, right here, right now.'* That was what being manager of Preston North End felt like to me.

It was where I was meant to be, like someone had put me there for that purpose.

It was the best of times and I know the next part of that quote is *' . . . it was the worst of times'*.

But for me, the only bad part of my time at Deepdale was leaving it.

I spent 10 years at North End as assistant, manager and running the academy. Without a doubt, it was the best 10 years of my life.

You'll have to forgive me, because I can get quite emotional when I talk about it.

But I can't help it - that's what Preston North End means to me.

It had been a strange old journey to get there but it was worth the wait - and more.

So if you want to hear about it, let's kick-off.

When I was a player . . . I was a defender, pure and simple. That was my job. I wasn't the most skilful player. I was a quick, strong full-back and my job was to stop the opposition playing.

But I was also able to make things happen, talk to the other players, organise things at the back and at most of my clubs they made me captain.

I suppose I led by example, too. I remember one time for Reading, I broke my ankle during a game but, in the days when we only had one substitute, I refused to come off as I didn't want to leave the lads short. They stuck me up front and as I hobbled about, the ball bounced off me and I scored with my good foot. I didn't play for a couple of months after that, but we got a result, so y'know . . .

That was the type of player I was. I never thought I was any good, but I was effective. I was a round peg in a round hole and started out at Reading. We had a back four where none of us were really good players, but we all complemented each other; some were quick, some were good in the air. We all liked a tackle, mind you.

We saw that if we worked together, we could overcome any individual shortcomings and be really effective as a unit. That was something that stuck with me all the way into my managerial career.

It's not about everybody being good at everything - it's about being a team.

Ian Branfoot had that when I was at Reading, then Dave Bassett had it when I went to Wimbledon and that's what I took with me when I was at Deepdale.

I'd been at the Royals for four years, before a couple of seasons at Fulham and then Dave took me to the old Plough Lane in 1982.

Malcolm MacDonald had been my manager at Craven Cottage and I'd had a falling out with him. I didn't really like the bloke, if I'm honest.

He insisted that I had to push wingers inside, when I knew that no-one ever beat me on the outside. *(Well, if they did, they wouldn't do it again.)*

Looking back, maybe he was right, but either way, he was the manager and I was out of the door. The fact he had Paul Parker coming through, who went on to play for England in the World Cup semi-final, probably had something to do with it, too!

When I got to Wimbledon, they were still in the Fourth Division and the infamous *'Crazy Gang'* was just taking shape: a young Nigel Winterburn was there, Dave Beasant, Alan Cork, Wally Downes.

Those lads already had a bit of a reputation, shall we say, but Dave introduced me to them on my first day by saying: *'Right lads, this is Gary Peters. He's your new captain.'*

Now, there were quite a few strong characters in that dressing room to put it mildly and you should have seen their faces - and mine. *Cheers boss!*

We were just setting off on a pre-season trip to Finland and I thought: 'Well, this is going to be interesting.'

True enough in the middle of the first night, I woke up with about six of them on top of me, shaving my moustache off: *'If we have to have you as captain, fine - but we're not having that flipping 'tache mate!'*

I hadn't even kicked a ball at that point (!) so on that trip they tested me quite a bit and lots of things occurred where I had to step up to the plate.

By the end of it though, I think they'd all accepted me as captain and we went on to win the league that year. To this day when I see those lads, they still call me *'Skip'*.

There are plenty of stories about the '*Crazy Gang'* days, but we have a rule not to talk about them in public - and they're mostly unprintable anyway!

We got promoted again in my second season there, going up into Championship level, on a shoestring budget and tiny crowds. It's one of football's great fairytales, really. We were the most physical team you could possibly be. That - and our togetherness - was our strength.

When I was manager at Preston, I tried to put all these lessons into practice; the team had to play as one unit - not 11 individuals. Loads of clubs have got 11 good individuals, but they don't make a good team. It's not because the players aren't good enough. But if they don't work as one, they fail.

You'd think that would be obvious, but all too often it isn't.

Finding the right players, the moving parts for the machine, is the key thing.

After Wimbledon, I went back to Reading, then briefly Aldershot and back to Fulham, playing a few games and helping out my old Dons mate Ray Lewington, who had taken over as manager.

The issue there was that I fell out with Jimmy Hill, who was running the club at that time. He used to get Ray and me and grill us after the game, in front of people in the boardroom, like he was some sort of football genius who had all the answers.

I wasn't getting paid or anything, I was just helping Ray out, so I had enough of Mr Hill and left.

Off the field, I'd done quite well for myself; I had two pubs and an office building that was working well for me financially, so I had no worries on that score, business-wise.

But around that time, I got a call from John Beck, who was doing well at Cambridge and wanted me to be his assistant. I'd known John from my first spell at Fulham under Malcolm McDonald. He'd looked at what Wimbledon had achieved by being direct and, well . . . he just took it to a whole new level.

He'd won promotion from Division Four, then when I joined we went up from Division Three and next we were flying in the old Second Division - again, Championship level now.

Round about Christmas time, we were top of the league and looking like we could go up for the third year running. We had the likes of Steve Claridge and Dion Dublin up front - a very good side. Now, this was 1992, and the Premier League was due to start the following season. Quite frankly, there was no way they wanted little old Cambridge in it - especially not playing the type of football we were playing.

We ended up in the play-offs, where we lost to Leicester, who then got beat by Kenny Dalglish's Blackburn in the final. So Rovers went up with Ipswich and Middlesbrough - and I'm sure someone, somewhere was very happy with that.

I think Kenny was a lot more 'marketable' than John Beck.

John was brilliant with his methods and his philosophy, but he struggled to manage players. He could fall out with them easy as anything and sometimes, well, often actually, he found it hard to be friendly with people. I never understood why, because I enjoyed working with him at Cambridge. I thought he had such good ideas, a great ambition and we were successful. What's not to like?

Eventually though, Cambridge sold players, John and I left and not that long afterwards, he got offered the job at Preston.

At first, I didn't know if I would go with him. I'd spent my entire career down south and, like I said, I had a couple of good businesses there.

But I looked at North End and thought the club was in the wrong position, struggling in the third tier. It wasn't like Cambridge, which was always going to have a natural ceiling to what could be achieved.

At Preston, you looked at the support, the potential and thought: *'This could be a whole different story. If we get this ball rolling, it could go all the way to the top.'*

At the time though, the club was in a mess. When we arrived, everything seemed *'off the cuff'*, all a bit amateur.

There was very little money, the stadium was decrepit and there was just an air of doom and gloom. The plastic pitch was there, but it was on its last legs after being down for a few years.

There was just no life to the place. The whole club just seemed asleep. It needed a short, sharp shock to wake it up and jolt it back to life.

Looking back, maybe that's what Becky brought, certainly attitude-wise. Because despite being sacked by Cambridge, he hadn't changed a bit.

He wanted to do everything just like he'd done previously; the way we'd play, the discipline, the mental side of things, the buckets of ice cold water before games, the ball boys cleaning the balls for us, everything.

He wanted us to be very direct, aim for zones on the pitch, make the most of throw-ins, do things in a very exact way, like it was a science almost.

For example, a forward was not allowed to take a player on in the inside - the thinking being that if he went outside and a tackle came in, you got a throw-in from it.

There was clearly a logic to his methods.

But he went into a dressing room that wasn't ready for him. These weren't lads who'd been on a journey with him from the fourth division to the brink of the Premier League. They had no relationship with him and because he didn't build one with them . . . it just didn't work.

The squad had its own mentality and there needed to be compromise, especially at first, but that wasn't John's way. He needed to get them onside, to buy into his ideas, but never really succeeded. On top of that, some big things that should have been used to our advantage weren't.

All visiting teams hated the plastic pitch - it should have been a massive advantage to us, we should have been winning every home game. But our lads hated it as much as everyone else, so we never really made the most of the advantage.

Also, the away fans were in the noisiest section of the ground - right behind the goal. There could be 50 of them making more noise than 500 of ours at the other end.

These things were staring us in the face.

So there was a lot to do, on and off the pitch. And some things he got right, some things were clearly wrong. He had a style of play that, being brutal, few players really enjoyed.

Players at Cambridge hadn't *enjoyed* it, but they did it because it was successful.

But it was the same as how we'd been at Wimbledon - if you're successful and it's working, players will go along with it.

So it was vital that we won the first few games at North End to get them onside, then they'll buy into things a bit more.

But we didn't win; we lost the first game 5-2 at home to Port Vale and that sort of set the tone. So after a while, you've go to adapt, have a rethink.

John wouldn't do that.

At Preston, with the plastic pitch and the way the ball ran off it, it just wasn't working and the players were getting frustrated that we kept on with it, game after game. It got harder and harder as each week went by and you could see the players thinking: *'What's all this about?'*

And all the time we were sliding worryingly down the table.

We hadn't been in a good position when we arrived, so there wasn't much leeway and as results didn't pick up we were heading towards the relegation zone.

When you're in a battle like that, you really need to have good man-management skills, to get everyone onside, fighting for each other and pulling in the same direction. You've got to have that Wimbledon-style togetherness.

Sadly, I think that was probably the weakest part of John's armoury. He was brilliant in how he approached games and ahead of his time in preparation, statistics and things like that, monitoring performance.

But, as I say, the whole thing depended on people buying into his ideas. If he couldn't carry them with him, it was doomed to fail. He just couldn't - or wouldn't adapt his approach.

Someone like Lee Ashcroft, for example - a really good young player, but a fiery little bugger. Becky would be hammering him in front of the lads and you could see Ashy just getting angrier and angrier. *It wasn't making him play better - it was making him want to wait for John on the car park!*

Lee was a young lad who needed a different approach.

Funnily enough, seeing his response back then helped convince me I could be a manager in my own right one day. Later on, I knew Ashy wouldn't respond to being criticised in front of his teammates, so I always used to do it behind closed doors, where he would sit, listen and be fine.

But back when we arrived at Preston, it wasn't just Lee Ashcroft - there were quite a few experienced players who were just not having it. At all.

It got to the stage where Becky would have conversations with the players and then they'd have a talk among themselves about their response.

Obviously, it shouldn't be like that but as assistant, I was that bridge between the two and as time went on, I ended up having a closer relationship with the players.

It wasn't a case of picking sides or anything, it's just the way things developed.

John took a lot of the training and wanted to force his ideas through, no matter what the players thought. Watching it unfold, I learned a lot from him; good and bad.

There was obviously more bad than good in that first season as we ended up being relegated on the last day, away at Bolton. That was a real sickener and a terrible day all round, we felt like we'd let the supporters down - and we had.

But when the club stuck by us, it gave John a chance to bring in his own players for the next time out. The lads he brought in were some brilliant signings; Ian Bryson, David Moyes, Paul Raynor - really good professionals and strong characters.

However, in hindsight, that eventually became part of the problem as well.

You could probably have signed a bunch of young lads who would have totally followed an idea, even if it's not working. You can't get senior players to do that.

The pressure was on us, as the management team, because when you get relegated and a club sticks with you, you've got to show pretty quickly that you can get back up. Thankfully, we had a good start and with the new lads settling in, we had the makings of a very good team.

The Town End was now the home end and the Kop was still North End fans too; I think we stuck the away fans in a corner of the old West Stand, where they could barely be seen, let alone heard.

Crowds had picked up and the supporters were making the most of the new set-up; the Town End was starting to be THE place to spend your Saturday afternoons in Preston.

There was ticker tape, a drummer turned up and the noise starting to come off it was brilliant for the team. We were up and about the top end of the table and things were going well overall.

We then hit a terrible result in the FA Cup though, losing 1-0 away at Kidderminster and that was a lesson again to everyone at the club.

We put out a good team that day; some really strong, experienced players. We had a fantastic following, but if you don't play as a team and don't stick together when things start going wrong, you're going to end up getting beat.

Eleven individuals won't beat one team - it's as simple as that.

So we had to take our medicine as a team and try not to let it affect us as we pushed on for promotion, ending up against Torquay in the play-offs.

That second-leg at home was incredible. We'd lost 2-0 down there but even before the kick-off at Deepdale that night, I looked around the stadium, took in the atmosphere and thought: *'Well, if nothing else, we've woken the place up.'*

Obviously, it turned out to be an incredible, dramatic night and by the end of it, there was so much emotion. I don't know what the fans were more happy about, getting to Wembley or seeing the end of the plastic pitch.

They were ripping it up with their bare hands at the final whistle and, to be honest, I felt like joining in!

We were playing Wycombe in the final and, while it was great for the club to be there, it led to probably one of the worst selection mistakes I've ever seen in football.

Stuart Hicks had been in the team for the semi-final and did brilliantly.

Jamie Squires was a good young defender, but he was coming back from injury and it seemed like an obvious choice to stick with Hicksy for the final.

I don't think Squiresy expected to play or that he was ready to play in such a big game. We'd prepared for Stuart all the way through the week but on the coach on the way to Wembley, John turned to me and said: *'Do you know what? I've got a feeling. I'm going to go with Squiresy instead of Hicksy.'*

I just said: 'John, you can't be serious. Don't do that. It'll kill everyone. We've all prepared for Stuart to play. We're all set up.'

I thought I'd talked him out of it, but when we got there before the game and were having a look around the pitch, I saw John jogging across to Hicksy to have a word.

I realised straight away what he was telling him by the look on the lad's face.

I felt for him, I felt for Jamie, who was being thrust into this massive occasion, and I felt for the rest of the lads, who took the decision badly among themselves.

It had a terrible effect. It just killed the morale and the excitement in the dressing room, I suddenly thought: *'This is crazy. It's like no-one wants to be here.'*

Hicksy was devastated and the other players were devastated for him. I was, too, for him and for Jamie; it was a hell of an 'ask' for a young lad. Even when we made a good start against Wycombe, we fell away and I think that decision cost us that day, it really did. But that was John - when he got an idea in his head, he just couldn't be talked out of it.

That summer we had another blow when we lost Tony Ellis. Whatever level you're at, you need a goalscorer and he had been our top scorer for the past two seasons.

He may not have fitted the perfect idea of a John Beck player, but if you put people around him, he'd shown he could still score goals in the system. So, irrespective of where he went or anything else, it was a big loss.

The following season, we maybe had a play-off hangover and just couldn't really 'kick on' from the season before.

Things were getting really intense and pressured between John and the players and things built up so much there inevitably had to be that release. The players had a meeting and wanted things to be softened a bit; they wanted John to be a bit more flexible in what they could do on the pitch.

They came up with some good ideas - Moyesie, Ian Bryson - things that wouldn't change the overall style, but just give them a bit more freedom.

I sat down with John and said: 'There's some good stuff here, which ones are we going to bring into the system?'

He just looked at me and said: *'None of 'em.'*

He added: 'Forget all that. We're going to do it our way, end of story.'

My heart just sank and I knew there was trouble ahead.

That was John's big weakness - he just didn't work as man manager.

Baxi had got involved with the club around that time and I don't think there were great relationships with John at board level either. Results were suffering and, in the end, everything just became too much for everyone; players, fans and directors.

I could sense the end was nigh and John was sacked in early December.

In all honesty, I was a bit surprised that they then offered me the job, as I'd come in with John and been part of his team. I hadn't fallen out with Becky, but I'd disagreed with him in a lot of situations.

I thought things could have been done differently and if I hadn't thought like that, I'd have left with him. Like the players, I thought we just needed to adapt things and soften the edges and we could all be successful.

I was genuinely sad that John couldn't see that and in the end lost his job.

If he'd have just given a bit of leeway, we could have got the team back on board. What stood me in good stead was that I understood what the problems had been, I knew how to solve them and I knew how to get more out of the team.

They were good pros after all, and it was a good club, starting to move forward behind the scenes. Baxi's investment was changing things quite dramatically; the directors before that were good people with the club's best interests at heart, but they just didn't have the resources. Now, with Bryan Gray as chairman, there was finally a bit of money around.

Another big factor for me was how much I'd grown to love the club and how well I'd settled in the area. I come from London and the south and it's hard to explain, but the people up here are very different.

Northern people are just lovely - I couldn't go back and live in the south now, I'll live up here for the rest of my life.

When I was at North End later on, I had job offers to go elsewhere, but I stayed because I loved the place that much, the club, the town, the people, the pubs, everything.

One of the very first things I did was appoint David Moyes as my assistant. Along with Brys, he stood out a mile. Those two could control the dressing room and keep things moving in the right direction. The funny thing was, we didn't do things very differently. We didn't change it a lot at first.

Don't forget, we'd brought in a lot of players to play a certain style - *lads like Neil Trebble and Mark Sale* - so we couldn't just flick a switch and start playing tippy-tappy football. But just making a few minor changes worked, as well as bringing in one or two new faces.

I pride myself on the hours I used to put in and would never sign anyone without seeing them three or four times in the flesh. You've got to know what he's like off the ball, what his body language is like, how hard does he work? Things that you can't get from videos or whatever. So I used to be here, there and everywhere watching games.

It had always been like that with Becky, to be honest. There were times when he would say: 'I want you to have a look at this lad playing for Plymouth tonight.'

I'd be like: 'But John, Plymouth's six hours away.'

'Well, you'd better get going then, hadn't you?'

I didn't want to treat Moyesie like that; I wanted to keep him as a player in my mind. So I wouldn't let him do those sort of trips - I still did them myself. I set out to be the hardest-working manager in the country and I think I probably achieved it!

I used to sleep at the training ground at times and God knows what my working hours were like - I was a man possessed. I'd been given an opportunity and a responsibility and I didn't want to let anyone - including myself - down through lack of hard work.

I did take Moyesie down to Walsall one time though, to see a young lad in Man United's reserves who I quite fancied taking on loan.

David Beckham was playing central midfield that night and as we drove back up the M6, it was clear Moyesie didn't really fancy him - he thought he was a bit lightweight. But I'd seen enough in the way he struck the ball to make up my mind.

The following day, I rang Sir Alex Ferguson up and asked if we could take him.

Fergie's response was interesting. He paused for a moment then asked: *'What position are you going to play him?'*

I said: 'To be fair, I know he plays centre midfield for your reserves, but I was going to play him wide right because it's a very physical division and I think it would be better for him to be out wide. Also, we'd get the benefit of his crosses coming in.'

I think that swung it, to be honest.

As we chatted, Fergie could see we'd look after the lad and, while it would be a toughening up process, we weren't going to throw him right into the mix in the middle.

It's probably a good job that I kept him out wide. In his second game for us, against Fulham, they had my old Reading teammate Terry Hurlock in the middle of the park. Trust me, you wouldn't want to put a young lad in there (!).

People ask if there were any other of those great United youngsters we could have had, but you couldn't get Scholes or anyone like that - they'd made their minds up on them by that stage. But not on David Beckham.

Obviously, he did brilliantly for us and I like to think that we helped him, even in that brief period, as much as he helped us.

He was on £400-a-week back then, with an extra £50 if he played, which was probably more than our lads were getting, but he was just so professional in everything he did, even as a youngster.

Right from the start, after our training had finished, he would be out there on his own knocking balls about with a goalkeeper. By the time he left a month or so later, there were five or six of our lads out there doing the same thing.

So he was an absolute dream to work with, totally dedicated, and he raised our standards for sure. I would have loved to have kept him for the rest of the season. I think it could have made all the difference - I think we'd have gone straight up.

But by that time Fergie had seen how well he'd done for us and made up his mind on him. When he went back to Man Utd he was in the first team almost straight away.

Obviously Becks was only on loan, but with the backing of Baxi, we brought in Simon Davey from Carlisle midway through that season. Simon had been captain up there and turned out to be a great player for North End and another good leader to have in the team.

We only lost four games until the end of the season and climbed up the league to finish fifth.

In the play-offs we were up against Bury, who finished above us by 13 points. They had just a bit too much for us in those games and we ended up losing out 1-0 on both nights (although they only scored late on in the second leg as we were chasing the goal we needed at the end). I was absolutely gutted that we didn't get through. It really hurt me that we'd worked so hard and got nothing really to show for it.

I never wanted to feel like that again, so set about planning for the next season straight away. I had to make sure that we got the right players in to get the job done - ideally without the flipping play-offs.

It meant a summer of players coming and going. Mike Conroy, who had been great for us, went down to Fulham and I also faced another really tough choice between two young players.

John Beck had taken over at Lincoln by then and wanted to sign Gareth Ainsworth from us. I loved Gareth. He worked hard, was pacy, fantastic attitude - he had all the attributes of a very good player. But I knew I wanted a settled team that was going to play every week.

So it was between him and Lee Cartwright on the right hand side.

I just couldn't see Gareth dislodging Carts in my team; Lee was such a hard worker, so quick and he could run all day. I'm not just saying that, the lad could literally run all day - and he never seemed to be out of breath. He covered back, got forward, he scored goals, whipped in good crosses - he just had everything.

It was one of the hardest calls I ever had to make.

I looked at maybe playing Gareth up front instead of Steve Wilkinson, who had just come in. But again, Wilks was brought in for a purpose to partner Andy Saville. It might have been a 'round peg in a square hole' situation for Gareth.

So in the end, with a heavy heart, I had to let Becky have him - it wouldn't have been fair to hold the lad back, especially as he went on to have such a good career.

But the fact that Carts played more than 400 games for the club and was a regular in the Championship shows the quality he had, too. Like I say, it was a tough, tough call.

As for Steve and Sav, they worked like a dream as a pair up front. I'd scouted them both separately but knew they'd make a perfect partnership.

Wilkinson was so intelligent with his runs, his passing and his football instinct, whereas Sav was a really good player - a lot more than just a battering ram.

The skinhead haircut and his big frame probably disguised his ability a bit. Defenders wouldn't be expecting so much skill from a 'traditional' centre forward, but he had really good feet and a fantastic football brain.

We got him from Barry Fry's Birmingham for less than half of the £250,000 they wanted so it was a great piece of business. I bumped into Barry recently he still goes on about how we robbed them with that deal!

Sav and Russ Wilcox came from the same neck of the woods and we always used to kid that we'd only signed Russ because he could give Sav a lift to training. *(As if!)*

All joking aside, those two were probably our best signings around that time - up top and at the back they were a key part of our spine.

So we were strong up front and at the back, but for me, we were outstanding in midfield. People might say Sav and Steve won us the league that year, but I think the midfield won it for us just as much.

We had Cartwright and Ian Bryson on the wings, Graeme Atkinson and Simon Davey in the middle and the funny thing was, they were all such good players, they could pop up anywhere and do anything.

They were all just as comfortable out wide as they were in the middle; they could all tackle, they could all get forward and they could all score goals.

As an engine room they were the heartbeat of the team and in those days, we didn't really go for squad rotation - you knew your best team and you played it if you could.

The way they interchanged during games, the opposition just couldn't keep track of them - they were popping up everywhere and must have been a nightmare to play against because it was all so fluid.

Behind them of course, we had Moyesie and Russ, two absolute rocks at the back.

Maybe not the quickest, but you would not find two guys who could read the game better than them. And *hard?* Neither of them would have looked out of place in my old Wimbledon team, let's put it that way.

Andy Fensome was a machine at right-back, just up and down all day long, and on the other side we had Ryan Kidd.

Kiddo was a centre half really, but we had him at left-back and he was another one who would run through a brick wall for you - he was just so committed to the club and the team. But he was a great defender too; again, the number of games he went on to play for Preston was fantastic and I know the fans loved him.

In goal we had John Vaughan, who had been with us at Cambridge. He wasn't the biggest - *only 5ft 11ins* - but he was known as The Cat for good reason. He was a consummate professional and made saves at times when you just thought: *'Bugger, they've scored here.'* And then he's plucked it out of the top corner. That's the real sign of a top goalkeeper; when they get to the ones you really don't expect them to.

So that was our team.

We were bringing through some good local lads around that time too; Kevin Kilbane, who had everything - pace, skill, workrate, the lot - and Dave Lucas, who was a really good young keeper; agile and with brilliant reflexes.

Once we got started, we gathered that momentum that you need. After getting beat on the opening day, we didn't lose again until January.

We were thrashing teams 3-0, 4-0, 5-0 and - on one brilliant afternoon - 6-0, when we beat Mansfield with Steve and Sav both getting three goals each.

It was just the perfect performance really, and while the strikers grabbed the goals, every single player that day was outstanding. The sun shone, the Town End was packed and it was one of those times when everything in the world was just perfect.

Same for the season really; I'm not saying it was easy, but over 46 games, we were the best team in the league, no question about it.

By mid-April we knew we could seal promotion by beating Cambridge, but - *fair play to them* - they put up a hell of a fight and beat us 2-1.

Thankfully, a few days later, we put that right by beating Leyton Orient at Brisbane Road, with Sav grabbing a couple of goals, then pulling his shirt over his head in celebration. *Don't ask me why he did that - as long as he was scoring, I didn't care!*

The fans were going wild and it was a just reward for everyone's efforts; players, backroom staff, board, fans, everyone.

I think one of the things we'd done that season is bring people together - everyone was now pulling in the same direction and that togetherness I go on about extended beyond the team and into the stands.

And who else was up in the stands, cheering us on that day? David Beckham and his dad. That's a measure of the man and what a diamond he is. He was absolutely thrilled for everyone at North End and couldn't stop smiling.

The following week, I gave Dave Lucas his debut away at Hartlepool as we won 2-0 and clinched the title. I remember the atmosphere on the bus going back home was just unbelievable and we stopped off in Scotch Corner to top up supplies.

We piled into this pub and as we went in there was this huge roar . . it was jam-packed full of North End fans.

We just dived in and went from there with them! Singing and chanting and having the craic, Baxi shirts everywhere you looked - absolutely brilliant.

Winning that league was a fantastic achievement and, without a doubt, the best time of my life. I probably had about 10 promotions in my football career, but that season stands head and shoulders above the rest.

I loved the club and I still do; I can't quite explain how and why it got its hooks in me the way it did, but there's just something about it.

The people, mainly, but also the stadium, the history, Sir Tom, the atmosphere, everything, right down to that famous white shirt. I felt a responsibility to all that and I knew it was a privilege to be in charge at such a special club.

That's what drove me on, this mission in my mind: *'We've got to be successful for these people, for this town.'*

We had to get the club out of the bottom division and back up the leagues. It was too good and too big to be down there.

At the last game of the season, we played Exeter at Deepdale and the new Tom Finney Stand was absolutely packed to the rafters.

There were just under 19,000 in the ground and God knows how many more locked outside, well before kick-off. Exeter had brought about 100 fans, but the away end was packed with North Enders who had raced round there to get on when the home sections had filled up.

Fittingly, Steve and Sav scored a goal apiece in a 2-0 win and we were presented with the trophy on the pitch on another beautiful sunny day.

I still have the pictures from that day hanging up in my house.

One of my favourites is a picture of the Town End, a sea of smiling faces, and bang smack in the middle is my wife Jill, with a North End scarf on, a 'Barmy army' hat - and a smile as wide as anything.

She could have been up in the director's box, but she wanted to be in among it that day, to experience it with the fans - and she loved every minute. We weren't married at that point and it's a funny story actually.

Towards the end of that season there was a game where we were struggling a bit and - out of nowhere, as I sat on the bench with the game going on - a thought came into my head: *'If we win the league, I'm going to marry Jill.'*

I never said a word to anyone. Like a true romantic - I didn't even tell her!

But at the end of the season, we went off to New Orleans and tied the knot. What with that and winning the league, I felt like I'd won the double. Jill was great; she'd even put up with my idea of a 'date' - watching someone's reserve team in the freezing cold.

She was a police officer and occasionally was on duty at our games. One time over at Oldham, we scored and she instinctively jumped up to celebrate. Problem was, she was working near the home fans who, *errr*, didn't appreciate it, and her boss quickly led her away to a quieter part of the ground. After the game I jokingly mentioned this in passing to Brian Ellis of the Lancashire Evening Post.

Typical Brian - he did a little story on it and by Monday morning, it was being read out on the Big Breakfast on TV: *'Football manager's wife gets arrested at game.'*

I nearly choked on my cornflakes!

Overall though, it was just an amazing period in my life and it all came back to North End.

I was emotional about it at the time and I still get like that when I think back to it now. I was just so proud and so grateful that we'd been able to achieve something like that, winning the league.

I had always felt like I was a North End supporter myself. I felt like I was one of them. We shared the same passion for the game, for the club - it meant so much.

I was the manager, but I lived in Preston, in among the supporters, I was in the pubs with them when I went out and I'd always have a chat with the fans.

On a Friday night, it was always: 'What's the team tomorrow boss?'

On a Saturday, depending on the result, it would be a big discussion about the day's game, win, lose or draw.

I loved it. I felt part of it. I'd never had that before down south.

So yes, the 10 years I spent at North End was the best ten years of my life.

I made friends there that will stay with me forever, I put down roots among the people because I loved them so much.

After games, we'd go in the pubs with the players - starting off at The Sumners and then heading into town. I used to tell the players to come up there after the games and they'd all be in, no problem.

Not only did it give us team spirit among ourselves, it gave us a proper bond with the people who were supporting us, who we were representing.

We'd be in there until 10 o'clock at night sometimes *(maybe later if we'd won)*. The call would go out that we were in there, the place would fill up with fans and we'd have a cracking night with everyone all there together.

To me, it's important that players have that connection. Both sides - players and supporters - needed to know that really, we're all the same; we just want Preston North End to win games and be successful.

Nowadays, I understand that it's not the done thing; players tend to drink less, they get paid a lot more and clubs have a lot more control over what they do.

Don't get me wrong, I understand the reasons behind that thinking and I'm not a dinosaur or anything - the game has moved on, for better or worse or just different.

But I'm telling you how it was in the 1990s. It's something that has been lost from the game in the modern era.

I still think most players are good professionals, working hard to make their way in the game that they love. But that spirit, that connection, that bond . . . it's not the same as it used to be. And I think if you asked supporters from back then who still go to the games now, they'd say the same thing.

You can't argue with all-seater stadiums from a safety perspective and the facilities at Deepdale now are absolutely brilliant. But you'll never get that old atmosphere back - and the price of tickets at some grounds now is just driving ordinary fans out of the game.

Football is a working class sport; you shouldn't be pushing those people away by charging nearly £40 a ticket. It's madness.

Obviously, it was a lot cheaper in 1996 and throughout our title season, I had to keep my feelings as a fan in check a bit because we had matches to win and, first and foremost, I was the manager.

But by the time we'd got the trophy in the bag and it came to the open top bus parade, well, I could be a proper fan then, loving it as much as the people who came out to see us. It felt like our celebrations had gone on for days as we set off on that parade.

And the thousands and thousands of people who came out to see us well . . . it still chokes me up to think about it now.

Standing on the steps of the Harris Library, looking out over the sea of white on the Flag Market, with the fans all singing *'There's only one Gary Peters'* . . . wow, I mean, come on . . .

It was just on a higher level, really.

No matter what else I achieved in my career, nothing gets anywhere near it.

My life, my entire football career, could have ended that day and I'd have been happy. That's what Preston North End means to me.

If I could relive those minutes over and over again, I would.

And I do, in my mind, quite often. I think back and just savour those moments with the players alongside me and the fans all around. Togetherness, right there.

At the time, as I came back to earth for a moment and tried to get my thanks across, I was a bit stuck for words, speechless, really.

So I suddenly realised there was only one thing for it.

I looked around, took a deep breath and then - in my best singing voice - asked the famous question: *'Who's that jumping off the pier?!'*

Of course, by the time I got to the second line, about 20,000 people had joined in and you could barely hear me over the noise.

You know the answer; I don't like to mention them . . . but they can't beat the famous PNE.

Everyone was loving it and we couldn't wait to get down there among the fans. We ended up going to as many pubs in the town as we could that day (and night) and sharing as much celebration bubbly as possible with them.

I just wanted to share the day with the supporters. There were no camera phones in those days, otherwise there would be some interesting sights, especially as the night wore on!

Again, in those days, the players had a bit more freedom. We could all let our hair down, without worrying about it popping up in the papers or on the internet the next day. So it was a great way to round off the season and everyone went away for a well-earned break.

But me? I knew I couldn't switch off.

We were going up a level and I had to start planning straight away for what we'd need in the higher league. We'd have to go again and I wanted to keep the momentum of the club going. When you go up, the first thing you've got to do is make sure you stay up, but I wanted us to aim for more than that.

It was a really tough proposition because I looked at our midfield and thought; how can we replace any of them? They were just so good as a unit.

But once we were up, quite quickly, I knew we had to strengthen. Mark Rankine came in from Wolves, but it didn't really go well for him at first. He really had to work at it to be successful at Preston in the long run and credit to him for sticking with it.

On top of that, within a few months, we brought in Sean Gregan, David Reeves and got Lee Ashcroft back to the club. Gregan had been playing as a centre half at Darlington, but we played him in midfield and, of course, everyone knows how good he turned out to be for many years at the club.

I'd seen Reevesy play so many times when I was out watching games and his movement was always superb; a real workhorse, a clever player and someone who I knew could score goals. Ashcroft was just Ashcroft; a real 'local lad' character and a very good player on his day.

Sadly, bringing these lads in meant some had to go out and it was with a heavy heart that Andy Saville went to Wigan.

He was a great lad and a good pro, but I knew we were going to be tested and maybe Reeves was a bit younger and a bit more mobile. It was a gamble to a degree, but I had to make these hard decisions to keep us moving forward.

Same with Gregan, he was replacing players who had done well for us the year before, but there's no doubt he improved us - he was a man mountain, who could also play, so he was the perfect combination really.

He made his debut against That Lot With The Tower in a memorable 3-0 win, under the floodlights on a Friday night, live on Sky, with Deepdale absolutely rocking.

I think the intensity of it all might have shocked some players, but Gregan just breezed through it, flattened one or two of their lads and it all went from there really.

Without a doubt, that was my favourite game in charge - hammering them on a Friday night and then going out celebrating in the town.

What a night that was - talk about special! There were times when I played up a bit on the M55 thing; but I genuinely didn't like them and still won't have anything orange in my house!

It's a proper football rivalry and I love things like that. Have an enemy and focus on being better than them. If you don't understand that, you're in the wrong job.

I'd been mixing with North End fans for a few years by then, so I knew exactly what they thought of the other lot.

One time, we were playing at their ground on a lunchtime kick-off *(very wise)* and I left just before the end to watch a player at Rochdale, starting at 3pm. Of course, when I got to my car, I was blocked in and almost straight away, the home fans spotted me.

That lot hated me and suddenly, there was about 20 lads banging on my bonnet and trying to turn the car over. Thankfully, the police showed up and I made a getaway, but it was just another reminder that I wasn't really welcome over there.

(A few years later, I had some trouble in a casino one night and a couple of them tried it on. I won't go into details - but it was another away win for North End at the seaside.)

Back on the pitch, we brought in Bobby Mimms and Kelham O'Hanlon as new goalkeepers. We were really just looking for experience as we brought David Lucas through. We also brought Tepi Moilanen in and he also added to us, though he was a bit of a character off the pitch - you were never quite sure how he was going to react to things. Good keeper, strange lad.

Neil McDonald was around too, a lovely passer of the ball, but really we were already planning to get Paul McKenna in the team. I remember the youth team had come back for training a few days before the senior lads and I walked across to watch them train.

McKenna and Kilbane were there and at the end of the session I went across to Chris Sulley, the Youth Team manager, and just said: *'Sorry Chris, those two are coming with me.'*

From there, we were gradually easing them into the first team more and more. Kilbane had already had a taste, but McKenna . . . you just looked at him and you knew he was going to be a great player.

The season went OK. We weren't able to push for promotion again, but we consolidated and finished 15th.

I think everyone could see we were improving and getting used to the higher level.

Kilbane had played most of the games throughout the season and it was no surprise that other teams were interested in him. That summer of 1997, we sold him to West Brom for around £1.2 million - a record for the club at that time.

Obviously, we were sorry to see him go but my immediate priority was re-investing some of the money to strengthen the team.

Luckily, I still had a good relationship with Sir Alex at United after the Beckham loan and had been down to watch his reserves play many times.

We also used to send teams over to play against United when Eric Cantona was banned after his kung-fu kick. It helped keep his fitness up and was good for our lads too.

It was from that relationship with Fergie that we got Michael Appleton, Jon Macken and Colin Murdock. It didn't cost us much to get them in.

I think we paid maybe less than £200,000 for Appleton and Macken in total, with Murdock on a free - that's how I remember it anyway.

The deal was loaded though, so that if we sold them on, United would get a cut and obviously that paid off for them in the long run.

Either way, it was a very good deal for Preston; Appleton later went for just under a million, Macken went for five million and Colin played 200-plus games for the club.

So it was a smart bit of business all round. I'm always very proud that overall, the club made about £9 million profit on players sales from my time as manager - so all those long trips on the motorway paid off in the end.

I also think that Fergie knew we would look after these lads and develop their careers in the right way. And when those three young United players came in, the professionalism they brought with them again lifted our standards.

They brought some of Fergie's philosophy with them; you had to be part of the club, you had to give it everything and do everything right.

People may say Macken lacked self-belief at first; but looking at the players he was competing with at United, can you blame him?

But I brought him in for a reason. He was a target man in the Mark Hughes mould; great movement, huge thighs, and a cracking shot.

He was quite good in the air, but if you look at his body, he had these short legs and a low backside, which gave him brilliant balance and close control.

Really, he gave us the replacement for Andy Saville that we'd missed in that 'hold-up' role the previous season.

But he was a young lad and you needed to be patient with him. I used to get frustrated at times when I could see how good these players were going to be, but the crowd would maybe moan when they didn't get it right every time.

It really planted a seed in my mind that I wanted to work with the younger players and help them develop, because I could see that the Mackens, McKennas and Kilbanes had all the attributes to be top players.

I was just worried that if we didn't look after them properly, it might never happen for some of them.

We made a decent start to that 1997/98 season and come October, we beat Carlisle away on a Friday night to push us up to third in the table.

In all honesty, I think that was a bit of a false position for us, because we'd played a day earlier than everyone else, but inevitably, it raised expectations.

We then went and lost four games on the trot - including two at home - and I started getting a bit of stick off the crowd.

The players were getting a bit of grief too, Jonny Macken hadn't really started scoring and we dropped down to about twelfth.

The drop looked worse than it was, as we'd only been third for 24 hours, and realistically we should have been bobbing around the play-off places, so there was a bit of grumbling for the first time really.

I know there's a difference between a lone voice in the crowd shouting nonsense *(let's face it, there's always one!)* to the majority of the stadium chanting for your head. But I never wanted it to get to that stage.

I didn't want anything to sour the relationship I'd got with those Preston fans - it meant too much to me.

On top of that, I had put a young side together and I had to find a way of protecting them. I wanted to make sure they weren't torn apart if I got sacked and someone from outside came in.

Around that time, there was a bit of a revolution happening in funding for youth development in football. Clubs could get £132,000 each year - a huge sum - if they were set up right behind the scenes and I knew we were looking for someone to take that responsibility on.

I also had Moyesie, who was coming on leaps and bounds on the coaching side of things and was obviously getting more and more ready to take a management job on.

He understood what I was trying to do in terms of improving the team; after all he'd had it first-hand when I'd brought in Michael Jackson as a younger player to replace him. If Moyesie went somewhere else and I ended up leaving, I feared that the young group we'd put together would be broken up. I didn't want someone from outside to come in and rip the place apart.

Like I say, I loved Preston and wanted to live there for the rest of my life, so I didn't want it to get to stage where the fans wanted me sacked and there was animosity and bad feeling. Mainly, I wanted to do what was best for the club in the long term.

And for me, that was me taking over the youth side of things and David taking on the first team. The fact that David did most of the coaching, knew the players and was definitely ready to be a manager made it the right thing to do.

And what a great job he did.

I didn't need to help David as he took the job to a new level and let me get on with building the centre of excellence.

Also with me in the background, I thought if Moyesie ever moved on in the future, I could maybe step back in as caretaker manager if necessary, or just be around to offer advice on the football side. I wanted to stay at Preston for the rest of my career and serve the club any way I could.

So I went to the chairman to explain my thinking and what I was proposing. Bryan Gray understood things and thought it was a sensible step. So that's what happened.

It was my idea and there had been no pressure from Bryan or the board.

It was just something that came about with the timing of the youth set-up, the development of David Moyes and the desire to keep that group of players intact.

On top of that, in all honesty, I think I'd probably taken the team as far as I could.

When you've had four years as manager and changed it round quite a bit, the fans, the players, everyone maybe gets bored with the same voice.

I think it's a good stint for a manager and knowing when to step aside for the good of the club is crucial. That's what mattered to me - *the club.*

There would be no point in me working so hard, putting so much in and then ruining things by hanging on when, deep down, I knew what had to happen.

And, as everyone knows, it worked brilliantly with Moyesie in charge.

I think eight of the team from my last game in charge - a 3-1 defeat to Gillingham - played in the play-off final against Bolton a couple of years later. So we were right to have faith in that group and David as manager.

Meanwhile, it worked well for me on the youth side too, for the next few years running the Centre of Excellence. We were really establishing ourselves, hitting our targets, developing young players and putting the whole thing on a professional footing. We made sure that all the child protection protocols were put in place and that youngsters were always in the right environment. Together with the team there, I thought we were really building something for the future of the club.

I had opportunities to go back into management elsewhere, but turned them down because I just never wanted to leave Preston. It was all going well and I genuinely thought I'd be at Deepdale for the rest of my career.

But then in 1999, Tony Scholes became chief executive. He hadn't been in that role when I stepped down as manager.

I hadn't got a pay-off or anything like that, I just took a big drop in wages in my youth role. It was more than people at other clubs might be getting, but there was a background to it.

In the end though, that didn't count for much.

I think he thought I was getting paid too much and he dug me out a bit.

It was around the time of the ITV Digital crash and the Centre of Excellence that I'd been running was being merged with the Youth Development Department to save money. I was told it was going to be me or Simon Davey that would have to go.

I'd signed Simon and he'd done a great job as player and a youth coach, so I said straight away it would have to be me.

No decision had to be made by the club.

Simon took over and I stayed on for a while to ensure a smooth transition.

I'll be honest, I was keeping up a bit of a front, because it was very hard to take.

I'd been at the club for 10 years as assistant, manager and then running the Centre of Excellence and it was a huge part of my life - it still is.

I had really thought I'd be there forever, with my own role, but stepping up if there was ever a crisis, helping out whenever and wherever needed.

If I was called upon I'd do anything for the club - from caretaker managing to cleaning the kit, anything at all. My heart is still there and I just wish I'd been able to carry on.

It was heartbreaking to leave - one of the saddest days of my life.

It hurt like hell, but it didn't change my feelings towards the club, the people or the city - nothing can.

I played for Aldershot, Wimbledon and Fulham and had eight years at Reading. I later managed Exeter and Shrewsbury and I'd been a boyhood Arsenal fan.

But for me, there is only one club - Preston North End.

I look back now with enormous pride on what we achieved at Deepdale on and off the pitch. I'm so pleased that when I go back I can hold my head up high and get such a warm welcome from everyone who was around back then.

I pray the club can get up into the Premier League soon, it would be fantastic and put North End truly back where it belongs.

But I tell you what . . . I don't think there will ever be a time quite like the 1990s.

I just feel so lucky that I got to experience the best days of my life in such a special place and share it with those brilliant fans.

Words alone can't explain how much North End means to me.

I love the club and I'll love it for the rest of my life.

It's in my heart and, yes . . . it's in my North End soul.

We hope you have enjoyed Keith Harrison's North End Souls 2 and the fascinating stories the PNE players of the past can tell.

Thank you so much also to Keith for his wonderful gesture to donate 10 per cent of the profits from North End Souls 2 to Baby Beat, the charity which supports babies and mothers being cared for at the Sharoe Green Unit at Royal Preston Hospital.

Every year 4,500 babies are born at the Sharoe Green Unit. Baby Beat funds specialist equipment, patient services, clinical care and research to ensure the best possible outcome for these babies and mothers. The charity was founded in 1987 by a group of midwives and a Consultant Obstetrician who wanted to provide more foetal monitoring equipment for the growing maternity unit at the old Royal Preston Infirmary.

They launched a fundraising appeal to raise money for the new equipment. And so Baby Beat began . . .

Baby Beat now supports four key areas:

- Maternity services to promote the best possible outcome for the unborn baby from conception to birth including the well-being of the mother.

- Premature and new-born babies requiring specialist care in the Neo Natal Intensive Care Unit following delivery until their discharge.

- Wide ranging research to improve health outcomes for pregnant women and their babies.

- Emotional and practical support of new parents suffering stillbirth and death of their baby.

Baby Beat seeks to save the lives of babies not yet born and give the babies born in our area the very best chance for life and the start of their journey into the world. Everything we fund is additional to what the NHS provides and makes a real difference to local families.

Maternity services at Royal Preston Hospital are at the forefront of new technology, with the vital support of Baby Beat. We are proud to support mothers and babies who are local to the Preston and Central Lancashire area, alongside families from across the whole of Lancashire and South Cumbria who need the care of the specialist Neonatal Intensive Care Unit.

If you would like to support Baby Beat's work, do get in touch. You can help by fund raising for us, making a personal donation, or even volunteering. Donations can be made by cheque, posted to the address below, by bank transfer or by cash to the Baby Beat office. You can also donate quickly and easily online to Baby Beat's Just Giving page which is www.justgiving.com/babybeat.

For more information visit our website www.babybeat.org.uk, email us at *babybeatuk@lthtr.nhs.uk* or follow us on Facebook or Twitter *@babybeatorg.*

Thank you for your support.

Cathy Skidmore

Baby Beat, Sharoe Green Unit, Lancashire Teaching Hospitals NHS Trust, Sharoe Green Lane, Fulwood, Preston, Lancashire PR2 9HT. (Charity no 1051194)

ACKNOWLEDGEMENTS

Sincere thanks to the following, without whose help this book would not have been possible: Gareth Ainsworth, Alex Bruce, Tom Clarke, Tony Ellis, Mike Elwiss, Simon Grayson, Peter Higham, Paul Huntington, Eric Jones, Ryan Kidd, Sean St Ledger, Paul McKenna, Jon Macken, Brian Mooney, Brian O'Neil, Gary Peters, Andy Saville, Ian Rigby, Hannah Broadley, Ian Robinson, Preston North End FC, Rochdale AFC, Hull City, Wycombe Wanderers, James Garratt, Dave Seddon, the Lancashire Post, John Kelly at pne-online.net, Jake Oates at fromthefinney.co.uk, John Thomas, Trevor Johnson, Michael Adair, Dave Nelson, my parents and family, my ever-patient wife Lisa and, finally, everyone who bought the first North End Souls book.

Thank you all.

COYW

PHOTOGRAPHIC CREDITS

Pictures courtesy of - Page 113: Paul Huntington (action) PNEFC/ Ian Robinson. 114: Gareth Ainsworth and Brian Mooney in action, Lancashire Post. Brian Mooney with fans, Michael Adair. 115: Sean St Ledger and Gary Peters 1996, Lancashire Post. 116: Tom Clarke, PNEFC/Dave Kendall. Andy Saville in action, Lancashire Post. 117: Jon Macken, Brian O'Neil, Lancashire Post. 118: Ryan Kidd, Lancashire Post. Eric Jones/ Peter Higham. 119: Paul McKenna, Mike Elwiss, Tony Ellis (action), Lancashire Post. Back cover: Sean St Ledger, Lancashire Post.

CHOOSE LIFE.
CHOOSE WHITE.
CHOOSE PRESTON NORTH END.
CHOOSE BEING TAKEN BY THE HAND FROM GREENLANDS TO THE PROMISED LAND
TO SEE BOBBY CHARLTON, COS HE'S GOOD, COS HE'S A GOD.
THEN NOBBY STILES, BETTER BY MILES.
CHOOSE LAWRO, MORLEY, ELWISS AND BRUCE,
GETTING BACK UP AND THEN RUNNING LOOSE,
IN THE HEN PEN WITH THE OLD MEN,
CHILLED TO THE BONE, LONGING FOR HOME,
TOO COLD TO CARE WHO'S UP ON THE THRONE.
CHOOSE THE DOC, NOW, NOW, DON'T BE CRUEL,
THEN KELLY AND BOOTH ON THE OLD DUCKING STOOL.
CHOOSE CHAOS, NO FLOODLIGHTS, NO MONEY, NO DIRECTION.
CHOOSE US OVER ENFIELD, FOR JUST ONE RE-ELECTION.
RESURRECTION, JOHN McGRATH, EN-TOUS-CAS,
THOMAS, BRAZIL AND A CAST OF SHEER CLASS.
LES CHAPMAN, BEYOND VENUS,
FRANK WORTHINGTON'S TOUCH AND HIS GOALS OF SHEER GENIUS.
CHOOSE MOONEY AND, YES, CHOOSE TONY ELLIS,
REMEMBER THE GOALS, NOT THE BIBLICAL REFERENCE,
DON'T CHOOSE JOHN BECK. CHOOSE PETERS, NEVER BEAT US.
CHOOSE GREGAN. GREEEGAN! A NEW DAWN WITH SEAN,
THRASHING THE LASHERS AT DEEPDALE 3-0,
JUST PAUSE FOR A SECOND . . . POP THAT LIKE A PILL.
CHOOSE MOYESIE AGAIN, AGAIN AND AGAIN.
A TRUE NORTH END LEGEND, A GIANT AMONG MEN.
CHOOSE GREZZA, MCKENNA, MARK RANKINE'S GOAL,
JUST THINKING ABOUT IT IS GOOD FOR THE SOUL.
CHOOSE CARDIFF: 'BELIEVE', THE FLAG AND SIR TOM,
DON'T THINK THAT IT'S OVER, DON'T THINK THAT HE'S GONE.
HE'S ALWAYS AMONG US, THE GAME'S CHOSEN ONE.
CHOOSE FULLER, LUCKETTI AND WE'LL COME RIGHT BACK,
GET NUGENT ON BOARD AND LET'S HAVE THE CRAIC.
CHOOSE BILLY THE MIDGET FOR A ROW EVERY HOUR,
WHO SAID SCOTSMEN WERE EVER SO DOUR?
CHOOSE GREZZA AT RIGHT BACK YA SILLY WEE SOD,
THAT'S ALWAYS YOUR PROBLEM BILL, YOU THINK THAT YOU'RE GOD.
AS FOR THE NEXT CLOWN, HE GOT IT ALL WRONG AND BLAMED OUR WOES ON AN OLD ELVIS SONG
THEN CAME ALAN IRVINE WITH TREVOR IN TOW,
WE LASHED OUT SOME MONEY, EVEN GAVE IT A GO!
FAREWELL FATHER TED, HELLO FERGIE JUNIOR,
THEN DODGY PHIL BROWN AND THE DROP CAME ON SOONER.
CHOOSE EXODUS! MOVEMENT OF THE PEOPLE,
THE GOSPEL OF WESTLEY,
A CHURCH WITH NO STEEPLE.
SAVE US PLEASE SIMON, THE YORKSHIRE MESSIAH,
YOU'VE NOT MUCH TO BEAT - WE'VE BEEN FLAMING DIRE,
OH, YOU'RE OFF ARE YOU MATE?
WE'LL CHOOSE ALEX NEIL AND HE'LL BE JUST GREAT.
ONE YEAR IS ENOUGH FOR THE PREMIER DREAM,
YOU CAN KEEP MAN UNITED AND THAT CURDLING OLD CREAM.
JUST SHOW US THE MONEY, COS I'M NOT BEING FUNNY,
WE DON'T BELONG IN THAT THRONG, WITH THE DAFT KICK-OFF TIMES,
THE SHOUTED HATE CRIMES, THE VAR LINES, THE SKY TV CHIMES.
CHOOSE COMRADES AND CAMARADERIE, COMEDY AND BLATHERY BITS LIKE THIS
IN BOOKS LIKE THIS ABOUT THINGS YOU MISS AND FOOTBALL BLISS.
CHOOSE YOUR TOWN AND YOUR TEAM.
CHOOSE CHASING THE DREAM.
CHOOSE PRESTON NORTH END.
CHOOSE LIFE.

KH 2020